ADRIAN PLASS
Classics

ADRIAN PLASS
Classics

Adrian Plass

THE GROWING UP PAINS OF ADRIAN PLASS

VIEW FROM A BOUNCY CASTLE

CABBAGES FOR THE KING

Marshall Pickering
An Imprint of HarperCollins*Publishers*

Marshall Pickering is an imprint of
HarperCollins*Religious*
Part of HarperCollins*Publishers*
77–85 Fulham Palace Road, London W6 8JB

The Growing Up Pains of Adrian Plass first published in Great Britain in 1986
by Marshall Pickering. Copyright © 1986 Adrian Plass

View from a Bouncy Castle first published in Great Britain in 1991 by Fount
Paperbacks. Copyright in the text © 1991 Adrian Plass. Copyright in the
illustrations © 1991 Dan Donovan

Cabbages for the King first published in Great Britain in 1993 by Fount
Paperbacks. Copyright in the text © 1993 Adrian Plass. Copyright in the
illustrations © 1993 Ben Ecclestone

This edition first published in 1998 by Marshall Pickering

3 5 7 9 10 8 6 4 2

Adrian Plass, Dan Donovan and Ben Ecclestone assert the moral right to be
identified as the author and illustrators of this work.

A catalogue record for this book is
available from the British Library.

ISBN 0 551 03138 7

Printed and bound in Great Britain by
Caledonian International Book Manufacturing Ltd, Glasgow

Contents

THE GROWING UP
PAINS OF ADRIAN PLASS

Introduction

God really brought me down to earth once. He's rather good at that sort of thing.

We'd gone to Cornwall for a winter holiday, something that we'd always yearned to do as a family. It was early December, bitingly cold, but brilliantly lit by one of those water-colour winter suns that seem to drip liquid light through the atmosphere. Our little white rented cottage overlooked an indescribably beautiful part of the northern coast. That coast must have been planned, built and illuminated by a creator with time on his hands, and a fine, excited eye for detail.

One morning, after a long, lingering, excessive breakfast, we all dressed in layer upon layer of the warmest clothes we could find, and set off, a procession of human barrels, to go for a walk in the ice-cream air. We went a new way. Through a white farm gate, and across an expanse of wind-flattened, metallic green grass, towards what looked like a cliff edge a few hundred yards away. Beyond that the sea stretched away for ever, merging with the sky in the strange pale distance.

I walked with Matthew, aged eight, whose every utterance at that time began with an interrogative. My wife, Bridget, strolled beside four-year-old Joseph, deep and thoughtful beyond his years. The smallest barrel, David, aged two, ran ahead of us chuckling delightedly, applauding the seagulls who keeled around us for a few minutes, performing impossible aerobatics with casual vanity.

As we neared the edge of the cliff, I reflected on the fact that we were happy – all of us. We are a close family, but it didn't often happen that we all achieved contentment, all at the same time, when we were all together. You have to work hard to keep a family of five reasonably happy. It's like the circus act where all those plates are kept spinning on the top of tall, thin sticks by someone rushing from one to the other at great speed. The difference with a family is that you never get a chance to stop and take a bow. You just carry on, and get tired. Holidays had always been an opportunity for Bridget and myself to enjoy an awareness of our whole selves, and to give some thought to what we needed to keep our plates spinning.

We had reached the edge. Far beneath us, enclosed by a horseshoe of unscaleable cliffs, lay one of the most magically secluded bays I had ever seen. Perfect shape, perfect sea, perfect sand, perfect rock pools. There was no way down. We could never use it. We could only look at it. It was as though one of God's successful creation prototypes had been overlooked when the workbench was cleared.

I forgot everything else as I gazed out over this hidden corner of the world. I felt a sudden surge of pride about belonging to the same world as the vast shining sea, the blue-white wash of the sky, and the massive, granulated bulk of the cliffs. These, surely, were symbols of God. Huge, beautiful, sublime, desirable, yet impossible to contain or define narrowly. I was lost in wonder . . .

'Daddy, want to go loo, daddy!'

My youngest son's voice arrived in my consciousness with urgent haste. David's little face was strained with the knowledge that disaster was imminent. As I struggled to reduce his Michelin-like proportions to an appropriate state of undress, I spoke to God in my mind with some trucu-lence.

'Goodness knows,' I complained, 'I get little enough time as it is to actually relax and enjoy beautiful things. Why should I have to come down from where I was to cope with little problems like this?'

'I did,' said God.

Chapter One

Early photographs show that I was little more than a huge pair of ears mounted on two long skinny legs. In most of those early pictures I look slightly troubled and very earnest.

Each week I attended the local church at the other end of the village, an activity that seemed to me to have very little to do with God. The Roman Catholic chapel in Rusthall was a converted private house, and therefore lacked the atmosphere of sublime mystery and divine confidence that I rather enjoyed on our occasional visits to St Augustine's, the huge and ornate mother church in Tunbridge Wells. There were few points of interest for a small child in an hour spent in one of three physical postures, listening to someone speaking a language that he didn't understand, to a God who seemed as distant and irrelevant as the dark side of the moon. Some of those services seemed to be several days long. Afterwards, my father, my two brothers and I would proceed sedately back along the path into the village, all my little springs of boredom and tension popping and pinging into relaxation as I looked forward to Sunday lunch and the traditional midday comedy half-hour on the radio.

Nowadays I have a great respect and fondness for the Roman Catholic Church and many friends who are members of it, but if you had asked me at the age of eight or nine to tell you what I enjoyed most about the mass, I could have named only one thing. I did rather look forward to that point in the proceedings when the priest placed a wafer in the open mouths of the communicants, as they knelt in a semicircle around him. There was a satisfyingly repellent fleshiness about all those extended tongues, and a fascinating vulnerability about the grown-ups, waiting like baby birds to be fed with something that, once inside them, (I was told) would turn into the body of Jesus Christ and nourish them in a way that I couldn't begin to understand.

That the church seemed to me to have very little to do with God may have had something to do with the fact that, while my father was a convert to the Catholic Church, my mother, whose religious background was the Congregational Church, remained a Protestant and didn't come to church with us on Sundays.

We frequently experienced our own domestic version of 'The Troubles' and I can recall how, as a small child, I felt painfully bewildered about the religious separation between my parents.

Why didn't mummy come to church with us? Did she know a different God? No? Well, in that case why didn't she come to church with us? I would understand when I was older, I was told.

The shadow of conflict darkened those Sunday morning services throughout my early childhood and had a strongly negative effect on my feelings about God, who clearly wouldn't or couldn't sort out our family.

If my poor father had been a more secure man the boredom of the services and even the parental conflict over religion might not have mattered too much. As it was, his inability to trust the love of his family resulted in twenty-five very difficult years for my mother, and, in my case, a very confused and troubled perception of what love, adulthood and Christianity meant. Two incidents spring to mind as being typical of the kind of emotional half-nelson that he was expert in applying and which must have contributed heavily to the emotional constipation which led to a breakdown in my own life years later in 1984, and from which I am only just emerging as I write.

The first concerned my father's black prayer book. It was a small, plump, much thumbed little volume, whose wafer-thin pages were edged with gold. As a child it seemed to me a miniature treasure chest, filled with immense wealth that had somehow been compressed into a tiny space for easy portage.

Dad's prayer book was part of him, like the little round boxes of Beecham's pills, the tin full of old and foreign coins, the trilby hat, and the tortoise-shell reading spectacles that made my sight worse when I was allowed to try them on, before they were put away again in the case that snapped shut with a pleasing hollow 'plock' sound.

One day we had all been naughty – all three of us. One of my brothers was two years older than me, the other was two years younger. I must have been about eight years old at the time. We seemed to spend our lives pursuing one of three activities. The first involved the consumption of vast slices of white crusty bread, spread thickly with butter and marmalade. We often accounted for three long loaves in a single day.

The second activity was simply playing together, and the third, which usually grew naturally out of the second, was simply fighting each other. Today, the eating and playing stages had passed all too quickly. We three boys had argued and squabbled and cried and fought for most of a long rainy Saturday. My parents' patience had been tried and tested in a way that, with three boys of my own, I now fully understand. They had tried everything: the gentle rebuke, the not-so-gentle rebuke, the appeal to reason, the bribe, the threat, the repeated threat, the repeated-yet-again threat, the last chance option and finally the shriek of fury. Nothing had worked. My father had long since abandoned any attempt to play an adult role in the proceedings. He was an angry child, hurt by our refusal to make it easy for him to be grown-up. His idea of an appropriate solution to this problem was bizarre, to say the least. He picked up his prayer book from its place next to the biscuit barrel on the sideboard, and holding it dramatically over his head, announced that if we didn't behave ourselves, we would drive him to the point where he would be forced to throw it at us, and if he had to do *that*, it really would be 'the end'.

Children believe things.

The end of what? Pictures flashed through my mind of the little book, stuffed with condensed divinity, crashing to the floor, bursting like some ripe, heavy fruit, and losing all its goodness for ever. Was that what he meant? Would I be to blame for that? Had I said or done something in the course of that long day of bickering, that was more serious — more wicked than I had realised? When he did finally, with a sort of orgasmic zeal, fling the book in the general direction of my younger brother and me, I was surprised to find that the world seemed unaffected by the gesture. No thunderbolts — no voice from heaven. The book lay, almost unharmed, on the floor, one or two pages detached by the impact and protruding slightly from the others, but otherwise, just the same.

I wasn't just the same though. I had made my father throw his prayer book at me, and he had said that it would be 'the end'. That book contained God. I had made him throw God away.

The devils grinned as they snapped home the padlock on another chain of guilt.

The other incident was so painful, that, even now, I find it difficult to record.

My father was a very jealous man. He found it almost impossible to believe that he was loved and wanted by those closest to him. Happiness and peace were just clever devices designed to lull him into a state where he could more easily be cheated and victimised, especially by his wife — my mother — who was, and still is, one of the most loving and innocent people I have ever met. People outside the family were 'all right'. They could never give him things that he feared losing in the same way. It was us, the family, and my mother particularly, who were obliged to trip and stumble through the dark forest of his fear and insecurity. In the middle of a pleasant family walk, when it seemed impossible that anything could go wrong, he would quite suddenly stop, and with that expression of tight-lipped anger on his face, that we all dreaded, announce that we were going back.

8

'Why, Dad?'

'Ask your mother.'

My mother, it usually transpired, had 'looked' at a man passing along on the other side of the road, or working in a field, or sitting on a gate, or driving a car. This kind of innocent glance was enough to shatter my father's self-esteem, and send him into a brooding sulky state for hours, or days, or even weeks. Eventually my mother would find a way to bring him round, but only by accepting and playing out the role of penitent, which was a very risky business, as he would only accept her penitence if she was innocent as well. He saw rivals everywhere. The man who came to build the extension onto our kitchen was, he told me, a 'naughty' man.

'What do you mean?'

'I'll tell you when you're older.'

'Why can't you tell me now?'

'It's not very nice.'

The man who took us for catechism lessons in a tall dark room in St Augustine's presbytery was also on the list of suspects. He was a big man with a large impressive moustache, a profound understanding of the catechism, and an almost total inability to communicate it to children. He was also, so my father said, not a good man.

'Bad, you mean?'

'Yes, very bad.'

'What's he done?'

'You wouldn't understand.'

'I would!'

'I'll tell you when you're older . . .'

There were so many things that I was going to be told when I was older! So many little clouds of half-knowledge were massing around my understanding, shutting out the light until much later in my life.

The most painful instance of my father's insane jealousy (most painful from my point of view, that is), happened just before my tenth birthday. I arrived home one afternoon after playing some sort of tracking game through the

9

bracken up on the common. Tired, hot and hungry, I came through the back door into the kitchen, and was about to get a drink of water and a wedge of the all-sustaining bread and marmalade, when I heard my father's raised voice coming from the other side of the dining room door. My very heart-beat seemed to fade, as it always did when I realised that 'it' was happening again. What now? I opened the door and slipped quietly into the room, thinking vaguely that I might be able to protect someone from something. My mother was shaking her head tearfully, sobbing out the words, 'It's just not true, it's just not true!'

My father, with an odd mixture of pain, anger and relish filling his face and voice, was jabbing his finger towards her and shouting, 'I saw you! I saw you with him! I looked through the window and saw you on the bed with him!'

My sympathy fluttered around the room like a nervous butterfly, uncertain where to alight, unsure where to lend the tiny weight of its concern.

'You can't have done – you really can't have done! It's not true. . . !'

Despite ample evidence from the past that plain denial was an absolute waste of time, my mother continued her tearful protest, until my father, suddenly inspired, took a step forward and pointed at me.

'Adrian was with me. He saw it too! Didn't you?'

There was a wild plea in his eyes.

My mother was crying.

They were my parents. You should support your parents. My father was appealing to me to lie for him. My mother needed me to tell the truth. Someone was going to be let down, and we were all going to suffer anyway. My voice was very small as I answered.

'I wasn't with you. I didn't see anything.'

I don't think I looked at my father's face. I had failed him by telling the truth. I was a cold mess inside. Angry, unhappy, and of course – guilty.

As an adult, I have come to understand how profoundly my father suffered through his inability to believe in

10

happiness, and I am now able to offer him posthumous for-giveness and feel more peaceful about the past. There is no doubt, though, that the development of my perception of God as a father was sadly distorted by the way in which he presented himself to me both as a Christian and a parent. It is fortunate that my mother was able to provide warmth and consistent care throughout my childhood, and for that I shall always be grateful.

The other great pleasure in my life, apart from eating bread and marmalade, was reading. I was an avid but non-discriminating reader. Various aged relatives died during my childhood, leaving large and generally rather sombre collections of books to my father, who placed many of them in a big dark-brown bookcase in my bedroom, presumably to aid the process of 'doing better than he did'. I read everything. I would sit, cross-legged, on the bedroom floor, in my baggy grey flannel shirt, and my even baggier grey flannel shorts, surrounded by little stacks of novels, poetry collections and biographies. Each book was like a stone in a rock pool. Lift it up, investigate closely, and you might discover something exciting – something alive! Nor was I handicapped by snobbery. There was no such thing as a classic. I was quite happy to give someone called Joseph Conrad a fair trial, but he had to succeed on his own merits, or be replaced by a really great writer, such as W E Johns, or Richmal Crompton. I was in love with words and ideas, but it never occurred to me, until one momentous day, that something I read in a book could actually change my attitude to real people in the real world.

It was my earliest encounter with the truth, although I certainly wouldn't have called it a religious experience at the time, and it happened on the top deck of the number 81 bus which used to run between Rusthall and Tunbridge Wells. The journey only took twelve minutes, but on this occasion that was long enough for a startling new truth to penetrate my ten-year-old consciousness so profoundly that it has affected almost everything I have done since that day. It was connected with something I had read that morning.

As I sat on the front seat of the big green Maidstone and District bus, a sixpenny bit and a penny clutched in my hand ready for the conductor, a phrase I had read earlier repeated itself over and over in my mind.

'Everybody is *I*'.

For some reason, I sensed an important inner core of meaning in the words, but I was unable to dig it out. I was frustrated and fascinated by the problem. If only the answer – the secret, had been a solid thing. I wanted to stretch out my hand and grasp it firmly – make it mine.

'Yes, son?'

So absorbed was I by the intensity of my quest for understanding, that the bus conductor's perfectly reasonable attempt to collect a fare from me seemed an unforgivable intrusion into my privacy. The friendly smile under the shiny-peaked cap wilted in the heat of a ferocious glare from this odd, skinny little boy. The poor man hastily took the two coins from my extended palm, turned the handle on his machine, and handed me a green sevenpenny ticket, before returning to more congenial company on the lower deck.

I stared out through the big front windows at the road ahead. We were nearly at Toad Rock. Didn't like Toad Rock very much. Why not? Didn't know really . . . Everybody is *I* . . . Everybody is *I* . . .

Everybody is I . . . Everybody is I . . .

We were passing the white frontage of the Swan Hotel now, turning slowly into the lower end of Tunbridge Wells High Street. Good old Tunbridge Wells, like a collection of huge dolls' houses. Lovely day, lots of people about – hundreds of people in fact. Probably going to the fair on the common. Everybody is . . .

Suddenly I stiffened. Body erect, hands flat on the ledge below the window, I pressed my forehead against the glass and stared in amazement at the crowds on the pavement below. The true meaning of those three simple, but puzzling words had exploded into my mind, destroying the illusion that I was the centre of the universe, and leaving me to cope, for the rest of my life, with the burden of knowledge. Every one of those people down there in the street, walking the pavements, driving cars, waiting for buses – every single one, whatever they were, whatever they looked like, whatever I thought of them, were as important to themselves as I was to myself! I shook my head, trying to clear it of this incredible notion. Everybody is I . . . That funny, bent old lady with the mouth drooping on one side – she mattered, she was vital – central. The bus conductor who had interrupted my mental churning earlier; he wasn't just a bit player in my world. He was the star in his own. He had a head full of thoughts and feelings; a life inside him; he was the reason that the earth went on turning. My own father and mother, my brothers, aunts, uncles, all my friends – all were 'I'. Everybody was I, and at that moment I was somehow aware that I would probably never learn a more important lesson.

This new understanding did not transform me into a nice person. It enabled me to understand a great deal more about others, but that understanding could be used to help or to harm. In the years that followed, the latter seemed more useful than the former.

Between the ages of ten and sixteen I was desperately engaged in the task of trying to cobble together something in the way of a usable personality. Other people seemed to have one. Why shouldn't I? Somehow I had to batten down the chaos, and construct a facade that would be both acceptable and impenetrable. I certainly didn't want anyone catching a glimpse of the earnest but confused little wretch that I felt myself to be. I discovered that sarcasm, skilfully used, was a means, not only of holding people at a distance, but also of acquiring a certain power. Lowest form of wit it might be, but it was also the most effective. I became an expert in the art of diminishing, belittling, and hurting with words. I blush when I recall the relish with which I applied this weapon at times, to people who can have had no idea of the yearning unhappiness that lay beneath such an alienating strategy. I had postponed happiness in order to concentrate on safety. I learned how to bob and duck and

13

weave in my dealings with school friends and adults, though with more and more difficulty as I moved into the highly competitive world of the boys' grammar school.

Things like homework, and PE kit, and pens that worked, and tidy school uniform, were constant nightmares. I felt grubbier, less equipped in all ways, and more disorganised than any other boy in the school. I had seen other people's houses and families. They seemed almost impossibly ordered and relaxed in comparison with mine. How did they manage it? I had no idea. Our house was a place of loud, moving bodies, swirling emotions and constant television. My mother always did her best, but it was not a place where you did homework. In any case, how could I spare any attention for things like homework or schoolwork, when every ounce of my inventive and mental energy was required for basic social survival?

I was still a voracious reader, and I had considerable natural ability in the subject of English language, but by my second year at secondary school I had already slipped gloomily down into the 'D' stream, the Hades of an establishment like ours, where academic achievement was the road to heaven. My reading nowadays was a way of escape, often into the world of those very dated public-school stories that used to be published in solid thick-paged volumes with a dramatic illustration etched on the front. In these books, clean-living, square-jawed chaps who inhabited something called the Shell, or the Remove, did and said manly things in a highly organised atmosphere of Victorian morality. They had names like 'Goodman' or 'Mainworthy'. Such cads as did exist were called 'Badstone' or 'Munger', and were either reformed or expelled in the final chapter. The teachers always included a young and enthusiastic ex-blue who unobtrusively guided the hero along his path to ultimate manliness, and a God-like headmaster who combined the wisdom of Socrates with the judgement of Solomon. The trinity was completed by a mysterious moving force known generally as 'good form'. Ridiculous though it was, I yearned for such a world. It offered so many things that I had never had.

My other avenue of escape was the fantasy of stardom as a film actor. I nursed a secret conviction that I was the greatest undiscovered thespian in the country, and that it was only a matter of time before, in one of the scenarios that I spent much of my time imagining, I would be discovered by an astonished director and immediately begin a glittering career on the silver screen.

I secretly bought a book entitled *Teach Yourself Amateur Acting*, and studied it in private, so that when the great day came I should be absolutely prepared. My first part would be a leading role in a film that also starred Hayley Mills, with whom I had been deeply in love ever since the day when I sat in the indescribably delicious darkness of the Essoldo cinema, watching *Whistle down the Wind* three times in a row. It was in connection with my passionate feelings about Miss Mills that I learned the second great lesson of my life.

One day, when I was thirteen or so, I made the fatal mistake of trying to turn fantasy into reality. At that time the Mills family lived a few miles away from my home, in a little country village called Cowden. I had often pictured myself accidentally bumping into my beloved in Cowden High Street. It is a fair indication of my naivety that I usually saw this romantic encounter developing from the fact that her bicycle tyre had gone flat. Her knight in shining armour would then pedal suavely on to the scene, flourishing not a sword, but a pump. She would be overwhelmed by my resourcefulness and charity, and subsequently bowled over by my natural charm, which, in my fantasy at least, was irresistible. Marriage would follow at an appropriate age. Large close-ups, glistening tears, stirring music – the lot!

One day I got tired of pretending. I wanted something real to happen for once. I had never actually been to Cowden, but on this warm, sunny, Saturday morning, I decided that the time had come. I set off on my shiny blue bicycle, tense with excitement, to make my dream come true. My belief in a satisfactory outcome to this expedition lasted for several miles, until the moment when I found myself confronted by a nameplate at the side of the road, which said simply, Cowden. I stopped my bike and, balancing on my left foot, reached over to touch the cold metal of the sign with my hand. It was real. Cowden really did exist. I straightened up again and looked around. Beyond the sign the road continued, bordered by trees, flowers and bushes. I could see the tops of one or two houses in the distance – Cowden houses. They were all real. Everything was real. By implication, then, Cowden High Street must be real, Hayley Mills must be real. She was a real person, who didn't spend her life hanging around the village street with an incapacitated bicycle, waiting for some scruffy little twit to rescue her with his pump. It was a sad moment. The world was real. As the full absurdity of my daydream dawned on me, I quietly turned by bike around and pedalled grimly back to Rusthall. Another lesson learned – hard but necessary. I would never find what I wanted in fantasy. That frightened me. Where *would* I find what I wanted?

By the time I began my fifth year at the grammar school, the whole area of education stank of dismal failure. I had never managed to acquire the work habit, and I was so far behind in all subjects except English language, that any hope of passing 'O' level exams had long since evaporated. I felt ugly, and awkward, and useless. The teachers were puzzled. I wasn't typical of the types who failed, but I was impossible to reach by then. It is also impossible to describe to someone who had not experienced it, the leaden misery of daily attendance at an establishment in which you are a legal obligation and nothing more. In all but fantasy (and that was discredited) I was worth nothing. The very school buildings themselves with their grand, mellowed, red-brick frontage seemed to mock my outer and inner disarray as I toiled through the big wrought-iron gates each morning.

I began to truant, setting off for school each morning, dressed in the distinctive grammar school uniform, and ending up walking round and round the recreation ground opposite the school, watching the old men playing bowls, or sitting with a book on the slowly revolving roundabout in the children's corner. Sometimes, at lunchtime, boys from the school would gather in a noisy group behind the bowls pavilion to smoke illicit cigarettes, often cadged from 'Jack', a highly questionable old character whose suspicious enthusiasm for the company of schoolboys was redeemed by his generosity with Kensitas cigarettes, of which he seemed to have an endless supply. Every school seemed to have its 'Jack'. Occasionally I would join this group, pretending to myself that I was normal and involved like them; that, after a morning's work in school, I was relaxing in an enjoyable, forbidden way before returning for the afternoon lessons.

When they left, the game ended, of course, and I would return to the intense solitariness of my truancy. I longed to be part of something, to be genuinely wanted by ordinary people, to be caught up in the warm casualness of relaxed friendship. Those endless months of morbidly aimless wandering while others were busy 'belonging', scarred my self-image more deeply than ever.

Eventually, and inevitably, I was 'asked to leave' by the headmaster. I felt no relief when this happened – only resentment, confusion and shame. I threw my school uniform away for ever, and stepped warily into the adult world.

Chapter Two

Tunbridge Wells in the mid-sixties was an experiential chocolate box. Every flavour of sensation was available in one form or another, and the notorious 'Disgusted of Tunbridge Wells' would need to take only a short walk through his own town to find ample cause for complaint. If you sat in a coffee bar at the lower end of the town, you were as likely to be offered marijuana as a religious tract. If you stayed long enough you would probably get both, and if you lingered even longer you might be approached by a glassy-eyed scientologist offering the chance to learn how to walk through walls in ten easy but very expensive lessons. If group violence was more to your taste, you would become either a mod, in which case you would wear a parka and ride a motor scooter, or a rocker, in which case you would need a leather jacket, long hair, and, at the very least, a regular place on the pillion of somebody's motorcycle. Membership of either of these groups effectively removed the problem of boredom at weekends and on bank holidays, which were spent planning, running from, or seeking mass conflict.

There were other possibilities. Eastern religions and philosophies were available in paperback, and once the jargon was learned, could be adopted as a way of life for a day or two. I remember experiencing some confusion over this when I walked into 'La Rue', one day. La Rue was a small cafe at the busy end of the town, where the pseudo-intelligentsia (of which I was one) met to discuss something called 'life' at interminable length, with no great profit to the proprietor who viewed with some coldness our tendency to sit in a group around one shallow glass cup of frothy coffee for hours on end. One morning I sauntered intelligently into the cafe, to find a friend called John sitting in the corner, with *I have undergone a change* written all over him. The ensuing conversation went something like this.

Me: You're early, John.
John: (*Unwilling to be drawn into small talk that might dissipate the impact of his new image*) Yes.
Me: Any fags?
John: (*Irritated by my failure to say he seemed different somehow*) No!
Me: Why are you out so early?
John: (*Dreamily*) Because the sky is blue.
Me: Pardon?
John: Because the grass is green, because birds fly, and hair grows.
Me: Right . . . hair grows . . . right. I'm with you now, John. (What the hell was he on about?)

SILENCE

John: (*Further irritated by my refusal to admit ignorance*) I don't see things in the same way any more.
Me: (*A generous concession*) Why not?
John: (*Triumphantly*) Because the world is round!

It turned out that John had sat up for most of the night reading a Penguin publication about Zen Buddhism, and his peculiar responses to my questions were evidences of his exciting discovery that, not only was he a Zen Buddhist now, but he always *had* been one without realising it. This made life a little difficult for him, as the book made it clear that the true adherent would never dream of actually stating crudely that he was a Zen Buddhist. Hence, the rather strange dialogue when I came into the cafe. I believe John went on to become a totally committed Marxist — for a week.

If the 'isms' failed to attract, one could always become a

novelist who also wrote poetry. The attraction of this occupation in the sixties, was that it was unnecessary to actually write anything beyond the first line or two of what would undoubtedly have been a great psychological work of fiction if it had ever been finished. In addition, one might compose a few lines of totally obscure poetry, unadulterated by such dated devices as metre, rhyme, or even meaning, and designed to break the stranglehold of the old classical poets like Milton, Dryden, and other people whose works one had never read. Today, twenty years later, there are still, to my certain knowledge, two people continuing to circulate the cafes and pubs of Tunbridge Wells with exercise books and biros, who were doing exactly the same thing in 1965. Tunbridge Wells can do that to people. It can allow them to decay with such a sense of style, that they hardly notice the process until it is too late.

This was particularly so in the sixties because educationalists thought they had discovered that each human being was, potentially, a creative genius. It would have been sacrilege for any one person to criticise another's artistic efforts. The real casualties were those who never recovered from flattery.

So, the choice was mine. Which flavour would I choose? I needed something badly, but it would have to go very deep to make a real difference. My facade of ironic indifference was brittle, but effective, and it was all I had. I sensed the shallowness of all that was on offer, but it didn't surprise me. Everybody is I. Did all these others carry around inside them the same tight ball of tearful chaos that I did? At one point my disguise included a violently checked jacket, a pair of dark glasses that I wore at all times and in all weathers, and a black billiard ball which I repeatedly threw up and caught with my right hand. Nobody was going to get inside me! I must have looked, to borrow a powerful expression of my son's, a real 'super-nurd'.

There were three good and important things in my life at this point. The first, my mother, had always been there, although on reflection I can see that my appreciation and treatment of her had been variable. Often, during this difficult period, I would arrive home very late at night to find that my father had switched off the electricity at the mains. This meant that the one light-bulb which travelled from room to room as it was needed, was useless to me. The dark house was doom-laden at one o'clock in the morning, but as I groped my way upstairs – still wearing the dark glasses – I knew that, nine times out of ten, my mother would have left beside my bed a little pile of sandwiches – usually Marmite – and a large glass of milk. People say they are curious about heaven. I have tasted heaven. It consists of reading escapist literature by candlelight while eating Marmite sandwiches and drinking cold milk, in a dark house in a dark world.

The second good thing was a real live girlfriend called Anthea. She was a talented, kind girl, whose parents were predictably aghast to find that the apple of their eye had trawled in an apparent lunatic, whose taste in clothes and obsession with dark glasses and billiard balls must have suggested that placement in a locked institution was imminent.

Anthea and I were together for four years, and I owe her a great deal. She was the first person outside my family to dispel my personal myth that I was unlovable, and she put up with a lot of testing in the process. I remember her with great affection.

The third important thing was my acquisition of three friends. The first, John Hall, had attended one of those traditional public schools I was so fond of reading about, though his description of life in his particular establishment bore little relation to fictional accounts. John's natural courtesy and generosity thawed me, often allowing the vulnerable little boy of six years ago to risk a brief excursion into the outside world. John is now an Anglican priest in the north of England, and still my closest friend. The other two friends were a married couple who lived in a rented cottage in the depths of the Sussex countryside, near Wadhurst. Murray and Vivien Staplehurst accepted me so unreservedly that I really began to feel – while I was with them at any rate – that life might be worth living after all. They switched me on with their approval, affection and appreciation of my sense of humour and fascinated me with their eccentricity and larger-than-life-ness. I value their friendship now, as then.

Every Sunday, the Anglican Church of St John's in Tunbridge Wells organised a coffee-bar evening in the upper room of a building called Byng Hall, next door to The Red Lion on one side, and my ex-grammar school on the other. In charge was a young and enthusiastic curate named Clive Sampson. He arrived after evensong each Sunday, accompanied by a small group of clean-looking teenagers to unlock the front door of the hall and admit the little knot of non-church attenders who usually gathered outside. I had got into the habit of coming along each week largely because there was very little else to do in Tunbridge Wells on a Sunday evening. The coffee was very cheap, and there were other, less material attractions. I sensed that, in a way I didn't quite understand, I was nibbling at someone's bait. Something in the studied casualness of the non-mini-skirted Christian girls, and the short haired, jerseyed Christian boys suggested that they were all expecting something to happen in, for, or to me, one of these days. It soon became clear that they were waiting – and perhaps praying – for my conversion to Christianity, whatever that might mean.

I took an odd pleasure in paddling on the edge of this sea of expectation, never going in too far, but never withdrawing completely. The only formal religious content of these evenings was a three minute talk or 'epilogue' near the end, but I rather enjoyed the sport of 'cornering the curate'. Every week I would have a different question to ask, a fresh objection to make, or a new argument to intro-duce. Clive battled manfully with the problems, clearly feeling a little inadequate as he sorted out the whole question of universal suffering for me, and explained, on behalf of God, how predestination and free will are,

22

actually, not incompatible at all. He half dreaded, half enjoyed these mind-stretching encounters. For me the whole thing had very little to do with God, any more than the Roman Catholic chapel had when I was a child. I enjoyed the discussions – I enjoyed seeing Clive out of his depth sometimes – but mainly I was just a sucker for being wanted. They let me talk and they seemed to want me in a slightly predatory sort of way. It was possible to relax and enjoy being large and different among these people who, though the same age as me, had skinnier arms and more innocent and organised lives.

Poor old Clive became aware after a number of weeks that talking me into any kind of Christian belief had about as much chance of success as striking a match on jelly. He had used all the illustrations, explanations, revelations and exhortations that he could think of. He was right out of '-ations'. The day came when his patience faded. His intellect stomped off in disgust, leaving his heart free to say something at last.

'I just love him!' he blurted out, smacking the palm of his hand down on the formica-topped coffee bar. 'I love him! That's all – I just love Jesus!'

This crashing service ace, coming at the end of a long succession of easily returned schoolgirl lobs, caught me totally wrong-footed. He'd broken the rules, hadn't he? Who said we were going to talk about things that really mattered to us? Because there was no doubt at all that Clive reacted to this Jesus from the gut. He'd taken a long time to say so, but it was a fact, and I was impressed. Not convinced, but definitely impressed, even a little shaken perhaps. Underneath Clive's words – and I knew all about words – lay a passionate feeling, or emotion, about someone who didn't exist, except as an historical figure.

Here we are, then, at a danger point. I can feel the temptation to embroider this incident and my reaction to it. I know how to do it. I would like to say that my spirit sensed the presence of the Lord. It didn't. I would like to say that from that moment I felt God calling me to him. I didn't. I would like to say all sorts of things that are not quite true. They might encourage people, but God wants the truth, and the truth is a funny, ragged old thing.

One instinct that Clive's outburst did arouse in me was curiosity. I was puzzled by the strength of his feelings and the process by which he had acquired them. Not that I equated strength of feeling with truth or goodness, necessarily. The Inquisition and the Nazi party were poor adverts for enthusiasm, to name but two. Clive had never burned anyone at the stake, or invaded Poland, as far as I knew, but, perhaps because of my father, I was very wary of emotion. I decided to maintain my air of indifference, and investigate as casually as I could.

I went to church. St John's was a very satisfactorily churchy-looking sort of church. Grey stone, and towers, and pointed arches, and dark wood and things. It was a heavy, comfortable, motherly sort of building, presided over by the Reverend Donald Edison, one of the sweetest-natured men I have known. Clive was his curate. I began to go to the service known as Evensong. This began at 6.30, and ended at 7.30, a long time for a devoted cigarette smoker like me, but I usually stuck it out for the hour. Soon I was settled into the new pattern. Tea at Anthea's house about five o'clock, down to the church for Evensong at half past six, and along the road to Byng Hall for the coffee bar at half past seven. The whole thing had a very pleasantly civilised feel about it. It was an oasis of order and freshness in the desert of unemployed gloom that filled the rest of the week. I remember my particular pleasure in the knowledge that Anthea's mother always ensured that Sunday tea included one of those beautifully labelled china pots of Patum Peperium – Gentleman's Relish. It was there for me.

The preacher at the evening service would usually be either Donald Edison or Clive Sampson, with the occasional visiting speaker.

One day a man called Denis Shepherd, from one of the London churches, came to speak to the evening congregation.

He was a tall, broad man, with a quiet manner and an air of inner strength. As far as I can recall he had been in the Merchant Navy for some years before being ordained into the Anglican Church. I was still very much a spectator, and I would have rejected with scorn the suggestion that what this man said was going to bring real tears to my eyes, and, for better or worse, change the whole course of my life.

The talk he gave was about the brief conversation between Jesus, as he hung dying on the cross, and the two lawbreakers who were crucified on either side of him, an event which is recorded only in the Gospel of Luke. The preacher read the relevant passage before beginning his talk.

One of the criminals hanging there abused him. 'Are you not the Christ?' he said. 'Save yourself and us as well.' But the other spoke up and rebuked him. 'Have you no fear of God at all?' he said. 'You got the same sentence as he did, but in our case we deserved it: we are paying for what we did. But this man has done nothing wrong. Jesus,' he said, 'remember me when you come into your kingdom.' 'Indeed, I promise you,' he replied, 'today you will be with me in paradise.'

The Reverend Shepherd went on to speak in more detail about the kind of interaction that must have occurred between these dirty, blood-streaked individuals as they hung side by side waiting for the relief of death. He spoke particularly about the man who had recognised something special in Jesus. He was a man who, to all intents and purposes, was finished. His life was over, and a wretched, useless life it had been. Any dreams of last minute reprieve had been shattered by the first of the executioner's nails, as it crunched through bone, sinew and flesh, impaling him to the rough wooden surface of his cross. It was the end of all reasonable hope. The dialogue between this fellow and Jesus was very uncomplicated. Presumably, it arose from what each saw in the other as they shared the same kind of physical agony. What did the criminal see in Jesus? Nobody knows for sure, but it was probably some kind of natural authority blended with deep compassion.

He obviously looked like someone who, despite his present circumstances, was going somewhere – an 'in-charge' sort of person, a grown-up. He must have known a bit about Jesus already, the conversation shows that: but perhaps he had never looked closely at him before, or believed it was possible to reach the heights of virtue that must surely be required from followers of such an uncompromisingly moral character. Whatever else he did or did not see, though, one thing is clear. He recognised a sudden, breath-taking opportunity to make everything all right. Morally naked as he was, there was no hope of convincing the Galilean that he deserved anything, nor was there time to live-a-better-life for a while in the hope of investing a little in his divine bank account. Perhaps what was happening was that the child in this hardened law-breaker, the part of him that still wanted to believe in something or someone, was yearning for the warmth and comfort that all children must have. In the eyes of the man beside him, he saw an invitation to be loved and wanted, not because of, nor despite, anything, but simply because that is what children need. Jesus' eyes, as they looked into the lost and dejected face of his neighbour, were full of the love of his father. They were saying, 'I don't care what you've done. I don't care what you are. I don't care what others say about you. I don't even care what you think of yourself. You're coming with me. Don't worry, everything's going to be all right.'

As I sat next to Anthea at the back of the crowded church, the preacher's words seemed to be meant specially for me. I felt like a child too. The puzzled little boy who had wanted so much to stop his mummy and daddy arguing so that they would be happy together, but had failed, not only at that, but at almost everything else since, wanted to shout out his hurt across the heads of the congregation, through the preacher who seemed a sort of conduit to God, and thence up to heaven itself.

'What about me? I'm lost too! I'm lonely and ragged inside. I've tried and tried, but I just don't know how to be like ordinary people. What about me? Do you love me like you loved that man on the cross? Will you be a father to me, whatever I am and whatever I say or do? Can I safely show you how hurt and wretched I am?'

Would Jesus look at me from the cross with those same loving eyes and say 'Don't worry, everything's okay. I know all about you, Adrian. It doesn't matter what's happened up to now. I'll look after you. I know you never wanted to be hurtful or sarcastic. I know how much you wanted to do well. I know you're not the person you wanted to be. It doesn't matter – I do understand.'

Suddenly my eyes were full of tears. How I wanted that kind of acceptance, the chance to start again and be real, to relax the constant strain that the maintenance of my artificial personality imposed on me. This man was saying that Jesus offered all these things in the twentieth century – right now. As I stood for the final hymn, my hands supporting my weight on the pew in front of me, I managed to control the tears, and after the blessing we joined the stream of people flowing down the centre aisle towards the big front doors where the preacher waited to shake hands with people as they left. Just before we reached him, Anthea and I looked at each other. Without speaking we knew that both of us had been affected by what we had just heard. As I shook hands with Denis Shepherd a few seconds later, I found myself saying quietly, 'Could we see you afterwards? We want to become Christians.'

Later, when the congregation had dispersed and all was quiet, we met him in a room at the back of the church and told him that we wanted to do 'whatever you did' in order to get 'whatever you got'. He seemed to understand this strange request, and suggested that we should say a prayer in which we asked Jesus into our hearts as Lord and Saviour. I didn't know what that meant, but I wasn't going to let mere technicalities put me off when real happiness was available. We found it hard to frame a prayer properly, so, in the end he prayed for us, while we joined in silently in our minds, and said 'amen' with him at the end. The prayer was short, but it included terms and concepts that, while appearing quite straightforward at the time, awe me nowadays with their depth and mystery.

'Heavenly Father, we know that we have sinned against you, like all mankind, by turning away from you. We thank you that Jesus died on the cross to pay for our sins and to offer a way back to you. We ask that Jesus will come and live in our hearts by the power of your Holy Spirit, and that we may be able to love and serve you for the rest of our lives, and be with you in heaven forever when we die. We ask this in the name of the Lord Jesus Christ, Amen.'

I didn't feel anything as I prayed this prayer – neither then nor immediately afterwards, but I had prayed it. My mind had said 'Yes' and I was a Christian.

There were many exciting Christian paperbacks on sale in the sixties. There are still, of course, but at that time it was something new. These books were so full of miraculous signs and wonders, that they made everyday life seem very drab and dull in comparison. After my conversion I, in common with many others, devoured this kind of literature in much the same way that large mammals are obliged to eat constantly in order to stay alive. They usually chronicled the background, conversion and subsequent spiritual adventures of a particular individual – often American. They made you gasp and weep and hope that, in time, God could use you in a similar way. Each new book that was published seemed to emphasise a different aspect of the Christian life, or a more reliable way to ensure that you had easy access to the divine machinery, and a working knowledge of its controls.

'Praise God in all adversity' said one. 'Don't be afraid to be angry and honest with God' said another.

'People who don't speak in tongues are not really Christians' claimed one writer. 'You don't need to speak in tongues to be a Christian' answered somebody else.

28

'God is working in the established church.' 'God had rejected the established church.'

All claimed to be right, all offered evidence to support their particular claim, and most included, somewhere on the front or back cover, the seductive phrase 'This is a true story'. I now know that there is a significant difference between a list of consecutive factual events, and an account in which things like atmosphere, interpretation and illustration have been woven – often very attractively – around those events. I try to do it myself. 'Truth' can be a very difficult thing to pin down. At the time, though, I was happy to collude with the writers of these books, which meant that I discovered the 'real answer', on average, about twice a week.

Many people were genuinely and lastingly helped, especially by such classics as *The Cross and the Switchblade*, but I fear that for me and many others, each new spiritual volume was like one more shot in the arm for an addict. It reassured for a time, and gave the world a rather tinny dazzle, but it didn't last for long.

One thing that nearly all these books had in common was the suggestion that conversion meant the end of the bad times, and the beginning of the good times. Much recent Christian literature, thankfully, avoids this grotesque and dangerous over-simplification, and is as honest as Jesus was, but at that time I got it firmly into my head that conversion equalled happy-ever-after, and there was little in the presentation of evangelical Christianity at the time to dispel this illusion. I had been converted. Go on then, God. Do something. Change me. Organise me. I've said the prayer. Away you go!

It wasn't working.

Soon after the day of our conversion, Anthea and I had been sent, through the post, a list of prayer meetings, Bible studies, and youth activities that were scheduled for the coming month. This list utterly dismayed me, and for some weeks I didn't go near the church. I felt confused and hurt. On the Sunday evening when Denis Shepherd had spoken,

I had been deeply moved and attracted by the possibility of acceptance and love from this man – God, Jesus. It had been an encounter between two personalities, and it had seemed to promise change. What had a typed list of activities to do with that? My resentment was on a hair trigger, and the flimsy piece of formality that I held in my hand was enough to fire it full-blast at a church which seemed to think that 'putting me on the register' would help in some way. God had offered me bread to eat because he saw that I was hungry. Now I was being told that what this amounted to was a course of cookery lessons. What had I expected? I don't know. I was full of bitterness and anger, quite unable to think rationally. I felt like the army recruit who, having responded to the charm of the recruiting officer, finds that things change drastically after signing on the dotted line.

In hindsight I can see the extent to which vanity played a part in my response. Like most people who despise themselves in private, I found it very difficult to be an also-ran in public. Perhaps I thought that the whole of Christendom should have rejoiced mightily to find such a valuable asset added to its numbers. Perhaps, in a local sense, it should have done. We who call ourselves Christians should be constantly aware that when someone responds to a call from God, we may have access to the particular kind of bread that was promised in that encounter. Let's give it. Let's ignore our prissy concern that we may be feeding someone's vanity. Let's be extravagant and let God sort the rest out.

Whatever the rights and wrongs of the situation, by the time I did go back to the church, a month or so later, I had reassembled my defences, and was ready to take on my old role of guilty performer in the new context of the Young People's Fellowship, and the Christian community of St John's Church. I learned the ropes and the language (what someone recently called 'Christianese') quite quickly. On one level I enjoyed being a part of the group, and yet being different – more 'of the world', but on another I still felt alienated and unreal. In the middle of meetings and services it was possible to feel good, to shout 'Praise the Lord!' with the others, and even feel that I meant it, but the nights were black. God never came home with me. I would return from a lively bout of rejoicing to find that, on my own, there was only fear, fear that there was no God; fear even that in some peculiar way I only existed when other people were present. My own consciousness was embarrassingly there with me, watching as some other 'I' wrestled with panic and doubt. I had never heard of holograms then, but that was what I felt like – substantial only as a projection of the beliefs, attitudes and responses of others. But how could I tell anyone this? I was a Christian. I was converted. If things weren't going right; if I wasn't experiencing the love, joy and peace that God *always* brought into the hearts of believers, there were only three possible reasons that I could think of.

(1) There was no God. I had made a mistake.
(2) I had done, or failed to do, something that was crucially important.
(3) After taking a closer look, God had said, 'No thanks very much', and decided I wasn't up to scratch.

I didn't want to believe the first, hoped vaguely that it might be the second, and secretly believed and dreaded that it was actually the third. Sometimes, I read the parable of the sower, in which some of the seed falls on stony ground, and after springing up quickly, withers away in the sun because it has no real roots. Was that me? And were all these mild, tidily dressed young people, who didn't smoke and were working for exams or preparing to go to university or college, the seed that fell on rich soil and produced a crop, some a hundredfold, some sixty, some thirty? I felt they must be. No doubt they all woke each morning and had the much discussed and strongly advocated 'quiet time' with God. I didn't. I said I did, but I didn't, any more than I had done my homework while at school.

In fact, the whole experience became a kind of parallel of schooldays. My uniform was evangelical language and behaviour – as scruffy and ill-fitting as ever – and the headmaster

31

was God, a distant being who was kind to those who succeeded, and eventually expelled the ones who didn't, or couldn't. What had happened to the Jesus who said he would look after me, and accept me whatever I was? I sang about him, discussed him, tried to talk to him. Where the heck was he? If there seems to be a lot of anger in these words, that's because there is. Even as I write, the memory of that feeling of angry disappointment floods into my mind and momentarily obscures the peace that I have now.

Now, of course, gentle reader, (I used to read a lot of Victorian literature as a child) I can see, as you can, that this scruffy, mixed up and over defended teenager was confusing God with middle class evangelical Christianity and that as long as I was trying to be like other people who were very different to me, I stood little chance of feeling that I was getting somewhere. Also, I recognise that my trusting mechanism had rusted with disuse, and was bound to require consistent applications of the oil of love, over a long period, before it ground into action again. Add to this my distorted perception of fatherhood and adult relationships, and it really is not difficult to account for the mess I found myself in. But I was by no means the only casualty. My heart goes out to all those others, who, in the sixties were attracted by Jesus, and tried unsuccessfully thereafter, to find him in the security of groups and jargon. In the group that I joined there was at least a handful of people who, because of difficult, painful backgrounds needed a special kind of love and discipline, but gave up in the end because the strain of copying was too great. They are at a particular disadvantage because, whereas most of the other attractions of the period – drugs or eastern philosophies or whatever – could be dropped without guilt, the abandonment of Christianity, as it was presented then and still is in many places, often left a shadow of guilt and failure darkening a corner of the spirit, that was not easily removed. This was intensified by the fact – puzzling and hurtful at the time – that whereas people in the church accepted you totally before conversion, they tended to find any deviation from the norm very annoying or unacceptable after you had 'crossed the line'.

So, the escape into reality that I had so longed for was simply not happening. Why *did* God disappear when I was on my own? Why was I still having to wear the masks that prevented people from coming close to me? Why, oh why was it all such a strain? I just didn't know.

Chapter Three

I arrived in Bristol after dark, clutching two badly fastened, string-reinforced suitcases, with not the slightest idea of where I would stay, or how I would look after myself. The city seemed terrifyingly large as I trudged out of the coach station, to find myself on one of those featureless roads that run dumbly behind large buildings. It was a viciously unwelcoming spot, and I was near to tears for a moment, as I put my bags down and tried to decide what to do next.

I suppose it was something of a miracle that I was there at all. Nearly three years had passed since I officially left school. After two or three disastrous attempts to enter the world of employment I had managed, on the strength of my ability with language, to enrol at the West Kent College of Further Education for a combined GCE and foundation drama course. Such a course could not have been better suited to one who, like me, was able to produce occasional flashes of brilliance in English Literature classes and drama exercises, this temporarily blinding tutors to the fact that I was doing next to no work at all.

A close friend, Hugh Card, wrote to me recently about those days.

We met in 1967, at a college Christian Union meeting. I was an engineering student. You were on a drama course. I noticed your size and untidiness. You sat at a table, dropping cigarette ash on the yellow formica, taking up more space than seemed reasonable. You talked rather than listened. As you explained your ideas, bits of paper spread across the table and on to the floor. An

Agatha Christie fell out of your pocket. You were the untidiest Christian I'd met.

For two years I enjoyed a feeling of relative significance in this setting, especially as the second year was spent in the comfortable knowledge that I had secured a place on the Bristol Old Vic Theatre School acting course, to commence in the autumn of 1967.

I left the college, finally, with a B pass at 'A' level in English Literature, which delighted and (secretly) amazed me, and a scraped pass in French 'O' level, which left me with the ability to converse in the present tense with close members of the family on such useful and diverse topics as writing implements and dining rooms, but very little else. Now, I was about to pursue that old fantasy of stardom in the acting world, and I had a real place on a real course at a real and reputable theatre school, over a hundred miles away in the city of Bristol. If only I had been better prepared. For some reason I never got round to arranging a place to stay when I arrived. It was so easy to rationalise my disorganisation. I called it 'walking in faith'. Christians didn't need to trouble themselves with such trivial matters as booking accommodation in advance. God would provide.

Now, as I stood dismally next to my luggage in the darkness of a strange city, I wasn't so sure. There was one chance, though. A friend in Tunbridge Wells had told me about a church in the Redlands area of the city. She knew the vicar well. He was, she said, a wonderful Christian. If ever I needed anything I should go to him. He would help.

'Right!' I said to myself, picking up my cases, 'Redlands it is.'

After many enquiries, and a fairly lengthy walk, I found myself, at last, outside the front door of a house situated to one side of the church my friend had named. On a polished wooden name-plate beside the door, I could just make out the reassuring words 'The Vicarage'. I was very tired by now, and aching with hunger, but these basic needs were as nothing compared to my desperate desire to make real contact with someone in this alien world. Ever one for the dramatic moment, I planned my lines carefully before raising my hand to the brass knocker in front of me. After all, this might be the beginning of chapter one in my own best-selling Christian saga one day.

The door was opened by a nicely-dressed lady, probably in her fifties, who peered doubtfully out at the tall dark figure standing between what must have looked in silhouette, like two over-stuffed cardboard boxes.

'Yes?' she said, rather nervously.

'I'm starting at the theatre school this term,' said I, 'and I've just arrived from Tunbridge Wells tonight.'

'Yes?' she sounded even more nervous than before.

Time for my punchline.

'I've got nowhere to stay and the only person I know in Bristol is Jesus.'

Now she looked positively terrified.

'My husband's out at the moment, I'm afraid . . . I don't know . . .'

Something crumpled in me. Never mind my Christian saga, I just wanted a little mothering. My voice broke a little as I spoke.

'A friend suggested I should come if I needed help . . .' I named the friend.

'Oh, yes, I know.' It obviously didn't make any difference. 'I'm afraid that my husband won't be back for some time.' The door was closing, she was drawing back. 'Try again later, perhaps . . .' The latch clicked into place. She was gone.

What had gone wrong? Wrong script? Wrong house? Wrong city? Wrong world? I was desolated. My last emotional and physical reserves had been spent in reaching that front door. All the old horror of not belonging flooded into my heart as I picked up my luggage and trailed off into the darkness. The magic words hadn't done the trick. Much later that night I did finally find somewhere to stay, but the moment immediately after the door shut on that autumn night in 1967 remained as a nightmare memory for years. Christians, God, Jesus – no one kept their promises.

I was, of course, totally self-absorbed at the time, otherwise I might have understood that middle-aged ladies on their own late at night are, quite reasonably, unwilling to admit very large religious maniacs with great armfuls of murder weapons in cardboard boxes. I'm sure that the lady concerned was as charitable as the next person, and, in one sense, she has affected me positively. Since that night I have never turned anyone away from my door.

I had not realised that it was possible to be as lonely as I was during my first term at Bristol. I used to lie on my bed in the lodgings I had found, alternately pleading and raving in the direction of this God who seemed to exist only within the confines of St John's Church, Tunbridge Wells.

Not surprisingly, perhaps, the year that followed was not a successful one in terms of the acting course. There was no doubt that I had talent, but my application and self-discipline were very poor. I soon realised that I lacked the kind of consistency required from students of what is a very tough and demanding profession. Once again, the reality trampled all over the dream. I stumbled through the days and weeks in my usual ragged fashion, still clutching my large Bible like a talisman in the most inappropriate situations, hoping I suppose that God would eventually flesh out the bones of the identity that I still thought the Christian faith might offer me.

Now some of those who have been following the story closely so far, will be aware, and are probably dying to point out to me, that 'Old God', as Bishop Peter Ball sometimes affectionately refers to him, had been putting in some pretty useful work on my behalf for some time, and getting no credit whatsoever for it. From the year before my conversion there were no less than five people who were offering me the kind of love and acceptance that God had seemed to promise on the night when Denis Shepherd spoke in the church. Whether they knew this or not, whether they liked it or not, it was so. My mother, Murray and Vivien, John and Anthea, all were keeping God's promise, and in their own way contributing to the process of breaking up the stony ground in my heart to create the kind of rich soil that would make real growth possible in the future. I didn't know this at the time, of course, but how well I understand it now. Later, in my work with children I met so many disturbed youngsters for whom security was just a rumour put about by social workers. They could be surrounded by love, and not see it. Their conviction that the world did not want them was not a belief. It was knowledge. They could not simply be talked into happiness, nor could they be bribed or lured into feeling 'all right'. Often, all that one could do was to go on loving them, practically as well as emotionally, sometimes for years without much, if any, response. They could be aggressive, rejecting, sentimental and apathetic by turns. I once sat with a fifteen-year-old boy sobbing on my lap after he had broken all my windows.

During that excruciatingly lonely period in Bristol, my head was so full of myself, scripture, spiritual gifts, charismatic speakers and Christianese gobbledegook, that I probably wouldn't have recognised Jesus if he'd jumped out in front of me on the pavement and performed amazing miracles before my eyes. Much less was I able to see the quietly persistent love of God in the eyes and arms and voices of those who cared about me.

Blinking God! I'd have broken all his windows if I'd known where they were. Then, perhaps, he would have let *me* sob on *his* lap!

It was in Bristol, in that year of failure at the theatre school, that God gave me the most valuable gift of all. Bridget Ormerod was a fellow student. Like me, she was capable of great mood-swings, but she had a kindness and sense of humour that I found irresistible. Her surname, she told me, meant 'snake in the clearing', which suggested a sort of unconcealed evil. How inappropriate for someone who has brought nothing but care and kindness into people's lives for as long as I have known her.

We spent all our time together after the first term,

sometimes spending the period from midnight to dawn in the all night cafe down in the Cumberland Basin, a place where the river and the main road met and crossed by means of a pivoting concrete bridge. The whole scene was lit up at night like a stage set, this appealing greatly to the sense of drama we had in common. It was a blissful time. After a long period of non-belief, Bridget had recently had a conversion experience of her own, and, for a while I enjoyed the novel experience of feeling that God and the world and I belonged to each other, and to Bridget of course. I was in love. We were in love. We felt like two children whom God was leading by the hand into a future that seemed much more promising than I had dared to hope. Perhaps God was all right after all? Fingers crossed.

The immediate question was what to do next. We would get married. We were quite sure about that. We were also quite sure that our future did not lie in the theatre. Eventually, we decided that, although we knew very little about it, we wanted to work in child-care of some kind. Indeed we believed that this was what God was leading us to do. After one or two false starts, and a brief but very enjoyable period as domestic workers at Burrswood, the Christian Healing Home near Tunbridge Wells, we started work as housefather and housemother in a County Council boarding school for maladjusted boys, in the little town of Dursley in Gloucestershire. The school provided places for fifty teenage boys with educational and emotional problems. We occupied single staff flats at opposite ends of the building, which was set in the beautiful green-sculpted Gloucestershire countryside. We were to be married in the following year. On the day we started work it was difficult to see how anything could go very wrong.

At last I seemed to be secure enough to let my childhood insight that 'Everybody is I' work for the benefit of other people. I suppose I envisaged the children I would work with as little, neglected, empty pots, into which I, a combination of Danny Kaye and Doctor Barnardo would pour care, affection and sympathy until they were full and overflowing. They would be pathetically grateful.

I cannot recall any single child being willing to take part in this touching scenario, and after only one day's work with the boys, I drastically adapted my fantasy to one in which a child, any child, was willing to talk pleasantly for five whole minutes to a painfully inept and lonely house-parent.

Within a few weeks my dignity was in shreds. All the techniques and ploys that had just about kept me afloat in the sea of adult interaction were virtually useless against the tidal wave of raw feeling that emanated from these hurt and needy children. With the uncannily accurate insight that is born out of disappointment and failure, they saw through my assumed air of calm confidence and provoked me into responses that frightened me in their violence and intensity. One boy in particular, was a past master in the art of finding my psychological raw spot, and twisting his metaphorical finger into it with relish. He had been alternately beaten and rejected by his policeman father, and he set out to prove that I, tall and dark like his dad, would do the same. His lengthy campaign of aggression and cringing apology worked in the end. In the centre of the football field one day, I knew that my frustration and humiliation were about to find expression. I would either burst into tears or hit him. As we faced each other at that moment the only real difference between us was one of size. I hit him very hard, twice. He had revealed me for what I was; a very immature adult with far too much chaos of my own to be able to cope with his. I couldn't face that at the time, though. I needed so much to be a person who loved children. The guilt and confusion I felt over this and other occasions when I lost control, remained unexamined and unresolved, and were to result in profound problems later in my life.

That first year of work was a nightmare of demolished dignity, lost battles and periodic retreats into the bottom of my wardrobe, where the enclosed darkness offered temporary respite from this world that seemed determined to prove to me yet again, that it was horribly real. Thank goodness I had Bridget. God seemed to have gone on holiday.

The second year was a little easier, but it was marked by an event of considerable significance: the death of my father. The news came by telephone one evening, as Bridget and I, married by now, were preparing to take ten of the most difficult boys away for a hostelling holiday. My mother said that the cancer which had been diagnosed two years earlier had finally killed my father. I didn't really know how to react, and the holiday, which we decided should go ahead as planned, was actually a rather welcome distraction. The constant activity required in the job I was doing enabled me to postpone the uncomfortable task of looking at my feelings for some time. When I did finally risk a peep round the wall of my busy-ness, I discovered that I was deeply unhappy. I was unhappy for a specific reason. My father's death had not been unexpected. We had known for some time that his illness was terminal, so whenever I journeyed from Gloucestershire to Tunbridge Wells to visit my parents' home, I made sure that we 'got on' well. I felt sorry for him in his diminished, crumpled state, all the old jealousies and insecurities seeming so trivial now that he depended on my mother like a helpless child. Also, if I am honest, I was deliberately trying to put together a reasonable collection of positive memories, ready to pile up like sandbags against the inevitable attack of guilt after his death.

But my immediate unhappiness was not about anything that had happened during his life, but about what was happening *now*. Had the plump prayer book worked? Had the Roman Catholic Church worked? Had God worked? Where was my father now? I wanted to know the answer to that question more that I wanted anything else. I remembered moments from the distant past when, frustrated beyond measure by the unbridgeable gap between what he was and what his religion said he should be, he had knelt on the floor pounding a chair with his fist, and shouting through clenched teeth, 'Oh, Christ, help me! Oh, Christ, help me!' Had Christ heard him, or was it all just a cruel, meaningless game?

By now, my father would know – if there was anything to know – all about heaven and hell. I had only the vaguest notion of what terms like that might mean, but I asked God about it again and again.

'Tell me . . . please tell me. Where is he?'

I began to think that I would never find peace, until, one night, I had a dream.

There were two parts to the dream. In the first part, I didn't feel as if I was dreaming at all. Perhaps I wasn't. The period just before sleep can be an odd mixture of conscious thought, and unbidden, dream-like images. Awake or asleep – it doesn't really matter. I saw the face of Jesus, just above mine, as I lay in my bed in the darkness. It was a face that smiled, and the smile was one that comforted and reassured. It was there for a few seconds, and then it was gone, like a light being turned out. Don't ask me how I knew that it was Jesus' face. I just knew.

The second part of the dream was quite definitely just that – a dream. It began with a muffled knocking sound, someone was knocking on wood with their knuckles, trying to attract attention. Gradually, I became aware that the noise was coming from my left, and, turning slowly in that direction, I saw a coffin. As I stared at the brown wooden container, I knew with the absolute certainty that is peculiar to dreams, that my father was inside, alive, and anxious to be released from the darkness. With that knowledge came the realisation that someone was standing quietly on my other side, waiting to speak to me. He was a traveller, a man from Tibet, the country I have always associated with hidden knowledge and mysticism. He had travelled a long way, he said, to bring me an important message.

I can hear his words as clearly today as I heard them that night, fourteen years ago.

'There is a rumour that your father has been resurrected.'

That was all; the dream ended with those words. In the

42

morning I remembered the details, but it wasn't until later in the day that I connected the dream message with my constant requests to God for information. As soon as that connection was made, I felt peaceful about my father's whereabouts, although I reckoned that at most, I had been given a divine 'hint'.

This experience is of course a very good example of the kind of incident that can be wrapped in the cotton-wool of spiritual jargon and exhibited from time to time in one's personal museum of 'things that show there is a God'. Thus, in the past, I might, and probably have, described the events of that night in the following way.

'I was lying awake – absolutely wide awake – when the Lord manifested himself to me, and ministered to me through his spirit in great power, with a mighty blessing. I was then shown a vision as of a coffin, and a great knocking came from within. A messenger of the Lord then appeared, and brought wonderful news that my father was gloriously resurrected. From that moment my soul was at peace, and I knew that my prayers were indeed marvellously answered.'

Notice that Tibet has disappeared altogether, and the whole thing is much tidier and more presentable. No, I seemed to see Jesus smiling at me; a man in a dream hinted that my father might be okay; the next day I was no longer troubled; I had been asking God for reassurance. These were the things that happened and they were enough.

Bridget and I worked at the boarding school for three years, and although there was some success and satisfaction, some good relationships made, and some painful partings at the end, it was an overpowering relief to walk down the drive and out through the gates for the last time. As we sat surrounded by cases in the little Dursley bus station I reflected on my amazing capacity for nostalgia.

'If,' I said to Bridget, 'you ever hear me say that I wish we could go back to the good old days in Gloucestershire, just remind me that at this moment I KNOW that's not the way it was!'

She promised she would, and has, of course, had to do so on a number of occasions since.

From Gloucestershire we moved to Bromley, in Kent, where I had been offered a place at a teaching college. In those days, the main qualification for promotion in the child-care world was a teaching certificate, and despite having been reduced to my lowest common denominators by the children at Cam House School, I wanted to continue in that kind of work. I also wanted to have a higher education qualification just for the sake of having it. Bridget had obtained a degree at Bristol University before starting at the theatre school, and, although very humble, was annoyingly bright. So – little Adrian had to have a badge to wear, just like her! I got my badge in the end, a not very impressive B.Ed degree, but by then it didn't seem to matter so much. During the three year course, our first son, Matthew, was born. I was totally enchanted with this little scrap of humanity. He was an enduring novelty, a source of endless fascination and pleasure. I loved his uncompromising, openly expressed need for us, his parents. Every sound he made, every new expression or movement was vitally interesting. Dear Matthew was, and still very much is, another link in the chain of God's loving concern for me. So too are a number of folk who were members of the local church youth club which we helped to run. They are all grown up now (they claim), but are still our very close friends, including Madeleine Dawson, who later became as regular a contributor to Company as her teaching commitments allowed.

St Augustine's, the church we attended in Bromley was one of the best kinds of Anglican assembly. By this I mean that the general ethos was more reminiscent of a family than either a morgue or an obstacle race. At the centre of the congregation was a minority of people who had a genuine faith, and a profound regard for God, while the majority came in a wide variety of temperamental and spiritual shapes and sizes. It was a very warm and caring community, and the first church in which Bridget and I felt genuinely close to, and part of, a worshipping body. The various dramatic productions and youth services that we helped with are among our warmest memories.

Despite all these positive aspects of life in Bromley, however, I still agonised over my relationship with God. I found myself doubting to the point of total disbelief. Okay, things were good at home, and very good socially at church; college was a strain from beginning to end, but I didn't have to be there much. Generally speaking, things were good. We were sharing the house of the curate, who was none other than my best friend from Tunbridge Wells, John Hall. Together we played bad but enjoyable golf once a week on the municipal course, and renewed our old practice of sitting up until the early hours from time to time, talking about everything under the sun.

I was happily married. Matthew was a constant joy. What more could I ask?

I wanted God. I still wanted that God who had made all those promises back in St John's Church when I was sixteen. In what form did I want him? I wasn't sure. I just knew that there was a knot of pain and anger in me that would never be untied (no matter how many good things happened) until I *knew* that God loved me in the way I had always wanted to be loved by a father since I was just a small child. And, as I still didn't know that, maybe there was no God after all.

It is supremely ironic that when, towards the end of our stay in Bromley, I did at last experience reality in my contact with God, I was so frightened by what he wanted me to do that I turned my back on him and 'did a Jonah'.

I had been reading an extract from the writings of Meister Eckhart, a German mystic of the Middle Ages. Particularly interesting to me was his view that repentance was a happy thing. God, he said, was overjoyed when people wanted to change their lives for the better, and more than ready to forget and forgive if it meant that a real friendship could be established. The parable of the prodigal son says exactly the same thing, of course, but perhaps now, I was more ready to accept this truth. Eckhart's words inspired me. I developed a sort of meditation technique, which had an amazingly releasing effect. I would imagine that I was standing in a mist or cloud, surrounded by all the bad or negative things in my life. I would then make a pile of these things – they were easy to stack – and stand on the top of the pile, as tall as I could. The stack was always high enough to allow my head to rise above the level of the mist into the clean, clear, light of the sun. God, in some indefinable way, was in that light. Neither he nor I could see the disreputable heap of baggage under my feet, in the mist, and neither of us cared. It was just good to be in the light, and it made all the difference. Prayer started to feel like conversation, like friendship. It was so new and unusual that I felt slightly hysterical about the whole thing, but it was real, and that was what mattered. Then, one evening as I sat alone in the sitting room at home, a thought 'punched' me in the brain. I can think of no other way to describe it, nor do I care to classify it too precisely. The words were few, but the meaning was clear.

'You must love Jason.'

Clear though the injunction was, I was still rather puzzled. The person in question (his name was not Jason) certainly didn't give the impression of needing my particular care or affection. He was strong, competent, one of those large, hand-carved, independent Christian types. Why should I need to specially love him, and what would it involve? The next day, Jason drove in from Central London where he ran a drug rehabilitation centre. He wanted to confide in me, he said. After my experience of the night before I was all ears, as you can imagine. A real job to do for God at last? He wanted to talk about a dark and difficult area in his private life, something that contrasted starkly with his public image as a professional worker and a Christian. For some weeks we met at frequent intervals. Our meetings did not feel very productive. He talked and I listened, or made feeble attempts to offer advice. His situation grew more complicated, the burden on me seemed increasingly onerous. I was out of my depth and floundering helplessly. I hated the thought that, now, when things in general seemed so much better, I might be about to fail yet again. I wanted to retreat into safety, and just at that time I was presented with a way that seemed to offer just the opportunity I needed. Since the completion of my college course I had applied for a post in a regional assessment centre in the midlands. Now, after a rather alarming interview in the big grey city of Birmingham, I was offered a job as housemaster in a unit of twenty-four delinquent boys. At the same time Jason suggested that I should join him in the work he was doing in London.

'You must love Jason.'

We went to Birmingham.

My new-found relationship with God was too fragile to withstand this deliberate evasion. I know now that, in fact, God being the way he is, he would have been quite ready to heave a sigh, forgive me unreservedly for letting him down, and start again in Birmingham, but I was not prepared to forgive myself, and that was that.

The following five years were dominated by the work I was doing in Birmingham, Norwich and finally Hailsham in East Sussex. Shift work with disturbed children split my existence into two parts – periods when I was working, and periods when I was waiting to go to work. Free time was not free of the shadow of the shift to come, unless it was lengthy enough for stretched nerves to relax, and clouds of worry to disperse. There never seemed to be time to stop and reflect on the strange tension-ridden life that I was leading. I learned to cope in the world of residential child-care. I was even able to appear fairly consistently calm and strong, compassionate and caring. I probably helped many children in the process, but every encounter was a role play involving the selection of a suitable personality from the stock that I had accumulated. The growing inner chaos was pushed deep and well controlled.

Meanwhile I was assembling my own little residential unit at home. Joseph was born in 1978, and David in 1980. It was not until 1982 that we moved off campus to share a house with a young teacher friend. For six years the sounds, sights and tensions of the work situation had infected our attempts to relax.

Holidays away were refreshing, but there is something soul-destroying about returning, and being accosted outside your front door by an excited child who passes on, with relish, the news that Fred has run away, Gloria has slashed her wrists, and there is an epidemic of pubic lice. Instant involvement – instant tension. The family frequently had to make do with the fag-end of my good will at the end of a shift, or after the second or third 'sleep-in' in one week. As a family, we were all paying a very high price for the maintenance of my public role. The nervous and emotional expenditure required for a lengthy working period was often so great that there was little time left for my wife and children, who needed their own share of my time and affection.

All my old doubts about God had reappeared during these years. I tried to rationalise the business of Jason and my abandonment of him. Sometimes I prayed. Occasionally I seemed to sense God trying to get close to me, but generally speaking I was in a spiritual desert, and, although I didn't fully realise it at the time, the growing tension of my work environment was running parallel with a steadily intensifying anger towards this being who either didn't exist, or didn't like me. Back to square one! When people asked me what I believed, I dragged out the old unwieldy package of evangelical clichés, but my heart was not in it.

Then, at the beginning of 1981, Bridget and I were involved in a new group that called itself The Hailsham Christian Fellowship. It was relaxed, informal and refreshing. Both of us experienced a lightening of our spirits as we became part of this little community of Christians from a variety of church backgrounds. Perhaps, through this group, I would find God again and all would be well.

Later in the year, Bridget and I wrote and produced a Christian revue for the fellowship, which was performed on the local secondary school stage to an audience consisting mainly of Christians from the local churches. It was called 'A Place For You', and was specially intended to reassure those Christians for whom Christian living had seemed like a long slog through ankle-deep mud. At that time the fellowship was a welcome refuge for such people. The production had a valuable unifying function for the fellowship, most of whom were involved in the project in one way or another. For us it was like rebirth.

We felt that God really was with us in the writing and rehearsal of the revue, and that, at last, we were coming out of the desert, and taking a few tentative steps into the promised land. It was a truly satisfying experience, and it left Bridget and me with a warm sense of belonging to this group of people whose lives were becoming so intertwined as the weeks went by. I had recently helped to establish a new unit for older children in the children's centre where I worked, and found myself enjoying work much more. Overall, things were looking good, and although God and I still had a lot to settle, at least I was keen to hear what he had to say again.

It was at this point, when both Bridget and I felt more confident and stable than we had done for years, that a friend phoned me to ask if I had noticed a small article in the local paper about the new television company that was due to take over from Southern Television in the new year. The company was to be called TVS, and the article described how Angus Wright, producer of religious programmes, was looking for six ordinary people to take part in a new kind of late-night religious programme.

'Why not write to him?' said my friend.

'All right,' I said. 'I will.'

Chapter Four

At various times, and in various parts of the country, I had found myself watching the late-night epilogue programme broadcast by the BBC, or the local independent television company. Occasionally they were interesting, but generally speaking I was not very impressed. They seemed to take one of two forms.

In the first, a single individual addressed the viewer with unstumbling ease, on subjects that were more or less religious in content. This kind of neatly packaged homily had a rather adverse effect on me. The speaker was heavily protected by the preparedness of his talk, and the fact that nobody was able to interrupt, or argue with what he was saying. At its best this kind of approach seemed harmless, but at its worst it could be positively intimidating. The impression often given was that the worthy person whose eyes followed you round the room as you collected the cocoa cups, had succeeded in tying up all the loose ends in his own understanding of the Christian faith, and was a living example of the way in which spiritual and psychological tidiness could be achieved. For people watching at home, whose lives were difficult and ragged at the edges, this was not always an inspiring example. If they had felt inadequate and confused before, they were likely to feel even more so now. The same thing happens, of course, in many churches, where there is a clear, if unspoken injunction to leave your 'shadow' by the door on your way in, before getting down to singing about how happy you are. There seems to be little room for people who desperately want to say, like Job, that life is wild and tragic

50

and they don't like it, so isn't it a good thing that God can be trusted.

The second kind of programme took the form of a one-to-one interview between a questioner, who was either religiously connected in some way or just suitably genial, and a guest, who would probably appear each night for a week, to answer questions about his or her life and work. The background set was always very simple, the participants usually emerging from near darkness at the beginning of the programme, and disappearing into it again at the end. Occasionally, these encounters had life in them, but most of the programmes that I saw looked like two people trying to reproduce a real conversation that they had enjoyed the night before. Worthy, but dull, they reflected the generally poor presentation of the Christian faith that we have all become used to.

Angus Wright was interested in trying a new approach, which, as far as possible, would allow the viewer to feel involved with what was happening on the screen. Instead of one or two people delivering over-prepared lines to the camera or each other, there would be three or four folk seated around a kitchen table, in a proper kitchen set, having a genuinely unscripted conversation about real happenings and events in their lives. Hopefully, the viewer would, as it were, take a seat around the table and become involved with the lives and views of the participants in as real a way as possible, bearing in mind the obvious limitations of television. The programme would provide a familiar and consistent way to end the viewing day for those in the TVS region who for one reason or another were awake and still watching at that time of night. It would offer company, and it was this basic aim which suggested that the new programme should be called, simply, 'Company'.

Although it was years since Bridget and I had left theatre school, and abandoned the idea of acting as a profession, we had never lost our passion for everything to do with performance. At work, at church, and with the youth club in Bromley, we had never really been happier than when we were caught up in the rich complexity of 'putting on a show'. We both find the stage – any stage – tremendously exciting, whether we are working behind the scenes, or actually taking part in a performance. When I wrote to Angus after my friend's phone call, the performer in me certainly hoped that we might actually be able to take part in this new project, but it seemed more likely that he would simply thank me for contributing my ideas, and that would be that. When he wrote back, suggesting that an associate producer, Frances Tulloch, should visit us for a discussion, Bridget and I were quite ridiculously excited. I can understand that it might be difficult to see why the prospect of appearing on a tiny programme that wouldn't start until most people had gone to bed should give us such pleasure. I suppose that, at the time, it seemed like a sort of confirmation that things were looking up. Life was changing for the better. The fellowship that we had joined, the revue, a general easing of tension at work, and now this. It was as if God was saying 'Right! You've done your time, now you can relax for a while.' Yes, you're right: I still didn't understand God at all!

After our meeting with Frances, who subsequently took over production responsibility for Company, we were invited to take part in an audition, to be held in Frances' club in London. We were still very excited, but also very, very nervous.

Travelling in the same carriage as us on the train to London that day was Lionel Blair, who was appearing in Eastbourne for the season. We reflected ruefully on the ease with which he would have handled the ordeal that lay before us, and which was causing us such nervous apprehension as we clutched our cardboard cups of British Rail coffee, and passed through all stations to Victoria. I'm not quite sure what we expected of our first step into the world of television, something a lot less gentle and civilised, I suspect. For the audition, Frances had obtained the services of a charming old gentleman and his equally charming wife, who usually hired out themselves and their simple video equipment for the purpose of recording Christian meetings and events. Angus Wright turned out to be a tall, thoughtful man, with a slightly distracted air, but a very pleasant manner. He was rather like a serious Derek Nimmo. Finally, we were introduced to Maurice Harper who was to direct Company. Maurice is a complex, attractive Irishman, who is still waiting for the world to deal him a really good hand. We were to become very fond of him.

The atmosphere was relaxed and warm as we took turns sitting in front of the single TV camera, but the five minute talks that we had been asked to prepare must have come over to our small audience as very tense and perspiring affairs. We were just learning how to breathe again when Maurice told us he was keen to see how we came over in conversation.

'Can you just talk?' he asked.

'Yes,' answered Adrian.

'No,' answered Bridget simultaneously.

Maurice ran a hand through his hair, a gesture that was to become familiar. He has always been able to subdue an oath when necessary. He subdued one now.

'Can't you discuss something that you both feel strongly about?'

We looked at each other.

'Well,' I replied tentatively, 'there is a problem we had a while ago when we did a church service. This lad. He was a bit of a nuisance – not turning up for rehearsals, that sort of thing. We weren't sure whether to get someone else or not. So we . . .'

'Fine, fine!' said Maurice. 'Sit at that table. Away you go!'

So away we went, having a discussion that was two months out of date, in a big, strange room, watched by a group of people we had only just met, terribly aware that every word we said, every over-sincere expression on our faces, was being recorded by the expressionless eye of the camera and the microphone on its stand between us.

The general reaction to our efforts seemed quite positive, but as we sat, exhausted, on the southbound train an hour later, we still didn't know the outcome of the audition. The days passed, and we heard nothing. Then, one day when I was out at work, Frances rang and talked to Bridget.

I came home from work that day in my usual, slightly manic state, and flopped wearily onto the settee hoping that a cup of tea and the newspaper might somehow waft themselves in my direction. Bridget, the most likely wafting agent, was sitting very still on the edge of her seat, and something about the quality of her stillness made me forget work and tiredness and cups of tea. Something was wrong. The children? I felt a cold shiver pass through me that I always experienced when I thought something bad might have happened to the boys. Bridget spoke.

'Frances rang.'

Not the children then. Why did Bridget sound so troubled? At the worst Frances could only have rung to say that we had failed the audition. Upsetting, but hardly tragic.

'Yes . . . and?'

'Well . . .'

This was getting silly. I got up, grabbed an upright chair from its place by the wall, carried it over to where Bridget was perched on the edge of her armchair, and sat as close to her as I could. She didn't seem able to let her eyes meet mine.

'Bridget, what's the matter? What did Frances say?'

She raised her head and looked at me at last, eyes wide with apprehension.

'She said they want to use me for Company, but not you.' Her face was creased with pain. 'Oh, Adrian, I don't want to do it if you don't do it. You wrote the letter and I thought . . .'

Poor Bridget. She really and truly was more concerned with how I felt, than anything else. So, how *did* I feel? I felt as though I'd been banged on the head with a very heavy object. Drat God! It was happening all over again.

Not wanted. Not accepted. Not good enough. Why not? Deep inside me the little boy collapsed in tears as his daddy let him down yet again.

Meanwhile, I was aware of Bridget's eyes searching my face for the slightest sign of hurt or upset. She has since told me that if she had detected the merest indication of what I was really feeling, she would have decided, on the spot, to ring Frances and say that she did not want to be included in the Company team.

Usually, I could not have concealed my feelings anyway. Like many husbands I am nothing more than a big baby at times, and if I get upset I make sure those around me know about it, or at the very least I carefully let them notice that I am concealing my feelings. But this was different. In the split second following Bridget's last speech I knew that the manner and content of my reply would either free her to pursue this interesting and novel activity, or prevent it altogether. It was not right or fair that it should be so, but it was a fact.

'Thank goodness for that. I thought it was something really awful for a moment.' I knew it sounded convincing.

'You mean you don't mind?' Bridget was puzzled, still wary.

I had myself completely under control now.

'In an odd sort of way, it's a relief,' I lied. 'Let's have a cup of tea. What about taking the children up along the old railway track for a picnic . . . ?'

It was the only truly heroic thing I'd ever done, but it didn't give me very much satisfaction at the time. I was used to engineering rewards for my virtue, but in this case I knew that I just had to keep my mouth shut, and suffer. Ironically, if I had not responded as I did, it is possible that neither of us would have been involved with the programme. As it was, only a few weeks passed before I was also asked to join the Company team, and I could relax from the strain of pretending to be genial but unconcerned about being excluded from Bridget's new activity.

The first Company participants were not actually as

'ordinary' as the original concept had envisaged. There was, for instance, Peter Ball, the Anglican Bishop of Lewes, already quite a celebrity in the south-east and elsewhere. Bob Gordon was a distinguished lecturer in Old Testament studies, and about to join Colin Urquhart as a co-elder at the Hyde Christian community near Haywards Heath. Ken Gardner was an Anglican priest from the parish of St Philip and St Jacob, Waldeslade, near Gillingham, and Ann-Marie Stewart was a Franciscan nun who had left her convent after twenty years to start a new form of Franciscan life in Canterbury. Ann-Marie supported herself by taking on cleaning jobs in the mornings, while devoting the rest of the day to prayer and the occasional preaching or teaching engagement. Next to this line-up of religious experts, Bridget and I were very conscious of being 'token ordinary ones'. I was an expert in spiritual confusion, and Bridget was an expert in living with someone who was spiritually confused, but that was about all.

For a time, it was a little intimidating. The TVS world seemed to be full of incredibly expensive machinery and highly trained technicians. The atmosphere in the new studio at Gillingham was one of great enthusiasm. We were in at the beginning of, not only a new programme, but a new television company. Everyone seemed to be on their toes. We were amazed at the number of people that seemed to be necessary for the making of such a humble pro-gramme. Whenever a technical problem occurred, they seemed to come out of the woodwork in their droves, each one an expert in something or other. Cameras, lights, sound, make-up, props, wardrobe; there seemed no end to the specialised knowledge required to make this five minute programme in a small corner of the vast ex-cinema studio. So what were *we* doing there? What qualified us to sit with experts, surrounded by experts, saying things that thousands of southerners from Maldon in Essex to Dorchester in the West would hear every night? Not, I hasten to add, that our fellow participants in any way deliberately made us feel inadequate. Bob was aggressively confident on behalf of all of us, Ken was always warm and self-effacing, Ann-Marie was, by her own admission and despite wide experience of public speaking, quite paralysed by nerves for the first few weeks, and Peter – well, more about Peter later. Helpful and friendly though everyone was, the question remained for Bridget and me: what right did two ordinary people have, to talk about Christianity in front of thousands of viewers, when so many others were better informed, and certainly more consistent in the way they lived out their faith? The answer was, of course, none at all, and in realising this we realised what our contribution should be. If we could manage to be honest and open about the things, good and bad, that happened to us, and resist the temptation to make excuses for God by papering over the cracks in our lives, then we might offer hope and reassurance to people whose lives were just as frayed at the edges.

In theory, ours sounds a humble role, but in fact, we weren't really feeling very humble at all. We just *loved* the palaver of production meetings and make-up and work in the studio. It all smacked of the 'telly'. We were on the 'telly'! We developed a sort of compensatory nonchalance about the whole thing, which probably deceived nobody, least of all ourselves. That feeling of novelty and rich excitement did not last very long, and perhaps it was rather silly, but I think it was a good and necessary thing. It made us feel like children again, and that is always a healthy experience for Christians.

Some of those early programmes must have been awful. I wouldn't be able to count the number of times that Maurice, sometimes running *both* hands through his hair, would threaten to strangle the next person who started a sentence with the words 'As a Christian . . .'. Then there was our tendency to be terribly, terribly polite to each other while the cameras were on us. There is nothing wrong with politeness, of course, but quite often the relaxed and strongly animated discussion which followed the programme, would have been far more interesting to the viewer than the cosy, religious head-nodding exercise that had just appeared on the screen. We were in danger (and it has remained a danger) of doing exactly what the old-style epilogue programmes had done, only more expensively. Added to this were our two great fears. We were afraid of silence, and we were afraid that a programme might finish without the opportunity for us to contribute our particular little nugget of insight or wisdom to the conversation. I filled many a silence with absolute blithering nonsense in those days, and probably still do at times. I also remember sitting at that kitchen table, waiting for a gap – any kind of gap – in the conversation, so that I could thrust my little set-speech into the proceedings, regardless of context. With a little ingenuity it was possible to force a connection of some kind. Thus, the following conversation might have taken place:

Ann-Marie: One of the most interesting things I ever saw, happened on a Monday, which is always a rather bad day for me.

Adrian: (Spotting a minute opening) Oddly enough, I was going to talk about something that happened on a Wednesday, which, as you know, is only two days after Monday. You see, my mother . . .

Bridget: (Determined not to be left out) Don't you think God is as much a mother as he is a father?

Adrian and Ann-Marie: (Both seething inwardly, but unwilling to display impatience in front of 50,000 people) Yes, yes, he probably is. How interesting . . . !

A slight exaggeration of course, but all these problems had to be faced. We discovered over the months that it *was* possible to be in conflict without throttling each other, and that a silence, if it was a natural one, was not only *not* to be feared, but could be more meaningful than a great deal of conversation.

The secret seemed to lie in two areas: honesty and listening. If the words we said came from the heart, and we really listened and responded to what others were saying, then it didn't matter whether we talked about potty-training or predestination. It would be real. As Angus has repeatedly said from the outset, people will only want to watch if something is *happening* on the screen. We are all still guilty of the same mistakes from time to time, but, one hopes, less often.

When Company first started, Bridget and I were naive enough to believe that the kitchen set, although obviously an aid to creating an appropriate atmosphere, was not something that would be much noticed by viewers. It was a rather basic kitchen as kitchens go, rather reminiscent of the fifties and not at all likely to attract attention. On the table at which we sat there might be a vase of flowers or a bowl of fruit, but generally speaking there was little that seemed interesting enough to distract viewers from our 'scintillating' conversation. We were wrong. One day, as we completed the purchase of a can of paint in a local shop, the lady who had served us cleared her throat in an 'I'm going to say something' sort of way, as we turned to go. She laid a hand on my wife's arm, and spoke earnestly.

'I do hope you don't mind me asking . . .' Her expression was very serious. Bridget smiled encouragingly. 'Only – you see, my husband and I have been watching your programme all this week and – well, we've got a question that we both want to ask. Would you mind?'

We were flattered. It was in the early days, and it felt good to be recognised in public. Now, here was this nice lady who'd listened, with her husband, to everything we'd said for a whole week, and wanted help with a problem. Some difficulty in their Christian lives no doubt. She and her husband saw us as people who might have some answers.

'If we can help, then of course . . .' Bridget's sincere tones matched the earnestness of the questioner.

'Only – it's been troubling us all week . . .'

'Yes?' Bridget was patience itself.

The lady leaned forward. She spoke even more confidentially than before.

'The fruit in that bowl . . . is it real?'

Later on, contact with viewers, through correspondence and in person was very important to us, especially in the very black days that were to come two and a half years after Company began, but at first, being recognised in the street was a strange and sometimes disconcerting experience.

One Saturday, Bridget lost her purse, containing most of our holiday savings, just drawn from the bank. Panic-stricken, she rushed around the town dragging our two pre-school children behind her. Her face smudged with tears as she searched in vain for the missing money, she was reaching a fine pitch of hysteria, when a voice at her shoulder said, 'Excuse me, but haven't I seen you on telly?' Bridget is a very modest lady, but not even the most inflated super-Christian TV image would have survived that moment. I ought to add that the purse was found and later returned to us by a very honest gentleman who stumbled over it on his way home from work.

Then there was the lady who flung her arms round my neck and kissed me on the cheek as I queued outside a cinema with eight-year-old Matthew. She fixed me with the intense gaze of the semi-inebriate, and spoke with deep, throbbing sincerity.

'Are you and Bridget as happy in real life as you are on television?'

As she departed unsteadily along the pavement without waiting for an answer, Matthew looked from me to her and back to me in wonderment.

'Gosh, Daddy,' he said. 'You don't 'alf make friends quickly, don't you?'

Sometimes, when we made programmes separately, one of us would mention that we had been going through an irritable, argumentative patch. I was standing in a super-market queue, one day, when a voice came from somewhere behind my left shoulder.

'Sorry to hear you and your wife had a row.'

It was a lady I had never seen before. Quickly, my mind made the necessary connection. Presumably Bridget had described our recent 'bad patch' to the south of England, late last night. What had she said? What did this lady in the queue know, that I didn't? I resisted the temptation to ask, and reflected on the fact that, while honesty on television might be the best policy, it could produce some very uncomfortable moments. Nevertheless, it became clearer than ever that it was just this willingness to be open about the darker side of our lives that would enable not just Bridget and me, but the Company team generally, as it changed and grew, to relate closely to viewers who needed to know that they were not alone in their experience of failure and difficulty.

Chapter Five

So what did we talk about evening after evening? Well, for a while we tried to solve most of the world's problems in double quick time. Death on Monday, forgiveness on Tuesday, suffering on Wednesday – we sorted them all out in five minutes or so each. Sometimes it was possible to have something approaching a reasonable discussion on these vast subjects in such a risibly short time, but I think we realised fairly early on that unless the things we said were grounded in experience we wouldn't sound very convincing.

Sometimes, for instance, we would pick up on the headline news of the day, and unless we had some specialist knowledge in a specific area, it was better to produce a kind of personal, uninformed response that the majority of viewers could identify with. Essentially, we were having a 'chat' rather than a discussion, and when friends chat they will probably talk about what they've been doing, making a passing comment on the day's news, and perhaps exchange gossip or 'have a laugh'. It is not easy to reproduce this kind of informality under laboratory conditions, as it were.

Apart from the specific area of child-care, the only thing I really knew about was 'being me', so for some time my contribution tended to be rather anecdotal. I suppose this was very fitting really, as my relationship with God had been rather anecdotal over the years. I enjoyed telling stories, and they did at least have the virtue of being true. There was the story, for instance, of the lorry driver and the rose.

It happened when I was hitch-hiking some years ago. I

was in the cab of a huge lorry, somewhere on the M4 heading west.

I've always loved hitch-hiking. It's a wonderful blend of adventure and legitimate inactivity. G K Chesterton said that he knew few things more satisfying than the experience of being stranded at a railway station. I know what he meant. The flavour of accidental solitude is tastier than Marmite, and I've experienced it most while standing on the side of the road waiting for a lift. I relish the fact that only God and I know where I am. Add to this the knowledge that every lift means contact with an unknown and quite unique human being, and you have the perfect occupation for someone with my twin vices of laziness and curiosity.

On this particular day I'd been dropped off on one of the motorway exits, and I had to wait some time on the corresponding slip road for another lift. It was late afternoon when a very large lorry squealed to a halt beside me. The driver leaned across and pushed the passenger door open.

'You'd better get in, mate. You'll never get a lift standin' there.'

I smiled as I hauled myself up to the cab. People said this to me so often, that I quite frequently waited at 'impossible' spots, knowing that some kind person would pick me up in the end.

As the huge vehicle rumbled on to the motorway, my new companion and I began the pigeon-holing process that always preceded real conversation. Once he'd established that I was well-spoken, slightly naive, and not at all threatening, the man behind the wheel leaned towards me and spoke in the tone of one who has made an important decision.

'I'm goin' to tell you somethin' I've never told anyone before!'

He paused, flicking a glance around the cab as though checking for eavesdroppers.

'I wrote this effin' poem.'

He shot a look at me then went on, apparently reassured by my quiet interest.

'I saw this rose, see? In an effin' park. I was just sittin' there, and I looked at this effin' rose, and I thought, "Blow me! Look at that!" So I wrote this poem, didn't I?'

His vulnerability attracted and frightened me. His was a fragile trust.

'Have you said it to anybody?' I asked.

'You must be jokin'! If I told my mates I'd written a blinkin' poem I'd never 'ear the last of it. Just see me goin' down the local and sayin', "Oy, I've written a poem about an effin' rose." I don't think so!'

'Could I hear it?'

After some inward struggle he bawled the poem out over the noise of the engine. When he'd finished I said something appreciative, and the journey continued for some time without further conversation.

As I gazed sightlessly through the wide windscreen in front of me, I wondered what God would think about all this. After a few minutes I had to turn my face to the glass beside me. I didn't want the driver to see the tears in my eyes. I felt that I knew what God must think. All the way down the motorway and into the setting sun he probably wept with me for all the people who have poems in them, and can't believe that anyone else wants to hear them.

That story was especially poignant for me, perhaps, as I have always enjoyed expressing my feelings through poetry, some of which I have shared with Company viewers. One poem, in particular, seemed to sum up the tension that was my legacy from an uneasy childhood. Sending these words out through the camera lens had an oddly cleansing effect.

When I was a small boy in a small school,
With endless legs,
And ears that widely proclaimed a head full of
    emergencies,
When I clung by bleeding fingertips to thirty-three
    plus nine,

And cognitive dissonance was a hard sum,
There were only two crimes.
The first was shouting in the corridors,
The second was to be a fool.
And when the bell, the blessed bell,
Let me fling my body home,
I thought I might, at least, one day,
Aspire to rule in hell,
But now I never hear the bell,
And part of me will always be
A fool,
Screaming in some sacred corridor.

A less poetic but no less meaningful account, concerned the way in which I coped – or rather, didn't cope – with the first day of my new job in Sussex, after moving down from Norfolk.

It doesn't matter how experienced you are in residential childcare, it's always nerve-racking to confront a new and horribly unfamiliar group of children and staff, especially in the intense atmosphere of a large children's centre. I was due to start at 2.30. By half-past one I'd run out of distractions, courage, faith and saliva. I wanted Armageddon to happen within the hour. Then, a decision, a solution of sorts, crawled into my mind. If I really shifted – if I took the short cut along the old railway line and across the school playing-field, I could get to the Britannia Arms in time to pour at least three pints of bitter into my stomach. That should drown the butterflies; poor little beggars – they wouldn't stand a chance. I hurried out of the house wearing the inevitable load of guilt like a haversack on my back. I had not had much to say to God for some time, but I knew what he'd think of my dash to the pub. Eyebrows raised, fingers drumming on a cloud. I challenged him 'bravely'.

'There's nothing you can do about it, God. I'm going for a drink and that's that. I want a drink, I need a drink, I'm going to have a drink. And if you don't like it, you'll have to stop me!'

As I sped along the footpath between bushes and trees, I offered a couple of suggestions to the deity.

'What about muggers, God? Why don't you get someone to leap from behind a tree and knock me out? Or maybe a dramatic soil subsidence. I could just disappear into a crack in the ground. Is that what you're going to do?'

I laughed rather wildly as I crossed the sports ground and jogged up the hill towards the town. I really wasn't very proud of what I was doing. Here was the main road at last. On the other side the pub; the beer.

'Last chance, God. Road accident? Needn't be anything serious. Broken limb perhaps?'

I negotiated the busy road without incident, and walked into the saloon bar of the Britannia. I ordered a pint. I watched it being pulled; I licked my lips. I put my hand out and took the brimming glass. As I drew it carefully towards me I felt in my jacket pocket with my other hand for some money.

'Hard luck, God! Cheers!'

Suddenly, I froze. Panic – horror – no money! I'd changed my jacket. I hadn't a penny. The barman didn't know me from Adam.

'I'm sorry – I haven't got any money,' I said pathetically.

'In that case, we haven't got any beer,' replied the man – clearly an Old Testament type, and he reached over and took my pint back from me.

I didn't start laughing until I was halfway back to the Centre. I was still laughing inwardly as I went into work at half-past two.

It was rather like – being drunk.

After telling this story one night, I discovered that we had a hitherto unsuspected audience of publicans. As I visited pubs in and around the area over the next couple of weeks, I found that landlords and their wives were intrigued by the details of the account. Which pub was it? What kind of beer was it? They usually watched Company, they said, because once all the clearing up was done, it was nearly midnight

66

anyway, and by the time they were able to put their feet up, our few minutes of chat was about all that was left of the evening's viewing.

It was also a good example of how openness can be a releasing agent. Having revealed that I was a Christian with a healthy liking for beer, and an unhealthy tendency to use it as a prop sometimes, it seemed easier for others to be frank about their own vices or failings. Although, at the time, I didn't know the answers to such problems, it did seem to me that it was better for people to feel free to talk about these things, rather than be paralysed by feelings of guilt. A similar effect was produced by Bridget's lively descriptions of times when everything went disastrously wrong, just as she particularly wanted to look like a calm, confident wife and mother. Those who knew what it meant to wilt under the disapproving stare of 'mothers-whose-children-behave-well' whilst wrestling unsuccessfully with their own rebellious crew, found it refreshingly easy to identify with these graphic tales.

Of course, me being me, it wasn't long before I began to see myself as God's gift to the late night box-watchers, put at that table to offer hope to an army of insomniacs. What I didn't realise was that God intended to sort *me* out over the next three years, and the first step in his campaign, using my participation in Company as a lever, was to do something that I had been trying to do for years. He found a way for me to give up smoking.

I was a dedicated smoker, and had been for sixteen years. In most of the photographs taken since I was sixteen, I was holding a packet of cigarettes and a box of matches in one hand, and a book in the other. Cigarettes were the only uncomplicated comforts I knew, little friends who were always available, never answered back, and didn't object to being trodden on. By the time I was thirty-three I was smoking at least sixty cigarettes a day; one every twenty minutes; one thousand pounds worth every year. I smoked when I got into bed, and I smoked before I got up in the morning. I lit up as I walked out of the door, and again as I waited for the bus. I smoked before, during and after a bath. Often I would leave a church service or an important meeting halfway through, ostensibly to visit the toilet, but actually to snatch a few reassuring drags before returning to the smokeless zone. Most delicious of all – oh ecstasy! – I smoked after a meal.

My smoking was conducted with a curious underlying intensity. I protected my addiction fiercely, realising, perhaps, that I was using it as a weapon in the battle to postpone real involvement with a world that was never quite satisfactory. At the same time, I had always felt guilty about being a smoker. It was one of the things a Christian *ought* to feel guilty about, wasn't it?

Nowadays, I believe that God is, in fact, quite nice, but for years I retained the image of something between a headmaster and a bank manager, before whom I played the role of a naughty boy with an overdraft. Now that I no longer smoke, I am quite sure that smoking, in itself, is no more of a sin than anything else, but I was a slave to the habit, and it was costing a fortune. I performed every spiritual gymnastic in the book. I made decisions at meetings, I went forward at rallies, I repented and pleaded and argued with the rigidly austere God that my heart had created. The only thing these experiences had in common was the pleasure with which I lit up the cigarette that invariably followed each decision to give up. Money, health, guilt – nothing was a strong enough motive to stop. For a couple of years now, I hadn't bothered to try.

Then, one day, as Bridget wrestled grimly with our dilapidated top-loading washing machine, something happened. She burst into tears of frustration as the appliance forced her, yet again, into a losing submission. She said just ten words.

'If you didn't smoke, I could have a new machine!'

She had never complained before. I walked round to the electricity showrooms and bought a washing machine on hire purchase. I calculated that if I cut down my daily ration of cigarettes to twenty, the money saved would cover the repayments. I decided to smoke one cigarette each hour, on the hour. I lived for the moment when, as my youngest son put it, the big hand was on the twelve. Each hour lasted several months. Each cigarette seemed to last a few seconds. My family hid. After a month of this, I knew that the moment of final decision had come. It was now or never. Give up altogether or go back to sixty a day. I decided to give up. The difference this time, was that I knew how to put a much more effective armlock on myself than at any time in the past. A few days later I talked at the Company table about how I no longer smoked. My heart sank as I burned my boats so finally. Relatively small though the Company audience might be, I knew that it was large enough for me to be 'leapt on' by regular viewers if they saw me smoking in the street. But it was my pride that would do the trick in the end. I had said I no longer smoked, and I hadn't the humility to fail. So much for sharing weakness!

The next few months were horrific. Each morning I woke, to remember, with a stab of horror, that I'd given up. I saw little point in getting up – in working – in doing anything. Like someone who has been bereaved, and that's how I felt, I could not be consoled. I resigned myself to suffering. Prayer? God? Don't ask!

Then, one afternoon, six months later, I could stand it no longer. By then I had moved over to work in the secure unit for violent and absconding children, and for once, everyone else was out. On the desk in front of me as I sat in the small staff office, lay a single cigarette, white and alluring, firm with tobacco – beautiful. It had been a hard day. I was tense and nervous. I had had enough. Company or no Company, pride or no pride, I was going to smoke that cigarette. I hunted feverishly through the desk drawer where the lighter was usually kept. As I searched, a small, feeble voice at the back of my mind repeated the same desperate prayer over and over again.

'Don't let it be there – don't let it be there . . .'.

It *was* there. The cigarette was in my mouth. I flicked the lighter. It didn't work. I flicked it again. It still didn't work. The stupid thing was out of petrol. I wanted that cigarette . . . !

Of course! Matches! Some of the children kept matches in the little pigeon-holes set against the wall on my right. I leaned over and started to pull out the contents of the little square wooden boxes.

'Don't let there be any . . . please don't let there be any . . .'

There were no matches in the pigeon-holes. Not a single, solitary match. Never mind. I was going to smoke that cigarette. The bin! The rubbish bin! You always found the odd live match among the rubbish. I had no dignity left. I emptied the metal container onto the floor and scrabbled through the messy heap of papers, orange peel, and general stickiness.

'Please, don't let . . .'.

Nothing! No live matches. I got up and almost ran down the corridor, out of the unit and down towards the kitchen that supplied meals for the entire children's centre. I knew I could get a light there. I stopped on the threshold of the large, busy kitchen, and looked around. On my right a gas flame burned brightly beneath the water heater. In front of me a huge, yellow box of matches sat fatly on a shelf. To my left, one of the cooks worked over the stoves. She was a smoker. I knew that she carried cigarettes and a lighter in her apron pocket. I took a step forward, then stopped. Quite suddenly, the madness left me. I slipped the crumpled cigarette into my side pocket, and trailed wearily back to the unit. Since that day I have not smoked a cigarette, but it was a year before it became easy.

So why was it so difficult? Why couldn't the desire to smoke have been taken away by some sort of divine surgery? That certainly seems to happen to some people. Why not me? I think there were three things I needed to learn.

First, there is no real sacrifice without suffering. I had known that, but only in my head.

Secondly, when you have reached the end of your own

70

resources, God does help – even if it involves 'fixing' lighters and removing matches. Sometimes a miracle is just the tiny puff of wind that makes it possible to go on toiling at the oars.

Thirdly, it allowed me to believe in change. It is not an exaggeration to say that, in my view, if weak-willed old me can give up smoking, then anybody can do almost anything.

So, stage one in the divine plan was completed. One of my most deeply rooted defence systems had been removed, and if it hadn't been for my 'declaration' on Company, it just wouldn't have been possible.

But that was only the beginning. From the start of my involvement with Company, I was meeting people who forced me to re-examine and overhaul my whole understanding of spirituality, Christianity and organised religion. The first and certainly one of the most influential of these was Peter Ball, the Bishop of Lewes.

Chapter Six

'I could sit and watch that man all day.'

As I sat behind the cameras in Studio two watching the three Company participants chatting quietly as they waited for the programme to begin, I became aware that the technician sitting next to me was gazing with a peculiar intensity at the still figure in the monk's habit, seated at the end of the kitchen table.

'What do you mean?' I knew what he meant.

'Well . . .' He leaned back in his chair slightly embarrassed by his own remark.

'It's like sitting on the edge of a lake. He doesn't even have to talk. It's just sort of relaxing to watch him.'

I knew exactly what he meant. Since the day when I first met him in February 1982, I had been intrigued and fascinated by the phenomenon that was Peter Ball, the Bishop of Lewes. I had never known a bishop before, and I had a vague and totally uninformed prejudice against ambitious prelates – princes of the church – that sort of thing. So too, I was soon to discover, had Peter Ball. I think I was fortunate in that I had never heard of him before we met as Company colleagues. When he drew up in his rather battered blue car outside our house in Hailsham, to drive Bridget and me up to the TVS studio in Maidstone, I felt under no obligation to be impressed or overawed by this man who, I later learned, is regarded by many as one of the wisest and most godly men in the Christian church. This was just as well, as his first words to me were, 'Hello Adrian, have a Mars bar.'

As I climbed into the front passenger seat, I registered

various obvious pieces of information. Middle aged, healthy looking but tired, dressed in a full length dark grey habit, rather charming boyish smile, perhaps a hint of toughness in the eyes. As we travelled northwards towards Maidstone, the three of us chatted very easily together. Peter didn't seem much like a prince of the church. He seemed more like a normal, but oddly happy human being who had somehow managed to achieve maturity without losing the excitement and playfulness of childhood.

'I expected you to talk about God all the time,' said I, rather crassly, as he negotiated the very busy Tunbridge High Street.

'You being a bishop I mean . . .'

Peter's smile lit up the car.

'People do seem to think that I ought to have a view on God all the time, and of course I have, but I do find it difficult when people assume that God is my sort of hobby. They talk to me about religion in the same way that you would talk to a philatelist about stamps, or a photographer about developing or something. Basically, they are not seeing me as a real human being.'

I was sure Peter meant what he was saying but his manner belied his words. I sensed that he had spent many many hours indulging the belief of others that he should talk to them about God.

Bridget leaned forward and spoke.

'But why is that Peter? Why don't people want you to be a real human being?'

'Ah, well . . .' Peter became serious. 'I think, Bridget, the problem is that we have got this attitude in the church at the moment, that the good Christians are those that spend a lot of time with religion. That's a load of junk! In fact there's too much religion.'

Listening to Peter was beginning to feel like a beautiful but unexpected cool shower on an oppressively hot day. As we turned onto the Hadlow road and headed out across the Kent countryside, the world seemed to me a slightly better place than usual.

'When you say "religion" . . . ?'

'I mean religious exercises. The more time you spend in church, the more Bible studies you go to, the more prayer meetings you attend, the better Christian you'll be. That's a load of junk. We're here for the transfiguration of the world, not to form a little cosy club of Christians who are all constantly involved in religious exercises. Of course we must pray — of course we must worship; those are at the centre of our lives, but then we need to live as fully as we can in a sort of joyful unselfishness, caring about people, and transfiguring ordinary life. We hope that we can touch everything and see it sparkle.'

Oddly enough, I didn't find Peter's use of the pronouns 'we' and 'our' discomforting or guilt-inducing. I couldn't honestly say that prayer and worship were at the centre of my life, and as for things sparkling when I touched them, well — they didn't seem to. Joyful unselfishness? Not a lot!

The curious thing was, though, that there seemed to be a power in Peter's words and presence that made me feel I could become all the things he had described; something that caused me to think that perhaps I wasn't such a bad chap after all.

This was quite new for me. Most of my Christian experience seemed to have emphasised the vast gap between the perfection of God and my own sin-ridden, worm-like existence. Often there had seemed to be some kind of ban on feeling 'liked' by God. It was all right to be loved, because that was *despite* everything you were. The atmosphere around Peter, however, contained a sort of rich encouragement that gave permission to relax and be warmed by something that is better described as fondness than anything else. This principle has held good with many people I have met since then. The nearer they are to God, the better they make you feel, without in any way suggesting that you should minimise or ignore your faults or weaknesses. I find this very encouraging. Presumably, God himself is the source and ultimate example of this quality. God is nice, and he likes me. What a thought!

When we arrived at the Gillingham Studio, we were able to witness the 'sparkling' principle, as Peter greeted cameramen, make-up ladies and security men in a way that suggested each one was vitally important to him. As he moved around the large studio building, he seemed to carry his own shining atmosphere with him. Later, in the course of the Company programme, I asked him about this.

'Peter, do you enjoy meeting people – all of them . . . ?'

He patted his flat hand gently on the table and nodded slowly.

'I do, Adrian. I honestly do enjoy people enormously. I am absolutely scintillating with excitement when I meet anyone; but it can cause problems.'

Bridget and I must have both looked puzzled.

'Well, you see, there are only two things that I am really any good at. One is squash, and the other is making people feel that they are special to me, and of course they are; but I meet so many people and you simply can't give yourself totally to everyone all the time. It gets very complicated, and I think sometimes its dangerous because people get very angry when I don't telephone them or write letters . . .'

He shook his head in dismay at the thought.

'Obviously,' said Bridget, 'they see something in you that's different, like I do; but you've only got twenty-four hours in your day, like everyone else. Do you think that what they're actually seeing in you, is Jesus?'

Peter's face shone again.

'I do hope so, I do hope so. I'm sure it doesn't happen all the time with me, but I wish it happened every minute of the day. We've all got a personality, and I believe that it can be transfigured by Jesus. We each must be a tiny little diamond in the kaleidoscope of the glory which is Jesus.'

Suddenly I felt personally involved in what was being said. The lights and the cameras drifted away from my awareness as I asked another question.

'The thing is, Peter, that diamonds are valuable, and one of the problems a lot of Christians have, is how to go on being valuable when they know what kind of people they really are. How should they go about learning to appreciate their value in God's eyes?'

I tried to sound detached, and interested in an academic sort of way. It wasn't easy, as I was actually hungry for his reply. Peter thought for a moment, his brows knitted. Then his face cleared.

'You see, the church has gone round saying that all humility means is that you think yourself a load of junk, a load of "garbage" as the Americans call it. In Lent, for instance, we all have to regard ourselves as garbage cans for forty days. We need to realise that, actually, God is totally fascinated by us. He took five thousand million years to, in a sense, evolve and create us. That's quite a long time even in terms of eternity – it's a second or two, isn't it? He is absolutely entranced by us. I love it! When I kneel down to pray in the morning, I don't say to begin with, "God, you're really great, you're wonderful." What I do feel at that moment, is that I am coming home. I know that he *is* really great, but I am coming home, and he is saying, "Oh, it's great to have you!" I don't understand it. You see – I know that I am very, very sinful, but I know something else as well . . .'

I was too much of an expert in controlling my emotions to actually cry, but I could feel tears swimming in my eyes as Peter's gentle voice continued, warmly enthusiastic about this God that I had difficulty in recognising.

'You see . . . I know that if I was to go out today and commit the foulest crime possible with every single person in the village where I live, and then went to prison as a result, then repented, and said sincerely to God, "God, I am so very, very sorry", he would say . . . well, what do you think he would say?'

We were like little children listening to a bedtime story. We shook our heads, wide-eyed.

'He would say, "Great! This prison is full of people who you can love with me, and I love you, even more than I did before!" So I would get on with loving where I was, and a whole new world would happen in that prison. God is all right! I really do believe that with all my heart, and I can't really understand why everyone doesn't.'

'God is absolutely real to you?' A statement of fact rather than a question. Peter leaned back, his hands disappearing into the sleeves of his habit as he folded his arms.

'Ever since I can remember, Adrian, I have never known a time when God has not been the realest presence in the world to me, more real even than human, touchable presences.'

'So when . . . I mean . . .'

Bridget paused, her hands outstretched as though testing for rain, while she searched for the right words.

'You wouldn't say then, that you have had what is usually called a conversion experience in the evangelical church? A point where you asked Jesus into your life, and then the Holy Spirit came into your life, and then you started to walk the Christian path – that sort of experience?'

'No.' Peter continued carefully. 'Not one in which I would be able to say, as evangelicals do say sometimes, "Before it I wasn't a real Christian and after it I was.' I find that way round difficult. I mean, I haven't any doubt that these are real experiences, given to them by Jesus Christ, and when I hear about it I rejoice. I haven't any inhibitions about it; but I believe that rather than me inviting Jesus into my life, Jesus is actually, very sweetly, taking me into his life. There have been very special times of course. I remember when I first realised that I hadn't got to try to "make-it" with God. There he was, and he accepted me totally. There was nothing I could do to work for my own salvation. I was just totally assured by him. It was a great *release* to know that I never needed to earn approval with God. I could totally relax. That was a big experience.'

After the programme had finished, we drank coffee in the canteen up on the first floor. I was beginning to see why people wanted to talk to Peter about God. Guilty as all the rest, I took up the conversation where it had ended a few minutes ago.

'Peter, why do you think people get so screwed up about

whether God loves them or not? What goes wrong?'
Another casual, disinterested question! Peter stirred his
coffee rather absentmindedly as he replied.

'God doesn't just *love* us. He loves us extravagantly. I
want to use the word extravagantly because people sometimes use the phrase "God loves us" in a way that puts me
off entirely. Sometimes it sounds like a sort of pressurised
love. "He loves yer, an' he's gonna get yer!" Or, he loves
you and you are going to become someone totally not
yourself. These testimonies you hear sometimes . . .'

He grinned wickedly.

'Sometimes I think people were far more attractive in
their old unredeemed state. No – I want to use the word
"extravagantly", because that's how God loves. After all,
that's how lovers love, isn't it? They don't love moderately,
or if they do there's not much point in getting married.'

He finished stirring at last, and took a sip of coffee, then
replaced the cup on its saucer and beamed at us.

'Extravagantly – profusely – outrageously – that's how
God loves us!'

It was extraordinary. After that first meeting I seemed to
hear about Peter Ball everywhere. So many people seemed
to have seen him or been confirmed by him, or been
changed by something he said, or simply impressed by an
encounter with him. The interesting thing was that these
were not just Church of England worshippers. He seemed
to have appeal for a wide variety of folk, including non-
believers, who were attracted by his informal style and the
sheer sparkle of the man. He related easily to people of all
classes, and to a wide selection of church denominations,
including the extreme evangelical ones, where even those
who weren't quite sure if Mother Teresa was 'saved' or
not, couldn't help but sense in him the spirit of a very
loving God. Peter himself, clearly did not enjoy some of
these occasions. I have never known a man in whom
nervousness and effectiveness were so strongly present
together, as in Peter when he addressed the monthly

'Growmore' meeting at the Congress Theatre in Eastbourne one Sunday evening. After the worship session, consisting largely of choruses led from the front, Peter, who finds that type of worship a little difficult, grey in habit and face, plodded from the back of the hall to the front to deliver an address remarkable for its humour, humility and insight, in contrast to the obvious feelings of woeful inadequacy in the speaker.

Impressed as I was by this unusual person, I wanted to find out what fuelled or energised him. How had he become the man he was? How did he remain the man he was? Was it the result of some kind of religious trick, or had God decided to smile on Peter for a particular reason? One day I visited Peter at his home in Littlington, a little Sussex village tucked away in the Downs, not far from the famous Long Man of Wilmington. There, in the homely sitting room of the rectory he talked about himself and his work.

Peter told me that he had been a monk for more than twenty years, as has his twin brother, Michael, who is the Bishop of Jarrow. Eight years ago, somewhat against his personal inclinations, Peter was installed as the suffragan Bishop of Lewes, and is now based at the old rectory in Littlington. Here he lives with a group of young people who are participants in the scheme that he devised to enable school leavers to spend two months at the rectory in work and spiritual training, followed by ten months in the community in teams of two or three, actively occupied in such areas as youth and voluntary work, while supporting themselves by part-time paid work.

Clearly, Peter's years as a monk under vows of poverty, chastity and obedience must have had a lot to do with the quality and steadfastness of his present life, but I wanted to know what kept him going now that he was a monk who was also a bishop, closely involved with all aspects of the real world. How did he cope with it? Peter settled back in the comfortable settee opposite me and talked about his daily routine.

'The first thing that happens each day, is my alarm clock going off at 4.15 am . . .'

He noticed my wince of horror.

'We get through a lot of alarm clocks in the monastic life, because the temptation is to throw them straight out of the window. But usually I manage to get up and the first thing I do is to make an act of devotion, saying, "Lord, this is the *best* day there's ever going to be in my life", and I mean it too, although I don't always say it with conviction . . .'

Peter chuckled reflectively.

'I want it to be – I really do. Every day I ask God that I shall go out to love and praise him with all my whole being, and over the last thirty years I must have managed that for . . . oh, at least five minutes.'

I was still wrestling inwardly with the idea of rising at 4.15 every morning.

'So, that takes you to – let's say, 4.30 am. I still don't see why you need to be up quite so early.'

Peter's eyebrows rose.

'Oh, well, the next thing I do is rush downstairs, do one or two ordinary things, then take the dog for a walk. That's the most beautiful part of the day really, walking down the lanes in the early morning. The shapes in the winter, the freshness in the summer. Then, usually at about a quarter to five, I hurry down to our little chapel in the cellar for about an hour and three-quarters of – hopefully – uninterrupted prayer or meditation, whatever you like to call it. I hope it is adoration. God embraces me in that time. I think he is always very pleased to see me.'

I was silent for a moment, thinking of my own fragmentary, undisciplined prayer life. By 6.30 each morning, Peter had already spent at least two hours being with, and being embraced by God. That was before the day got going. I sighed rather ruefully.

'Right, so what happens at 6.30?'

'We say ordinary morning prayer . . .'

Good heavens. More prayer!

80

'. . . then we hold our daily celebration of the eucharist and then it's time for breakfast.'

Breakfast – common ground at last. I had breakfast too!

'We have our very simple breakfast in silence, always in silence, because the devil likes to get at people after they have prayed, especially at the beginning of the day, in order to spoil the rest of the day. The silence means that you can only *think* a person is horrid rather than say it.'

'Is it all right to think it?'

'Well, it's only half a sin.' Peter burst into laughter at the expression on my face. Still smiling he went on.

'After breakfast we wash up, and then we clean the house from top to bottom every day, and we do it with a feeling of absolute urgency because we are on the border line between heaven and hell, where we believe we have been called to be the mouthpiece of creation in a big way. Every Christian is, but in the monastic life perhaps more so. In Christian prayer and service we are at the centre of life. Not the periphery as many think.

'We are here to stand between the world and the devil, to fight him before he corrupts and destroys, and sometimes it's a real old struggle against his infernal majesty.'

I was out of my depth. Breakfast, cleaning and the devil?

'Why is the cleaning so important, Peter?'

'In all things, Adrian, we aim to do a perfect job. Each one of us must be super-Harpic round every bend. You see, the Lord is here. His spirit is with us, and we know that we want to do it as perfectly as we can because the king of kings arrives every minute of the day – even in you, the king of kings has arrived.'

'Even in me?'

Through the sitting room window I could just see the top of the Downs in the distance. For some reason I found Peter's comment, light though it was, profoundly comforting. Even in me, the king of kings had arrived . . .

I wanted to pursue Peter's comment about not being on the periphery of life.

'How can a monk be at the centre of life?'

Peter suddenly looked very serious.

'Adrian, I have got to say honestly, and I mean it most sincerely, I am not a holy man, but if you spend hours and hours with God, you may very well see things more clearly and with more real knowledge than the person who lives on what I would call the periphery. That's why people go to holy men for help even if they've been shut up in a monastery for twenty years, because they sense that here is a chap who lives in the middle of life, and is able to, for instance, discern right and wrong, in a quite different way. Why, I've known people go to a monk who has been closed away for years just to ask him what kind of petrol they should use.'

'And would he have known the answer to that?'

Peter smiled. 'I don't know about that, but there is no doubt that one does get communications about things.'

I was intrigued. I tried not to sound too interested.

'Like. . . ?'

His voice was very quiet as he replied.

'On two occasions when I have been talking to someone, I have known that they were going to die.'

'Really?' I said foolishly, and probably a little nervously.

'Oh, yes, I could see death around them. I remember one chap – he wasn't particularly ill – I went back to the brothers and said, "He'll be dead in six months", and he was. I saw death around him.'

'And this is part of seeing the world from the centre?'

'Yes – and I recall another time.'

Peter sat forward as he suddenly remembered.

'There was a lady. Doreen was her name and she was very pregnant. One night I woke up at a quarter to twelve, and something – "within me or without me, I know not which" as Paul would say – said I should get out of bed and pray for Mrs Flag because she was just having her child. So out I got. Later, I heard that her baby had been born at just that time.'

'Was that in the form of a thought that came into your head, or . . . ?'

He clasped his hand thoughtfully.

'To quote Paul again, "In the flesh, or out of the flesh, I know not." But I do know that there wasn't any doubt about it.'

What a meal some Christians would have made out of these experiences. It didn't seem to bother Peter whether they were labelled or classified. They were just a natural feature of this vision from the centre that he was talking about. I wondered how Peter viewed the way in which other churches dealt with spiritual gifts.

'You hear a lot nowadays about things like prophecy and speaking in tongues. Word of knowledge is another gift that seems to be "in vogue" as it were. How do you feel about these things, Peter? The idea that God can zoom in on a service and say, "I've got a message for Fred, and this is it . . ."'

For the first time I felt the bishop was not altogether easy in his reply. His words were slow and carefully considered.

'Yes . . . I am happy. Paul makes it quite plain that everything must be done decently and in order and it's very difficult to get this balance. The Catholic Church, on the whole, has made the liturgy so frameworked and stereotyped, that it's actually very difficult to get these bits of informality in. On the other hand, some of the evangelicals have made it such a "hats in the air affair", that it's difficult for people to be able to concentrate on God, on giving themselves to him in sacrament, and in his word. It's very difficult to get it right. On the whole I think we need eucharistic worship and we need informal worship, but we probably ought to keep them distinct.'

It was a very careful reply.

'And the gifts themselves . . . ?'

'I am sure that there are people who have gifts of knowledge or prophecy. I've been to a lot of churches where it happens . . .'

His voice took on a more definite note.

'What worries me about prophecy is that it always seems to be jejune.'

I didn't know what he meant.

'Well, here we are, living in a world which could be on the edge of a nuclear war, where the wealth of the West is absolutely gross compared with the starving world, and you don't hear people saying any of the real strong stuff which I believe we should expect from prophets. It amazes me. Most of the prophecies I hear are saying that God is love and he loves you a lot. Well, of course he does, but is that what prophecy is for?' He paused, gazing into the distance, then smiled and relaxed back into his chair with a bump, his feet see-sawing into the air as he landed.

'I like tongues! I like to hear people singing in tongues. I've always said that if you have a special friend then there are two things which you must be able to do. You must be able to be silent with them and you must be able to talk nonsense with them . . .'

I laughed, remembering how, when John Hall and I met, we often talked complete but enjoyable rubbish for hours on end.

'. . . and the nonsense is not nonsense. It's because the love is so big, it bubbles out, and tongues is that freedom of bubbling out in love. It's lovely, you just go on and on.'

There was a short pause as I watched this bishop giggling with his legs in the air. No one who got up at 4.15 every morning had the right to be this happy.

'Have you ever doubted the existence of God, Peter?' He became quiet and serious again.

'Not doubts about the existence of God, no. Times when holding on was very difficult though, times when there was a great temptation to disobey, or seemingly disobey God.' Peter became very still, his voice so low that I had to lean forward to make sure I didn't miss what he said.

'I very much wanted to be married once . . . when I was about twenty-three. And God seemed to be saying, "Become a monk." I remember the whole time over that Christmas – they were very very black days.

'The balance was so fine. I only had to pick up a pen, and in thirty seconds write to this girl and say, "OK, it's on

84

again. When shall we meet?" Just a thirty second job it would have been, and it would have made all the difference between two totally different lives.' There was an expression of wonder on his face.

'When I think of Jesus calling Matthew "as he passed by". Amazing isn't it? Fifteen seconds to decide. Jesus looked over his shoulder and said, "Hi, Matthew. Come on – follow me!" Then he just walked on. He probably didn't even look behind him to see whether this geezer was coming. . . . Amazing!'

'Who made that choice about your future? Was it you, or was it God?'

'We made it between us, I think – together . . .'

He raised his voice in mock anger.

'He suggested it and I agreed, and I've got a bone to pick with him about it too!'

Suddenly he was laughing helplessly.

'I'm not a resentful creature,' he said, his mirth subsiding, 'but I get close to it.'

'So you've come to terms with celibacy then Peter?' I queried.

He looked at me for a moment, his eyes twinkling.

'Adrian, as I've already told you, God loves me extravagantly. I'm not just a celibate. I'm an extravagant celibate!'

Peter often returned, and still does return to the twin themes of extravagance and transfiguration. He is fond of quoting the story of Jesus feeding the five thousand, and points out that twelve basketsful of food were collected after the meal. A sign, he says, of God's extravagant giving.

He maintains that the church has a responsibility to transfigure the community instead of just forming a holy huddle once a week. For instance, he says, local churches should be as interested in producing a good football team, as in organising a good Bible study group. He is an inspiration to many, a puzzle to some.

As for me, he was the initiator of my understanding that

Christianity is not about *systems* and God, but about individual people, and the relationship they build through raw, prolonged contact with a creator who is genuinely and warmly interested in them. Peter is a man who has real discipline, a real prayer life and a real joy. He is one of the small group of people I know, who has gained his experience of God from God.

Unfortunately, Peter was involved with Company for a relatively short time before pressure of work and other responsibilities made it impossible for him to continue, other than for very occasional guest appearances. Three years later I was still meeting people who remembered things that he said in those early programmes. Peter is just the same today. Whatever he touches seems to sparkle. He even makes me fizz a bit.

Chapter Seven

One of the problems about saying that you're a Christian through a public medium like television, is that people have an awkward tendency to believe you, and neat organised expressions of faith seem to wilt rather, in the heat of real human need.

My friend and colleague, Ian, was really going through it. His father, who over the years had been loving parent, first-choice fishing companion and close friend, was dead. Cancer. For the last few months, Ian and I had worked together in a locked treatment unit, dealing with violent or chronically absconding teenagers from all over East Sussex. I had grown very fond of Ian; a warm, vulnerable, complex character, for whom pipe-smoking was a rich and absorbing activity, well suited to a nature that swung from deep contentment to heavy depression. He had a great talent for expressing affection, and real gifts with difficult and distressed children. I hurt for him when I saw his grief. I wished there was something I could do or say to help. There was something; but when I learned what it was, I felt quite frightened.

It appeared that in the seven months since Company had first come on the air, Ian's mother, Mrs Figg, had seen Bridget and me on a number of occasions as she sat up late watching the television, and was able to identify with much of what we said. Ian and I had only rarely talked about such things, but he asked me if I would deliver the address on the day of his father's cremation. He wanted me to do it, he said, first because I was his friend, and secondly, because, although I was a Christian I wasn't very religious. (I think this was intended to be a compliment, though it made me think at the time.) I agreed of course, but it was from that moment that I began to feel uneasy. I'd given talks before, but never on occasions like this. It was all very well to sit in that little island of light in the TV studio throwing out my views on God, left, right and centre, but this was going to be a real human event, full of pain and tears and the fear of death. What did I really know about God? What, for that matter, did I know about Ian's dad? Was he a Christian? If not, what would I say? Something vague but comforting perhaps. That would be the easy option; but would it be right? Or should I scratch the old evangelical itch, preach the 'hard line' gospel, and let people make their own minds up? It seemed to me that in a peculiar way I was neither humble nor arrogant enough to say very much at all.

As the day of the cremation drew nearer I felt more and more troubled. On the day before the service, I travelled down to Brighton to meet Ian's mum and stay the night with Ian and his wife, Sue.

Mrs Figg was nearly broken by her husband's death. I took her hand as we sat side by side on the settee in her sadly cheerful little sitting room.

'Tell me about Frank,' I said firmly. 'I want to know what he was really like.'

'He was the first person who really loved me,' she replied.

She told me that as a child she'd had a very strict religious upbringing. A lot of ritual, a lot of meetings, a great deal of church attendance and no love at all — no softness. Then, as a young adult she met Frank. He was the first person to offer her real affection and warmth. They fell in love and were married. Frank, a carpenter by trade, had always been popular at work and in the local community, especially as he had a great gift for settling arguments and disputes. She pointed to photographs of the smart, pleasant-featured man who had meant so much to her, and wept a little. She said that Frank would not have described himself as a Christian, and Ian, who had been listening quietly while his mother spoke, added that he might well have resented anyone attempting to stick that label on him after his death. I sighed inwardly. It wasn't going to be easy . . .

That night, I lay awake on my bed in Ian and Sue's spare room, gazing up at the ceiling and wishing that God would write the end of my talk for me. On the little table beside me lay the sheet of paper on which I'd jotted down headings and notes for tomorrow's address. But I couldn't write the ending. Lying there in the darkness I realised what a jumble of half-formed beliefs, feelings and thoughts still made up what I so easily described as my Christian faith. I just didn't know what I could say to all those people tomorrow without compromising God, or Frank, or myself or . . . I was still asking God for ideas when I fell asleep.

Sleep is a strange thing. The mind seems to go on working while the body takes a few hours off. In my case, the 'night shift' often seems more efficient and effective than the daytime one. Or perhaps God is more easily able to introduce ideas and suggestions when I am less defended and aggressively conscious. Whatever the reason, when I woke the next morning I *knew* how to end that address. The words were printed clearly on a sort of mental ticker-tape; all I had to do was transfer them to the sheet of paper beside me.

I was still nervous about the unfamiliar task awaiting me, but the central truth, the kernel of the event, was in my grasp, and as I stood in front of the mirror that morning, knotting, unknotting and reknotting the necktie that always seemed to half throttle me on these formal occasions, I knew that everything would be all right. My natural nervousness was not helped, however, by an absurd interval just outside the chapel of rest, when the undertaker asked where the minister was, as it was he who would lead the procession into the building. We had all spent a few minutes gazing around tensely, waiting for him to appear, when it suddenly occurred to someone – clearly brighter than the rest of us – that I was the minister on this occasion. Sweating slightly with embarrassment, I led the mourners into the cool interior of the chapel and after a hymn and a prayer, I began speaking to the fifty or so people who seemed to completely fill the available space. For a few minutes I spoke about the things I had learned about Frank from his wife and son. How very much they loved him, how he had many friends, how much he would be missed, how significant it was that Ian, in his thirties, would still rather go fishing with his old dad than with anyone else. I didn't have to make any of it up. It was all true. As I neared the end of the address, I lowered my notes to the table beside me. The last paragraph was still printed in my mind – I didn't need to read it. I spoke directly to Ian and his mum as they sat opposite me like two lost children, hands interlinked, eyes wet with tears.

'I am not sure what Frank thought about Jesus,' I said, 'but I am sure about one thing. They'll have met by now. And I'd guess that Jesus looked straight into his eyes, and smiled, and said, "Frank, you brought love into someone's loveless world, you were a peace-maker, and you were a carpenter. That's three things we've got in common. I reckon we've got plenty to talk about."'

On the following Wednesday night I described this event to Company viewers, pointing out how vulnerable I had felt when Ian first asked me to take the service. I had feared failure of some kind, failure to deliver the Christian 'goods', failure to make the event memorable and meaningful, failure, as well, if I'm honest, to impress. It occurred to me after the programme was finished that I was still playing games about honesty and openness. I had often said to people that I was quite happy to lay myself open at the Company table; to be truly vulnerable; but was I really? Later, as I settled comfortably back into my seat on the southbound train from Victoria, I frowned through the murky glass of the window and conducted an inner dialogue with myself.

'What do you mean when you say I'm not vulnerable on Company? I've just told goodness knows how many people about my rotten selfish feelings when Ian asked me to . . .'

'Ah yes. So you have. Did you tell Ian that at the time?'

'Well, no – but . . .'

'And isn't it a fact that you rather enjoy running yourself down about things that have already happened? It makes you feel good, and it protects you from real criticism.'

'Well . . .'

'Doesn't it?'

'I suppose so – but, look. What about the way I've talked about the arguments and problems Bridget and I sometimes have. They're real enough.'

My internal inquisitor chuckled. 'Oh, yes. I know what you mean. You mean when you and she sit there full of confidence and looking crackers about each other, and talk about the terrible problems you have.'

'But we do have problems! Surely it must be worthwhile to talk about things like that.'

'Oh, yes. I've no doubt it is. But that's not what we're talking about. We're talking about your claim that you're vulnerable sometimes. Let me ask you a question.'

'Yes?'

'Has it ever really cost you anything, mentally or emotionally to say the things you say round the kitchen table?'

East Croydon flashed by. I sighed.

'No – it hasn't.'

'Aren't you actually determined not to show your real feelings to anybody, let alone television cameras?'

I inadvertently vocalised the irritable 'Yes!' with which I answered this question, slightly shocking a precise looking elderly lady on the other side of the carriage. Perhaps she thought that I was practising being positive.

The next day I described this conversation to Bridget, and we decided to raise the question of 'being vulnerable' with the rest of the Company participants as soon as possible. We had our opportunity very shortly after this when the whole team, including Frances, Angus and Maurice met to discuss all aspects of the programme and its development so far. By now the team had changed and

91

grown significantly. Peter Ball was no longer with us, but we had a 'replacement' bishop in the form of George Reindorp, a very sprightly seventy year old, who had recently retired as the Bishop of Salisbury. He was now looking forward to an active retirement with his doctor wife, Alix. Other newcomers included Steve Flashman, an unusual combination of Baptist minister and highly talented rock musician, Robert Pearce, who worked for Christian Aid, Shirly Allan, an actress living in the Maidstone area, and Ann Warren, already well known as a Christian writer and broadcaster. At an appropriate point in the agenda Bridget brought up the subject of openness and vulnerability, and there was a general discussion about the advantages and difficulties of the expression of genuine feelings on television. It was finally agreed that the programme could only benefit from real communication, especially as the whole team had recently fallen into the trap of merely expressing agreement about rather unexciting truths. We all solemnly nodded our heads and vowed to be *really* vulnerable in the future. I, of course, nodded my head with all the rest, as one does in large meetings of that kind but I seriously doubted that, after all my years of being so well defended, I would really be able to open up. Less than two years later I was to be surprised by the extent to which I did reveal myself at my very lowest, but back at the beginning of 1983 it was George Reindorp who took the first step, when he told viewers about a tragic event that had happened many years earlier.

George Reindorp seems to have been in training all his life to become a grandfather. After only one encounter with this slim, white haired, vivacious character, Bridget and I knew that here was a man in whom children would delight, and there are few higher compliments than that. George, in his own way – and although it's not the same way as Peter Ball it is just as valuable – was able to make events and people sparkle with his infectious brightness and impish sense of humour. When I first knew George however, although I thought him very charming and competent, I also, rather arrogantly, suspected that he was more Anglican than Christian. He appeared to have responses and comments about all aspects of the Christian faith neatly labelled and filed in his mind for easy reference when required. Indeed, it appeared to me that, in his scheme of things, the Church of England was God's outer office, scrupulously tidied and cleaned, and presided over by highly organised reception-ists like George, who were employed to ensure that things ran smoothly; not to create problems where there were none, by asking unnecessary questions or exploring alternative ways of operating.

In my great wisdom I decided that George had never really been exposed to suffering and was effectively cushioned from real life by the privileges of high office in the church. Little did I know that George had already experienced one major tragedy in his life.

One night, soon after we had first met, George and I enjoyed an evening meal together at a hotel in Rochester, prior to a Company programme the following day. We ate and drank well, talked quite a lot (George is very good company), and then moved over to more comfortable seats for coffee. It was then that he told me about the death, in 1947, of his beloved baby daughter, Veronica Jane.

George was a parish priest at the time. He had married Alix in South Africa during the war and they were now living in Vincent Square near Victoria, with their small son Julian, in a house only three doors away from the flat which he later occupied in his retirement. Life seemed very full and good then. George was more than ready to tackle parish work after a long and eventful period as a navy chaplain during the war years. His was a large parish, including twelve thousand tenement dwellers, as well as the idle or industrious rich. There was ample scope for the use and development of those delicate skills of communication which he is able to use like a magician at times. George has always maintained that if David Jenkins, the controversial Bishop of Durham, had been able to experience life as a

93

parish priest earlier in his life, the knowledge and understanding of ordinary people thus gained, would have balanced his academic training, and perhaps resulted in a more careful and caring expression of his views on events such as the virgin birth and the resurrection. George felt, as a working vicar, that it was necessary to get really involved with such issues as the flower-arranging rota, and the debate about whose turn it was to clean the pews, for it was in these apparently trivial, day-to-day concerns that one could meet and learn about people, and perhaps earn the right to stand six feet above contradiction to preach to them. He is the same today. Somehow he learns about the personal lives and problems of many people who others hardly notice. Often as we have walked through the TVS building together, he has called out a cheery greeting to a cleaner or cafeteria assistant and added a query about the health or progress of a friend or child or parent.

In addition to the stimulation of his work, George was deeply in love with his blue-eyed, attractive wife, who as well as being a successful doctor was an ideal clergyman's wife, although she never allowed herself to occupy a stereotyped role.

Her only fault in George's eyes was her inability to give up cigarettes. He estimated that she smoked 'half a curate a year'. In all other ways though, she was perfect for him, being – by his own admission – less self-centred, and more controlled than he ever was.

Their joy was made complete by the arrival of a second child, Veronica Jane, a beautiful baby girl, in 1947. George adored her. Four hundred people were present for the christening of this special 'Parish Baby', none prouder than little Julian who thought his tiny sister quite wonderful.

Up to now, George had chatted lightly and easily as he recalled those first, pleasant, post-war years, but now a pattern of pain, like a much-used map, spread over his face, and he stared past my shoulder into the far distance as he spoke quietly about the death of his daughter.

'She was lying in her pram, just as she often did. I was in

the drawing-room talking to another clergyman, when the door suddenly opened, and Alix came in. She's a very unexcitable person, and she simply said, "Get a doctor quickly!", which struck me as being a very odd thing, because of course she's a doctor herself. Anyway, I went and got a doctor who lived close by. I knew by then that there was something wrong with Veronica Jane, but I took it for granted that everything was going to be all right. They both went upstairs, and after hanging around in the hall for a while I followed them . . .'

George's eyes misted slightly as he went on.

'When I first saw her I thought she was moving. I realised later that she wasn't really. It was just the effect of the artificial respiration they were doing on her. Alix knew in fact, as soon as she picked her up, that the little one was dead. Alix wept. I was just stunned. I cry a lot about all sorts of things, but that was . . . I don't know . . .'

He shook his head slowly from side to side, reliving the shock of that moment.

'She was a blue-baby you see. Nowadays, of course, they could have done something, but then . . . well . . .'

Dear George. As I looked at him I felt ashamed. I thought I knew about people, but I knew nothing. Never suffered? I thought of my own children and experienced just a hint of the pain that the death of any one of them would cause Bridget and me, and their brothers, of course.

'What about Julian, George? How did he cope?'

He smiled and relaxed into the warmth of the memory.

'Veronica Jane went on being very real to Julian. I remember he had a little friend round to play with him one day, about three months after the death. They disappeared up to the bedroom, and a little later we heard Julian screaming at his friend, so we rushed upstairs and it turned out that this other boy had picked up a little woolly toy, and Julian was screaming, "You can't have that! You can't have that! It belongs to Veronica Jane!" In the mind of that little five-year-old, you see, she was still very much alive. And, in fact, very much later, when we had had three more children,

I recall somebody saying to Alix and me one day, "How many children do you have?", and when I replied that we had four, Julian, who was of course much older then, interrupted quickly and said, "No! Five! You're forgetting Veronica Jane!" And he was right of course.'

'And how about you? Was she still there for you?'

George took a folded sheet of paper from his inside jacket pocket, unfolded it and passed it across to me.

'When she died we were devastated, naturally, and for a while I found it difficult to see where God fitted into what had happened. Then a dear friend – a saint really – wrote this to me.' He pointed at the paper in my hand. 'That's a copy of the letter. It brought peace to me, and since then it's been amazingly helpful to lots of others to whom I've given copies.'

I read the letter.

It was with great sorrow that I heard today of the death of your child. The religion of Christ was always sincere and clear-sighted. He refused to obscure the fact that tragedy was tragedy; and wept at the grave of Lazarus. It must therefore be in the circumference of His love that we recognise our torn hearts when we part with a child who has held all that was best in us in fee.

The fact that He could weep over the death of a loved one when He knew that in so short a time He was going to supply the answer which made hope the sequel to every tragedy, even the tragedy of sin, surely shows that here in time and space, grief and hope can come to us side by side.

Thus I pray it may be with you and your wife.

It has been given to me to see our progress to God as a road divided in the middle by a low wall, which we call death. Whatever our age or stage of development, or relationship with other human beings, there is no real change involved in crossing the low wall. We simply continue in a parallel course with those who loved us in our development and relationship. I do not believe that

God has altered one whit your responsibility or service for your child.

I do believe that she will grow side by side with you, in spirit, as she would have done on earth; and that your prayer and love will serve her development as they would have done on earth. There is nothing static about the other life.

The difficulty is that our spiritual sight is so little developed compared with our earthly sight. We cannot watch the development and growth as we could on earth. Yet much can be done by faith, by the realisation that what we hope is true, and that we can train our minds and imaginations to think in terms of truths, even if they are pictured in earthly forms. The companionship which was given you, you still have. The growth to which you look forward will still be yours to watch over and care for.

You will be much in my prayers at this time. What I have written I know to be true and I pray that you may be enabled to live in that truth and to find the answer to your tragedy.

When I had finished reading, I refolded the paper and handed it back to George.

'Thank you,' I said. 'Thank you for telling me about what happened to your daughter and for letting me see that.' I paused.

'Are you going to talk about Veronica Jane on the programme tomorrow, George?'

'Yes,' he replied brightly, 'I thought I would. It may help others who have lost someone they love very much.'

The following evening George repeated the story of Veronica Jane as we sat around the kitchen table in the Gillingham studio. It clearly cost him a lot to go through the whole thing again, and I felt glad that there was a cushion of thirty-five years between him and the tragedy. There was an unusual stillness about the studio as the programme came to an end. Those working on the studio floor and in the control room had been deeply moved by

George's story, and so, presumably, had viewers at home. It had been an event rather than a performance. Bishop Reindorp had undoubtedly pioneered the vulnerability that we all thought to be necessary, but suppose, I reflected, one wanted to talk about a tragedy that was happening in the present, and not thirty-five years ago. Would that be possible, or even desirable? Not very many weeks later we had a chance to find out, when George talked in a Company programme about the second major disaster in his life. This time we were quite unprepared for what he said, and it was not an incident from the past. It was happening to him right now.

We didn't associate George with tragedy. It was fun preparing and making programmes with him. He had a fund of stories that were very amusing and always well told. What was more, he never seemed to mind being stopped in the middle of his attempts to repeat them for the second or third time. His ability to switch from being avuncular to being like an excited small boy was very endearing and enriched our gatherings greatly, especially when we all felt rather limp and formless. George stacked untidy bits of the world very neatly when necessary. We indulged in a little playful sniping at times. I noticed that George had developed a very effective conversational ploy which he used in argument or debate. He would state his point of view with great force and panache, then, thrusting his chin aggressively towards the person he was addressing, say, in a tone implying that any attempt to put forward an alternative view would indicate advanced mental decay, 'Don't you agree?' I kindly pointed this out to George who was as grateful as one might expect, but I did notice that he modified the query thereafter to '*Do* you agree?', which does at least have the virtue of sounding like a real question. He bided his time, awaiting an opportunity for revenge. It came one day when I started a Saturday night programme by describing a thought that had occurred to me while I sat in the local pub on the previous evening.

'I was well into my second pint,' said I, 'when I really saw what Jesus meant when . . .'

George's sense of humour was so tickled by the idea of divine revelations beginning to occur at the two pint mark that he never allowed me to forget those few words.

'You know, Adrian,' he said one day. 'You're very fortunate. Most people have to drink all evening before they start to see things.' He paused, then stuck his chin out, his eyes glinted. 'Don't you agree?'

It was so enjoyable working with George, and he seemed such a happy man that the revelation of his great sadness was a real shock. We had decided to make a programme about the year that had just finished, and although we hadn't discussed the content in detail, Bridget and I assumed that most of the conversation would be about events that had made news in 1982; politics, sport, significant social change – that sort of thing. George was due to start the ball rolling, and sure enough, when the floor manager cued him he began to speak. But it wasn't what we'd expected.

'The most important thing to happen in my year never got into the newspapers or onto television,' he said. 'As you know, my wife Alix and I were hoping to retire into the country when I finished full-time work, but it is not going to happen now because Alix is suffering from Pik's disease, and she's going to move into a nursing home.' George's voice broke slightly as he went on. 'The thing is, you see, that the disease involves progressive deterioration of the brain, so . . . so she will need to be there for the rest of her life.'

Bridget and I sat in stunned silence, temporarily incapable of taking in what he was saying. We had never met his wife, but we had heard so much about her. Alix. The girl with the vivid blue eyes; the lover of flowers, the marvellous mother, wife and friend, full of inner sympathy and strength, the hostess who had entertained a thousand people a year. George's 'thought-mate', and an eye to catch across the room when someone said something ridiculous and you wanted to share your secret laughter with the only other person who would really understand . . . She was not to be with George in his final years.

He went on to describe how Alix had become more and

more withdrawn over a long period until it became clear at last that something was terribly wrong. When the illness was diagnosed, George's first concerns were practical ones. Where would she live for the rest of her life? Fortunately (George said that it was like Christian losing his burden in *Pilgrim's Progress*), someone presented him with an anonymous gift at this point, and through the generosity of that unknown person it was possible to arrange first-class care for Alix for an indefinite period. The next, and greatest task facing George was learning to live alone and face his retirement years without the steady, loving support of his wife.

'It's not the big things, you understand. You've had a good day – you've maybe had a bad day. You go home and she says, "How did it go?", and you say what happened and who said what, and she says, "How do you feel about it . . . ?" That's what you miss, that sort of ordinary, comfortable chat. And then you miss having someone to hold in your arms; and quite apart from that, you were such good friends . . . such good friends.'

At the close of the programme, Bridget and I and Frances, the producer, were in tears. But behind my tears all the old anger flared up again. I found myself saying silently to God, 'Well? Explain that one then!'

Over the following weeks, George came to terms with his situation quite remarkably, although a basic level of sadness remained of course. He seemed to have gained a new understanding of God's love for him as a son and a friend, quite apart from the official and ceremonial relationship that had existed over the years.

I probably had more difficulty accepting what had happened than George did. Perhaps this wasn't so surprising when one considered the fact that he had been pursuing a clear path of duty for more than half a century, and had good reason to trust God. Much later, over lunch one day in his Vincent Square flat, I told George how I had felt on hearing about Alix, and asked him the question I had wanted to ask at the time.

'Where is God in this, George? Has he allowed it? Has he got a point to make in it? What's going on?'

'I did ask a lot of questions like that,' he replied slowly. 'You go all through the possibilities. Is it because I have to learn something? Is God saying, "You've talked a lot about faith, now–what about it?" You ask yourself all those questions.'

For a few moments he studied the end of his fork, then laid it gently down on the table.

'In the end I simply have to say the same as old Polycarp, the Bishop of Smyrna, who was a holy man–rather different from me! They said to him, "Now, we really don't want to have to put you to death, so be a good chap and throw a few grains of incense on the altar for the emperor just to make it all right, then he'll let you live." And he said, "Lo, these eighty and six years have I served God. Shall I cast him off in my old age?" Well, now, God has been marvellous to me. We've got wonderful children and we're a very happy family. We've got nine and four-eighths grandchildren! So, although at first I did ask all those questions, and I still don't really understand it, I know that in it somewhere–God knows where–and I mean that literally, God IS, and I hold on to those words from scripture: "God has prepared for those who love him, such good things as pass man's understanding, that we loving thee *above all* things . . ." I've said that–talked about it a thousand times. I have to go on trusting.' He stopped for a second. 'Good heavens. It sounds as though I'm saying it's so *easy*. I get very very lonely still, especially as Alix is so out of character now, and when I do visit her each week, she quite often seems to lack interest in me, and draws the visit to a close after a very short time. It's hard sometimes when I go down there, longing to see her and then . . .' George straightened his cutlery neatly on his plate.

'Do you believe that you'll meet Alix, as she was, in another place, after death perhaps?'

There was more passion and certainty in George's voice when he replied, than I think I had ever heard before.

'Oh, Adrian . . .' For a moment he was lost for words. 'Somehow – if Christ is what I'm convinced he is, and believe and know him in my heart to be, so far as my little mind can take it in, I'm absolutely certain that all will be well. Shall we see again those whom we love? Yes! What will they be like? We do not know! When I wake up after thy likeness I shall be satisfied!'

Each sentence that George quoted, sounded like a girder that strengthened him. I realised that these words had a meaning for him that brought far more than intellectual reassurance.

'A bond of love like the one between Alix and me could never be completely shattered,' he continued. 'My God is not capable of such a capricious whim. We shall somehow be together again, not as husband and wife but in some other, better way. For the present I can only live a day at a time, but for what I've had, I give thanks.'

I had one more question. 'If Jesus was sitting here in this chair beside you now, and you wanted to say one thing to him about all this, what would it be?'

Through the big front window of George's sitting room we could see on the other side of the road, two of the masters from the famous nearby public school, hitting golf balls across the school sports field. One of them gave his ball a mighty crack, and I watched it sail into the blue, and disappear, to land somewhere on the far side of the grassy expanse. George's voice, as he spoke, was very gentle.

'I think I'd say, "For the past – thank you *very* much." Why?'

The 'Why?' was not a demand, just a simple question. George trusted God. I knew that now. And could it be, I wondered, the reason he had been able to be vulnerable on Company, was that he was accustomed to being vulnerable to God? An interesting question.

And what about me? Would I ever be able to let people see *me* broken and bruised? Never!

Chapter Eight

Peter Ball, George Reindorp, and other Company regulars and guests all shed their own particular light on the truth. Father Tony Cashman, for instance, brought my understanding of the Roman Catholic faith right up-to-date when he described how spiritual gifts such as tongues and prophecy are increasingly common among Catholic Christians nowadays. Robert Pearce, a regional secretary for Christian Aid, has broadened my understanding of international issues, especially when describing his trips abroad and his personal reaction to the sight of people in acute need. I particularly enjoyed meeting Mother Frances, an Anglican nun who runs Helen House in Oxford, the only children's hospice in the country. She was a delightful mixture of strength and freedom, with a sense of humour that seemed, somehow, to invigorate the air around her. Another welcome guest was the Roman Catholic Bishop of Arundel, Cormac Murphy O'Connor, an ex-rugby player and a man with a deep commitment to the building of bridges from denomination to denomination. I'm sure Cormac won't forget Bridget and me in a hurry. After we had made our programmes on that Tuesday, he kindly offered to give us a lift home to Hailsham on his way to Arundel. Unfortunately my navigating skills deserted me when we were about halfway home, and we wandered through endless Sussex lanes for what seemed an eternity. We did get home in the end, and Cormac was very patient!

When Vishal Mangalwadi joined us as a guest, I was determined to get his name right first time. Vishal works on behalf of the poor people in his part of India, and has suffered imprisonment and violence because of his quiet determination to be a true follower of Christ in that situation. As the run-up to the first programme began, I repeated Vishal's mouthful of a second name over and over in my mind, to make sure it came out smoothly. 'Mangalwadi – Mangalwadi – Mangal . . .' The floor-manager cued me and I spoke confidently to camera three.

'Hello. It's nice to have a special guest with us tonight, and it's . . .' My mouth opened and shut like a fish. I'd forgotten his *first* name!

All of these people were Christians of one variety or another, of course, but the time came when Frances announced that there was to be a new member of the team who was not a Christian, but a Jewish Rabbi. His name was Hugo Gryn.

Hugo turned out to be a bundle of fizzing activity, a short, physically dynamic, clean-shaven man with a crackling sense of humour, enormous energy, and a gravelly voice with an attractive combination of transatlantic and Central European accents. Like me in the past, he smokes incessantly, and with something akin to dedication, as though each fresh cigarette wards off the resolution of some fearful issue. With others he is rarely still, always watchful, studying and learning from eyes, adapting a little here and there in his responses, still employing, perhaps, in a modified form, the survival skills he learned in the harsh schools of Auschwitz and other camps during the war. Highly educated, multi-talented, a fascinating speaker and supreme teller of stories, Hugo is a congregational rabbi in the West London Synagogue, which has a full membership of thousands, and is a constituent of the Reform Synagogues of Great Britain. He seems to have been to most places and met most people. He is always on the move around the city, the country, the world. A skilful user of the media, he is familiar with both television and radio broadcasting, and he has brought a new dimension of interest and entertainment to many many Company discussions. Hugo always 'delivers'. He is not a man who would find it easy to be at a loss, and I have only very occasionally seen him display anything but buzzing competence. I don't think Hugo believes that many people would be interested in his sadness when it occurs, and, as he said to me once, when he does get hurt, he tends to go inside himself, rather than turn to others.

I had often wondered, before meeting Hugo, where all the Jewish jokes came from. I now believe that, even if he doesn't make them all up, Hugo is largely responsible for giving them currency. Whenever we meet nowadays, I look forward with relish to the latest story. I don't interrupt, but I recall that, when I first met him, I stopped a joke after half a sentence.

'These two Jews were on a bus . . .'

I interrupted pompously. 'Do they have to be Jews, Hugo?' What a wonderful non-racist person I was.

Hugo's expressive face twisted into concentrated thought, then relaxed, one eyebrow raised humorously. 'Okay, I'll start again. There were these two Chinamen on their way to a Barmitzvah . . .'

I collapsed.

A story that was much appreciated by Company viewers was Hugo's account of the elderly Jew who desperately wanted to win the weekly lottery that was organised in his community. This man stood before the open ark in the synagogue and called out with a loud voice.

'God! Let me win the lottery this week. I need the money. Please let me win!'

To his dismay there was no reply, and someone else won the cash that week. On the following week he came back to the synagogue, and stood before the ark once more, beating his breast and calling out in an even louder voice.

'Oh, God! You must hear me! I've been a good Jew all my life. I've done what you've told me to do. I've been in the synagogue every week. Now I'm asking you to help me. Please! Please, let me win the lottery this week!'

Again there was only silence, and again the prize-money went to another man a couple of days later.

The next week he prostrated himself before the open ark, pleading and begging God to answer his prayer, and let him win the lottery, just once. After a few minutes of this, he lay exhausted and speechless on the floor of the synagogue. Suddenly a voice came from the open ark. It was the voice of God.

'Look, meet me halfway, will you? Buy a ticket!'

My mother, well into her sixties by the time Hugo joined Company, and a very reliable barometer for the programme generally, took a real shine to the rabbi. She thought him kind, good-looking and original; very high praise from her.

On a more serious level, I wondered how we would handle the gap between Hugo's beliefs and those of the rest of the team. Most of us were Christians of one denominational shade or another. He was a Jew. Should we confront? Should we compromise? Should we ignore the differences and talk about something else? Generally speaking, discussions tended to be very polite and non-controversial when we did talk about our contrasting faiths. Hugo was asked on one occasion to say something about the enormous variety of faiths that exist in the world. Were they all misguided, or perhaps, all true in their own way? Hugo subscribed to the latter view. Just as a crystal will throw out different facets of the same light, so, he maintained, each religion or like-minded group receives a facet of the single, central truth, which is God.

It was a good answer, and a diplomatic answer, but I couldn't make up my mind when I saw that programme, whether Hugo really did believe what he was saying. What would I have said if I had been involved in that discussion? I would have been polite I expect. I'd have nodded, and said, 'How interesting'. What did I believe? Did I go for the crystal idea? Or did I believe that, unless they turned to Jesus, all Jews would be rejected from God's presence on the day of judgement? I imagined Hugo and me walking side by side into the presence of God. I tried to picture myself being accepted and the rabbi rejected. My mind wouldn't do it – the other way round, perhaps, but not that way. I could sense a piece of the love of God in Hugo – nothing to do with his religion. It was just there. God would surely welcome home that piece of himself. Who was I to judge after all? There was little to show for my faith. Hugo's had survived experiences that I could only guess at. What did I know about suffering, compared with this man who had not long been a teenager when he first entered a Nazi death camp, and saw his younger brother taken away to be executed because he had no useful function for the Germans? Why was Hugo not only still a believing Jew, but a rabbi, after coming through experiences that might be thought to deny rather than affirm the existence of a loving God? There was never enough time or an appropriate opportunity to explore these areas with Hugo during the Company broadcasts, but I really wanted to know the answer to that question in particular. Also, what was the difference between Hugo and George in relation to the way they coped with personal tragedy? Or Peter Ball for that matter, who had given up the warmth and fulfilment of marriage and family life for the sake of serving the same God as Hugo. Why did they all continue to follow him whatever happened? The only way to ask Hugo these questions was to actually book time with him. His diary was always packed, but he named a date and on that day, a strangely significant one as I learned later, I met him at his London office.

Hugo was oddly ill at ease that morning, partly because he had been following what was, even for him, a very rigorous and demanding schedule, but also for another reason which I was to learn as we talked. People were clamouring for his attention in person and via the phone up to and beyond the point where we finally sat down. He fumbled with the telephone as he replaced it on its rest at last, half-dropping then retrieving it, glancing up quickly to see if I had noticed his uncharacteristic clumsiness.

Finally he was settled, with the inevitable cigarette safely lit, leaning back in his chair and narrowing his eyes as the smoke rose in front of his face like a thin grey screen.

I had with me a book called *Returning*, a collection of exercises in repentance by past and present Jewish writers and poets. One poem in particular had moved me more than anything I had read for a very long time. I knew Hugo was familiar with it, because he had chaired the RSGB Prayer Book Committee which had assisted Jonathon Magonet, its editor in his compilation of the anthology. I read the poem out loud.

The house of God will never close to them that yearn,
Nor will the wicks die out that in the branches turn;
And all the pathways to God's house will be converging,
In quest of nests the migrant pigeons will come surging.

And when at close of crimson nights and frenzied days,
You'll writhe in darkness and will struggle in a maze
Of demons' toils, with ashes strewn upon your head,
And lead-shot blood, and quicksand for your feet to
     tread.
The silent house of God will stand in silent glade.
It will not chide, or blame, or scoff, will not upbraid,
The door will be wide open and the light will burn,
Ane none will beckon you and none repel with stern
Rebuke. For upon the threshold Love will wait to bless
And heal your bleeding wound and soothe your sore
     distress. . . .

I finished reading and looked up. Hugo was nodding vigorously.

'Yes, I know that piece well. Actually, it's about abandonment – the kind of abandonment that we experienced in the camps. It reminds me of . . . did I ever tell you about the postcards?'

I shook my head.

'It was in a relatively small camp in Silesia. About four thousand prisoners I think. It must have been in . . .' Hugo frowned as he tried to remember, then stabbed the air with his cigarette in triumph. 'It was the summer of forty-four!

We were made to work from dawn to dusk for six and a half days a week. I think it was Sunday afternoon we were allowed off, and then, absurdly, sometimes the camp orchestra would play. Can you imagine that, in the middle of death? Anyway, one day, to our great amazement we were all supplied with a postcard each, and some pencils, and told that we could write to *anyone* we liked, *anywhere*, and they would be delivered via the Red Cross.

'So, there I was, standing with my pencil and my postcard, and gradually I realised I had no one to write to. My father was there in the camp with me, but I had no idea where my mother was. The rest of the family had all died in Auschwitz. Everybody dead. Grandparents, brother, cousins, aunts, uncles, everybody from my part of the world, by that time they were already dead. I knew I had some relatives somewhere in America, but I didn't know their names, and I certainly didn't know any addresses. I really tried to think of someone, but, in the end, I was one of many who handed in a blank card. I had no one to write to, and I didn't think there was anyone in the world to whom it mattered if I wrote, or didn't write, if I lived or died. There was a sense of being totally abandoned.'

'Was that very hurtful?' Another great 'Plass' question.

'It was *so* painful. I came face to face with the fact that I didn't matter to anyone outside that camp. Thank goodness I mattered to me, because plenty of people around me soon stopped mattering to themselves, and then, well . . . the suicide rate was very high.'

'But you did have your father there with you?'

Hugo stubbed out his cigarette.

'Yes, I did, and it was really because of him that I managed to avoid the excesses that many other prisoners were driven to. He was a very sane, very intelligent, very good man and he kept me from doing really bizarre or shameful things. I don't mean that I was particularly good. I just had that peculiar dimension of luck in having him with me. He kept hope alive, you see. I remember he once saved the margarine ration for weeks, and he made a little bowl out of clay, and a wick from strands of cloth, just so that he could light a candle to celebrate the festival of Hannukah. "One way or another," he said, "we *are* going to celebrate!" And he got all the people together to light the Menorah.'

'Did you understand why he did that?'

Hugo threw his hands out and opened his eyes wide. 'No! I thought it was a waste of margarine. I said so. Especially as the candle didn't even light when it came to it. It just sputtered and died. But he took me on one side — I was about thirteen or fourteen then — and he said, "Understand this. You and I have gone through a lot. A long, forced march with next to no food, and once we lived for a couple of days with no water. You can live for quite a long time without food. You can even live without water for a day or two, but I am telling you that you cannot live for three minutes without *hope*. You've got to have hope!" And he was right. As long as people were taking that much trouble to make a single candle to use for a religious ceremony — well, there must be hope, even in the middle of suffering. He taught me that.'

'Did your father die in the camps?' I flinched inwardly as I waited for Hugo's reply.

'Actually, he survived the whole war, but . . . you see, we ended up at this camp in Austria, a really vicious place, just a few days before the end of the war. We had been on a forced march to get there — more than half of the march died on the way — and in this camp there was not just hunger, but raging typhoid. Everybody had it. When the Americans liberated the camp on May the fifth, there were unburied corpses everywhere, and those who were alive were all sick. All those still living — and my father was living — were taken to a kind of makeshift hospital, although I'm not sure that they really knew how to treat us. And my father and I shared a bed in this place . . . It was then that he died.'

'So he died after . . .'

'Yes! After liberation! When they came to take him away, and I knew for sure he was dead — I wouldn't let 'em! I was hysterical – beside myself. It was the ultimate in being cheated, you see. He'd actually survived . . . the sight of him being taken away was very bad. I had typhoid too, and everything seemed blurred and confused. I do know though, because they told me afterwards, that at that moment I attacked one of the German SS men that they were using as orderlies. I mean . . . I really wanted to kill him. I was completely out of control. And after that . . . it was just oblivion. I wasn't even able to be there when they buried him, presumably in some sort of mass grave . . .'

Hugo selected another cigarette from the packet beside him, and flicked his lighter expertly. He was in control, but there had been a glimpse of a very young and desperate Jewish boy for just a moment.

'Do you know the date of his death?' I asked.

He thrust a hand towards me, palm downwards, fingers outstretched, patting the air, a characteristic gesture. 'Adrian, you're catching me on a very, very, peculiar day. After I came to, some pious Jews who had been there when my father died, gave me the date and told me not to forget that my Yahrzeit – that's the anniversary of my father's death – was the fourth day of the Hebrew month of Sivan. Whether they were right or not, I'm not sure, but that's the date I've got.'

'And that day is . . . ?'

Hugo nodded energetically. 'Today!'

No wonder he had looked distracted – less together than usual. Time heals, but scars can ache terribly. Should I go on?

'So . . . is this a bad day to talk about . . . ?'

Hugo interrupted, leaning forward and smiling. 'Peculiar! Not bad, just peculiar.'

I took the plunge again. 'What happened to your mother, Hugo?'

'She survived. She went through Auschwitz, just as we did, and then on to another camp, where she not only survived, but helped to organise an escape group of women.'

'She wasn't with you when your father died, then?'

Hugo's response to this question was a strange, gentle, sweetly-growled 'No-o-o-o.'

'When was she freed?'

'She was released a few months earlier – in March I think, so she had already made her way back to our home town, and eventually, I made my way there as well.'

'Do you remember your first meeting with her when you got back?'

He replied vehemently. 'I remember it very, very, *very* well!' He settled back in his chair. 'I had a very complicated journey home from the camps. Transport in Europe was all over the place at the time, and you just had to travel as best you could. It was a very odd time. I went by train, I went by boat, I walked, I even stole a horse and cart with a couple of other people once, and used it for three days then abandoned it in some town. Eventually, I came to Budapest. I wasn't home yet, but I suddenly remembered that I had relatives in that city. I managed to find out where they lived and presented myself at their door.'

Hugo paused for a few moments, his hand arrested in mid-gesture, his eyes focused on the image in his mind. It didn't look like a happy memory. He went on in tones that sought to excuse the people who had opened that door to him.

'I must have looked very peculiar . . . and I think they felt very ill at ease with me. They never even invited me in. . . .'

Hugo threw the last sentence away, but I caught it, because it triggered the memory in me of that doorway in Bristol, and the abject misery of being turned away when I most needed to be taken in. That had been bad enough. How must Hugo have felt after so many years of desperate survival, so much loss and death, when people who might have laughed and wept with him, however distantly they were related, didn't even ask him in? I didn't know how deeply that had hurt him, and for some reason I couldn't face asking him. For my own sake, I think.

I realised that Hugo was going on.

'. . . and this train went and went and went until we reached a point about three or four stops from my home town in Russia. Before the war it had been in Czechoslovakia, but now the borders had changed, and suddenly I lived in Russia. No matter! Wherever it was, it was home, and I was nearly there. Anyway – the train stopped at this station a few miles from my destination, and a man got on and sat in the same carriage as me. We got into conversation, and after a while it turned out that he knew my family.

'"Did you know," he asked, "that your mother is at home?"

'Well, I didn't know, of course. It was the first time I'd heard of it. I told him so.

'"Yes!" he said. "She's there and she's fine, and she's waiting for you, . . . and your father. Where's your father?"

'He told me that someone had come back from the camp where my father and I ended up, just after it was liberated by the Americans, and given my mother the news that we had *both* survived. So I now knew that my mother was sitting at home waiting for me to walk through the door with my father. Well . . .'

I stared at Hugo in silence, moistening dry lips with the tip of my tongue as I tried to imagine how he had felt. No fiction writer could have concocted a more tortuously dramatic situation.

'When the train stopped at my home town,' went on Hugo, 'I didn't want to get off. I said to this man, "Look, I'll just stay on for a couple more stops, and have a think about things, and then I'll come back." I was afraid to get off! But . . . they wouldn't let me stay on the train. Whether they actually held the train up for a while I don't know, but somehow they persuaded me – conned me – into getting off the train, and I started to walk towards my house. Believe me, I didn't have much luggage! So, I'm walking down the road towards the house where this man said she was staying. It's a summer afternoon, and, you can imagine, I'm nervous. Then, I looked up, and there was my mother, watching me from an upstairs window as I trailed along the road towards her – alone. And when we were finally face to face, she didn't ask me anything. She looked at me and took it all in, then we embraced. And then . . . you know, we have a tradition that when someone in the family dies, you sit Shivah. That means you sit on a low stool for seven days, and that's the formal mourning. But if the news of death is delayed, you still go through this ritual of mourning, but for just one hour. So my mother just looked around, found a low stool, and sat in silent mourning for an hour. At the end of the hour she got up – she still hadn't asked me anything – and she said to me, "Hugo, you're the son. You say Kaddish." That's a prayer of praise that we say, and it doesn't actually mention death at all. It starts "Magnified and hallowed be the name of God . . ." So I said it. And then, when I'd finished – then, we started to talk. I didn't really understand it then, but I do now. You see, the language of religion and ritual was, if you like, the mediating influence.'

'You mean that the ritual *was*, in a sense, the conversation between you and your mother?'

Hugo nodded. 'That's right, and we didn't need anything else. It wasn't until days later that she said "Now, what exactly happened?" There was too much to say at that first meeting, so we didn't try. The most important thing, she knew anyway, just by looking at me.'

Coffee arrived. After a little clinking and stirring we were settled again.

'Why, Hugo . . .' – it was the question I had wanted to ask – 'why, when you had seen so much suffering, so much misery, did you decide to become a rabbi?'

'Well, it's a good question, because, actually I always wanted to be a scientist – I *am* a scientist, I've got a degree in maths and bio-chemistry – but I agree with Emil Fakenheim when he said that Hitler mustn't be allowed a posthumous victory. He invented an eleventh commandment . . .'

'Which was . . . ?'

Hugo wrote the words in the air with his hand. 'Thou Shalt Survive! It wasn't enough to stay alive physically. It was just as important that Jewish values, and above all, Jewish learning should be preserved. And the thing is, Adrian, that in the Jewish tradition, learning and spirituality go hand in hand. Most of us come to spirituality through learning – not the other way round. I was very lucky to have a great teacher . . .' He pointed to a picture on the wall beside us. 'Leo Baeck. In the end, he and another rabbi who was coaching me, sensing that I was beginning to believe I was the only person in the world who was still seriously interested in Jewish studies said, "All right, if it's so important, then go ahead and devote yourself to Jewish learning!" So I did.'

Hugo chuckled richly. 'I was bluffed – dared into it, and I was lucky really. They stopped my bitching just like that. It just shows how important it is to fall into the right teachers' hands at the right time.'

'So you became a rabbi?'

'I became a rabbi.'

'But you didn't feel a call from God in the sense that Christian priests talk about it sometimes?'

'I might have been *sent*, but I don't think I was called.' Hugo was laughing again. 'I don't really know . . . I believe that God actually rules all our destinies, so, in that very general sense, perhaps he sent me. More specific than that I wouldn't like to say. I don't quite see God picking me out and saying, "Now, Gryn, I think you ought to do so and so . . ." No, it's not my notion of God.'

'But if . . .'

Hugo interrupted. 'We have free will! I have it, you have it. If you abuse yours you might well diminish mine. That's where it all goes wrong. But . . .' He leaned forward, one hand raised, but flat, to separate heaven from earth.' I can't blame God for *my* getting it right *or* wrong. For me, that equation just doesn't work. The things that I saw in the camps, the suffering I experienced can be wasted or not, according to how I exercise my will. I am able to know more

115

accurately than some, perhaps, what hurts, causes pain in others. My aim is to simply *not* do that which is hurtful.' He waved his cigarette as if to attract my innermost attention. 'The Golden Rule is different in the Christian and Jewish traditions. The Christian tradition says "Do unto others as you would have them do unto you." But the Jewish tradition says "Don't do unto others what is hateful to you." There's a difference, and it's a difference that I learned through suffering.'

'And God is involved with suffering.'

'I think that God wept with the Jews in the camps. I think that God weeps with all who suffer, and I mean *with*, not just *for*!'

I was still having great difficulty in understanding Hugo's relationship with God. I felt I had grasped the importance and significance of learning and the need to preserve tradition and ritual, but there was so much in him, and in the stories he had told, that spoke of a God who did take a personal, caring interest in this person who had been 'lucky' enough to find a teacher like Leo Baeck, whose influence had changed the course of his life, and 'lucky' enough to have his father with him through the camps.

Perhaps it was just the conditioned Protestant in me, but I couldn't dismiss the strong impression that at some point in his life Hugo must have encountered God in a very close and profound way. Was it I wondered, that I simply needed to have my own image of God reinforced?

'Has God ever spoken to you, Hugo?'

'In so many words?'

I adapted hastily. 'Not necessarily, but has there ever been an occasion when God gave you a nudge, or a push?'

'Yes there was. Yes. Quite clearly.' No hesitation at all. I sat very still and listened as Hugo went on.

'It was Yom Kippur, and I was in prison, and I had a kind of bolt-hole in this place I worked in. I knew that if I worked the twelve to fourteen hours a day they demanded I wouldn't last. There just weren't enough calories coming in to keep me going. By that time I was a cunning, experienced prisoner – I knew the ways of the prison world anyway. So, I used to disappear for a few hours at a time, and just sit in this bolt-hole of mine. It was in a builder's yard. You can do things in a builder's yard. Well, it was Day of Atonement, and all the Jews in this camp knew that, and I knew it, so I got in there – into my hiding place. Well . . . I didn't have a prayer book, but I remembered some of the prayers, and I . . . I decided I'd pray. So I did.' Hugo's voice was a soft growl. 'Half-remembered prayers . . . bits and pieces, and I ended up really crying. I just cried and cried . . .'

It was a vivid picture. Hugo, already forced to be old beyond his years, sitting in the darkness, weeping for Judaism, for his family, for himself.

He went on, his voice low but very firm. 'I was convinced then, and I remain convinced to this day, that my cry was heard. I'm not saying it saved me, because that was a chance thing, but I *know* I was heard, and I in turn also heard . . . understood that the ways in which we hurt each other, these are not God. Actually, that's when I became religious, in that bolt-hole that day. It never left me. I could draw a picture of that place now. It's that clear. On that day, I understood, for the first time, the reality of God; understood that he is not just an extension of me – that he is wholly "other". And, yes, I can communicate, and it's not a one-way thing . . .'

'And that principle continues?'

'All the time.'

I felt surer than ever that there was something that Peter and George and Hugo had in common. Something about trusting, despite not really knowing. Something about not claiming more than was actually true . . . I couldn't quite put my finger on it. I glanced up at the clock – nearly time to go. One more question.

'Hugo, you said that today might be the anniversary of your father's death. What would he think of you if he was here now?'

For a moment I witnessed a rare sight – Hugo at a loss.

'I want notice of that question!' He considered for a

moment. 'Well, first of all he would be surprised that I was a rabbi, and not a scientist. He would say I have reverted – my grandfather and his father before him were both rabbis. He wouldn't be displeased about it, just surprised.' He blew a long stream of smoke towards the ceiling. 'Then I'd set out to show him he could be pleased. I think we'd get on well. I don't think he would be particularly ashamed.'

I didn't think he would either. In fact, I thought that he would probably be very proud of the way in which this son of his had kept the eleventh commandment.

Chapter Nine

As 1983 got under way I was feeling rather shell-shocked. So many things had been happening in all areas of my life. I had given up smoking more than a year ago, something I had always thought impossible. Then there was the television programme which seemed to fill up a large proportion of my free time.

The bulk of my time and energy, however, was spent on the work I was doing in the newly opened locked unit at the Children's Centre in Hailsham. Planning and running this treatment facility had proved to be an intense and often stressful experience for all concerned, as we were dealing with extremely difficult teenagers in a very small and restricted environment. One child in particular was very disturbed. She had been with us for many months, a fifteen-year-old girl who, after a disastrous early life had been unable to settle for very long in any of the county establishments or foster homes that had been tried over the years. Placement after placement had failed, and now Meryl was an expert in institutional disruption, unwanted by her family, and unsuited to any but our small physically secure wing catering for no more than five children at the most. Meryl was able to wind up and manipulate adults to screaming pitch. On more than one occasion I arrived at work to find a staff member alone in the office, shaking with tension and anger after a few hours with Meryl, who seemed to feed on this kind of response.

Generally speaking there was a relatively peaceful atmosphere when she and I were together but there were times when she tested my self-control almost to breaking point with her finely judged, spiralling hysteria, and constant attention-seeking ploys. I was no longer the very immature personality who had hit out at that boy in the middle of a field ten years ago, but that was really only because I had learned more techniques and knew how to stack tension away in some inner space that, although I didn't realise it at the time, was already dangerously overpacked.

A typical incident occured one autumn afternoon, when Meryl and I were the only two people in the unit. I was ensconced in an armchair in one corner of the multi-functional dayroom while she, rather moodily, pushed snooker balls around the half-size table that stood in the centre.

Meryl desperately wanted to find foster parents who she could live with, but, predictably, the search for these 'super-humans' was taking rather a long time.

Already, that day, she and I had talked about how much progress had – or rather, had not – been made and I knew that she was feeling angry and frustrated. Poor Meryl, despite a succession of horrendous failures, always managed to whip up a froth of optimism and excitement about 'The Next Place'. Everything would be different! Oh, yes it would! She would change! Why couldn't it happen tomorrow? It wasn't usual for her to use aggressive tactics with me, but today was different. Her mind and body were aching with the strain of containing such heavy, jagged emotions, and I was the only available means of off-loading some of this intense feeling.

Sitting comfortably in my chair, absorbed in a newspaper, I was suddenly aware of Meryl's voice, filled with a sneering challenge.

'What would you do if I put this effing cue through that effing window?'

I knew how essential it was to think very quickly in these situations. Indeed, it was the extra half-second's thought that often made the difference between a successful outcome and disaster at times like this. I had been the author of enough calamities in the past to know that. In the moment

120

after Meryl's question, the following thoughts flashed through my mind. Firstly, she was quite capable of doing what she threatened, and there was a real danger of injury, leaving aside the less important matter of damage to the building. She was on the far side of the snooker table, and therefore out of grabbing range, even if I came out of my chair like a rocket. Also she would expect me to react angrily, or nervously, or to reason with her. Any of these responses would have suited her well, offering as they did, the possibility of tension-filled dialogue, culminating in an emotional 'splurge' of some kind. I had learned to avoid predictable responses. And lastly my stomach was knotting up, as it always did when 'aggro' loomed, no matter how confident I might feel about the outcome.

The pause before my reply must have been imperceptible. As I spoke, I didn't move my eyes for even a fraction of a second from the open newspaper that I was holding.

'Just a minute.'

It was hardly a response at all. There was a short pause. Meryl must have decided that I couldn't really have heard what she said. She repeated her threat in a slightly louder voice.

'I *said*, I'm going to put this effing cue through that effing window!'

Still without looking up I answered her, trying to put into my voice the mild, abstracted irritation with which one reacts to an annoying, but trivial interruption.

'Look, Meryl, I just want to finish this little bit in the paper, then I'll be with you. Okay?'

The newsprint swam before my eyes as I waited for her next move. There was another, longer silence. When Meryl spoke finally, it was with a rather pathetic, baffled wistfulness. I wasn't keeping to the rules!

'Yeah, but I said I was going to put the effing cue through the . . .'

My raised hand interrupted her. I folded the newspaper, placed it neatly on the magazine rack beneath the coffee table, then turned deliberately in my chair to face her,

121

crossed my legs, folded my arms and demonstrated my readiness to give her my full attention.

'Now, Meryl, I'm listening. What can I do for you?' It was the polite bank clerk with his next customer.

Meryl was a little muddled by now. She held the snooker cue up and replied quite quietly and politely, 'I'm going to put this effing cue through the window.'

'Yes . . . and?'

Meryl looked blank. I was supposed to supply the 'and'. She collected herself a little. 'Well, I'm going to do it! I am!'

I nodded soberly. 'I'm sorry, Meryl. I don't quite see what you want me to do. If you've decided to break a window with that cue, then I expect that's what you'll do. You must make your own decision about whether it's a good idea, or not. I'd like to be able to help, but . . .' I spread my hands in a helpless gesture. 'What can I do . . . ?'

Meryl raised the cue, her eyes fixed on mine. Was I bluffing? 'I am gonna do it!'

I looked up at the clock above the sink over on my left. 'Look, Meryl, I really have got to make some phone calls. I'd better go and get on with it. You stay here and decide what to do, and I'll be in the office.'

I stood up and strolled casually past the end of the snooker table, down the passage on my left, and into the little unit office a few yards along the corridor. As I passed within 'striking' distance of Meryl, I sensed her sudden increase of tension. I knew that it would happen now if it happened at all. I waited for the sound of smashing glass . . . but it didn't come. Instead, the disconsolate figure of Meryl appeared in the office doorway, the long wooden cue now dangling loosely in her hand. I snatched the redundant weapon from her, and shouted loudly into her face as all the pent up emotion of the last few minutes burst out.

'Don't ever do that to me again!'

After this explosion, we sat and reviewed what had happened, looking for ways in which Meryl might have expressed her feelings more appropriately.

Meryl had many difficulties after her placement at

Lansdowne but Bridget and I became very fond of her and she continued to visit and stay with us as a friend in the years that followed.

Work with children like Meryl was very stimulating and exciting – you never knew what would happen next – but it was also rather wearing.

Nowhere was the God who came, and comes down in the person of Jesus, more needed than in the lives of these children I was working with. Children like Meryl, and many others, were already emotionally crippled before they reached their first or second birthdays. Theoretical compassion was useless to them. Their experiences did not generally make for an attractive presentation and success in caring for them demanded a carefully balanced mixture of warmth and firmness. This could occasionally take extreme forms, as in the case of Miranda, another long-term resident in the secure unit, a very powerful girl, full of passion and chaos. On more than one occasion I was able to defuse the violence in her, only by putting my arms lovingly around her and whispering bloodcurdling threats into her ear at the same time. It worked because she knew I was sincere about both. I suppose – on reflection – that God operates in a similar way. The Bible has always struck me as being largely made up of God's love on the one hand, and his blood-curdling threats on the other.

Both Meryl and Miranda were victims of cruelty and mismanagement. I have always strenuously resisted the argument that says people cannot be held accountable for their crimes because of difficult childhood experiences, but there are notable exceptions, who, by the time they have struggled through and arrived wild-eyed at the age of sixteen, deserve a full apology and a pension for life.

Many people, however, do not actually commit crimes or anti-social acts as a result of early problems. They do, however, often end up with an emotional limp, an inadequacy in one area or another. Perhaps Jesus' statement that people need to be 'born again' has a special meaning for those who would welcome the opportunity to start life again and get it right this time round.

I was interested to see, as the months went by and people started to be more open, how many of the Company team had suffered as young children, and had seen, or wanted to see, God coming down into their lives to change the consequences of early trauma. Ann Warren, for instance, lost both of her parents at a very early age, and has been a refugee from her past ever since. It is her insight into her own situation, and her determination – with God's help – to overcome the darkness inside her that has enabled her to help so many others through her books and counselling. Peter Timms, the prison governor who made headlines when he left the prison service to become a Methodist minister, lived with the conviction that he was unloved for years, after his mother's early death, and formative years spent with a family who, although very caring, never really succeeded in making him feel that he belonged. Sue Flashman, one of the brightest contributors to the programme, has been very open and honest about the fear and insecurity that has dogged her all her life, and that is only now beginning to ease after much expert Christian counselling. Again, the roots of her problem lie in child-hood, and any attempt to find a solution without reference to that fact would fail before it began. Frances Tulloch, Company's producer, has much in common with these folk. She also sustained a lot of inward injury as the result of her parents' broken marriage, and has had to slowly and pains-takingly reassemble a shattered self-image over the years.

Does God come down and help? How does he do it? I'm sure he does it in many ways, but one of the most striking examples that I have seen is in the case of Jo Williams, my good friend and Company colleague. Of all the team, she is the one whose background most reminds me of the children I have worked with.

When Jo was 'discovered' as the newspapers put it, she was working as a cleaner in the TVS studios in Southampton and running a local scheme offering help and friendship to old, sick and desperate people. She called it Neighbourly Care and appeared one day on the TVS community services programme PO Box 13 to describe her work. Angus Wright immediately asked Jo if she would like to join the Company team and, slightly bewildered, but willing to have a go, she agreed. She became even more bewildered when the national press ran a story about her elevation from cleaner to TV star, especially as there was no question of her giving up her cleaning job to live on the 'huge' income she would receive from her television appearances. Whoever wrote that story clearly knew nothing about the kind of budget usually allowed for late-night religious programmes.

On the day Jo was due to make her first trip to the studio as a broadcaster, there was a ring on the doorbell, and on opening her front door she discovered a uniformed chauffeur standing smartly to attention beside a vast white limousine looking oddly out of place in the very ordinary little Southampton back street where she lives. With great ceremony she was ushered into the cool interior of the sleek vehicle and soon found herself gliding smoothly across the South East of England in the direction of Maidstone. Feeling very apprehensive, Jo leaned forward eventually to timidly ask her charioteer if it was 'all right to smoke'. Sensing her unease the driver abandoned his air of respectful detachment and suggested she ''op in the front with 'im', an invitation which she gratefully accepted. On the outskirts of Maidstone, however, he stopped the car, and insisted that she returned to the back seat in order that her arrival should be suitably regal. As the car purred to a halt outside the big glass doors of the TVS building, Jo reached out with her hand to pull the door lever and felt her heart suddenly leap into her mouth as the driver hissed violently out of the side of his mouth, 'Don't touch that handle.' Jo, suitably chastened, sat like a pudding while the chauffeur stepped smartly out of the car, marched smoothly round to the side and released her with the dignified servility peculiar to his profession. From there, she ascended to the press-room, where interviews and photographs awaited her. That was the end of that kind of super-star treatment, but it was the beginning of something much more valuable for Jo.

Jo's very first memory is a violent one. She was three years old at the time, sitting on the kitchen table at home in the middle of being washed by her mum. An argument sprang up between her parents, increasing in intensity as the little girl, in her birthday suit, forgotten for the moment, watched and listened nervously hoping that things would soon be all right again.

Eventually, her mother picked up an alarm clock and flung it at Jo's dad. Jo doesn't remember whether it hit him or not, but she does know that following that argument, she was sent to live with an aunt in Wales for a time, completely bewildered about what was going on, and more importantly, about whose fault it was. From Wales she moved to another aunt in Portsmouth, and from there back to her mother in Southampton only to be evacuated to Bournemouth almost immediately because of the war.

When the war ended, Jo, aged nine, was at last able to come back home, and she must have hoped against hope that she would never have to leave again. About a year later, however, her hopes were dashed when, as a ten year old, she arrived home from school one day to find that her mother had left for good. On the table was a brief letter, telling her to go with her younger brother and sister to another member of the family, and a pound note, presumably for bus fares. Jo had no idea where this other person lived, so pocketing the letter and the money, she led her brother, aged six, and sister, aged nine, round to the lady next door, who took them in and called the police. When a very kindly policeman and policewoman arrived, Jo was taken to a local reception centre, where she lived for about six months as one of a group of children in the charge of a house-mother, before being transferred to a Doctor Barnardo's Home, far away in Liverpool, where she stayed until she was fifteen.

Jo's memories of life as a child 'in a home', are not good

ones. She already had the idea firmly fixed in her mind that she was a 'horrible' little girl. She must be. If she had been a nice little girl her mummy would never have sent her away when she was three, or at least she would have got her back as soon as she could. And then, later on, that note on the table had been the final proof. Her mummy didn't want her, and in that case, how could anyone else ever want her? She was *horrible*! Her experiences in children's homes did nothing to dispel this lack of self-value. As a twelve year old, Jo used to assemble with the other children in the home every weekend to await the arrival of local people who would 'select' a child to invite to their homes for tea on the Saturday or Sunday. Each time, Jo presented herself, scrubbed pink, and wearing her very best clothes, longing to be the one who was picked for this treat. 'Let it be me!' she would say silently to herself, 'Oh, please! let it be me!' But, for some reason she never was picked. Not that she ever really expected to be. After all, what else could a horrible little girl expect?

At school there was a different kind of problem. Jo was sent off each day from her children's home, wearing the regulation issue black gymslip and stockings to mix with girls from ordinary families who seemed to have an enormous variety of clothes in all sorts of lovely colours. Noticing the curious glances directed at her sombre attire, which remained clean but unvaried as the days went by, Jo decided that something had to be said. Unwilling to confess to the shameful crime of not having a family, she invented a baby, tragically lost before birth by her mother, and explained that she wore black because she was in mourning. This very sad tale attracted quite a lot of sympathy, but two months later someone became curious about the fact that the period of mourning seemed inordinately long. Poor Jo, remembering how well the story had been received the first time, and having only the scantiest understanding of the facts of life, invented a *second* lost baby which, on this occasion, did not go down at all well. Jo laughs now when she tells this story, but it requires little imagination to see how excruciatingly embarrassing it was at the time.

At fifteen, Jo was transferred yet again, this time to Didcot in Kent, where, as a quite unreligious attender at the local Anglican church, she found herself rather fancying a good looking young curate, whose name was David Shepherd. From there she was moved to a hostel in Reigate, where she was taught housecraft, followed by yet another move to a working girls' hostel in Norwich, where she found a job selling fruit for a firm called Sexton Brothers. The effect of all these moves should not be underestimated. Each one involved breaking bonds with friends, with a distinct locality, with an environment which, even if not particularly pleasant in itself, offered the security of familiar sights and sounds from day to day. By the time she was sixteen, Jo had moved at least ten times.

One of the regular customers at the shop where Jo worked was a 'little old lady' who lived nearby. They got on very well and it wasn't long before Jo left the hostel to move in with her new friend, who became not only her foster mother, but a little later, her mother-in-law, when Jo married Netta's son, Joseph, a sailor in the Merchant Navy. Jo was blissfully happy for the first time in her life. Her husband was sixteen years older than her, and she didn't actually love him at first, but she had a home. She was wanted by nice, good people. She had married for security, and found it. Later she did fall in love with Joseph, experiencing what she calls 'tummy feelings' when he was due to return home from sea after a trip.

Joseph turned out to be a very good husband. He looked after Jo, made all the important decisions for her, and even cured her of the worst effects of her bad temper. She used to break things when she got angry. One day Joseph carried a complete china tea-set out into the garden and very calmly and methodically smashed every piece. When Jo, puzzled and aghast, asked him what he was doing, he replied quietly and reasonably that if she could do it, then so could he. She stopped breaking things.

In 1957 their daughter, Karen, was born. Jo was

twenty-one and determined that Karen would not suffer the kind of neglect that she had. She admits she overdid it. Karen became a spoiled and difficult teenager. It was a problem, but Jo also had Netta and Joseph who continued to provide a place where she really belonged, where she could feel secure.

In August, 1978, Jo was in hospital having treatment for back problems. At 10.30 one night, as she lay in the ward, unable to sleep, someone brought the news that Netta had died that day. Netta was dead! Jo could hardly believe it. Thank goodness Joseph was all right. She knew he was at home feeling rather poorly, but it couldn't be anything very serious. It couldn't be! She needed him to be all right, to go on looking after her.

Less than two months later, on Sunday, October the first, Jo knew that her husband was about to die of cancer. Suddenly she was filled with overwhelming panic. She phoned the local Roman Catholic priest, and begged him to come to the house. As she waited for him to arrive she feverishly hunted out every candle, every holy statue, every religious emblem she could find and placed them on a table in the same room as the dying man. When the priest arrived at last, she dragged him into the house, up the stairs and into the bedroom, crying and screaming for him to pray for a miracle to save Joseph. They both prayed, but there was no miracle. At 2.55 on the following Sunday, Jo's husband died. His last words to his wife were simple but true. 'We've had twenty-five good years.'

The only emotion that Jo could feel was anger; deep bitter anger. She was angry with Netta for dying, angry with Netta for taking Joseph with her, angry – so very, very angry with Joseph for going with his mother when Jo needed him so desperately. The people she loved had done it all again – gone away, leaving her lost and alone. They didn't care – they'd never cared! She'd known it all along, and she was stupid to think it could ever really change. She *was* horrible! She was a horrible little girl . . .

Jo sat down one evening soon after Joseph's death with a

half bottle of whisky and more than a hundred codeine and aspirin tablets. Carefully, she crushed the tablets between two sheets of paper and poured the powder into a tumbler. She then poured whisky into the tumbler, stirred the powder in with a spoon, and swallowed the mixture straight down. She wanted to be dead. Fortunately, her attempt to swallow such a huge quantity of tablets all at once resulted in vomiting, and instead of dying she lay unconscious and undiscovered for the next forty-eight hours. When she eventually came to, the impetus to die had diminished, and over the following month, a month in which she was virtually deaf as a result of the suicide attempt, Jo did a great deal of thinking about her situation. She realised that the only way out of her darkness and depression was through offering help and support to others, and it was out of this realisation that the Neighbourly Care Scheme was born, a scheme that resulted in enormous benefits to many sick and troubled people in the Southampton area.

Jo worked hard and found it easier to live with her own grief as she became involved with the lives and problems of others.

In 1980 she married again, somewhat on the rebound, but her new husband, Don, was a very charming and intelligent man, and it was good to feel secure again. Three weeks later, she arrived home one afternoon to find Don hopelessly drunk and very abusive. He was a chronic alcoholic. Jo was horrified: there had been no hint of the problem before their marriage. Now she was confronted with a situation that was as frightening as it was unfamiliar. There followed a dreadful year of conflict and despair. Jo, terrified by the intensity of the hatred she now felt for Don, but relieved to hear from others in the same situation that her feelings were not abnormal, decided that, for the sake of her own sanity, Don must leave.

Alone again, Jo threw herself with even greater energy into her Neighbourly Care work, and the studio cleaning job. Then, came the appearance on PO Box 13, followed by Angus' invitation, and, in a little flurry of publicity, Jo became one of the Company team.

By the time Jo joined us we had moved from the Gillingham studio to the brand new TVS building at Vinters Park near Maidstone. Here we shared a studio with the news and current affairs programme, Coast To Coast. At one end was the news desk, at the other, the Company kitchen.

Frances had managed to find a flat in the country, out at Harrietsham, where the four participants for each week were able to catch up on news, discuss programme topics for the coming week, and generally relax together. Sometimes there would be a special guest joining us for a few programmes, and he or she would usually stay at the flat with the regulars, helping out with domestic tasks like everyone else, regardless of rank or status. This was very useful as it helped to create a closeness between members of the group, which resulted in a more natural interaction in the studio itself.

We had some good evenings at the flat. Bridget and I particularly enjoyed being there when George was staying. He always entered into the occasion with tremendous zest and good humour, invariably teasing Frances about what he described as her 'posh Islington life-style', and christening her 'Black Rod' at an early stage in the proceedings. We grew very fond of many of our fellow kitchen-dwellers as we came to know them better through time spent in that informal environment. The friendships we have established with some of our colleagues will last long after Company is gone and forgotten. Certainly, we shall never want to lose contact with Jo Williams.

We liked Jo as soon as we met her, although she tells me that I 'put the fear of God into her' when she came up to Maidstone for an audition. She remembers thinking that I was very aggressive in the programmes she had seen in the past. She soon realised that I was a softy really, and once we were able to get to know each other in the relaxed atmosphere of the Harrietsham flat, we became good friends. Jo is a very motherly type, and I must confess that I do enjoy being mothered, especially in the mornings. Jo shares with George Reindorp and Peter Timms, one supreme virtue that probably gives them the edge in the race to heaven. They all get up early in the morning to take tea to everyone else. It is a mark of my greatness that I am happy to lie in bed and let these three store up riches in heaven through this charitable act. It is a sacrifice, but I do it.

During Jo's first evening in the flat, she told us about some of the events in her past, concluding with an account of her second, disastrous marriage. Later that same evening, after our production meeting was over, and we had eaten together, she talked in more depth with Ann-Marie, who is a very sensitive listener. Ann-Marie listened quietly as Jo told her that she could never have Don back again, then promised to pray for both of them. This was quite a new idea for Jo, who had always believed that prayer was for emergencies and special occasions.

That week's programmes went well. It was clear that Jo was going to be a valuable member of the team. She was quite unselfconscious about asking the 'obvious question', unlike one or two of us who had perfected the art of looking as if we knew the answer really but were generously allowing others the chance to talk!

A few weeks later Jo received a phone call at home. It was from a hospital in Bristol. Don had jumped from a bridge in an attempt to kill himself. Obviously it was a genuine attempt; his body was wrecked by the impact of the fall and there was a strong chance that, if he lived, he would be confined to a wheelchair. Did Jo want to see him? Everything in her wanted to say 'Never!' but she didn't. She said 'Yes.' Later, seeing him broken and helpless in his hospital bed, she felt pity for Don, but not forgiveness. That year of misery was too clear in her memory for that. Nevertheless, she agreed that he could come home when he left hospital. The day before Don's return, Jo remembered her conversation with Ann-Marie, and said a prayer about the future. The next day, standing on the platform at

Southampton railway station, she watched Don as he alighted from the Bristol train, and felt a wave of forgiveness and compassion flood through her, washing away—for the time being at any rate—all the anger and bitterness she had been feeling. She took Don home.

That was far from being the end of Jo's troubles. Don was still an alcoholic, and he was still drinking. Jo herself was ill much of the time, and often very depressed as the old bitterness began to creep back in and poison her efforts to find peace. In addition there were problems in Jo's relationship with her daughter who now had a lovely little boy called Joseph.

But something else was happening as well. Both inside the studio, and at the Harrietsham flat, Jo was asking a lot of searching questions—desperate questions, not for the sake of theological debate, but because she wanted and needed to know.

She had never read the Bible. What was it like? She read it in a modern translation and understood it for the first time.

She asked on the programme one evening why no vicars or priests had visited when Joseph died. Over the next few days she was inundated by ministers of various kinds.

What was all this about healing? Could Don walk again if she prayed for him? She did pray, and gradually he did walk again.

Did God listen to all our prayers? What about all the suffering? Jo wanted to know everything. They weren't unusual questions, but there was a childlike quality in the way she asked them, and in the way that she received the answers, that I frankly envied. George was wonderful with Jo, but she seemed to attract great warmth from everybody, including James Blomfield and Roy Millard, two young men who had become very much part of the team. They developed a very soft spot for Jo—James once zooming across country from Dover to Southampton at a moment's notice when Jo hit a really bad spot.

Once, she phoned Bridget at home, when she was feeling

suicidal, and said, 'Give me one reason for staying alive.' Bridget could think of nothing very logical to say, but what she did say was enough. 'I love you, Jo. As long as I love you, you just can't die.'

It was clear that Jo was beginning to see the Company team as a sort of extended family; her trips to Harrietsham and the studios were a refuge from the storms of everyday life. Whether this was desirable or appropriate, I really don't know. I think that many viewers enjoyed becoming part of this 'family' of Jo's. Over the months she had shared the whole of her life story with people at home.

There came a day when Jo had simply reached the end of her tether. The doctors had just examined Don in hospital after yet another drinking bout. Their verdict was chilling. There wasn't much of his liver left to function. He was unlikely to live for very much longer, especially as he was still drinking. Not only that, but Jo was ill herself. That was how she felt – ill, lonely and useless. That night the Company participants were Jo, myself, and Prabhu Guptara, a freelance writer and journalist and a man for whom I have a great liking and respect. Jo wept openly as she told Prabhu and myself how close she was to giving up altogether. She couldn't pray, she said. God was angry with her. I reached across the table to take her hand, and Prabhu joined his hand with ours as I prayed for Jo and Don, for their peace and health – for some deeper kind of healing in both of them. I don't think I felt much faith in my prayer being answered, but I said the words, and we all said 'Amen'. After the programme, Prabhu put his arms round Jo who was still crying, while I stood by with a heavy heart. I'd said so many prayers in my time, often for children whose lives were just like Jo's and Don's – a mess. How many of those prayers had been answered?

I shook my head and compressed my lips as I watched Jo regain her composure. I prayed again silently. 'Please, God! Please do something for Jo! For Don!'

Had he heard? Was he going to do something? I couldn't have guessed at that moment, how much was to happen to me before I knew the answers to those questions.

Chapter Ten

I knew why I felt so hopeless about praying for Jo. It wasn't just the memory of children in care who had stumbled from disaster to disaster, regardless of what I did or prayed, although that was certainly part of it. It was something else – something that had happened earlier in the year, to someone I hardly knew.

Just after I was converted at the age of sixteen, I travelled to Bakewell in Derbyshire with the other young people of St John's Church, for their annual weekend house-party, organised by Clive Sampson, the curate, and featuring a very impressive guest speaker, a young Anglican curate whose name was Ross Patterson. We arrived in the conference room for our first meeting, to find that Ross had rigged up a system of strings across the top of the room to support a very large, and very vicious-looking kitchen knife in such a way that, if it should fall, the point would plunge straight into the top of his head as he stood talking to us from the platform. We liked that. After all, it *might* fall. It was a powerful visual aid in his talk about the need for salvation, and he was a good speaker, strong and humorous. He was also a good tennis player and all-round sportsman. One of those people, in fact, who seem to have a magic touch in everything they do, and a vivid illustration of the truth that not all Christian men are effete.

During the course of the weekend Ross invited as many of us as were interested to come to a mission meeting a few miles away, where his vicar who had travelled down from York for the occasion, was due to speak. I was quite intrigued. I suppose I reckoned that if Ross was only the curate, then his boss must be Patterson cubed; some kind of superman. It was with great interest, therefore that I filed into that church hall somewhere in Derbyshire to see and hear David Watson for the first time.

He wasn't like Ross. He wasn't like anybody. There was something in his speech and delivery that was quite unique. I was fascinated. Most of us keep words and sentences stacked carelessly in untidy piles in our minds ready to throw around haphazardly. There was a bespoke quality about every word and phrase that this man used. It was as if each tiny component of his speech had been carefully cut and polished by hand before being inserted into sentences that seemed to shine with a sort of translucent purity of intention. I had never heard anything like it before, and although I soon forgot the content of that particular talk, I never forgot as the years went by, the feeling that I had listened to someone who not only *believed* what he was saying, but was able to translate his thoughts into words of crystal clarity.

Over the following nineteen years, David Watson became known all over the world as one of the most effective communicators in the Christian church, through books, television appearances and missions. The unusual combination of a strong simple faith and an ability to show clear and cogent reasons for his beliefs, meant that he could appeal to people on all levels including those who might previously have felt that the Christian faith required an abandonment of intellectual integrity. Personally, I found his books much less appealing than the man himself, although they have obviously been very helpful to many many people. For me, he was a reminder, sometimes irritating, and sometimes reassuring, that there were Christians around who meant what they said for reasons other than that they had some personal emotional or psychological axe to grind.

At the beginning of 1983 it was announced that David Watson had cancer. The prognosis was poor. Unless a miracle happened he would die. All round the world people

136

prayed for that miracle. I think some people would have jettisoned God and kept David if that had been an option. Perhaps that was the problem. Friends from a church in America, where many healings have reportedly occurred, flew specially to England to pray for him. David spoke in interviews about how he felt a strange warmth pass through his body when they laid hands on him for healing, but neither he nor they ever claimed to *know* that he would be healed, only that God could, and might make him better.

One night we asked Company viewers to join us as we prayed, like thousands of others, for David's peace and recovery. Later on that year, in July, Frances invited him to join Bridget and myself and George Reindorp in Company for seven evenings to talk about how those prayers had, or had not been answered, and how he viewed the future.

George had met David on a number of previous occasions, but for me it was rather strange to encounter a distant memory in the flesh. I was not disappointed. There was that same clarity of expression and delivery, and a much greater depth of peace and confidence. I marvelled once again at the differences in people who followed God closely. David was very much himself, however much he might have in common with other Christians. He didn't look or behave as if he was terminally ill, and during the evening that we spent in the flat out at Harrietsham, there was no visible sign of his energy flagging.

As we left the flat on the following morning, the owners of the property, Lord and Lady Monckton, appeared from the main house, and were introduced to David, who shook hands warmly with them. As we were about to move off, Lord Monckton, who is a Roman Catholic convert and an endearingly lordish sort of Lord, took a small transparent paper packet from his pocket and held it out towards David.

'Like you to have this,' he said with a gruff cheerfulness.

David looked at the little envelope. Peering over his shoulder I could see that it contained a small square of cloth of quite unremarkable design.

'Relic of Padre Pio,' went on Lord Monckton.

I had heard of Padre Pio, an Italian priest and mystic, now dead, who was said to bear on his body the marks or wounds of the crucifixion. Others had experienced the same strange phenomenon – Saint Paul, Francis of Assisi, Dorothy Kerin and others. Presumably this little piece of cloth was a fragment of some part of the old priest's clothing.

'That's extremely kind of you,' responded David. 'Thank you very much.'

Lord Monckton smiled happily, pleased with the way his gift had been received.

'He's very active in Kent and Sussex y'know.'

I was a little taken aback by this. The Roman Catholic belief in the significance and influence of the dead on our day-to-day lives was not something that I could identify with at all. I was pretty sure that David would feel the same way. I wonder why it is that the way in which he reacted to this last comment of Lord Monckton's has been my most abiding and personally helpful memory of David. It wasn't *what* he said, it was the way that he said it.

'Really! How *very* interesting.'

Those few commonplace words conveyed an enthusiastic respect for the other man's point of view, and were not followed by one of those words like 'but', or 'however', or 'nevertheless', which usually lead quietly into total disagreement. It may seem rather trivial, but I learned something quite new at that moment about meeting people where they are, and not dragging them crudely into the arena of my own beliefs in order to club theirs to death.

We recorded seven programmes in the studio that morning, watched by Michael Harper, who was a close friend of David's and a religious adviser to TVS. Most of the programmes were indirectly or specifically connected with the illness and its effect on David's faith and family, and attitude to God. The atmosphere in the studio and the control room was one of hushed concentration as he spoke about the panic of waking at midnight, drenched with sweat, wondering if there was a God after all; of examining

138

his faith to find out what remained when all else was shaken away, and of finally reaching the point where he wanted to go to God, but was willing to stay if necessary, instead of the other way round. He spoke of his present conviction that the best was yet to be, and grinned, like a child on Christmas Eve, when he said it.

'God's love,' he said, 'will not necessarily transform the situation – the sickness itself, but it will transform our reaction to it, and that's what really counts. I am responsible for either giving way to self-pity, which actually becomes a problem for other people as well as myself, or letting God's love and peace transfigure my reaction.'

We asked David what his central message to people would be at this stage in his life. He didn't hesitate.

'The most important thing is that people really need to *know* that God *loves* them. An awful lot of people are hurting for one reason or another. Down at the roots you find that they are not *sure* that they are loved and accepted – by anyone. To know that God loves them, that's the important thing.'

At the end, David prayed aloud.

'Father, we thank you that you have shown yourself to be a God of love. Help us, and all those in pain and need, to realise how *much* you love us, and to trust you whether we understand or not, for Jesus' sake, amen.'

As we left the studio that day, David was looking so well, and sounding so strong and optimistic that it was difficult to imagine that the cancer existed in his body, let alone that he could be dead in the near future.

Later in the year Bridget and I met David again, when we visited him and his wife Anne at their house in London with Frances Tulloch, to discuss a Sunday morning worship programme scheduled for the following spring. It was interesting to meet Anne. She struck us as being very real, and refreshingly practical about spiritual matters. Our discussion went well, although David didn't seem as well as he had done earlier in the year. We were quite excited about the prospect of making a programme that would last for an hour instead of less than ten minutes, and I think that I had developed a rather unreal expectation about the way in which personal spiritual problems might be resolved through frequent contact with David.

When I arrived at the TVS studios one evening, early in 1984, to learn that David Watson had died, it was as though some kind of heartless trick had been played on me. I know it seems childish and selfish but I felt cheated. Of course I felt for Anne Watson and her children as well, but they were strangers to me. I just wondered why God had, apparently, snatched away the man who could have solved my problems. Rational or irrational, that was how I felt, and the little fire of anger that had always burned deep inside me, flared up dangerously as this fresh fuel was added to it.

We went ahead with 'Meeting Place', as the Palm Sunday programme was called, and we were fortunate to have David MacInnes, a close friend of David Watson's, to take over the task of leading the service, but it was not a happy occasion for any of us, including little David, our youngest son, who was also taking part in the programme, and developed German measles on the day of the recording. I don't know who was more unhappy, him or me!

The period from Easter to autumn that year, I remember as a series of manic highs and miserable lows. Everything was losing its worth before my eyes, so it didn't really matter what I did or thought, or said. I was heading for some kind of crisis, but on the way to it there were two 'moments' that were to seem very significant in the future.

The first happened as I sat in church one Sunday morning. A picture started to form in my mind of a huge lake surrounded by plots of land, each one occupied by a single person. Behind the plots that gave access to the lake were more plots, again occupied by individual people. As I explored the picture mentally, I saw that the lakeside dwellers were made up of two kinds of people. The first kind rushed to and fro from the edge of the lake to the boundary between their own plot and the one behind, carrying cups of water to their landlocked neighbours. Most of the water got spilled in the process, but they worked on frantically, doing their best. The other kind were not working frantically at all. They were simply digging steadily on their plots of land, with no apparent interest in the fate of the waterless tenants whose land adjoined theirs. One of the cup-carriers stopped, red-faced and breathless, and spoke with some annoyance to one of the diggers.

'Why don't you do as we do? Why don't you get a cup and carry water to those who have none? It is selfish to work only on your own land as you do.'

The digger leaned on his spade for a moment and smiled. 'You don't understand,' he said, 'I'm digging a trench.'

The second moment was a moment of prayer. Like most people I had always had great difficulty about talking to God. It was all right sometimes, but more often than not my prayers bounced off the ceiling and the walls like a badly hit ping-pong ball, rolling to a halt eventually at my feet. On certain rare occasions though, a particular prayer seemed to pierce the barrier between myself and God with the kind of sweet certainty that one experiences on hitting the perfect off-drive in a cricket match (equally rare in my case). This prayer was like that. Bridget and I, realising that the kind of Christianity we were living out fell very short of the picture painted by Jesus, decided to say a very risky prayer.

'Father, we know that we haven't done very well with anything much up to now, but we really want to go all the way with you. We realise that we don't even understand what that means, but, whatever it costs, and however much it hurts, please let it happen. Amen.'

If I could have grabbed that prayer back as it zoomed off to its heavenly destination, I think I would have done. But I couldn't, and it wasn't long before God started to answer it in an unexpected and alarming way.

Chapter Eleven

'The police are here.'

My head was spinning as the nurse put yet another stitch into my injured wrist, but the words penetrated my brain with needle-sharp clarity. I was going to be arrested. After years of collecting children from police stations, and countless discussions about how to avoid getting there in the first place, I was about to find out how it felt to be 'nicked'. I relaxed my head back onto the pillow, and tried again to make some sense of what was happening to me. What had the doctor put on my sick note three weeks ago? 'Severe stress reaction.' They were just words.. What had really happened?

When my three sons were all 'little' children, I used to wake in the morning sometimes to find that there were five people in our king-size double bed. Matthew, long and well-built, would be draped across the foot of the bed, forcing me to take up a near-foetal position, while Joseph was usually jammed firmly into my back, thus causing me to throw my head back and create space just under my chin for little David, who, during the night, was little more than a heat-seeking device. I ended up lying in exactly the same posture as a long-jumper in mid-leap; arms stretched above my head, back arched, legs bent, the classical position for gaining maximum distance. Poor Bridget would just be a shapeless form, crushed against the far wall by this living jigsaw of human bodies. In the morning I had to painfully ease and straighten out all those parts of me that had been adapting for most of the night to the unyielding bodies of my three small but solid night visitors. Being very tall, the pain could sometimes be intense, and on occasions I would abandon my own territory and either get up very early, or seek refuge of a sort on a vacated, two-foot-six wide bunkbed in the children's room. Anything to ease my aching bones.

This is the best way I can think of to describe what was happening to me in the summer of 1984. My mind and emotions were cramped and strained by the constant need to adapt to the varying demands and expectations of people, situations and attitudes that never seemed to allow me to stretch and relax, to be unashamedly myself, whatever 'myself' turned out to be. Whether I was under more pressure than others in similar situations I don't know. I only know that the 'act', the ability to go on playing all these complex games that normal life seemed to involve, was using up all my inner resources.

Even as my faith and belief in God and myself was draining away from me, there seemed to be an increase in what was wanted from me as a social worker, as a father and husband, as a Christian, and as someone who appeared often on television talking about God as though I had something worthwhile to say.

I was tired of locking children up for a start. Ironically, in the two years that I'd worked in the secure unit, I had finally begun to accept that it was safe to relax and be genuinely concerned about the people I was caring for. I enjoyed the challenge that each child's needs presented, and I began to believe that I might be on the verge of becoming real in my dealings with them. But real people are vulnerable, and for years I had disallowed, repressed, and postponed the expression of feelings that were too deep for words. Now, I cared desperately about the fate and future of these children, and although we did have some success, it became increasingly difficult to live with the failures, especially as I, like the other staff in the unit, was turning the key on them daily. By then, Meryl had gone to a psychiatric hospital, and Miranda had gone to prison. So many children had passed through the 'sad-mad-bad' cycle even before reaching us, and all too often a custodial sentence seemed to be society's relieved response to a conveniently concrete crime. The whole exercise began to appear a vastly expensive, cynical game, and I, who had pretended so much in the past, simply could not pretend any more. At work, in the six months before I finally broke down, I had felt mounting inner hysteria, and detachment from an institution which, although excellent in comparison with other places I had known, now seemed ridiculous; a place where we supervised the disposal of social rejects and colluded with social-service higher management in playing the 'professional and caring people game'. No doubt my vision was distorted by tension and role-play fatigue, but now, as I view things more calmly and objectively I see it in the same way. There were some good people working in a system that was top-heavy with bureaucracy, and too often expedient rather than caring.

The other game that I had become very bad at was being-a-Christian-and-going-to-church. I didn't seem able to keep to the rules any more. I wanted to say that I was sad when I was sad, happy when I was happy, non-believing when God didn't seem to exist, angry when I was angry, and bad when I was bad. I wanted the freedom to be all of me, and not a little, spineless, spiritually arthritic version of myself. I wanted to break away from the awful, simpering, Christianese language that seemed to obscure and stifle passion and human-ness whenever it threatened to break through the carefully organised spontaneity of meetings, services and conversations.

I wanted to shake off the arid virtue which had taken the place of real goodness for so many years, and force a full-frontal collision with reality; to dive naked into the dark waters of the risk-infested non-religious world, from which God – if he was God – would rescue me because he loved me, and not because I strained to conform to precious group norms that depended for their maintenance on unspoken agreements that nobody would mess things up by telling the whole truth. These were not clearly specified or dignified needs at the time. They were ragged, wild longings to find the reality of God that had been promised all those years ago on a Sunday evening in St John's Church. No more systems, no more pretence, no more props. I had been conned and compromised for long enough. Let the props snap, and let God do whatever he was going to do – if he was there!

For more than thirty years a great shout had been building up in me, a shout of tearful protest that I couldn't manage, that people *didn't* seem to mean what they said, that I felt like a small person trapped in a large actor's body, that all I wanted was to collapse, and be allowed to be useless. As for God, and most of those who claimed to represent him, they – in my mind – were the arch-offenders, the 'smiling' ones who had deceived themselves just sufficiently to be able to deceive others. I hated and despised the neat middle-classness that allowed them to pose as Christians without significant effort or cost. It was my turn to do, be and say what I liked, and the rest of the false, smiling, stupid, bloody world could go hang!

One night I returned home late after going out for a drink with friends. As I walked through the front door, something snapped. I started to scream and shout, punch the walls with both hands, and sob uncontrollably. My wife, who, with a friend, wrestled through the whole thing with me for hours, tells me that I shouted the same phrases over and over again.

'I can't lock them up any more! I can't lock them up any more! I've tried to be good – I've tried to be good! I want to be me! I want to be me! I can't lock them up any more!'

And indeed I couldn't. Children, feelings, hurts from the distant past, agonies I'd never shared, bitter anger against God, the church, and everything connected with it – I couldn't lock them up any more. Down went all my defences for the first time since I was a little boy, leaving me raw and vulnerable to whatever temptations and influences might be around.

The weeks that followed were a nightmare, not only for me, but for Bridget as well. No work, no church, no stability, no reason for me to do or not to do anything other than what was immediately stimulating or sense-dulling. The darkness had a thick, sweet attraction difficult to resist. I would disappear for hours at a time, returning home late at night, usually drunk, still wanting only to drown thought and feeling in loud, powerful rock music, or more drink. And the anger continued to rage in me, making it impossible to meet most of the people I knew, especially those who wanted to tell me I had 'stepped outside the Lord's will' and could step back in again by applying some formula or other.

There are aspects of that period that are very difficult and painful to remember. For some reason I seemed to need to abdicate completely from commitment to previous close relationships. My family, more important to me than anything else in the past, suffered and watched, and waited for some light to appear in the darkness. Every day offered new potential for disaster as I wrestled with the strangeness of a world that, in some ways I was seeing for the first time. I would stand on the pavement in the High Street, watching people as they passed to and fro, and wonder with genuine amazement how they could possibly have discovered a strong enough motive for moving in such a purposeful way. I recall sneering sceptically at the girl in the Chinese take-away when she responded to my order in a normal, pleasant way, 'You almost sound as if you really care!' The whole world felt like the setting for a wearisome game in which everyone cheated.

One day, I arranged to meet a friend, someone who I could still communicate with, in a pub in Eastbourne. I arrived late to find that he'd gone. I boiled. Disproportion-ately angry and tense, I slammed out of the pub and crossed the road, intending to call Bridget from the phone box and unload some of the blackness that was building up in me. As I stepped into the kiosk, a hot wave of anger surged through me. Part of me, oddly detached, watched, hypnotised, as my fist arched towards one of the small square glass panes, and smashed through. I drew my hand back, all the anger gone now, and gazed disbelievingly at a long and sickeningly deep gash in my wrist. Oddly enough, at that moment, I felt only relief as I watched the blood drip onto the floor of the box. It was so good to see some external evidence of the gaping wounds inside. Fear followed immediately. Why had I done it? Was I really going mad? Suddenly I was very calm. In a nearby shop I got someone to call a taxi for me, and a few minutes later, I wrapped a piece of cloth round my wrist and climbed in. Before long I was in the accident and emergency ward of the local hospital.

The nurse put a final tape on the dressing, and grimaced sympathetically at me as I swung my feet onto the floor. I realised that the old, tired coping mechanism was grinding slowly into action, just as it had in so many difficult situations over the past years. But this was different. I was the one in trouble, not some desperate teenager needing me to get them out of a fix. My 'crime' was not a major one by any standards, but the situation was a completely new one for me. How was I going to handle this encounter with the law? I automatically selected and rejected options. 'Sullen and disturbed', maybe? Or perhaps 'weary and resigned' would be more effective. I finally settled on 'surprisingly calm and pleasantly co-operative'. The receptionist led me to a small side room where two young policemen were waiting. Politely, and with a hint of embarrassment (it turned out that both of them were Company viewers) they informed me that I was arrested on a charge of criminal damage, and that anything I said would be taken down and might be used in evidence against me. Later, in the bowels of the police station, I was fingerprinted, photographed, and left to sit in the corner of a small room containing nothing but a table, a bench, and a couple of posters on the wall. For some reason, this bleak little room seemed familiar. Then I remembered. This was exactly the same room in which I had found Miranda on the last occasion

147

that I had been called to collect her from a police station. I was a rank amateur in crime and violence in comparison with her, but as I sat on the same bench as she had, waiting for someone to return, I felt the sting of tears in my eyes as I realised for the first time, why she, and other children I'd known, had shown such violence in similar situations. Why were two young, pink people in blue uniforms, so obsessed with a piece of glass? Didn't they know about the last thirty years? Didn't they *want* to know? I wanted to ask them, to argue with them, to *make* them understand, because they were the visible, official representatives of punishment without passion, the hard words without the loving arms. By now, if it had been Miranda, the place would have been in uproar. I was lucky. I had been around longer, and back home I had four pairs of loving arms to balance the inclination I suddenly felt to shout and punch and kick and swear at the mechanicalness of justice. I was thirty-five; not fifteen. I held my tongue, and smiled, and wasn't charged, and went home.

Richard Wurmbrand tells of a judge, placed in the cell next to him in an underground communist prison, who spent much time asking forgiveness for the way in which he had passed sentence on so many convicted criminals without any genuine understanding of what imprisonment really meant. For any arrogance or self-righteousness that I have shown towards children in trouble in the past, I also ask pardon, realising that we all stand together in the need for mercy and compassion. God help us all.

The difficulty and despair of this time is well illustrated by two pieces of writing that have survived the turmoil somehow. The first is a poem, written at the point where I realised that the particular kind of Christianity I had tried to embrace, was more likely to prolong the agony than cure it.

Who made these poison pools
In desert lands
So sweet and cool?

A welcome lie;
The chance to die with water on my lips.
I've seen how others try to die unpoisoned in the sun,
I do not think that I can do as they have done.

The second, and far more graphic illustration is provided
by an extract from a letter written by Bridget to a very close
friend at the time. I include it here, with her blessing, in the
hope that others who find themselves in the same position,
will see that theirs is not a unique experience, nor a hopeless one.

. . . if anyone else asks me how he is, I think I'll scream. I
don't know how he is. I don't know *him* any more. He
keeps saying this is the real him, and only my memories
of fourteen years keep me from believing him. He is still
lovely to the children, and they, thank God, seem by their
cuddles and hugs to be able to reach him in a way I can't.
All I seem able to do is wait and pray, and I seem to do an
awful lot of both!!! I just keep on and on at God all the
time, it feels like bashing on his door until he finally
answers, and every now and then I get a total feeling of
peace, as if he has done just that. When Adrian is out, and
I don't know where he is, I just beg and beg God to just
hold on to him and keep him safe and bring him home –
Whatever state he's in.
I'm living one day at a time now. I only wish everyone
else could. They seem to want instant recovery, and I feel
a ludicrous sense of failure when I have to say, 'He's
about the same, really . . .'
. . . Sometimes I just feel hurt and angry that it's
happening. I love him so much, and it's my life he's
wrecking as well as his. – I know that's horrible, and I
hate myself, but I do feel it, especially when he says he's
glad it happened. I wish to heck that *I* understood what's
happening to us all. I can't see any future at all at the
moment . . .
. . . sometimes all I can do is hold him like a child, and I

149

can feel the agony in him. I must try not to keep crying – it makes everything ten times worse, because he feels so guilty about what's happened – so sorry for all of us. I wish God would hurry up and *do* something, anything! . . .

Bridget was quite right when she said that some people wanted my instant recovery. They fell into two groups. The first was made up of those who had used *me* as a prop until now. There was almost an air of annoyance in their response to the news that I could no longer offer support. I understand that now, but it hurt me then. The second group, not large, but significant, was composed of those Christians for whom non-recovery seemed to constitute an attack on their faith.

God knows, I was a million miles from being as innocent as Job, but there was no doubt that as far as one section of the church was concerned, I was 'spoiling the game' by not recovering quickly and testifying to the healing power of God. I had shared their creed, and now I was threatening the theology of that creed by stubbornly refusing to get better, and protect their religious confidence. One or two were visibly angry, not just with me, but with others in a similar situation, who were letting the side down by being chronically unwell. Rightly or wrongly, I felt that such people had what Oswald Chambers calls 'The ban of finality' on them, the result of theology – albeit lively, active, theology – being put before God. After one or two very negative encounters of this kind, Bridget deflected approaches from people who wanted to tidy me up spiritually, not least because I had abandoned politeness, and was quite likely to say exactly what I thought in strongly unreligious terms.

On the positive side, I look back with enormous pleasure at the wide and sometimes surprising variety of folk who supported and loved and put up with me, not because they had a particular axe to grind, but simply because they cared. Some were Christians from our own church, some were from others. Some were not Christians at all. There were friends from the past and the present, one or two from work, others who, previously, I had felt I hardly knew. They had one thing in common. They gave something of themselves to me, and asked for nothing back. They were glimpses of God in the desert.

The image of the desert is particularly appropriate as, shortly after I stopped work, my perception of myself in relation to the church was crystallised in my mind by a daydream, or mental picture in which I found myself in a vast desert, standing on the edge of an oasis full of excited, cheering people. They were all facing inwards towards the centre of the oasis, and, try as I might, I just couldn't break through the tightly packed bodies, to see what was causing all this noise and activity. In the end I asked someone on the edge of the crowd to tell me what it was he was trying to see, and why everyone was pushing and shoving and jumping up and down so excitedly.

'The king!' he said. 'It's the king! He's there in the centre!'

'Have you seen him?' I asked. 'Have you actually seen him?'

'No,' he replied. 'I haven't seen him, but we all know he's there! Isn't it exciting!' And he went back to his calling and waving.

Disheartened, I turned my back on the oasis and walked slowly away into the desert. As the commotion gradually faded behind me, I became aware of a dot in the distance, which, as I came closer, seemed to be a heap of rags, piled untidily on the sand. At last, I was near enough to see that it was a man, his eyes large and dark with suffering, his clothes in tatters.

'Who are you?' I asked.

The man smiled a smile of deep, sweet sadness, and spoke softly. 'I am the king. I couldn't get in either.'

There were other glimpses of God. A friend suggested I should visit the Anglican vicar of a small, nearby country church, a man who might be regarded by many people I knew as 'unsaved', or 'uncommitted'. At one time I might have thought him so.

So why, I wondered, as he and I walked his dogs along the old disused railway track, and took shelter from the soft autumn rain under one of the tall, brick bridges, did I feel a relaxation and a peace that I had not found elsewhere?

'What do you think of God, then?' I was still rather graceless.

Frank smiled imperturbably. 'I've never met him,' he said quietly, 'but,' gesturing around him with his stick, 'if he made all this, and was the one who gave me my talents, I think I would love him if we met.'

What was all this? If we met? Was this any way for a Christian to talk? Not where I came from! And yet, on the two occasions that I walked through the countryside with this gentle, peaceful man, I sensed, even in the midst of my confusion, that Jesus walked with us, and that he and Frank were old friends.

I saw God, too, in the support of my fellow Company participants, when I arrived in Maidstone for the first programmes I had made since the night I had lost my 'props'. In many ways this attempt to continue with Company was an experiment. Just about everything else had fallen apart, and neither Bridget nor I were very confident about my ability to hold things together enough to cope with production meetings, studios and cameras. It was providential that my colleagues on this 'test run' were Hugo Gryn and Prabhu Guptara, a rabbi and a 'Hindu follower of Christ', but, more importantly, two compassionate and warm human beings who, with their own kindness and control, held me in a stable frame of mind, and enabled me to get through the meeting and programmes without too many problems. Some have thought it strange that I should have been able to go on making television programmes throughout this period. I can only say that it was the best anchor I had for a time.

The flat in Harrietsham, and the kitchen table in its little pool of studio light, were familiar, safe environments, that were detached from the rest of my life, and always had been. My visits there provided an ongoing reassurance to me that I wasn't going completely round the bend, and that I was still – if only minimally – useful to someone. I soon realised though, that I could only carry on with Company if I was prepared to be honest about what was happening to me. It wasn't a welcome prospect. I had never exposed or shared pain and hurt before, and in my present fragmented condition, I couldn't be sure that I would control my emotions.

On the occasion when I did first describe what was happening to me I very nearly ended up in tears, but I managed to get through it somehow, and I was very glad I did. The response from viewers to that programme, and subsequent ones in which I talked about what was happening to me, was so warm and supportive, that it was like having a whole other family behind the cameras. Letters and messages from people 'out there' offered prayers, hugs, shared experiences, and constructive advice. It isn't easy to put into words how much the concern shown by those letters meant to me during this time.

Meanwhile, what about God? For a quite lengthy period, the answer to that question was very simple. There *was* no God, and if by any chance it turned out that I was wrong and he did exist, then I hated him with all the newly released passion in me. Other people, like George Reindorp and Peter Ball believed that he had been with them, helping and directing them, throughout their lives. Not me! With me, God had really screwed up, and I preferred the simple conclusion that he didn't exist, to the impossible task of reconciling my situation with the active concern of a loving, omnipotent presence.

Now here, as some comedian used to say, is a funny thing. I had dismissed God. He wasn't there. I was doing all sorts of things that my dry morality had woodenly prevented in the past. I was feeling and choosing and sinking and rising without any reference to any religious rule-book or its author. But, try as I might, there was one thing, or rather, one person, who I just couldn't shake off. No matter how far I penetrated the darkness, no matter how low I went, no matter how much I drank, there was Jesus.

One day, I was sitting in a pub with a man I had known in the past. He had moved away, and was back just to visit. He can't have known anything of what had happened to me, and we had met by accident that day. He was a farmer, and his name was Bill. He'd always had the disconcerting ability to see through lies and insincerity. He was about as tactful as an avalanche, but he had a sort of rich agricultural charm, and I liked him. Bill knew that I was a Christian. When he was resident in the TVS region, he'd often watched me attempting to put the world to rights at midnight on TV. Now, there was something about the way he was gazing into his beer with knitted brows and pursed lips, that suggested he had something to say about it.

After a sudden swift gulp from his pint glass, he banged it back down beside him, rested his elbows on the table, and pointed both forefingers in the direction of my eyes, unconsciously indicating that in them he would read the truth, whatever I might say.

'You still doing that programme?'

I nodded.

'I don't understand you,' he said. 'I can't understand why a bloke like you wants to be a Christian. You always seemed quite sensible – normal. I don't see how you can believe it.'

He watched me closely – waiting. Our eyes seemed so rigidly locked together, that I had the absurd fantasy that if he leaned back quickly he would pull my eyeballs out. Had he complimented me, or was it an insult? A bloke like me? For a moment I felt the old tension grow in me, the tension that invariably preceded my regurgitation of the undigested lump of evangelicalism that I'd swallowed in my teens; a congealed mass of guilt, half-remembered scriptures, and fear, that until recently had neither nourished me, nor passed out of my system. It was different now. In the old days I would have searched for words to keep me in the good books of both Bill and God. Quoted John 3:16 perhaps, like a magic charm, to ward off real communication. I realised that, now, I could answer truthfully. I was not bound to produce either a bon mot, or the paralysed jargon that had clogged the arteries of my spirit for so long.

'I just don't see how you can be a Christian,' repeated Bill, doggedly.

'Nor do I, actually.' I seemed to hear bells ringing, people cheering.

Bill's gaze relaxed a little. He looked more puzzled than accusative now. The fingers drooped.

'I mean – what about the church? I mean – surely you can't think the church is much good the way it is – surely?'

'The church is a mess,' said I, remembering my old set speech about it depending what you meant by 'the church'. I was beginning to enjoy myself. Realising that I wasn't going to enlarge on what I'd said, Bill ploughed on.

'Some of the people who say they're Christians – don't you find it embarrassing – people thinking you're like them, I mean?'

'Yes.'

'On that programme you do – Company. That bloke who seems to think everything's evil – I mean, do you agree with that?'

'No.'

Bill had almost reached the end of his furrow.

'Some Christians,' – the fingers were up again – 'some Christians believe the whole Bible is one hundred per cent historically accurate, every word. I mean – how can they?' He paused. 'Well, is it?'

'I don't know.' I wasn't sure. I realised that I never had been sure.

Bill was leaning back in his chair, rubbing the small bald patch on top of his head, (the one that had never bothered him at all) his face contorted by the search for comprehension.

'But in that case, if that's all true . . . what's left? Why *are* you a Christian? Why bother?'

My euphoria faded suddenly. Why bother, indeed? Bill didn't know it, but he'd got the question wrong. Not—*why* was I a Christian, but *was* I a Christian at all? Was anything left? I suddenly remembered a rather frightening thought that had occurred to me one day, not long before I broke down, as I sat in church watching people come in before the start of the service. Supposing, I thought, each person came to church with a regulation black briefcase containing, in some impossible way, their personal evidence that the Christian faith was true. Every Sunday, we would nod and smile at each other, indicating our briefcases with genial confidence as if to say, 'Lots in mine, brother. No problem here!' One awful Sunday, though, the minister would announce that, today, we were all going to open our cases in front of each other, and examine this mass of evidence. One by one, in a heavy silence, the cases are opened. They are all empty . . .

I had opened my 'case' in front of Bill. Was anything left in it? Could there be anything real and truthful tucked away in a dark corner somewhere? To my surprise, there was; but it was such a raw, indefensible, insubstantial piece of truth, that neither cleverness nor jargon could express it. It embarrassed me to say it, and Bill reacted as though I was some kind of spiritual flasher.

'I don't bother at the moment, Bill, but if I ever bother again, it'll be because I love Jesus. Do you want another drink?'

And it was true. Even in the deepest darkness, like the faintest of nightlights, he was there, not trying to make me do, or believe, or feel anything in particular, not even causing me to believe in God, absurd as that may sound, but simply 'being there'. It is not rational. It is a humble fact. Much later, I wrote some words to a friend's tune in an attempt to capture the essence of this experience. The title is simply 'Song to Jesus'.

156

I didn't have to see you,
In the darkness, there by the side of me,
I knew it had to be you,
Knew you loved the child inside of me.
You smiled in the darkness,
It seemed to blind and burn.
But when my eyes were opened,
I smiled in return,
For you were there.

I didn't have to hear you,
In the silence, you were a part of me,
I knew that I was near you,
Knew your love was deep in the heart of me,
I knew that you were saying,
'Our happiness has grown,
For prayer is only friendship,
You never were alone,
For I was there.'

I didn't have to hold you,
Tried to trust you, trust in your care for me,
The secrets I had told you,
Hoping you would always be there for me,
So let the darkness gather,
And let the silence roll,
The love that made you suffer,
Is burning in my soul,
And you are there.

In one sense it was this constant, unbidden awareness of
Jesus, that led to the activity that was instrumental in my
regaining stability, and an interest in relatively normal
living. I started to write; and the first thing I wrote was a
series of six stories called *The Visit*. They chronicled the
experiences of a fairly ordinary church member, confronted
with Jesus, in person, paying an extended visit to a church
of vague denomination in 1984. Not surprisingly, the

157

stories are littered with allusions to my own experience, although the central character is quite unlike me.

Writing helped. It was a discipline and a therapy. The love of my family helped. They never stopped supporting me. Friends helped, especially perhaps, Ben Ecclestone, an elder at the Frenchgate Chapel in Eastbourne. He never preached at me once, and was – and is – refreshingly honest about his own faith and life. Company helped. It sustained a faint belief in me that I might not be totally useless. All these things contributed to a gradual process of rebuilding, or, more accurately, reassembling. I became calmer, more disciplined, readier to accept that I had to fit into the world as it was, albeit with a much freer outlook and a far greater flexibility in my view of myself and others. But I didn't know what to think about God. God, the father? He wasn't my father, and never had been. Despite the strange reality of Jesus, I still felt far removed from accepting the reality, let alone the concern of the senior member of the Trinity. Until, that is, one day when I took a very expensive taxi ride, all the way from Polegate to Haywards Heath.

Chapter Twelve

'Damn and blast!'

I cursed loudly as the London train disappeared infuriatingly into the distance, then flopped down on to the wooden bench behind me, rubbing my bruised knee and sucking air through my teeth as the pain started to make itself felt. I'd missed the train! Only by seconds, but that made it worse somehow. Anger and frustration crashed crazily around inside me, looking for an outlet. Perhaps I could throttle the ticket inspector, sitting inoffensively over there in his little box at the top of the steps. As long as the jury at my trial was made up of twelve people who had at some time in their lives missed a train by a hair's-breadth, I had no doubt that they would bring in a verdict of justifiable homicide. As I passed him on my way out of the station, my imagined victim nearly hastened his own end by calling out genially, 'Missed it then?'

'Yes,' I replied, baring my teeth, 'that sums it up nicely.'

As I limped off down the steps, he called after me, encouragingly, 'Never mind, there'll be another one along in an hour.'

In an hour? That was no good. I was supposed to be in Haywards Heath by four o'clock, and I'd just missed the last train that could get me there in time. As I stood outside the station, still fuming inwardly, it seemed to me that someone or something was doing everything in its power to stop me reaching my destination that day. Well, whoever it was, they seemed to have succeeded. I wasn't going to make it. I leaned against the wall, gloomily watching people arriving and departing from the taxi rank on the station forecourt, and wondered why this particular trip had come to seem so very important.

It had started a couple of weeks ago when I was thumbing through the dog-eared little volume in which Bridget and I recorded addresses and phone numbers. For some reason I had written down Michael Harper's address in Haywards Heath a long time ago, but had never had cause to contact him either by letter or phone. In fact, that meeting in the TVS studios during the recording of the David Watson Company programmes, was the only occasion on which I had met or spoken to him. Now, as my eye caught his name on the 'H' page of the little book, I remembered how impressed I had been by the depth and sensitivity that I sensed in his personality. Was it possible that he might have something to say to me that would assist, or speed up, or perhaps just encourage the process of reintegration that had already started?

Following the impulse before it had a chance to escape, I took the book over to the phone and dialled Michael's number. When I finally got through to him, all I could think of to say was, simply, 'I've had a sort of breakdown. Would you mind if I came to see you?' He responded warmly, suggesting a date and a time that happened to suit both of us. As the days passed, I looked forward to this meeting, although I had no idea just how crucial it was going to be.

The day of my trip started well. I didn't have to be at Polegate station until about ten past three, so there was plenty of time to relax and organise myself. After drawing some money from the bank after lunch for the coming weekend, I walked slowly down to the precinct in the centre of Hailsham to catch the 2.55 bus, which I knew from experience would arrive at Polegate in plenty of time for me to get the London train.

The bus arrived late. Not very late, but enough to set up a sort of nervous ticking in my stomach as we lumbered out of Hailsham and turned heavily on to the south-bound dual carriageway towards Eastbourne. The ticking increased to a frenetic whirr, as the bus breasted a slight hill and I saw the lines of stationary traffic before us. Of course – roadworks! I'd forgotten that they were taking the road up just before the Polegate turn-off. It put another five minutes on the journey, and by the time I got off near the Horse and Groom pub, I was almost whimpering with frustration. I still had quite a distance to walk – or rather sprint. I flew along the path towards the station, so panic-stricken at the thought of losing my train, that I lost my footing and fell heavily onto the ground, cracking my knee against the kerb, and shaking my innards into a jelly. With hardly a pause, I hauled myself up, and staggered onto the station, only to see my train standing tantalisingly by the platform, passengers boarding and alighting with impossible casualness. I could still make it! Unfortunately, the man at the ticket office refused to let me through without a ticket, and I had made the fatal mistake of letting him see that I was in a tearing hurry. With excruciating, deliberate slowness, he gave me my return ticket, took my money, and counted out my change. By the time I reached the platform the train was pulling out of the station, and all I could do was swear.

Now, as I watched taxis come and go on the forecourt, I felt miserable and defeated. There was nothing left but to find a telephone and let Michael know I wouldn't be coming. I knew that he had only an hour to spare, as he was going away the following morning. There would be no point in getting a later train. I trudged slowly up the road towards the centre of the town, knowing that there was a nest of phone kiosks just outside the Post Office.

As I walked, though, a wild thought occurred to me. Why shouldn't I go to Haywards Heath by taxi? Well, why not? I counted the money in my jacket pocket. There was twenty pounds exactly. Would that be enough? I didn't know, but I could find out. I hovered, undecided for a moment, imagining Bridget's reaction if she knew that I was contemplating using a sizeable chunk of our available cash for a taxi fare. I decided to take a chance. Turning round, I hurried back to the taxi rank, and asked one of the drivers if he could get to Haywards Heath by four o'clock. Yes, he thought he probably could. How much would it cost? He wasn't sure. About twenty pounds perhaps. I climbed in, and away we went.

I can remember only two things about that journey. One was the fare meter, displaying the cost of the journey as the miles rolled away beneath us. After a while I saw nothing but the red-lit numbers beneath the dash board, changing alarmingly every few minutes as another ten pence was added to the total.

The other thing was what seemed like an endless monologue by the driver on the subject of how he dealt with people who were sick in the back of his taxi.

By the time we reached Haywards Heath I felt as if I was going mad. My mind was in a surrealistic whirl of red lights and vomit. We stopped outside Michael's house. It was five minutes past four, and the meter showed eighteen pounds, fifty pence. I gave the driver the whole twenty pounds, and hurried up to the front door My feelings as I rang the front door bell were rather similar, if I'm honest, to the way I had felt all those years ago when I stopped my bicycle next to the Cowden sign, and asked myself what on earth I thought I was doing. What was I doing *now*? Was it really going to be worth all that money and effort, just to spend an hour with a man I hardly knew?

Someone who I took to be Mrs Harper answered the door, and showed me through to a study at the back of the house, where Michael sat working at a pleasantly cluttered desk. He greeted me very warmly, and seemed genuinely concerned about the difficulties I had been experiencing. His depth and gentleness had an oddly softening effect on me, but it wasn't until we prayed together at the end of the hour, that I realised why it was so necessary to be at that place, at that time, with that person. God wanted to speak to me. After praying quietly for a little while, Michael was silent for a moment. Then he spoke again.

'The Holy Spirit is showing me a picture of a field,

Adrian. The field is your life. It's going to be a bigger and more beautiful meadow one day, but at the moment it's being cleared. There are rocks and brambles and bushes that are being shifted and uprooted to make space for useful things to grow. But I'll tell you something . . .'

'Yes,' I thought, 'please *do* tell me something.'

'Nothing has been wasted—nothing! The soil underneath all these things is rich; richer than it would have been if they hadn't been there. It's going to be a *beautiful* meadow.'

As Michael opened his eyes and looked up, he must have sensed that his words had reached me on a level that had been untouched for years. I was fighting back tears as I said over and over in my mind the words that had meant most to me. 'Nothing has been wasted—*nothing* has been wasted.'

He smiled. 'Dear Adrian.' The words were from God, care of Michael Harper, and they conveyed the love of a father.

I left, and as I walked through the darkness towards the railway station, all the tears I had been holding back were released. God had spoken to me. He cared about me. He was *nice*. How did I know it had really been God speaking? I can't say, but believe me—I knew.

As a matter of history, Bridget reckoned it was a pretty good twenty pounds worth too.

That day marked the beginning of a new kind of hope, and was the first in a series of events and encounters that led me, slowly but surely, into a quite different understanding of what a relationship with God might mean. Some were quite dramatic, while others, apparently, were too trivial to be worth noticing. There was my bike, for instance.

I hadn't had a bicycle for years, not one of my own. As a kid I'd had several, including the shiny blue one on which I had set out to find and captivate Hayley Mills back in the sixties. Since my teens, though, I had hardly ridden one at all, apart from an old boneshaker belonging to John Hall, which, I seem to remember, I lost, somewhere in Bromley. Perhaps I thought they were one of the less dignified modes of transport, I don't really know.

Now, in 1985, at the age of thirty-six, my mother was quite convinced that what I really needed was a bike. A nice big bicycle would offer more relaxation and therapy than a hundred books, or a thousand conversations, in her view. I knew better of course. Every time we spoke on the telephone, and she said for the umpteenth time, 'Have you got a bike yet?', I would smile indulgently to myself and make vague promises that I *would* get one eventually.

Then, one day as I was glancing through the local advertising journal, I noticed an ad in the 'For Sale' section.

Gent's blue bicycle for sale.
Large frame. Very good condition.
Used only six times. £50.

I think it was the 'blue' that did it. A shiny blue bike of my very own. The years fell away, and I was an excited teenager again. I'd almost forgotten what innocent excitement felt like. I rang the number at the bottom of the advert, walked round to the bank to draw the money out, and within an hour I was the proud possessor of a large Raleigh bicycle; not, admittedly, with seventy-five derailleur gears, or however many they have nowadays, but nevertheless a 'good bike'. How nostalgic the words 'Sturmey Archer' seemed as I read them on the gear-lever housing attached to the handlebars. How strange to be back in the world of tyre-levers, cotter pins, saddle bags, chain guards, brake-blocks and, of course, puncture repair outfits. How satisfying to recapture the feeling of relish when negotiating the narrow gap betwen the kerb and the lines of cars doing the rush-hour crawl, or waiting for the lights to change. But most of all I just liked riding around like a kid or enjoying the whiz and swoosh that usually rewarded a bit of grinding uphill work. I had always hated the A-to-Bness of life. Now, I could go where I liked. I could start at A, head for M, and stop off for a while at F if it took my fancy. If I changed my mind at F, then I might forget M and pay a little visit to Q, which, as we all know, is only just down the road from R. It was lovely, and I loved it. I felt about as sophisticated as Pooh Bear on my bike, but I didn't really mind. In the course of just riding easily to and fro, I made real contact with the child inside myself, and in the process learned a simple but profound truth about contact with God. I discovered that prayer didn't have to start at A and end at B either. I learned or started to learn, that it's quite legitimate, and – dare I say – enjoyable, to meander aimlessly around, just enjoying the nearness of God, in the same way that you don't have to arrange special activities in order to enjoy being with a friend or a parent. God sat quite happily on his back doorstep, watching me as I pedalled happily around in my prayers, looking up occasionally to smile at him, and feel reassured by the way in which he smiled back. It was a new experience, and a very pleasant one, despite the occasions when I fell off my metaphorical bike and bawled like a kid with a bruised knee.

It's odd how different things affect different people. I talked about my bicycle in a Company programme a few weeks after I got it, and as I left the studio one of the cameramen stopped me to talk about *his* bike. Like me, he had at first felt rather foolishly adolescent just cycling to and fro, purely for the fun of it. He experienced the same nostalgic sensations of youth and innocence, and now, as he described the difficulty of confiding this to anybody without feeling a complete idiot, an expression of real pain contracted his features.

'What happens to us? Why do we lose all that? I was happier then than I am now that I reckon I know what's what.'

I knew exactly what he meant. One of the most moving aspects of parenthood is watching your children as they discover for the first time, things that have become so familiar that you hardly notice them. I had often prayed that the spirit of excited discovery would not die in my children, as it had in me for so long. When the oldest, Matthew, was five, he and I had taken a walk through the January streets one morning, to get to the park. When we came back, I tried to preserve part of that experience in the following lines.

I wish I was my son again,
The first in all the world to know,
The cornflake crunch of frosted grass,
Beside the polar paving stones,
Beneath the drip of liquid light,
From water-colour, winter suns.

Now, I was recapturing my own sense of discovery and excitement, especially in connection with natural things; flowers, skies, textures, the seasons. For some years I had been saddened by the loss of my ability to experience first-hand enjoyment of these things. A walk through a flaming autumn wood, for instance, produced only memories of the feeling I had once known of being right in the centre of a passionate, tragic symphony, full of sadness and hope. All seasons had their own character and poetry, but the spiritual vasectomy I had performed on myself a long time ago, had somehow prevented creative involvement with the world around me. It gave me real joy to discover that sense of wonder once more; to find, for instance, that I could gaze, astonished and enraptured, at a single daffodil bloom for several minutes, just absorbing the beauty of its shape and colour.

Daffodils are not flowers
They are natural neon from the dark earth,
Precious metal grown impatient,
Beaten, shaped and dipped in pools
Of ancient, sunken light.
Folded, packed and parachuted through,
To stand and dumbly trumpet out,
The twice triumphant sun.

It was my growing appreciation of natural things, and in particular perhaps, things connected with the season of autumn, that provided an almost immediate bond with a new member of the Company team, who first appeared on the programme at the turn of the year, and has since become a dear friend and valued adviser.

I know that the idea of the Christian life being a kind of journey, is an old and rather hackneyed one, but sometimes the metaphor is refreshed by encounters with fellow-explorers, who really seem to know where they are going. My new friend, Philip Illot, was one of these. My own journey had always been more of an undignified safari than an organised tour, and until now I had been hopelessly ill-equipped for the expedition. Like many Christians, I had tended to crash through the spiritual undergrowth, stubbornly clothed in my strange denominational and temperamental costume, refusing to discard the tools and weapons that seemed so essential. Now, most of my props had gone, but I was still physically fit. I still had the ability to stand and walk and move about freely. Philip had lost even that.

As a young man of eighteen, newly come into the Christian faith, and working in post-war Germany, Philip had a very strange dream one night. In his dream he was travelling across Germany in a train, when, unexpectedly the locomotive was halted by Russian soldiers who were searching for a particular man. Suddenly, Philip knew with total certainty that he was the one they wanted. Terrified, he hid by the window, hoping to be passed by. It was no use. He was aware of his fellow-passengers looking on helplessly through the windows of the train as soldiers forced him down onto a wooden cross lying on the grass. His hands and feet were nailed to the wood, and the cross was raised to a vertical position. Philip woke up screaming.

As the years passed, and he became an ordained minister in the Church of England, Philip never forgot that dream, assuming that one day in the future, he would be able to understand its meaning. He was a 'hyperactive' priest, always on the move, always busy, his life full of people and activities. There were many good, productive years, and a few very hard and difficult ones, but eventually, Philip, with his wife Margaret, and their two children, came to a parish in Bexhill, a seaside resort on the south coast, where, as usual, Philip threw himself into the life of the church, quickly earning the liking and respect of people throughout the town.

For some time Philip had been troubled by intermittent illness. At times it was so bad that he ended up in a Sunday service, lying across the alter, wondering if he was going to die there and then, and reflecting in the midst of his suffering that it wasn't a bad place to go! The symptoms continued, and became more frequent. Eventually, whilst in hospital, Philip learned that he was suffering from multiple sclerosis. He lost the use of all but his head and arms, and is now confined to a wheelchair.

That sounds like the end of a story, but it was actually the beginning of a completely new adventure in Philip's life. It was autumn when the illness was diagnosed, his favourite season. He sensed that, just as the natural world accepts change without panic or resistance in that season, so he was being called to be obedient to what was happening. To let it be. It was as though God was bringing him to a place that had been prepared from the beginning. He acquired an inner stillness that was the stillness of arrival. He was in the right place. The strange dream of many years ago seemed connected somehow with what was happening. But *why* was it happening? Philip dreamed again.

This time he dreamed that he found a key at the foot of the cross of Jesus. Choosing to pick up the key, he was then faced with a very low door, over which the word 'BEWARE' was written in large letters. Using the key, he unlocked the door and passing through in his wheelchair, discovered a vast crowd of troubled and broken people, waiting for the special kind of ministry that a man broken in body, but not in spirit, could offer. The dream is now a reality. Philip is constantly in demand as a counsellor, a speaker, and a leader of missions. What little strength he has is poured out for others, often in ordinary ministry, but sometimes with strange and amazing effects, one of which, too private to record yet gave me a greater sense of the absolute reality of God than anything I had experienced before.

For me, Philip is the smile on God's face. His joy, in the midst of what must be terrible suffering at times, is absolutely genuine, perhaps because of a different kind of intimacy with God, that can only be experienced on the other side of pain. He tells me that 'the darker side of God is brighter than the light side', a knowledge gained through long sleepless nights, when God feels as close to his heart as the darkness is to his face. For some reason I have been able to tell things to Philip that I could tell to no one else, knowing that they (and I) are safe with him. Most of all, perhaps, I love his sudden laughter. My relationships with people who lack a sense of the absurd, are necessarily limited; but there is no such limitation with Philip. Laughter erupts out of him at times, and is invariably infectious. The combination of strength, tenderness and humour is irresistible.

I asked Philip once during a Company programme, a rather idiotic question. It was the kind of question that a lot of people would like to ask, but don't, for fear of giving offence. I knew he wouldn't mind.

'Supposing,' I said, 'you could choose to have the spiritual insights and growth that you've gained since you became ill – or – you could have your health back, and walk and move normally. Which would you choose?'

True man, and true Christian, Philip smiled as though he had asked himself the same question many times, and replied firmly, 'I would, without question, choose both!'

Another whole book could, and probably will, be written about Philip's life, but the important thing for Bridget and me is our contact, not just with Philip, but also with Margaret, who has also suffered, of course. She is pure gold. We have much in common with them, and at a time when we needed people who would really understand, God gave them to us for real, no-nonsense ministry, and for a very special kind of friendship.

My visit to Michael Harper, my new bike, a new appreciation of natural things, and the ministry and friendship of Philip Illot; all of these things played their part in turning me gently towards the God that is, rather than the rather unpleasant image of the deity that I had strived with for so long. I had space to explore this new direction, as I took early retirement from my employment with Social Services, and I was not being confused or distracted by regular attendance of any one church. Each day I did little more than pray and write, and hope that the relative calm I had found would last. I really was beginning to feel that peace might be possible. I felt it even more after a surprise phone call from Jo Williams one day.

'Do you realise,' she said, 'that it's a year since you and Prabhu prayed for me and Don on that programme?'

I remembered my faithless prayer, and the feeling of hopelessness that had followed it.

'Yes, Jo. Of course I remember it. Why?'

'Well, do you realise what's happened since then?'

Jo went on to describe, over the phone and later when we met in Maidstone, how that prayer had been answered. Don, close to death a year ago, had been off the drink since that time. They say, 'Once an alcoholic, always an alcoholic', but for Don to stay away from alcohol for a year was a miracle in itself. Later, Bridget and I and the three children stayed in Southampton with Jo, and had the opportunity to meet Don for the first time. We found him to be a very charming and intelligent man, with a particular talent for getting on with our children, who thought Uncle Don was 'terrific!' That is high praise, believe me! It was a heartwarming weekend for everybody.

Then there was Jo, herself. Since the night on which we had said that prayer, something had happened to change her life. Jo decided to visit her auntie in Wales, the one she had stayed with as a very little girl all those years ago, after the big row between her mum and dad. She'd never thought of visiting her before, but now, for some reason, she and Don decided to make the long trip to Wales so that

Jo could meet her mother's sister for the first time in over forty years. While they were there, Don asked a very important question.

'Was Jo difficult and horrible when she was a little girl?'

Jo's heart must have missed a beat as she waited for Auntie Vi's reply.

'No!' said the old lady without hesitation. 'No, she was a very caring little girl. When her baby cousin was ill with rheumatic fever, I remember Jo laying a nappy out on the floor, and saying that maybe if the baby stood in the middle of it, she'd get better. She was like that. Very quiet, but a really nice little girl.'

She turned to Jo. 'Don't you let people put you down, you hear? It was your mum's fault, what happened, not yours.'

In all important ways, Jo is very uncomplicated. This information from the past changed everything. All her life she had blamed herself for anything that went wrong. It was only right. What else could a horrible little girl expect? Now, suddenly she had discovered that all her guilt had been based on a lie. She hadn't been a horrible little girl. It hadn't been her fault. She was a lovely little girl – a very caring child.

Auntie Vi had said so, and she should know. In a peculiarly real way, it was like being born again.

At the end of this year, Jo's attitude to God had changed radically. As far as she was concerned, the trip to Wales had been 'set up' by God, who had been trying for a long time to show Jo how much he loved and cared about her.

'Now,' she said to me late one night over coffee in the Harrietsham flat, 'it wouldn't matter to me deep down if nobody loved me, because I *know* that God does, and that's that!'

My faithless prayer had been answered, and so had that 'once for all' cry that Bridget and I had sent up to God in the summer of 1984. Trenches had been dug through our lives; it only remained to wait, and see the water flow.

171

Chapter Thirteen

Company has now completed its fourth year. Only Ann-Marie, Bridget and myself remain from the original team. George is no longer a contributor, but is very much alive and kicking at his flat in Vincent Square. Hugo is still with us, still telling stories, entertaining and educating. Jo Williams makes the trip from Southampton to Maidstone every month or so, and Peter Ball joined us quite recently to take part in a week's broadcasting. Peter Timms is a central figure for viewers nowadays, while Roy Millard has made it a real family affair by marrying James Blomfield's sister, Jane. There are new faces, including Ruth Soetendorp. Ruth and her rabbi husband, David, have become good friends of ours, especially as I no longer feel a neurotic need to switch on my evangelising machine every time I meet someone from a different faith. That man in the wheelchair still appears from time to time, and every now and then Bridget and I spend a very enjoyable half-day with Philip and Margaret at their house in Bexhill. Frances Tulloch, the major architect of Company, continues to produce the programme with the assistance of her hardworking secretary, Wynn Steer, who is beloved by all of us for her patience and good-humour. Angus Wright has now left TVS, and, at the time of writing, no one has been appointed to take his place.

Bridget and I calculate that between us, we have sat at the table in the Company kitchen on at least seven hundred separate occasions. So much has happened to us through the four years of the programme's life, and a great deal of it has been mentioned during those midnight chats. It has been a rich and productive experience – one we would not have missed for the world.

Company's fourth birthday sees me at a turning point, a point where I haven't the foggiest idea what's going to happen next. I don't know where I'm going, or how I'm going to get there; I don't know what I'm going to do or how I'm going to do it; but I feel an odd mixture of uneasiness and anticipation.

When I told my eldest son, Matthew, that I was about to write the final chapter of this book, he paused for a moment in his activity of transferring great wodges of dried mud from the bottom of his football boots to the kitchen floor, and nodded with all the wisdom of the modern twelve-year-old.

'Oh yes,' he said, 'that's the bit where you have to say everything's all right now, and you and God get on very well and all that.' Matthew has read his share of Christian paperbacks!

He was right of course. Many, if not most, of the huge number of testimonial books that exist nowadays, end with a tidying-up chapter in which God, man and the universe are slotted firmly into their proper places, and the reader is invited to submit himself to a simple process that will ensure spiritual growth or transformation.

I would *love* to be able to write a chapter like that. If only it was possible to pass on the information that Jesus lives at Number Ten, Gorringe Road, Luton: ring three times and say that Adrian sent you. I know that many people would like it to be that easy, and I know that some folk think it is that easy. I even know a few people for whom it really does seem to have been that easy, but they are very few. Nothing in my recent experience has made me any happier with simplistic formulas for spiritual living than I have ever been, nor, I'm afraid, am I much more patient with those who peddle such recipes.

Not very long ago, for instance, a Company viewer stopped me in the street and asked me why 'that man in the wheelchair doesn't say the prayer of faith and get up on his feet'. I was almost dumbstruck. Philip Illot believes in, and has had experience of miraculous healing, but God is using his physical situation in a particular way, just as St Paul's physical suffering was clearly part of his ministry. I'm glad that Jesus didn't say the prayer of faith, and come down from the cross to live out his life quietly in some Jewish suburb. Neither Philip Illot, nor St Paul, nor Jesus, for that matter, actually wanted to suffer physically; only loonies want that; but more important to them was discovering what God wanted of them and obeying him despite the suffering that obedience would bring. I told Philip what this lady had said one day, and asked him what he thought about it. He answered without any hesitation.

'If you should happen to see that lady again, I'd like you to tell her, with my best wishes, that I say the "prayer of faith" every single day!'

Of course we should pray for healing, anoint with oil and lay hands on the sick, but they won't always get better. They *don't* always get better. Everyone knows that they don't always get better, and it requires a peculiar form of corporate dishonesty to claim that they do. God will do what he will do, and sometimes we can only live in the mystery of that fact, waiting for it all to make sense when the right time has come.

The disciples had this problem of course; wanting to develop systems and rules to make life safer and easier to handle. Every now and then they really thought they'd got Jesus pinned down.

'She could have sold the ointment and given the money to the poor!'

He was always going on about the poor. Surely they'd got it right this time. Sorry lads – wrong again!

'Shall we call down fire from heaven on this village, Lord?'

Jesus told them not to be silly.

'I shall never let you be killed, Lord!'

Peter really got an earful for that.

174

'Tell Mary to help me, master, she's no use to anyone sitting there!'

Poor, likeable old Martha was wrong as well.

God cannot be reduced to a set of simple propositions, however simple his dealings with any individual person might be. This was, in hindsight, a large part of my problem in the sixties. When the church tried to compete with other 'instant cures', or means of establishing identity, it was, and still is, offering a version of Christianity that is, in one sense, too simplistic, and in another sense too difficult. The hippie movement tried to say that love is free, that it can be given away with a flower. This was no more true than that Jesus saves without cost or complication. I don't mean that he doesn't want to—far from it! But an honest and genuinely open reading of the four books that record what Jesus said, shows me that there are two essential parts to the message he wanted to put over.

First, I read that God is passionately committed to a world that he is absolutely crazy about, and there is no doubt that he would go, and has already gone, to the most extraordinary lengths to open up the channels between him and us, channels which are *so* blocked nowadays that only a very few people are genuinely and specifically hearing God talking to them. A lot are pretending or imagining (I've done so often), but very few really hearing.

The other part of what Jesus says is about counting the cost, keeping one's hand to the plough, loving your enemy, using talents properly, and being able to lose or give away all that you value most, if that's what is required of you. In other words—turning your own world upside down! I believe that these things need to be preached as part of the Christian message, instead of being the small print that you notice with dismay after committing yourself to receiving the free gift. I can't believe that Jesus said them all for fun. He must have meant them.

The problem for me, and for many others, was how to reconcile these two areas in my life from day to day. I was glad that God loved me—although I, in company with countless other Christians, probably never quite believed that he did – but I was quite unable to comply with, or even comprehend, the awesome demands that were being made on me. This is made even more difficult by the way in which God is all too often presented in evangelical and charismatic circles. He tends to come over as either a sentimental softy with such a pathological need for human affection that he doesn't really care what we get up to, or as a harsh, vindictive, austerely pure being, more concerned with narrow moral issues than people. I have seen so much fear and guilt transferred from speaker to listeners, disguised as 'conviction' and 'divine chastisement'. I recall one man who put an empty chair in the centre of the church, and invited us all to imagine that Jesus was sitting in it.

'Wouldn't you feel bad!' he said, 'wouldn't you want to hide your face and creep away, knowing the sin that's in you – the things that would make it impossible to meet his eyes!'

All I could think of as I stared at the empty chair, was how marvellous it would be to fling myself at him, like Peter dashing through the shallows to have an exciting breakfast with the risen Jesus. He didn't think of his own sin first, and remember, the denial business still hadn't been sorted out yet – he just wanted to get to Jesus because he loved him. Not want to see Jesus? I thought there must be something wrong with me!

I have begun to understand the way in which God is both loving and meticulously demanding by exploring an image used consistently by Jesus. He knew God as father. Now, as anyone who has read this book so far will know, that image presents problems for me, but there are good fathers around who I have been able to 'see in action', as it were, and I have been involved, directly or indirectly, with many children in care who needed to be fostered or adopted by families other than their own. Saint Paul says that Christians are the adopted children of God. God is their new father; so what does a really good father look like?

Well, first of all, joining a new family, adoption into a

different kind of environment with different rules and different expectations, needs careful thought and preparation by all concerned. It isn't like joining a club; more a matter of deciding where to put down your deepest roots. The candidate for adoption will need to visit the home in which he has been offered a place so that he can see the head of the household in action, without the pressure of immediate decision or commitment. He will see this prospective father of his being very firm, punishing his children at times. He will see him being very loving and forgiving as well. He might well see him rolling on the floor with the kids, laughing and joking. He will see how he weeps when one of the family is hurt or lost, how everyone is encouraged to love and look after everyone else, and how all have direct access to their father, but show different degrees of trust and confidence depending on what kind of people they are and what their backgrounds have been. He will be intrigued by how different the children of the family are; some quietly, deeply affectionate, others loud and boisterous in the way they show love to their father, a few can manage only a small smile because they hurt too much to do anything else for a while. Some may just sit in the furthest corner of an empty room, paralysed with fear of rejection, but nursing the tiniest of tiny hopes that the smile they glimpsed on the face of the man in charge was meant for them as well as everyone else. They are all in the house. They all belong. The most fearful will be loved into happiness in the end.

If our candidate likes the place, and is happy to take the rough with the smooth, do what he's told when necessary, and accept his adoptive father's control and guidance as a sign of his care, then he'll probably move in. He doesn't have to be perfect, or even good, to qualify, and even after he's arrived, space will be allocated, allowances will be made, time will be spent and given. He'll be left in no doubt about what the house rules are, but everyone will be aware that it takes time to learn and adapt. Adopted children take ages to settle in sometimes. He'll be all right in the end. He might leave, but the offer of a home is forever; he will always be able to come back if he wants to; his new father will never stop loving him, however annoying he may be. Eventually, the spirit of the place will get right inside him; he will mature and learn that he really is wanted. The rules will suddenly seem much easier to keep, in fact they won't seem like rules at all. He will probably be given one or two responsible tasks to perform on behalf of his father. In the end, he will be so well tuned in to his dad's voice, that a single word will bring him flying to his father's side, saying excitedly, 'Yes! What do you want me to do?'

The family image is reinforced for me by what I see in those who really have learned to trust the head of the family. They don't become narrower and more condemnatory, they become broader and more loving. They show little interest in gifts, but are profoundly fascinated by the giver. Their spirituality does not seem loony, it feels real; it fits, on some crucial but undefinable level, with everything else that is real. They may be travelling on the hard road that Jesus said was the only road for his followers, but something makes them smile even when their feet hurt. They have usually paid dearly for their joy, and the price seems to be, quite simply, everything. They are convinced that they are the worst of sinners, but equally convinced that they are the most forgiven of men. As far as they are able, they organise their priorities so that God is at the top of the list, knowing that an honest reading of the gospels makes it quite clear that all other things begin from that starting point. And yet, as I've said in connection with Peter Ball, the effect is not to make someone like me despair, and study my sins in a misery of self-loathing, but to feel that the source of all this love and warmth must be able to do something, even with me. I catch sight of God's optimism and feel cheered and encouraged. I remember visiting Peter once with my friend James, whose Christian life has followed an agonised path, not unlike my own. The three of us talked for an hour or so, then, as James and I drove away towards Hailsham, he said with a sort of wistful puzzlement, 'He knows a different God to the one I do. His God's nice!'

He didn't mean soft, he meant 'nice'. Warm and caring and consistent and reliable and firm and forgiving and competent – like a father. That same sense of rich, compassionate, intelligent care can be found in the works of Paul Tournier, a Christian writer who, again and again, has preserved my spiritual sanity. His book, *The Adventure of Living*, is an invigorating invitation to get off the Circle Line of religion, and explore the mystery of *really* living as a follower of Jesus in the *real* world. Because we do live in a huge and thrilling mystery. Whatever I may say here, the things that happen to me are not the things that will happen to the next man, and I have no right to try to crush him into the little box of my own experience. It is so easy to be wrong, so easy to decide that because God did 'X' on Tuesday, he will do 'X' on Wednesday; so easy to preach our own salvation as the way things should be, instead of acknowledging the excitingly complex and creative nature of God's dealings with men. I know a lot of Christians, they're all different – gloriously different. I used to think, for some strange reason, that our ultimate goal was to be exactly alike, but now I don't. I love the differences, and so, I believe, does God. Despite the fundamental similarities in faith, who could be more Paulish than St Paul, more Peterish than St Peter, more Jesus-like than Jesus? I don't want to be like anyone else, nor do I want to force anyone into being like me – God knows I don't want that! I want a hair-raising adventure of cosmic proportions with this God whose aim is to make me the best possible 'Adrian' that I could be. In the process I might even become a useful member of the family, and be able to lend a hand with the newcomers. I'd like that.

Meanwhile my own adventure doesn't look much like an adventure from the outside. Each day, after sharing the arduous task of producing three reasonably dressed and equipped children out of the morning chaos, I settle down to do three things.

First, I read a chapter of the New Testament. I read it in the Jerusalem Bible because I like the print and the headings and the lay-out. I have never read the Bible in a disciplined way before. When I have tried to do so, I've usually taken a couple of verses only, and squeezed them pessimistically in my mind, hoping to extract a drop or two of meaning or significance. Now, I read in order to grasp the broad intention of a chapter, happy to stop and consider a point if it catches my interest. I am reading the gospels at present because I am suddenly fascinated to know what Jesus really said. With my mind still cluttered with prejudices and preconceived notions, this isn't easy, but even I can see that the full gospel of Jesus Christ wouldn't go down too well in most churches that I know. I can also see, though, that he himself would bring healing and tenderness to individuals in those same churches who carry inside themselves a deep-rooted conviction that they are too bad or too insignificant to enter what Jesus calls the Kingdom of God.

Interestingly, as I discover a new freedom to be disciplined in Bible-reading, a close friend has discovered a different kind of liberty through his conscious and careful decision to postpone, for a few months only, the daily study of scripture that has been has habit for many years. I relish the contrast between the ways in which our individual needs are being fulfilled.

Secondly, I pray. At last I have found a way of prayer that is not excruciatingly boring or meaningless, or hopelessly fragmented. On the desk in front of me as I write, lies a pile of about thirty long brown envelopes. On the outside of each is written one or more names. Inside each sealed envelope is a written prayer for the people concerned. Each day I pick up each envelope, hold it up to God, and ask him to do whatever is needed for them. If I am in a grumpy, or sulky mood, I flick through them quite quickly, saying, 'Bless him, and him, and her, and them . . .' If I am feeling more peaceful, I try to be creative in my prayers. I might, for instance, imagine Jesus administering communion to each person, and try to see what happens in the encounter. I might, on another occasion, hold the hands of each one in my mind, and say a prayer for both of us. Sometimes I picture Jesus standing by an open door, greeting people individually, and inviting them in. They all respond to him differently. Sometimes I see strange things occurring in these 'mind-pictures'. Whether they are purely imagination or something else, I have no idea. I begin to feel, nowadays, a real sense of responsibility towards this little group of people, and I enjoy meeting them and God every day. I usually say a prayer of confession before doing anything else, and perhaps spend a few minutes after this trying to float in the warm sea of God's love for me. I try to do these things however I feel. In the old days I would have abandoned the attempt to make contact with God if I had been unpleasant since getting up, or if things seemed generally bleak, or if Bridget and I had gone through one of our monumental arguments over some trivial issue. I'm now much more aware of the difference between temperamental and spiritual failure, and far more conscious of the fact that God is as anxious – more anxious probably – to meet me when I've been a berk, as when I fancy I'm one of his little sunbeams!

Thirdly, I write – or try to. We have frequent visitors, and as others who work at home will know, this is a sweet-and-sour dish. I love seeing people – first, because I simply like people, and secondly, because they are a welcome addition to the long list of 'things that prevent you from getting started on filling up the horrific blank sheet of paper'. The list includes such essential activities as going to the lavatory, making coffee, answering the phone, scratching your ear, combing your hair, anything to avoid the moment when the pen first touches the paper.

As I've said, it doesn't look much of an adventure on the face of it, but I feel a growing excitement about the prospect of living in an upside-down world, presided over by a passionate, humorous God, who wants people to be as free and involved and creative and committed and tough as

181

Jesus was. God forgive us for the way in which we have presented Jesus as a 'wet-willie' over the years; as an 'A-stream/doesn't play sports' type, who can't wait to leave this nasty world and get back to the sanitised environs of heaven. As I read the gospels now, I find a Jesus who was passionately involved, physically, mentally, and emotionally with people and with the natural world. Healing and helping and feeding and getting angry and weeping and eating and drinking and sweating and dying. His message to the world was uncompromising and impossibly demanding, but his way with hurt and sinful individuals was tailor-made and tender, unless the sin happened to be hypocrisy in church leaders, in which case he could be devastatingly angry. As far as I can tell, the invitation to continue his adventure and mission in this world is open to everybody, but it seems clear that nothing very startling happens in anybody's life until they start to do what Jesus laid down as a very clear condition of growth. Namely, to make the number one priority in your life, 'Seeking the Kingdom of God'. That's why I do what I do each day. I want to be in on the adventure. I don't want to huddle with other Christians twice a week for the rest of my life, indulging in religion as a hobby. I want God to take this grumpy, jealous, critical personality of mine, transfigure it somehow, and send me out to get my hands dirty in the real world, on his behalf. It's 'mission impossible' at the moment, but as Jesus himself said, 'What is impossible for men, is not impossible for God.'

My heart goes out to all those for whom 'being a Christian' has been like a marathon walk through ankle-deep mud. Some drop out, some keep going, all wonder what on earth it's all about. Why so many peaks and troughs? Why so little peace? Why do some Christians seem to have 'got it', whatever *it* is?

I've got no smart answers. I'm still trudging along myself most of the time, but I'm excited by three things. One is the person of Jesus, one is the fact that God likes me and wants me in his family, and the other is his assurance that nothing is wasted. To all my fellow-stragglers and Christian delinquents I say, with tears in my eyes as I write, God bless you in whatever way you need. Be wary about those once-for-all solutions, but hang on – he'll rescue you.

'That day – it is Yahweh who speaks – I will finally gather in the lame, and bring together those that have been led astray and those that have suffered at my hand. Out of the lame I will make a remnant, and out of the weary a mighty nation. Then will Yahweh reign over them on the mountains of Zion from now and for ever.'

Micah 4:6–7.

VIEW FROM A
BOUNCY CASTLE

Contents

Bouncy Castle

You hear some funny things when you eavesdrop on your own thoughts. It happened to me the other day. I had been chatting to a very stolid, repressed sort of bloke, a nice chap but not easy to get close to. As I shook hands with him and said goodbye, I found myself thinking: 'You're a long way from the bouncy castle.'

It took me a while to focus on the origin of this homespun phrase or saying. But when I did track it down it was rather interesting.

A couple of years previously Bridget and I had been invited to the summer christening of Alex, the baby son of close friends of ours. The service went well, Alex was satisfactorily dunked

– to use a theological term – and the outdoor party afterwards was quite a grand affair.

There was lots of food, a lot of people, lots of sunshine and, in the middle of a grassy space at the back, a highly coloured, fully inflated, un-policed bouncy castle.

Fed by a constant stream of stabilising air, it stood wobbling gently in the slight breeze, just waiting for small, excited children to clamber up and abandon themselves to bouncing, rolling, leaping ecstasy.

It didn't have to wait long, of course. The kids, hearing that the only rule was 'Take your shoes off!', were soon swarming all over it, relishing the fact that because it was hired 'without owner', there was very little in the way of restrictive supervision.

Nor was it long before the adults got in on the act as well. I was one of them.

I imagine that most parents will identify read-ily with my feelings about bouncy castles. We have four children, ranging in age from sixteen years old down to three and a bit (I shall be in trouble if I don't mention the 'bit'). In one and a half decades we have visited countless numbers of fêtes, fairs, school functions, agricultural shows and other open-air events, many of which fea-tured the aforesaid attraction – but only for children!

Many a frustrated half-hour had I spent watching my offspring ricocheting wildly around on their inflated playground, while I smiled be-nignly, concealing my fierce inner desire to join

190

them. Always I was thwarted by the unrelenting presence of the proprietor, usually smoking one of those eternally dangling cigarettes, and occasionally coming out with professional phrases such as: 'Nobody over eight!' or 'This lot off – that lot on!'

The contrast between the dispassionate tone of these utterances and the tumbling joy of the kids used to depress me somewhat.

Now, for the first time, it was possible for fifteen years of frustration simply to disappear as I indulged my deep-felt need.

I have to confess that it took me a while to shake off my dignity and my shoes, but once I did it was wonderful. What the children thought about 18 stone of middle-aged man bouncing crazily from one side of their paradise to the other, I don't know. I wasn't too concerned at the time.

Most people got on during the afternoon, but there was one chap, Richard, who just couldn't seem to relax enough to have a go. He was one of those large, not very well co-ordinated men who look as if they were born in a suit. Now that he was grown up he wore it like a coffin. Very smart, very uptight, very dignified. At first he dismissed the whole idea of his using the bouncy castle as silly.

You could see him mentally picturing himself taking his heavy, well-shined black shoes off and leaping foolishly around like an inflated child.

But, as the afternoon wore on, I noticed that Richard was making gradual, unobtrusive moves in the direction of the castle. He would go and get another drink, for instance, then come back and stand just a little closer than before.

Every now and then his eyes would flick round and study the noisy bouncing mob with an odd mixture of fear and yearning.

Eventually, towards the end of the afternoon, he managed to stroll up to the castle apron, sit with tremendous nonchalance on the edge, and very casually remove his shoes, carefully unlacing them first. The jacket was next to go, folded neatly and placed on the ground beside him.

He then climbed carefully onto the castle itself and sat quietly at the side as though he was there in some sort of benevolent supervisory capacity.

He didn't sit for long. There is magic in the bouncy castle.

Before a minute or two had passed, that mass of congealed human dignity was flinging himself around wildly with the best of 'em, in a way he probably hadn't done for years. Down below, his large shoes stood neatly side by side in the middle of a jumble of other shoes. It occurred to me then how appropriate that was.

Rather like Moses at the burning bush, Richard had removed his shoes before treading the hallowed ground of joyful abandonment. For a short time he allowed himself to be a little child again and, as we all know, Jesus said that unless we become like little children we cannot enter the kingdom of heaven. I am quite sure that he did not intend this condition to be regarded as some kind of cold and arbitrary rule. Rather, he was saying that until we do acquire a child-like perspective we simply cannot see or understand the things of God, whether they be secular or specifically religious aspects of living.

The shedding of false dignity can be a very painful process (although the fear is often much worse than the fact – it was difficult to get Richard off once he'd got going) but every now and then, when we tread that hallowed ground for ourselves, we realise the wisdom of the Good Shepherd's words. Everything looks different from the vantage point of the bouncy castle. Get on

with me now – there's no age limit – and we'll take a look.

Gardens
A Skip Full of Memories

I am not a keen gardener, to put it mildly. Every now and then, I dismally plod around our lawn behind the mower as it snarls and rips and chews at the grass like a toothless old lion. I might, if I am feeling more energetic than usual, do a bit of strimming as well. You know what strimmers are – those long things that buzz like demented insects, and drive you mad because you have to pull the nylon cord out a bit further every two minutes unless you've got the posh sort, which we haven't.

The only other thing I do in the garden is sit in it, usually just after I've finally got round to giving the lawn its short back and sides. I may not be very good at the practical side of things, but when it comes to occupying a garden chair with, say, a bottle of wine and half a cold chicken to keep me company, I am capable of displaying a concentration and single-minded persistence that would amaze many of those who think they know me. These latter talents have been very infrequently exercised however (a prophet in his own country, perhaps?) so, generally speaking, a little mowing, a spot of strimming, that's about the limit of my gardening activities.

My wife, on the other hand, is devoted to all growing things. A dedicated digger, planter-out and pruner, she has to be almost physically restrained from weeding the central reservations of motorways and the moss-filled grooves under the windows of other people's Morris 1000 Travellers. A real fanatic. She claims that if Paul Newman had proposed to her at the same time as I did, the deciding factor would have been the degree of horticultural commitment offered. An unlikely story, in my view, but there we are.

After a long early holiday a couple of years ago, my wife pointed out that the garden behind our house was beginning to acquire a sort of Matto Grosso quality. Would I do something about it? After a one-man safari into the undergrowth I went into the garage to look for a machete, or some other equally suitable tool. The garage was in a worse state than the garden. There might have been some tools there, but they were buried under about five years' worth of things-you-put-in-the-garage-because-you-can't-think-where-else-to-put-them. I realised that, before getting the garden done, we needed a skip.

It arrived after lunch, a huge metal bucket like a spare part for a tank. They delivered it, we would fill it up and they would collect it and dispose of our rubbish – at a price. It was lowered slowly outside the garage in a cloud of pink petals from our Japanese flowering cherry. I rolled my sleeves up and got started.

It sounds silly, but I got a bit emotional after a while. Some of the things I chucked into the skip were horribly concrete reminders of failed intentions, half-completed projects and even broken promises. Worst by far was the jumbled mass of wood, wheels and bits of wire that constituted my abortive attempt to construct a go-kart for my son Matthew when he was much younger. I remembered little Matthew waiting eagerly for it to be finished, and I remembered my own deep frustration as my ham-handed efforts resulted in complete and utter failure. My eyes were misting a little as I heaved this particular memory into the depths of the metal bucket. I've kept most of my other promises, and Matthew and I have a very good relationship now, but it was a painful moment.

As the afternoon wore on, the skip vultures descended. A friend who lives a little further down the road sauntered up and after some incidental conversation, mentioned that he had a fridge to dispose of. Would it be all right if he dumped it in my skip?

'Go on,' I said, 'shove it in!'

So he did.

Less than an hour later another friend who lived along the road the other way arrived with a little 'rubble problem'.

'Go on,' I said, 'bung it in!'

By the time a third supplicant had dumped his garbage in *my* skip, I was beginning to feel vaguely resentful. I try to be perfect but I'm not.

I wondered if a good night's sleep would produce a little more charity in me. It might have
done but for the fact that on inspecting the skip
the next morning, I discovered that some person
or persons unknown had used the cover of darkness to deposit even greater quantities of refuse
in my giant yellow dustbin. I hopped about
furiously on the pavement in front of my house
like one of those 'angry people' in a Charlie
Chaplin film. I was seething.

'Why should they be allowed to put their blinking rubbish in my skip?' I muttered to myself
when I had calmed down a little. 'Why should
they? After all, I'm the one who has to pay for it in
the end. Forty quid! It's not fair!'

'Big deal!' said the other end of a rather disturbing dialogue that occurs in my mind sometimes. 'You're paying forty pounds, are you? You
may think that's an awful lot of money to spend
on getting rid of other people's rubbish – '

'Yes, I do think exactly that!'

'Do you want to see a human skip?'

Then, in my mind's eye, I seemed to see a hill.
And on the hill, nailed to a wooden cross, was a
man in agony.

'Come on,' he called out, 'bring all your garbage up here, all your mistakes and failures and
broken promises, all the things you can hardly
bear to look at or think about, whatever they are
and whatever you think about them; shove them
on me – I'll get rid of them for you.'

'But who's going to pay?' I asked.

'I've already paid,' said the man. 'You go and get on with your gardening.'

The Gift of Weeding

I don't know how much Ascension Day means to most people. As a significant day in the church calendar it doesn't get much of a press, usually. Perhaps this is because it falls on a Thursday (nothing religious could possibly happen on a Thursday, could it?), and, let's face it, there are no chocolate eggs, pancakes, or gift-wrapped presents attached to its celebration. If we were a little more imaginative we might arrange to hire tall buildings for the day, so that Christians could make symbolic ascents in the lifts (or Vertical Personnel Distributors, as the Americans call them sometimes).

Ascension Day is, of course, the time when we remember Jesus' final farewell to his closest band of followers, the disciples. He had already, much more dramatically than Sinatra, made a number of comebacks, but now it really was 'goodbye' for the last time, and the Bible tells us that he was taken up and away from them in a cloud.

I saw a film once where they had obviously strapped a camera to the bottom of a helicopter for the Ascension scene. The disciples' hair was waving wildly in the wind from the rotor blades as the machine lifted.

I don't know how it happened in reality, but, however it was, he was gone, and that little collection of very ordinary people was left to wonder how on earth they were going to tackle the problems of the world without the power and charisma of his leadership. He had said something about sending a comforter to strengthen them but he had also warned that they would suffer more than he had, and he had made it very clear that the baton was being firmly passed to them.

It must have been a very thoughtful and somewhat worried little group of world-changers who drifted sadly away from the last, strange farewell.

And that is precisely how I feel when I try to pray for huge, impenetrable problems such as the situation in South Africa or the Middle East – thoughtful and somewhat worried, to put it mildly. How can I make any difference to the vast, complex set of difficulties that accompany political change in South Africa? Such a massive task: such – apparently – unresolvable issues. Surely my small prayer would drown in that sea of violence and prejudice and misery. It can seem a very dark world at times.

Fortunately, God does send us rays of light from time to time, and some of them, like little pocket torches, are re-usable. The one that helps me with this question of small prayers and big problems is a memory of something that happened to a friend of mine called Doreen.

Doreen and her husband, Geoff, are members of the house group that meets in our sitting-room each Thursday evening. We have become very fond of them over the years. Now at retirement age, they have qualities of cheerfulness, loyalty and ungrudging industry that are quite exceptional. One of the most reassuring sights that Bridget and I know is our two friends plonking themselves down on the big settee in our upstairs sitting-room every week at eight o'clock. They are good people.

One evening, Doreen arrived at the usual time for house-group clutching two big bottles of champagne, and with a great big grin stretched across her face. When the group had finally assembled, corks had been popped, and we each had a full glass, Doreen explained.

'Tonight', she said, 'we're celebrating the fact that I've weeded my neighbour's garden!'

Doreen had read the Bible passages in which Jesus says that we must love the people we don't like, as well as the people we do. Suddenly, as she read, she thought of the person who lived just down the road from her, a terribly bad-tempered old lady who talked endlessly when she wasn't being angry, and was popularly supposed to be very stingy.

Plucking up her courage, Doreen marched round to her irascible neighbour's house and offered to sort out her weed-ridden flowerbeds. The offer was received with predictable surprise, but quite unexpected enthusiasm.

'And it works!' said Doreen. 'It works! It really does! She's not bad-tempered at all when you get to know her. She's become so nice, and she's not stingy at all. She made me take some money for some plants I got her. Oh, and the lady up the road's doing a bit of gardening for her as well and – I don't know, there's so much love in it all!'

I know that the Gift of Weeding is not mentioned in Corinthians, but what a gift to have! There were tears in my eyes as I downed my champagne.

Doreen was celebrating her discovery that the Spirit of God still works in a suburban street in southern England in the nineteen eighties, and it inspired, and inspires me still, to believe that what could happen in a small way, could happen in a large way.

It is worth praying for South Africa. Every tiny defeat of prejudice that happens in that sad country as a result of the tiniest of our prayers, will justify the trust that, on Ascension Day, Jesus places in ordinary men and women using the power of his Spirit.

I don't know if drinking is allowed in Paradise, but, if it is, I would guess that, every time someone like Doreen lets love overcome hate and fear, the champagne corks must be popping all over heaven.

Trains
The Six-Forty to Charing Cross

Jesus once said: 'If your right eye causes you to sin, pluck it out and throw it away. And if your right hand causes you to sin, cut it off and throw it away.'

'It's better', he said, 'for an eye and a hand to be lost than for your whole body to end up in hell.'

Knowing what a lust human beings exhibit for the formation of new denominations and sects, it amazes me that we have not seen the development of groups of people whose members literally lop pieces off themselves and each other.

When I was going through my own very literal phase, the rather drastic approach to combatting sin that these verses suggested was very alarming, especially when I considered my own personal failings. If I had decided to remove the parts of my body that caused most problems, I would have ended up a decapitated eunuch – at least!

If, however, we agree and accept that Jesus did not intend us to interpret his words literally, what *did* he mean? I'm sure there are many shades of explanation, all quite valid. How about this one?

A friend of mine, whom I shall call Veronica, worked in a London office each week from Monday to Friday. Every morning she drove to the little country railway station near her home in time to catch the six-forty to Charing Cross. She didn't have to catch that particular train. The one that left at seven o'clock would have done just as well, but Veronica was one of those people who like to arrive early at their place of work, so that there's time to relax and take stock before launching into the business of the day.

The salary that Veronica earned was just what she and her husband Derek needed to keep their joint income at a reasonable level (Derek was a self-employed sculptor who worked from home). They were a very happily married couple in their mid-thirties, not just in love but also very good friends, an excellent advertisement for commitment.

The months passed and, in the course of her regular daily commuting, Veronica developed a nodding acquaintanceship with a fellow traveller – a man – who invariably boarded the same train as she did, but at the next station along the line.

Gradually, almost imperceptibly, a friendship began and was deepened each morning during the hour-long trip to London. The man who sat on the opposite seat every day was civilised and charming, a very attractive person. Veronica was forced to face the fact that she had become that rare creature, a happy commuter. Her heart beat a little faster each time she boarded the train and found herself facing her new friend once again. She was on the verge of falling in love.

This is not, of course, a rare phenomenon in married people, and in many other cases might well have been an indication of neglect or thoughtlessness on the part of the husband, but Veronica and Derek really were very close, and they valued their relationship highly.

Veronica was troubled, and unsure what to do. After much thought she decided to ask for advice from her best friend – her husband. On the Saturday morning following that decision, she sat Derek down with a whisky and soda in the living-room and told him exactly what she was feeling.

Honesty compels me to admit that if I had been in Derek's position that morning I would almost certainly have produced some kind of ragged, emotional response. I used to tell myself that I was the civilised, level-headed type who could handle any crisis with deep, dark-brown-voiced calm. Experience has shown, however, that a small high-pitched hysteric usually takes over on these occasions.

Not so in Derek's case. He is a pipe-smoking, philosophical chap, the sort of man who enjoys pondering contentedly over a pint. He listened carefully to everything that Veronica said, sipping his drink occasionally and nodding in an understanding sort of way. Finally, she ran out of words and sat anxiously on the sofa waiting to hear what her husband would say.

There was a long pause, then Veronica spoke once more.

'I don't know what to do, Derek – tell me what to do.'

Slowly, deliberately, he rose to his feet, crossed to the sofa and sat down beside his wife. Placing his arm around her shoulders he spoke gently, but firmly:

'Darling – change trains.'

That was Derek's solution, and in this case it worked. If the six-forty to Charing Cross causes you to sin (don't cut it off exactly, British Rail will probably do that for you), go on the seven o'clock. Change trains.

Now, even I'm not naïve enough to believe that all or even most problems of this kind can be solved so simply. Even in Veronica's case, it cost her quite a lot to abandon the growing relationship that had brightened her mornings. It was worth it for her. For others there will be such complex considerations and so many difficulties, or perhaps things have gone so far that the 'changing trains' option is just not feasible.

But for people, Christian or otherwise, who want to avoid problems in the future, it is worth considering the proposition that it is easier to steer our lives and temperaments *round* obstacles, rather than meet them head-on, wrestle desperately with them, and probably lose the contest. Most of us know only too well the areas in which we are weak, or likely to be tempted. Often it takes a lot of courage and determination to change direction when sweet darkness is only a step away.

I know that Veronica's story doesn't sound much like the New Testament verses that I quoted, but it comes down to the same thing in the end, and the general principle holds good in all sorts of different situations. If you run into trouble, and it's not too late to do something about it, don't mess about – change trains.

The Four-Fifteen from Paddington

There was a time, not all that long ago, when I made sure that I never went anywhere, or did anything, that could possibly result in my looking foolish. As a result, you will not be surprised to hear, I rarely went out, and didn't do very much at all.

Far from producing humility in me, this limited approach to life made me into something of a clever-dick whenever I *did* do anything that was remotely useful. I have been coaxed, pummelled and persuaded into a much more vulnerable state over the past few years, but the clever-dickness (what an elegant expression!) is still part of me, and still has to be squashed by God from time to time.

One of the most memorable of these 'squashings' happened at London's Paddington Station when I was attempting to catch a train to the West Country – the four-fifteen to Taunton, as far as I can remember.

A very large number of people were queuing on the station concourse that afternoon, all keen to find seats on the fast inter-city train that was already being cleaned in preparation for departure.

I was as keen as everyone else. I wanted a seat in the second-class carriage adjacent to the buffet, so that I only had a short journey to fetch my coffee, sandwiches and – as a special treat on this particular day, I'd decided – a danish pastry. So intent was I on achieving this objective that I was prepared to sprint, suitcase notwithstanding, in competition with my fellow travellers, to make sure I got what I wanted. If there had been any starting blocks available I would have been crouched and ready for the gun.

Frustratingly, there were three false calls over the public address system as I waited near the front of the line of passengers. Three times a voice announced: 'The four-fifteen is now ready to board', and three times the same voice announced: 'We apologise for an incorrect call. The four-fifteen to Taunton is not yet prepared for boarding. Passengers are requested to return to the station concourse until further notice.'

Goodness knows what was going on behind the scenes. I never did find out what caused this rather excessive break-down in British Rail communications, but there was no doubt about its effect on the people in the queue. They – or rather, we – were muttering and fretting and tutting with impatience and irritation against the common, corporate enemy.

Then, just as I was preparing myself for the fourth attempt, the other end of that same disturbing (but familiar) dialogue, began to speak in my mind.

'Why are you racing against all these people?'

Feebly, I replied, 'Because, er . . . I want a seat next to the buffet so that I can get sandwiches and er . . ."

My reply trailed off pathetically.

'You're in the wrong race!' said the other end of the dialogue, and again – 'You're in the wrong race.'

As I turned these words over in my mind, I realised that the O.E.O.T.D. was absolutely right. I had become so taken up with writing books and making broadcasts and speaking to groups of people, that I was beginning to lose touch with the roots of all this activity, namely, my relationship with Jesus and my responsibility to God.

'Right! Okay! Good lesson, God,' I said brightly to the now clearly identified O.E.O.T.D., 'Buffet time now, eh?'

But to my horror, the same voice now said, 'I want you to walk round to the end of this queue of people, then, when the time comes, stroll down to the train, and I will save you a seat in the carriage next to the buffet.'

Full of faith, I said, 'No chance!' After all, I reflected, creating the universe was one thing, saving a seat on the four-fifteen to Taunton was something else. Obviously, God had never travelled by this train before . . .'.

Besides, I'd always found this business about 'God saves parking spaces for me when I ask him' extremely difficult to accept. Now, typically, I was being artfully manoeuvred into testing out a very similar principle. I decided that I'd better do what I was told.

Moving round to the back of the queue, I felt very foolish. When the fourth call to board came through the loudspeakers and I started my slow-motion amble towards the train, I just felt annoyance.

'I know what happens now, God', I said. 'I get to the train and there's no seat for me, and I'm expected to say "Hallelujah" anyway! and oh . . . I've been here before!'

The rest of the passengers were doing precisely what I'd known they would do. They were heading, as one man, for the buffet region of the train. I was heading for it too – very slowly, every muscle tensed with the effort of not running. When I boarded the carriage at last it was exactly as I'd expected, packed solid with people sitting and standing. There was just one vacant seat, right at the end of the carriage, immediately next to the buffet.

I stood beside the empty seat for some time, waiting for its rightful occupant to return from wherever he or she had gone. Eventually, when nobody claimed it, I spoke to the girl in the neighbouring seat.

'Is anybody sitting here?'

'No,' she said, 'it's free.'

So I sat down.

'I told you so!' said the other end of the dialogue. There is no smugness in the divine nature of course, but the O.E.O.T.D. did sound rather satisfied with itself.

Once again my clever-dickness was squashed, but I never really mind when these things happen. There is such wit and wisdom in the workings of the Holy Spirit. He is never dull.

I should add that my experience on Paddington Station is not an indicator that God will invariably reserve seats for his followers whenever they use public transport. I wish he would! It would make my life much easier. Rather, it was further evidence of the way in which God uses living parables to teach his children, and a reas-

suring reminder that those parables are engi-
neered with individuals in mind.

Children
A Bedtime Story

It is possible to find hope in the most desperate situations sometimes.

The subject of homeless children in London and other big cities seems to come up frequently in news and documentary programmes nowadays. These are youngsters who have quite literally run away from difficult home situations, or from County Council homes for children in the care of the local authority. Some of them are frighteningly young. Not much imagination is needed to picture the kinds of pitfall awaiting naïve twelve- or thirteen-year-olds who are homeless and penniless in the big city environment.

These references always attract my attention because until I changed course a few years ago, my working life had been spent with children in trouble. I hesitate to describe them as 'disturbed' children, as an awful lot of my charges were – potentially – quite normal kids who had been struggling desperately to survive among highly disturbed and inadequate adults. They had, as Jesus puts it in the parable of the sower, no root in them – none of the good soil that is produced by consistent care and warmth and discipline and approval. I would be the last to deny that each person is responsible for his or her own actions, whatever the effect of background and circumstances, but there was a bleak inevitability about the downward progress of the fortunes of some of those children that was heartbreaking.

In the late seventies I spent eighteen months working in a secure assessment unit in the Midlands. This 'locked facility', as it was rather grimly called, existed to cater for children who were either too violent or too likely to abscond, to be placed in one of the open units that existed on the same campus. During their stay of a few weeks each child was assessed, and eventually despatched to a long-term placement of some kind.

Reasons for placement in this double-locked, seven-bedded little world were sometimes bizarre in the extreme. One boy, a harmless enough looking lad, was in the habit of collecting together stray dogs from the area around his home and setting them on little girls for 'fun'. I well remember my mother-in-law bravely visiting the unit and chatting to this particular boy for some time. Afterwards, totally unaware of his strange hobby, she said, 'I really can't think why he's in here. He seems a very normal sort of boy. We had a lovely chat about dogs – he's very interested in them, isn't he?'

Another boy, no more than twelve years old, was admitted to the unit after failing in his attempt to kill, by drowning, a little girl of six who had tormented him for a year by calling him 'Fatty' every time they met. His account of how he lay in wait for her, pushed her into a stream, then held her head under the water with his boot until she seemed to be dead, was chilling, to say the least.

Some of the older teenagers, seventeen- or eighteen-year-olds, were hard, unrepentant delinquents, who could never be fully trusted in that environment. There were never fewer than two staff members working with that little group of seven 'visitors', although the atmosphere could actually be very warm and pleasant at times, depending on which staff were working, and the particular mix of kids at the time.

I have such a jumble of memories of that place; moving, grotesque, depressing, all kinds, but one that always comes to mind when I look back at that year and a half is the memory of an incident that might contain a little bit of inbuilt hope for all of us.

It was an evening when an outsider had come into the unit by special arrangement to show the boys how fluffy toys could be quite easily made as presents for mothers or little sisters or girlfriends. Four of the toughest residents had opted for this activity, and were soon deeply absorbed in the sewing and sticking and stuffing of various toy animals. Having made it quite clear to me that their efforts were purely directed towards the happiness of those who would eventually receive the toys as presents, they worked with quite unprecedented care and concentration for the whole session. It was one of those nice, quiet evenings.

Later, when supper had been eaten, and the unit tidied up, each boy washed and went into his single bedroom for the night. It was then my dismal duty to go from room to room, locking the door of each one securely after a brief chat with the occupant. The four boys who had been involved in the toy-making happened to sleep in the same row of four rooms.

In the first one I found that Ben, a villainous and battered fifteen-year-old, had sat his newly assembled squirrel up in bed beside him, and was reading it a goodnight story. I closed the door quietly and moved to the next room.

Sammy, a dangerous and unpredictably violent lad, was just kissing his rabbit goodnight.

In the third room Peter, a genuinely charming fellow who seemed completely unable to refrain from running away and pinching things, was already fast asleep, a little woolly head on the pillow next to his.

In the fourth room was Brett. Brett was certainly not a sentimental type. The grinding difficulty of his early life and clashes with authority figures of various kinds ever since had convinced him that life was a dark and unfriendly jungle, a place where you simply couldn't afford to show any weaknesses at all.

Brett was lying back, staring at the ceiling. The squirrel he had made earlier was dropped carelessly onto the chair beside his bed.

'Your squirrel not going to bed with you then, Brett?' I asked seriously. 'He looks a bit lost lying on the chair there.'

'Don't be daft!' grunted Brett. 'I'm seventeen – I'm not a kid any more.'

'No,' I thought, as I locked the door, 'you haven't been allowed to be a kid for a very long time.'

Half an hour later, when I peered through the little square glass window in Brett's door, I saw two things. First, he was asleep. Secondly, there was a shoe-box on the floor next to the bed. Inside, tucked up cosily beneath tissue paper and a handkerchief, Brett's squirrel slept beside his maker.

What is hopeful about all this? It reminds me that in all the years I worked with children and young adults in trouble, I never met one whose inner child had been completely extinguished. However tough or hardened, there seems to be a part of every individual that could still, potentially at least, respond with the simplicity of a small child, and that is the part of us that God calls to himself, whether it is lost in a city or in a lifestyle.

'Suffer the little children to come unto me,' said Jesus, knowing that many of them are locked up inside people who have not been kids for a very long time.

Sportsday

My children asked me the other day what I enjoy watching most on television. After thinking about it for a bit I realised that the answer was sport in general, and athletics in particular. My special favourite is the relay. There's something about all that bursting energy and the giving of everything in a co-operative effort that really touches me. And it doesn't have to be the Olympics or anywhere near that sort of standard. Nor does it have to be on television of course; live events are always exciting.

It was exactly the same when we used to hold our own sports day at the boarding school for maladjusted boys where I worked many years ago.

What is a maladjusted boy? Well, basically he is someone who is unable to cope with, or adjust to, the situation he is living in, often through no fault of his own. In fact, it would be fair to say that in many cases known to me, the parents were far more maladjusted than their children, and only too happy to project their own unhappiness and disturbance onto a son who could be removed like an amputated limb and despatched to boarding school. Other boys came from homes where parents genuinely loved and cared for their children, but through grindingly negative circumstances had been unable to hold their families together as they would have wished.

The boys at this particular school all came from difficult backgrounds of one kind or another, and they were almost invariably more experienced at losing than winning. Consequently sportsday was a very tense and important occasion, especially as some of the participants would have parents coming along to watch.

We had some incredible characters taking part in these races. I remember one lad called Vincent, a very amiable kid, and the most incompetent criminal in the world. He always got caught, but never seemed to mind very much. He came out on a trip to Bristol in the school van once, together with a couple of the other boys, and cackled loudly and suggestively when we stopped to allow a pregnant girl across the road.

'I don't see what you're laughing about,' I said, 'all the people you can see around us are the products of pregnancy.'

'Oh, I know,' said Vincent, suddenly very earnest, 'I used to live in Bristol.'

Whether he believed that birth through pregnancy was a phenomenon peculiar to that city, or whether he was claiming to have fathered the entire population of Bristol, I was not absolutely sure.

Vincent had never won anything. Fifteen years of being an unwanted extra in his own home had left him with no genuine confidence at all. He had to act big.

Then there were kids like little Donald. Donald was a few years younger than Vincent, but, if anything, he'd probably had it even harder. His dad had knocked him about every day for years, and he'd ended up a bit like Piglet in Winnie the Pooh books, quivering with willingness to please, but very nervous, and sort of wispy to look at. Donald used to go out first thing in the morning to hug the trees, and he quite often wrote letters to himself. He wanted a real friend more than anything else in the world.

I found him once in the boys' telephone room trying to get a bewildered operator to put him through to his father. I tried to help for quite a long time until Donald happened to mention that there was no telephone in his dad's house. Even after I explained, he didn't really understand.

'The other boys phone their dads,' he said, 'why shouldn't I phone mine?'

I did my best to describe the telephone system in as painstaking a manner as possible, but he still remained unconvinced, and clearly thought that some kind of deliberate unfairness had been perpetrated on him. Secretly, I considered it a blessing that he had no easy access to the harsh and uncaring words that he would certainly have heard from his father if that kind of regular contact had been possible.

Donald would love to have won something in the school sports – anything really – preferably with his dad watching. For despite everything that had happened, his father was still the only person whose approval really counted.

It is a matter of record that neither Vincent nor Donald ever did actually win a race on sports day. Vincent was a very tall, skinny lad whose feet stuck out in the quarter past nine position. He ran like a penguin – not a born sprinter.

Donald was not exactly a natural athlete either. When he accelerated his legs seemed to be trying to escape from his body to left and right, while his trunk moved in an averagely straight line. I swear that his ears streamed in the wind like Piglet's when he picked up speed, though.

They never won – but they didn't half try! That's what used to bring the tears to my eyes, the desperate, red-faced, trying to win against all odds. I admired it then, and I admire it now.

There's an awful lot of talk in the Church nowadays about TRIUMPH and OVERCOMING and VICTORY, but that sort of talk often (not always, but far too often) comes from church leaders and speakers who have talents and ambitions and vested interests that leave the Vincents and Donalds of the Christian world puffing away hopelessly at the rear.

One of the things that infuriated people about Jesus was his refusal to enter the kind of political, social or religious races that they wanted him to win. He turned the accustomed social order upside down, too busy with the Vincents and Donalds, the so-called losers, to win other people's races for them.

He is the same now, and the words he used two thousand years ago are a promise for ever to those who try hard, but just can't manage to win.

'**The first shall be last, and the last shall be first.**'

Pistols at Dawn

Earlier this year our house group was divinely inspired (well, we were inspired to decide – oh, all right, it just seemed like a good idea) to study some of the parables. Parables might be broadly defined as stories that keep you entertained on the front door-step while the truth slips in through a side window, and Jesus was of course a master of the genre. There's always something new to be discovered in these expertly crafted little tales.

We opted to begin with the parable of the wheat and the tares which, for those who are interested, is recorded in the thirteenth chapter of Matthew's gospel. In it, we learn how a farmer's enemy secretly sows thistles among his wheat during the night, and how the farmer decides to let the thistles grow until harvest time, because uprooting them might harm the genuine crop. Later in the same chapter Jesus explains to the disciples that the wheat represents the children of the Kingdom, and the thistles are people belonging to Satan, sown by the Evil One to disrupt God's chosen ones.

Naturally, every member of our group is a dazzling example of total transfiguration, but I did wonder, as our discussion progressed along very satisfactorily interesting and stimulating lines, whether any of my fellow pilgrims had experienced, as I had, an involuntary spasm of self-doubt as they listened to the story.

'You're a tare! You're a tare!' screamed the loud voice of my old insecurity. 'Call yourself wheat, you weed? You must be joking!'

'Calm down,' said the quiet voice of kindness and reason. 'You may be a bit stunted and defective in the ear department, but you are wheat. You are *my* wheat. Understand?'

It's taken me a good many years to hear and trust that quiet voice. Goodness knows what I'd do without it nowadays, though.

I don't know if any of the other group members were actually wrestling with inner fears that they might be sons of the evil one, unconsciously planted to do damage to the saints, but I do know that a lot of Christians find it much easier to believe they are condemned than forgiven and wanted. I meet people all the time who have spent their lives feeling guilty about everything under the sun. They probably apologised at birth to their respective midwives for taking up so much valuable time. This particular vulnerability, the tendency to take on the 'Jonah' role in any and every situation, does not make life easy, to say the least.

When my oldest son, Matthew, was a little boy, he went to a small junior school in Norfolk. Mrs Shaw, the headmistress, was small in stature, but a mighty force in the little world that she ruled with awe-inspiring competence and total assurance. One day, Matthew, only just five years old, climbed down from the school van at half past three with a doom-laden expression on his normally cheerful little face. Half an hour and two tear-dampened jam sandwiches later, we knew what the problem was. He had been walking along in the playground that afternoon just before coming home, when he happened to put his hand in his pocket and discovered a coin left over from the weekend. Pulling it out too quickly he lost his grip on the ten pence piece and dropped it onto the tarmac. Immediately he was pounced upon by a representative of that awful race, the 'Big Girls'. She reminded him, probably with a great deal of relish, that Mrs Shaw had said some very cross things last week about children who brought money to school.

'You wait', said the big girl, 'till I tell Mrs Shaw you had some money. You'll be in trouble tomorrow.'

Matthew was petrified. In his mind Mrs Shaw made the Spanish Inquisition look like the Red Cross. Tomorrow was going to be the worst day of his life – and possibly the last. We were quite worried really. Matthew obviously thought that his headmistress was going to kill him. What should we do? After much thought I decided to write a letter to Mrs Shaw, in which I would challenge her to a duel. It was the only thing that sprang to mind. As far as I can recall, it began as follows:

Dear Mrs Shaw

Matthew is terrified that you might kill him in the morning because he accidentally brought money to school with him yesterday. I am therefore challenging you to a duel on the hill overlooking the school. I am happy to allow you the choice of swords or pistols. If you win, then you may punish Matthew's abominable crime in any way that you see fit. If I win, then he remains unpunished . . .

My only worry as I sealed the envelope was that she might accept my challenge. I'm quite sure she would have won.

The letter seemed to do the trick. The head-mistress wrote back to say how much she and the other teachers had enjoyed the letter, but she also commented on how it had made her realise that loud public condemnations aimed at real offenders, might sometimes bring terror to small, innocent people who hadn't quite understood. Mrs Shaw was really quite nice after all.

Some of the statements that Jesus made are very frightening. They were meant to be. He never pulled punches or compromised the truth when something hard needed to be said. But how tender and forgiving he was with individuals who were conscious of their sin. He still is, especially with worried wheat like you and me.

I'm quite sure that when Jesus was here on earth in his physical body, there must have been many small, nervous people who would have tugged the master's sleeve after one of those awesome speeches about hell-fire and gnashing of teeth.

'Err . . . excuse me,' they would have said, 'I don't think I'm going to make it.'

'Don't worry,' he might have replied through the side of his mouth. 'I'll see you later. It's that lot I'm after.'

And 'that lot' were the hypocrites, the pharisees, those who claimed to be getting everything right, the ones who placed impossible burdens on the shoulders of those same small people, who wanted to be good but knew they weren't succeeding.

We do not pray for the rigid justice of Christ, the dislike of God and the unfriendliness of the Holy Spirit to be with all of us. Grace, love and fellowship are the attributes of God that warm us and draw us together. God hates all sin, a fact that he makes abundantly clear, and the law is the law. But when it comes to the crunch, he's almost as nice as Mrs Shaw.

Heads and Hearts

More than thirty-five years ago my grandmother died. For the whole of her married life and since the death of my grandfather, she had lived in a detached house called 'Cabinda' near the top of a hill in the little Sussex town of Heathfield. Next to my parents I loved Nanna more than anyone else in the whole world. She was the only person, for instance, other than Mum and Dad, who was allowed to see me with no clothes on. Travelling the fourteen miles by bus from Tunbridge Wells to visit her was always an enormously thrilling adventure, sometimes I thought my heart would burst with excitement and joy as my mother and I passed through the front gate and caught our first sight of the familiar thin figure waiting to greet us at the door.

When I think about her now a wave of images flood my memory. Her face was a bright light ringed with grey hair, and she always seemed to wear the same green cardigan. She had a spinning top that belonged to my mother when she was little, but still hummed as if it was new. There was a big cardboard box filled with a wonderful assortment of items to make things with, and a drawer full of blown birds' eggs, and a garden that rambled down to a pear orchard at the bottom, and stone hot-water bottles, and a Bible like a pirate's treasure chest with big brass clasps. Nanna always had plans for being nice to people that you could help with, and lots of time to read stories, and things to do in the kitchen that involved using funny old-fashioned tools and containers, and a scullery that was one step down from the kitchen, and a discarded pre-war car in the field beside the house that I used to sit in and pretend to steer. So many memories gathered in such a short space of time.

I was only six years old when Nanna died. It was the age of the stiff upper lip. 'We all have to be very brave,' my mother said, but I couldn't be at all brave when I heard the news. It was like a blow to the head, shocking and painful beyond belief. Almost immediately afterwards, though, a numbness replaced the pain. Somehow, unconsciously, I managed to hold the unwelcome piece of information in the back of my mind without letting it touch or affect my heart, the place where you really believe things.

Some time after Nanna's death I set out one morning to walk the fourteen miles from Tunbridge Wells to Heathfield. At the time I seemed to be motivated by a stubborn determination simply to visit the town that had always been so special in my life, but in retrospect, I am quite sure that I was actually setting out to prove to myself that my grandmother was still alive, whatever anyone said. Armed with fivepence worth of sweets I embarked on my journey. I told my parents where I was going, but, quite reasonably, they didn't take me at all seriously. Children of my age just didn't do things like that. They thought I was playing a game.

All through that day I trudged along the bus route that I knew so well from those countless trips to see Nanna, every now and then eating one of my little stock of sweets, and hoping that it wouldn't be much further.

Meanwhile, my frantic parents had contacted the police, who were searching the area around my home on the assumption that I was lost, or had been abducted from some local spot.

By five o'clock that afternoon, sweetless and weary, I had walked as far as Mayfield, nine miles south of Tunbridge Wells, and still five miles short of Heathfield. It was there that the truth hit me at last. Nanna was dead. There was no point in going on. If I reached Heathfield and walked up the hill, Cabinda would still be there, but it would be no use going through the front gate and knocking on the door because there was nobody to open it any more. Nanna was dead. I turned round and began the long journey back to Tunbridge Wells.

Much later I arrived home to be greeted with overwhelming relief from my parents and a telling-off from the police.

It hadn't been a wasted journey. The truth about my grandmother's death had now made the eighteen-inch journey from my head to my heart. Because of the particular way I was made I had needed my Mayfield walk for that to happen.

We are often painfully insensitive to this need in other people when they appear stubbornly unresponsive to our gospel-spreading endeavours. For many folk it is not just a matter of receiving information about the Christian faith. There often has to follow a journey – emotional, intellectual, spiritual, or all three – which allows that information to become a personal reality in their lives. Stomping around impatiently with size sixteen evangelical boots at this stage is unhelpful, to say the very least.

I am reminded, in this connection, of an incident involving my son David when he was about seven years old. We were on holiday in Wiltshire at the time and visiting a village not too far from Salisbury. As usual we drifted into the parish church and began that slow-motion perambulation peculiar to church explorers. After roaming around for several minutes I came to a small side-chapel. Inside I discovered David, standing with the stillness of deep concentration, in front of an old oil painting of the crucifixion. Peering over the top of my son's head I studied the picture that was so absorbing his attention.

It was not one of those idealised, rather unreal portrayals of Jesus on the cross. The artist had obviously set out to demonstrate the appalling physical suffering that this barbaric punishment inflicted on its victims. The Jesus in this picture was haggard with pain and exhaustion, flecked with blood from the wounds caused by a cruelly depicted crown of thorns, and sweating with malarial profuseness. It was a painting of someone who could only welcome death.

David has been hearing tales and talks and readings about Jesus since he was a baby; about his life, his teaching, his death and his resurrection. The facts about the crucifixion were certainly known to him, but the expression on his face as he turned around and spoke was an unfamiliar one. Shock and compassion filled his voice.

'They didn't half hurt Jesus, didn't they, Dad?'

The knowledge had entered his heart. They really did hurt Jesus, and he really did die on that cross.

But he really did come back to life as well.

Jesus is dead. Nanna is dead. But David and I expect to see both of them again one day.

What Katy Said

The best Easter present I ever had was my daughter Katy.

I must be honest and confess that, far from being planned, our fourth child was what one might term an 'after-not-thought'. Bridget and I already had three sons and we loved them very much, but we very definitely did not want another one. When Bridget discovered that she was pregnant in 1979 it was very hard for her or me to rejoice and be thankful. On the contrary, we felt weary and apprehensive about the prospect of adding yet another infant to our collection. We already felt disorganised enough with three.

Additionally, Bridget was at an age when health problems for mother or child could easily arise during pregnancy, so quite frankly, both of us were frightened and nervous about the whole thing.

As the nine months passed we gradually cranked our attitudes up onto a rather unstable level of optimism, talking with brittle brightness about the baby boy who was due to be born in March. Very rarely did we allow ourselves openly to consider the possibility that it might be a girl. Instead we shrugged, as people do, and said, 'Well, just as long as it's healthy we don't mind what it is'.

I can't speak for my wife, but as far as I was concerned, every repetition of that well-worn cliché was a twenty-four carat lie. I wanted a girl. Oh, how I wanted a girl! By the time that nine months was up, the heavenly in-trays must have been piled high with applications in triplicate, signed by me, and all saying the same thing: 'Let it be a girl!'

The birth took place at about four o'clock on March the ninth. It was hard work for Bridget, but there were no complications. At the moment when the midwife held our fourth child up to be inspected by its mother, Bridget was so geared up to joyful acceptance of a boy-child, that, despite the evidence of her eyes, she cried, 'Oh, the little darling, it's a boy!'

I have made some famous mistakes in my time, but not on this occasion.

'No, Bridget,' I said, checking once more with a quick glance, 'I'm pretty sure that's a girl. . . ."

The midwife agreed, and with a majority verdict against her, Bridget soon changed her opinion.

It was a girl. It was Katy. And what a gift she was. To the three boys, because she quickly became a focus for love and affection. They changed her, they looked after her, they cuddled her and they adored her. They were utterly entranced and captivated by her.

To Bridget, for most of the same reasons, and because having Katy meant that she was no longer stranded in a house full of males.

To me, because something brand new had come into my life. I was one of three brothers, one of them two years older than me, the other two years younger. I knew nothing about little girls and how they grow up. It was enormously exciting to have this small jewel of a person living in the same house as me, sharing my life and teaching me so much. As Katy's personality developed, so the things that she said and did began to suggest all sorts of other ideas and connections.

I recall, for instance, a train journey from Polegate to Brighton when Katy was still very much a baby. As the train approached a tunnel, just after leaving Lewes Station, she put her thumb into her mouth. Our carriage happened to hit the darkness at precisely the same moment. By the light of the sixty-watt bulbs that dully illuminated our carriage, Katy removed her thumb from her mouth and stared at it in amazement.

'Good heavens!' she was obviously thinking, 'all I have to do is stick this in my mouth and the daylight gets switched off!'

The train emerged from the tunnel and, full of expectancy, she popped her thumb in again. Nothing happened of course, but she was un-dismayed. All the way down to Brighton, and all the way back later on, she repeated the experi-ment with little loss of enthusiasm.

I couldn't help but reflect that many de-nominations are founded on less . . . .

Much more recently, in the year when Katy became three, I strolled into the garden one sparkling April morning, to find my diminutive daughter pushing one arm up as far as it would go towards the sky. In her outstretched hand was a single bluebell, newly picked from the border beside the lawn. As she offered her flower to the shining early sun, she identified it with loud ecstasy.

'DAFFODIL!!' she shouted, 'DAFFODI-I-IL!!'

I am as tediously obsessed with accuracy as most parents. I corrected her gently.

'No, darling' I said, 'it's a bluebell.'

Not one inch did she reduce the length of her stretching arm, not one decibel did she lower her volume: 'BLUEBELL!!' she shouted, 'BLUE–BE-E-ELL!!'

Katy's joy was in being part of the morning and having a beautiful flower, not in anything so trivial as being right. She accepted my pedantic correction, but it didn't change anything important.

If only those of us who are Christians were more like Katy in the garden, less concerned with how right we are in our individual emphases and dogmas than with the joy of being one with Jesus.

'YOU HAVE TO SPEAK IN TONGUES TO BE A CHRISTIAN!!' one of us might shout ecstatically.

'No, you don't', God might correct us gently.

'YOU DON'T HAVE TO SPEAK IN TONGUES TO BE A CHRISTIAN!!' we would shout with undiminished joy.

Not long before the incident in the garden I took Katy to a show performed in a nearby hall by a local amateur dramatic society. This year the special attraction for children was an afternoon performance of *The Wizard of Oz*. Katy was excited and a little bit scared. She knew the story well, and liked all the characters except one, the Wicked Witch of the West. This was the character who had sent her scurrying to safety behind an armchair when the story appeared on television in cartoon form. Like most children of her age, Katy was not yet able to separate fact from fantasy in some areas.

Now, as I dressed her in woollies, ready to walk down the road to this live presentation, she tried to reassure herself.

'Daddy,' she said solemnly, 'there won't be a Wicked Witch of the West this time, will there? Eh, daddy?'

'Well, I think there will be, darling,' I admitted, 'but why don't we think of something to say to her when she comes on, so that we won't be scared?'

Katy considered this suggestion seriously for a moment, her brows knitted in concentration. Then her face cleared, 'I know what we'll do,' she said brightly, 'why don't we just say "One – two – three – BOO!" when we see her, then we'll probably be all right, won't we?'

'Sounds good to me, Katy,' I replied, 'let's just practise a few times before we go.'

A little later, word perfect in our defensive ploy, we set off in the exciting darkness to walk to the hall, Katy still whispering 'One – two – three – BOO!' at intervals, just in case the witch might be hiding behind a garden hedge or in the branches of an overhanging tree.

The inside of the hall, when we arrived, was filled with light and noise, lots and lots of children laughing and chattering with their mums and dads. Such a cheerful atmosphere was it that Katy forgot all her earlier fears as she gossiped with acquaintances and contemporaries.

At last, the lights dimmed, the curtains opened, and the show began.

Katy loved it. She pointed everything out to me as if I was blind. There was the little girl called Dorothy, and there, a little later, was the scarecrow, then the tin man, and finally the lion (the 'nice' lion, as Katy hastened to point out). So far, so good, but eventually there came the inevitable moment when a green spotlight was switched on, and the wicked witch appeared, cackling horribly, her long bent nose almost touching her long, bent, wart-covered chin.

Amateur dramatic societies are not always able to produce convincing portrayals of benevolent or morally neutral characters, but when it comes to evil caricatures they really go to town. They did on this occasion. This witch was very unpleasant indeed.

Katy was terrified. Forgetting all about 'One – two – three – BOO!', she dived under my overcoat and pressed against my chest as if she was trying to get right inside my rib-cage. Nothing I could say or do would persuade her to come out until it was absolutely guaranteed that the witch would not reappear.

Later, after the show, she treated my explanation that the witch was just an ordinary lady dressed up with the scorn that it deserved. An ordinary lady is an ordinary lady – a witch is a witch. Silly Daddy!

I wondered, as we arrived home, if it had been a mistake to take Katy at all, but already, as her coat was being removed, she was telling her mum all about the entertainment with great animation. Clearly, the fear was a part of the whole experience, and probably wouldn't do her any harm.

Looking at my daughter a little later as she tucked into her fish-fingers and baked beans, I thought about the Wizard of Oz, and how the story closely reflects what I want for Katy, and what God has always wanted for each of us.

Like the scarecrow, I want her to have a brain that is creative and strong. I would like her to have a heart that is generous and loving, like the tin-man. And, of course, I hope she will be as brave as a lion, especially when the wicked witches of this world appear. I'm sure she'll find something more effective than 'One – two – three – BOO!' with which to defend herself.

Most of all, perhaps, I would like Katy to carry through life the same urgent and excited desire as Dorothy (and, incidentally, the prodigal son); and that is, quite simply, a yearning, in the end, to go home.

Coming Home
A Near-Fatal Encounter

If Jesus decided to pay an extra-curricular visit to claim the accrued royalties on his parables, more than one publisher would disappear in a cloud of holy smoke. Just about every Christian preacher in the world would have to shell out ten per cent of Caesar's own as well. For two thousand years now these sparkling little stories have been used to comment and illustrate and prove and disprove and reinforce and undermine and entertain in an endless variety of publications, pamphlets and sermons.

Take the Prodigal Son, for instance. I began to take a special interest in this character one autumn evening after I had been speaking at a college in Manchester. I was staying in what I can only describe as a grotty hotel room, deep in the heart of some nameless suburb. It was the sort of hotel where they chain the television to a water pipe fifteen feet up the wall so that it can't be easily pinched. It was only possible to see the screen properly by lying flat on my back on the bed, staring up towards the ceiling.

No doubt, on some deep level, I thanked God for my accommodation, but on a superficial and worldly plane I was absolutely cheesed off. Lying there in my rented tomb, almost breaking my neck in an attempt to watch some rubbishy TV programme, I started to have a very bad attack of good old-fashioned homesickness. One by one I pictured the members of my family – Bridget, Matthew, Joseph, David and Rosey the dog. A wave of misery engulfed me as I imagined them all moving and having their being in the warmly familiar surroundings of the house and town where we live.

For a time I ceased to be a complex human being. All that I was or had ever been was concentrated into one yearning desire. I just wanted to go home. I wanted to be in the place where I really belonged, where I slotted into a shape that was *my* shape, a perfect fit through constant use. And it was when that uniquely painful sensation was at its worst that I thought about the prodigal son, ragged among the pigs, suddenly feeling what I was feeling only much more so, and deciding it was time to go back.

The story is so well known now. That feckless lad has been leaving home loaded and light-headed, then returning broke and bowed, over and over again for twenty centuries. Every detail of his briefly-recorded history has been drawn out carefully with the theological tweezers and laid under the bright lights of exegetical study to be examined from all conceivable angles.

The story of his dramatic fall and rise (did you know that 'Prodigal Son' is an anagram of 'No-God spiral?') has brought comfort, repentance and simple understanding to millions of souls over the years, not least because of the eternally heartwarming picture of a God who picks up his skirts and runs with a passion much greater than forgiveness to embrace the miserable broken specimen that used to be his son.

There's no mistaking the joy with which he offers a cloak and a ring where a harsh word and a blow are expected. Then the dash back to the house, the bustle of a hastily-prepared party, and the famous fatted calf feast. An orgy of happiness and relief, too bright to be dulled by the Pharisaical elder son's moaning.

The whole tale is a stunning revelation of God's excited willingness to displace sin with love.

'So what?' you may ask. 'We knew that.' The thing is, lying in that Manchester hotel room, I began to feel rather puzzled. Why do so few church-going people seem to have experienced that joyful collision with God? What about the ring and the cloak and the fatted calf? How come lots of Christians I meet feel that God is graciously but rather distantly allowing them to hang around on the edge of the kingdom on sufferance, instead of showering them with affection and signs of his love?

It's as if God had taken the prodigal back, but treated him according to his self-valuation as a hired servant rather than a son. What goes wrong? Consider this . . . .

The Prodigal Son abandons his job with the pigs, just as in the parable, and sets off towards his father's house, nervous about his reception but determined to go anyway. Not long after the start of this journey he is intercepted on the road by an enthusiastic but deluded individual who has heard only a distorted account of the father's habit of forgiveness.

He doesn't quite believe in it, but he thinks he does, and he'll feel a lot happier when he's not alone.

'Hi!' he greets the trudging penitent. 'Good news – you've been forgiven!'

'Great!' says the prodigal.

'Here you are', says the deluded one, and he wraps an imaginary cloak around the lad's shoulders. He mimes the action of putting a ring on his finger. Together they sit down to eat a nonexistent fatted calf with invisible knives and forks.

'Isn't it wonderful!' he enthuses.

'Oh yes!' responds the prodigal, intensely relieved that he is to be forgiven so painlessly. 'Yes it is!'

They meet regularly for mime sessions. They become very proficient at mime. At last the young man manages to express a growing concern.

'The, er . . . cloak and the ring and the calf – they're not actually, er . . . real, are they?'

His lack of faith is rebuked and disciplined. He feels guilty and unhappy. He knows the things are not really there, and he doesn't actually feel forgiven. Where is the father?

Eventually he either settles for the troubled half-life of tediously repetitive mime sessions, or he goes back to the pigs; or, if he's got any sense, he leaves his mime instructor behind and moves on down the road to risk a genuine encounter with his father, who is anxiously awaiting him with a real cloak, and a real ring, and a real fatted calf.

And real forgiveness . . . .

Death by Atrophy

The 'mime' thrives where religious activities are atrophied and conducted only out of a sense of duty.

Jesus wasn't interested in captive audiences. He didn't need to be. The people heard him gladly. So gladly did they hear him that thousands of them forgot to make lunch arrangements on at least two occasions because they were so captivated by the things he said and the way he said them. It didn't matter about food. The loaves and the fishes turned up, and Jesus was very resourceful when it came to trivial essentials.

Is it foolish and shortsighted to ask why the Body of Christ on Earth – the Church – demonstrates so little of this natural drawing power nowadays? Why are so many Christian communities locked into the monotonous repetition of those 'mime' sessions that I mentioned in the last section? You do see a Christ-like attractiveness in some groups and individuals: famous ones like Billy Graham, and completely unknown ones like a little old lady who lives half a mile from me. People like this attract without bribe or coercion because the life of Christ has become an indistinguishable part of *their* lives. They glow unselfconsciously.

Perhaps that's the problem with our religious activities, that we allow the sacred and the secular to become unhealthily separate. Take Bible study and prayer groups for instance. Malcolm Muggeridge once said that the Church is man's way of keeping God at bay. An exaggeration perhaps, but well illustrated in many home-groups that I've experienced, where such exercises as Bible study, prayer and hymn/chorus singing actually act as walls to prevent the wind of the Spirit from blowing change and adventure in people's lives. And it happens in every kind of denominational setting, from very traditional to very modern.

My own denomination, the Church of England, is far from guiltless in this respect. Revival has come to many parts of the anglican world, but we are still prone to be rather stiff and resistant to necessary change.

There comes a point in the communion service, for instance, where, in many anglican churches, a strange tension creeps into the atmosphere, a tension compounded of fear and apprehension. A Martian or a Baptist would be very puzzled. What could possibly be causing the clammy palms, the nervous glances to left and right, the troubled shifting from foot to foot, the shallow breathing, the white-knuckled grip on the service book?

The answer, of course, is that the congregation is about to be encouraged to 'Exchange The Peace'. A friend of mine tells me that every muscle in her body tenses when this moment arrives. 'Well, I'm not hugging *him*,' she mutters to herself as she glances at her left-hand neighbour, 'and I'm certainly not kissing *her*! A couple of handshakes and a quick mumble and that's my lot – back to pretending to read the service book!' I realise that a great many people *do* enjoy the Peace, but an awful lot of others are still going through an unfreezing process. Habits die very hard in religious communities, including bad habits.

Have you, for example, ever been in the following kind of House Group or Bible study meeting?

Leader: (*Nervously*) Right – well I've got the vicar's/pastor's/elder's questions here, and we've just read the passage, so here goes. (*Reads from a sheet of paper.*) Do we think the leper was er,

pleased or er, upset to be healed?
(*Pause as everyone drops into the shampoo position to study their fifteen different versions of the Bible and find the answer to the question 'in the text'.*)

Doris: (*Uncertainly, with her finger keeping the place in her Bible*) Er . . . I think he was pleased.

Leader: (*Nodding impartially*) Hmm . . . interesting. Er . . . Richard – any thoughts?

(Pause)

Richard: (*Bent frowningly over the passage*) Er . . . I think he was *very* pleased.

Leader: (*Nods slowly for a few seconds as if turning over these responses in his mind*) Okay . . . right . . . well, I think we've probably gone about as far with that as we can go.

Such a meeting will then proceed to a bone-shatteringly tedious time of prayer, during which numerous half-hearted requests twitter uselessly against the brass heavens and flutter back to earth unanswered. Finally, there is only Mrs Bissington's elbow to be prayed for before the 'religious' part of the evening is properly concluded. At last, the elbow is duly interceded for by some public-spirited volunteer, the Grace is said with a sincerity fuelled mainly by relief, and all those present relax into the blessedly natural atmosphere of 'coffee and biscuits time'. If only some of the warmth and energy of this latter period could have crept into the 'God bit' earlier. Perhaps if the group had allowed their spiritual activities to grow out of relationship with God and each other, instead of vaguely assuming that such things were obligatory from week one, the quality of the whole meeting might have been quite different by now. An awful lot depends on leadership that is secure enough to explore, and wait, and build patiently, and see God's hand in *everything* that happens.

Deadly Dim-Dominant

Negative and atrophied leadership styles are by no means confined to the traditional denominations. In those churches where spontaneity is much more carefully organised, the incessant need to maintain an optimum spiritual blood temperature can result in some strange behaviour.

I have quoted elsewhere (and it is an entirely authentic quote) the worship leader who, carried away by his own enthusiasm, told his congregation that, after the next chorus, he wanted to hear a 'spontaneous round of applause'.

That kind of thoughtless comment arises, more often that not, from a fear that things are not 'buzzing' spiritually in the way that one might expect if God was really present in the service or meeting. Insecure leaders will occasionally project their fears onto those they are leading. I once knew a church elder who almost invariably stopped the service, usually in the middle of a chorus, to announce that he sensed a 'spirit of heaviness' in the room, that was preventing people from worshipping freely.

His confidence could only be restored by something blatantly spiritual happening, preferably accompanied by tears of grief, relief or repentance on the part of some co-operative individual. (Tears have always been rather popular in some sections of the Christian world, perhaps because the release of emotion in one person reduces the pressure on all the others.) I'm certainly not suggesting that the Holy Spirit doesn't or can't work in situations like that, but inciting others to produce spiritual-type behaviour as a means of reassuring ourselves is surely not terribly constructive.

I have already suggested that religious activities such as Bible study and prayer can actually keep God out of small group situations. This happens especially when such activities have not grown out of relationship, and where (particularly in the kind of church I've just been describing) the leader is unable or unwilling to allow genuine discussion.

Let me introduce you, for example, to a character called Mister Dim-Dominant, or DD for short.

DD has been selected to lead a housegroup mainly on the basis that he says the right things in the right sort of religious language.

In public his air of assurance is so great that some people slip into a miserable awareness of their own spiritual inadequacy for as long as they're in his orbit. Highly intelligent or well educated people are particularly vulnerable in this respect.

Somehow DD manages to convey that his shining persona is made possible by the light of the Spirit passing directly through a heart and mind unshadowed by the dark forms of knowledge and reasoning power.

'My knowledge', DD seems to be saying, 'is supernatural in origin. Lay down your flimsy, worldly tools of intellect and creativity, and I will instruct you.'

The truth about DD is that he is neither as naïve, nor as spiritual, as he appears. He has simply discovered a role which glosses over some yawning cracks in his faith, life and temperament.

In the meantime, rather unfortunately, he has been placed in a position of leadership and authority over a group of Christians who need more solid help than he is able to offer. DD's housegroup is not a happy affair. It usually consists of everyone sitting in a circle miserably telling each other how good God is, and how rotten they all are.

DD, with his crinkly smile and air of assurance, is like a small, one-bar electric fire at which the group members attempt to de-ice their frozen faith.

DD maintains his dominance through well-orchestrated discussion sessions. In the following example he has pinned a large rectangle of white paper to the wall by his chair, and a black marker-pen is poised in his hand.

DD: (*Nodding significantly and smiling insightfully at members of the group.*) Okay! Now, we're going to have a real old brainstorming session. I've got a question for us to think about, and I'll just stick the answers up on the wall here. Okay?
(*The group makes a noise like a herd of depressed cattle, indicating agreement.*)

DD: Okay, and here's the question. Who is Jesus?
(*Dismal silence*)

FRED: (*Meekly, knowing he's almost sure to be wrong.*) Er . . . He's the Messiah?

DD: (*Showing pastoral kindness to Fred.*) Yep! Okay! He's the Messiah . . . (*Writes* Messiah *in tiny letters at the edge of the paper*) . . . but, Who is Jesus?
(*Dismal silence*)

MARY: (*Not very hopefully.*) He's the Saviour.

DD: (*Writes* Saviour *in even tinier letters at the edge of the paper.*) Mmm . . . yes, he's the Saviour . . . (*in deep, meaningful, authoritative tones*) . . . but Who is Jesus?
(*Beams around with shining, questioning eyes.*)

BOB: (*Trying to hurry along the coffee and biscuits.*) Is he the mighty counsellor?

DD: (*Writes* mighty counsellor *in minute letters along the top edge of the paper.*)

251

Thanks Bob, he's the mighty counsellor, but . . . (*puts his bottom lip between his teeth in an expression of
fatherly, playful chiding*) . . . come on
folks – WHO IS JESUS?

BRENDA: (*Preset for failure.*) He's not the Son of
God, is he?

DD: (*Delighted and thrilled.*) The Son of
God! Jesus is the son of God! (*Writes
THE SON OF GOD in huge letters that
cover the paper on the wall.*) Jesus is the
Son of God! What's Jesus . . .'?
(*DD conducts with his arms as the group
recites the correct answer like a class of
infants learning their tables.*)

GROUP: Jesus-is-the-Son-of-God.

DD: I think that's from the Lord!

In junior schools this is called 'focused questioning'. It is heavily discouraged by those who
train teachers. Why is it all right in the Church?

Mister Dim-Dominant is not malicious, just
misguided.

But when leadership of this kind is allowed to
continue, a lot of people can get hurt and
confused.

The example I've given portrays a caricature –
but only just!

Breakage in the Pickle Aisle

Outsiders are unlikely to be attracted by church
communities which are stuck in the 'mime'
situation.

252

Some time ago I walked into a supermarket to buy a pound of sugar. It was one of those huge places where shoppers drift trance-like, with wild eyes, down the wide aisles as strange music softly plays. Ghastly – and fascinating.

As I set off to hunt down the sugar (supermarkets 'hide' the sugar for obvious commercial reasons) I noticed a huge sign hung above the tills. Its message was printed in large, vivid, red lettering This is what it said:

CROSSROADS VALUES CUSTOMER CO-OPERATION. WE WOULD BE WARMLY GRATEFUL IF SHOPPERS COULD REPORT BREAKAGES OR SPILLAGE IN THE AISLES. THANK YOU!

I registered this information vaguely as I trailed dismally around the store searching for my humble purchase, but just after I discovered the sugar (tucked away between toilet rolls and garden compost) I remembered it with sudden clarity, for there, in front of me, lay a beauty of a breakage or spillage. A big fat jar of Piccalilli sauce, the yellow glutinous stuff with chunks of something-or-other in it, had fallen on to the floor where it had burst like a huge ripe fruit. The resultant mess, a yellow, glass-littered sludge, was quite spectacular.

'Time', I said to myself, 'for a bit of customer co-operation. Here's where I earn some of that warm gratitude.'

Clutching my pound of granulated, I made my way unerringly to the 'Twelve items or less' queue, anxious to report my discovery. Idly, I found myself counting the purchases in the basket held by the lady in front of me. 'One – two – three – four . . .'' The discovery that she had thirteen items to pay for filled me with a quite irrational fury. For some reason, taking thirteen things through the 'Twelve items or less' exit seemed, at that moment, a much greater crime than murder or genocide.

I wanted to proclaim loudly to the whole world the depths to which human nature was capable of sinking. But I didn't. Instead, I contented myself with imagining the warm gratitude with which my co-operative gesture would be greeted. At last, the criminal in front of me having accomplished her evil designs, I arrived at the front of the queue and paid my money to the female cashier, a girl who looked as if she might have just passed her ninth birthday.

Then, with what I considered to be rather suave nonchalance, I proceeded to co-operate.

'Oh, by the way,' I said, 'there's a big jar of Piccalilli all over the floor round the corner there, in the pickle aisle. I just thought – you know – I ought to tell you.'

Without a single word or change of expression the girl jabbed her thumb against the button beside her. A bell rang somewhere in the distance. She waited, her eyes wide with bored vacancy. I had the uncomfortable feeling that I had ceased to exist. Eventually, a young man wearing a little green trilby and a bow-tie of similar shade arrived at the till with an expression of mechanical enquiry on his face. He was much older than the girl – fifteen at least judging by his moustache.

'What?' he said.

The girl spoke, her words emerging in little leaden lumps of weary exasperation.

'Customer complainin' about a breakage in the pickle aisle.'

The young man, clearly a master of verbal economy, emitted a single grunt, which managed to express annoyance, impatience, and scornful distaste for the whole pathetic customer race. He started to move away.

In most situations of this kind I am rendered impotent by the disease of politeness. Sometimes, when our car comes back from the garage in as bad or worse condition than it went in, I swear to my wife that *this* time I'm really going to give them a piece of my mind.

'This time', I snarl, 'they're going to get the rough edge of my tongue! I'm going straight up there and I'm gonna tell 'em!'

Breathing threats and imprecations I stride up to the garage full of angry lion-like confidence. As I walk in through the door, though, something happens. I turn into a sheep.

'Hello, there!' I bleat cheerily, 'the old car's playing up again. Not your fault, of course. I just wondered if I could pay you some more money to fix it again. Ha-ha-ha! What a silly old life, eh . . .?'

This time it was different. I was too annoyed to be polite. I wanted my warm gratitude.

'Excuse me!' I said, catching up with him, 'I wasn't complaining, I was co-operating. It says up there' – I pointed – 'that you will be warmly grateful to customers who report breakages or spillage in the aisles. That's what I've done. Now, how about a bit of warm gratitude?'

He stared at me for a moment, searching for words with which to seal this unexpected breach in the surrounding wall of his small world. His reply, when it came, was triumphant.

'Well, you don't have to clear it up, do you?'

So stunned was I by this startling piece of non-logic that I couldn't think of anything else to say.

'Breakage in the pickle aisle!'

The cry rang out from the bow-tied one, and was taken up and passed on with ever-decreasing volume until it could be heard only very faintly somewhere in the bowels of the shop. Finally, a diminutive member of the shop staff (probably a university student on vacation) arrived with a selection of cleaning implements and attacked the problem, muttering as he did so about 'people who make trouble for other people'.

'So who,' I asked myself later, 'actually meant what was said on that sign over the tills?'

Perhaps if the managing director of Crossroads had been present when I 'co-operated', he might have shaken me by the hand and formally thanked me on behalf of the board of directors for my wonderfully public-spirited act. But he wasn't there, and clearly no one else was prepared to represent him.

I fear that many churches have exactly the same problem as that branch of Crossroads. The huge sign that hangs over the church – the Bible – promises love and healing and adventure and miracles and dynamism and involvement in an urgent rescue operation. Too often it is impossible to find people who will represent the promises that Jesus made. He still keeps those promises in all who genuinely follow him. How sad that so many outsiders who venture past the portals of their local church are greeted with the equivalent of that young shopworker's query – 'What?'

We'd better be careful. Our managing director will make his next visit without any warning.

Happiness

Can we expect to find lasting happiness?

I'm afraid this is not a subject that my family readily associates with the grumpy recluse who squats in his caravan at the bottom of the garden, getting more and more irritable as he tries and fails to write something funny. From a distance, I am told, I look like a caged muppet.

The gap between public and private presentation has always been a problem for Christian communicators.

My wife, Bridget, for instance, is all too aware that she is married to an average Christian whose job happens to involve exposure to the public through books and broadcasting and speaking

engagements of various kinds. Those of us who *do* stand on platforms to bleat at others tend to get a bit carried away at times. We are so anxious to give God a good reference, as it were, and so fearful that the humble crumbs of our Christian experience will not be sufficiently nourishing for the baby birds who wait, open mouthed, to be fed, that we inflate the truth, not realising that in the process it may become hollow and insubstantial. At least, that's what happens to me, and the temptation is upon me again today, even as I write this.

Can we find lasting happiness?

'Of course we can!' whispers the neurotic professional Christian in me. 'Tell 'em! Tell 'em! All you have to do is ask Jesus into your life, pray, read the Bible, go to church, be nice to your mother and you'll be happy for ever and ever, amen, hallelujah, praise the Lord! Go on – tell 'em! You'll be letting God down if you don't!'

But a moment's reflection suggests that I'll be letting God down if I do. I know lots of Christians, all of varying denominational shapes and sizes, each one a different, but essential part of the body of Christ; some of them, me included perhaps, those 'odd parts' that Paul talks about in Corinthians.

Now, if I'm absolutely honest, the thing that all these people have in common is *not* happiness. Many of them, an awful lot of them, are living and trying to cope with hurts, and problems in relationships, and illness, and doubt, and conflict, and personal failure, just as much as they are enjoying the more positive aspects of life and faith. Of course it may just be that I happen to know a particularly unfortunate load of Christians – but I don't think so. The thing they do have in common is that they are human beings who are trying to follow Jesus.

Let us look at Jesus for a moment – God, but also a human being, who was once described as 'a man of sorrows'. It is a matter of record that Jesus experienced grief, anger, hunger, weariness and, when the disciples failed to stay awake at Gethsemane, a profound disappointment that they had let him down. Again at Gethsemane, he sweated drops of blood as he agonised over the choice between life, which must have seemed very sweet to him, and a horrible death, for him the inevitable consequence of obedience. Later, on

the cross, Jesus learned for the first time in his life
what rejection and despair really meant.

'My God, my God, why have you forsaken
me?' can hardly be described as the cry of a happy
man.

The apostle Paul fared no better. In the
course of his ministry to the Gentiles he was
shipwrecked, imprisoned, starved, beaten, re-
viled and finally executed – probably beheaded
by his Roman captors. Stephen was stoned to
death. Peter was crucified upside down – at his
own request.

Leaping the centuries to our own time, I have
a friend called Mike, a Christian, who was recently married for the second time. His first marriage failed largely through his wife's inability to
accept the inconveniences and demands of a successful acting career. She left him eventually and
later they were divorced. Mike was devastated by
this failure, and not at all comforted by the fact
that, whereas God seemed happy to extend forgiveness to all concerned, some of his fellow
worshippers certainly didn't. He changed
churches, and a couple of years later fell in love
with and married his present wife. Very shortly
after their wedding she developed a chronically
debilitating form of arthritis which has prevented
her from working or walking without the aid of
sticks ever since. Not a happy situation on the face
of it. Rather, the contrary.

My friend Philip Illot, an anglo-Catholic priest
whose biography I have been privileged to write,
has suffered throughout his life. Through his

ministry people have been healed, miracles have happened, amazing events have been witnessed; yet he has gone through a succession of appalling experiences beginning with abuse as a small child, and continuing to this day with emotional and physical trauma and hardship that are in stark contrast with the relief and healing he has so often brought to other people.

Now, before we go any further, I'm well aware that certain spiritual brothers and sisters, particularly, perhaps, members of that fast-growing denomination 'The Holy and Apostolic True Church of the Abundant Revelation of Living Stones' will be just aching to tell me a) that Jesus, Paul, Stephen, Peter, my friend Mike, and Philip Illot must have experienced plenty of happy occasions as well as the rotten ones – well, that's probably true; and b) that even when they *were* feeling unhappy, a sense of inner joy, the joy of the Lord, would have been present at the same time. This response has become one of the greatest and most oft-repeated clichés of the Christian faith, and, like most clichés, it has its roots in the truth. Jesus is quoted in John's gospel as saying: 'Peace I leave with you; my peace I give to you; not as the world gives do I give to you. Let not your hearts be troubled, neither let them be afraid.'

Jesus was offering the 'shalom' peace, that sense of well-being and wholeness that comes from the knowledge that one loves and is loved by God; a peace that cannot be disturbed by worldly hardship or suffering; and, as countless folk can witness, it really does exist, and it really can sustain our spirits inwardly when things get rough on the outside. The problem with the clichéd, simplistic expression of this great truth, is that there are times in the lives of nearly all the Christians I know when suffering is so intense or prolonged that they lose their peace and have to fly, as it were, on automatic pilot. Whether or not this ought to be a fact isn't very relevant, because it *is* a fact. People *do* get troubled, and they *do* become afraid. At such times they are not happy.

The answer to our original query about lasting happiness may lie in the consideration of two other questions:

(1) Why do people continue to follow Jesus *despite* suffering and unhappiness, and (2) What, ideally, does following him really mean?

The answer to the first question seems to lie in relationship. Jesus endured the sorrows and agonies of the world, not out of theological or nationalistic loyalty, not because of some vague personal philosophy about the efficacy of suffering, and not only because of the benefits that his death and resurrection would bring to mankind; but because, with a passion too deep for us to comprehend, he really did love his father so much that he was prepared to be obedient way, way beyond the point where it started to hurt. In his heart he knew that lasting happiness lay in the perfect preservation of a relationship that meant everything to him.

About his disciples he prayed: 'Father, I desire that they also whom thou hast given me, may be with me where I am' and therein, I suggest, lies the motivation for Paul, Stephen, Peter, my friend Mike and his wife, and Philip Illot. They are all prepared to follow Jesus to the place where he is, through failure, triumph, ecstasy, despair, certainty and doubt, not because they are driven by a misty, theoretical religious instinct, but because, in the end, they want to be with him; and they want to be with him because they love him and are fascinated by him; and they know that, ultimately, it is only with Jesus that lasting happiness will be found.

My friend, Mike, for instance, tells me that although his wife's illness is a heavy burden for them both to bear, and although it does cause them both a lot of unhappiness, their relationship with each other and with Jesus is such that their over-all calm and optimism is quite inexplicable to those who see only the tragedy in their situation.

The answer to the second question, about what following really means, might be divided into 'doing', and 'being with'.

What do I mean by 'doing'?

I fear that modern pharisaism, like ancient pharisaism, would have us believe that the Christian approach to life is a very negative one – a list of don'ts. And, of course, Jesus did make it abundantly clear that God hates sin and finds any and every expression of it totally unacceptable. But Jesus' entry into the world brought Grace, and a new perspective on the problem of sin.

In the twenty-second chapter of Matthew's gospel we find Jesus lopping off the negative commandments from the original ten, to leave only two – the ones that begin with the words 'Thou shalt. . . .'

'Thou shalt love the Lord thy God with all thy heart and with all thy soul and with all thy mind.' And secondly: 'Thou shalt love thy neighbour as thyself.'

'On these two commandments,' says Jesus, 'depend all the law and the prophets.'

In other words, the 'shalt nots' are swallowed up in the 'shalts'. Later in the same book he tells the parable of the sheep and the goats. The sheep get into heaven because they have visited the sick and imprisoned, clothed the naked and fed the hungry, not because they have not got drunk, or not fornicated, or not been covetous. The positive Gospel of Jesus Christ says that we will be justified by our faith in him, and that *that* faith will result in us doing things on God's behalf for the benefit of others. Constant, neurotic, spiritual and moral self-analysis is not usually very relevant in this context. The narrow path that Jesus speaks of elsewhere is the way of loving, caring – doing. Sins are the seductive gateways off the path on to the broad and easy road of not loving, not caring, doing nothing.

As well as the 'doing' there is the 'being with'. We shall not want to follow Jesus unless we know him well enough to think him worth following. I'm talking about prayer, but a great deal of prayer is simply friendship, and God desires our friendship more than we can imagine. Having said that, I know only too well how prayer and Bible study can become dry and difficult to maintain. That is a whole other subject really, and a very important one, but there is one practical way of establishing or re-establishing this friendship with God, that has worked for a lot of people.

Take the gospels – or one of the gospels, John perhaps – clear your mind as much as you possibly can of everything you thought you knew about what Jesus did or said, then read the book and find out what he really *did* say and do. The result can be quite a shock, and if you keep your spiritual ears open you may be surprised at how much the Holy Spirit speaks to you through your discoveries. If you feel you want to answer back, and a dialogue gets going – well, you're praying.

Someone once said that we should pray as if prayer was the only thing that worked, then work as if work was the only thing that worked. It sounds a pretty good recipe to me, as long as we allow some space for a few miracles.

I doubt whether most of us are able truly to find lasting happiness in this world. There are those who, either because of their particular temperament or because they walk specially closely with God, enjoy a consistent contentment and peace. They make wonderfully good ambassadors for the Christian faith; but I also believe that for all of us, at our different stages and in our different states, it is possible, between and around and through the trials and tribulations that beset us, to taste the joy of heaven, and that there, in heaven, our happiness will be unalloyed and eternal.

I must confess that I get very low sometimes; that's the effect of my temperament; but when people say to me, 'How can you be so low when you're a Christian? Why don't you abandon Jesus?' my response is very similar to that of the disciples two thousand years ago when all but that small band had deserted him.

'Where else would I go? He has the words of eternal life – and happiness.'

Football
Joe

No one who witnessed it in 1989 will ever forget the disaster in the Hillsborough Football Stadium when ninety-five people were crushed to death. One of them was a ten-year-old boy. There must have been many fathers who like me, on that awful day, looked at their own ten-year-old sons and appreciated their value even more than before.

My Joseph was ten at the time. He was, and still is, definitely a one-off. Joe is a quirky, sensitive character, full of complicated thoughts and feelings, but not a great chatterer like the others, until you get him on his own, that is. He's not as physically demonstrative as the other three either, perhaps, but when he does come and put his arms round you and kiss you on the cheek, it feels like an enormous privilege, something really special.

Joe eats, sleeps and breathes football. He plays it, he watches it, he has an encyclopaedic knowledge of it that is far in advance of my own. He happens to support Manchester United (a team some of you may have heard of), but it's the game of football itself that he loves more than any individual team. On the Saturday of the Hillsborough tragedy, at tea-time, our family prayed for everyone who was bereaved or hurt by the things that happened at the Liverpool-Nottingham Forest match, and Joe's 'amen' came straight from the heart. He cared.

The other thing about Joe is that, like my other children, he's done more to help me understand myself in relation to God than almost anyone or anything else. Take the whole business of repairing friendship, for instance. I love Joe very much, but he's capable of making me more angry than just about anyone in the entire world. I suspect that's because he's not able to pretend or play games about relationships. He just responds as he feels, and if I've been very busy, or away from home a lot, he tends to retreat into himself and present me with a rather blank face and a total absence of those special cuddles that I mentioned earlier. If I'm feeling guilty about my absorption in activities that take up family time, I'm quite likely to get very angry when this happens. If the

pattern is then repeated a few times my relationship – my friendship – with Joe dries up almost
completely. It just atrophies. And then, somehow, the friendship has to be repaired. The question is – how?

Now, you can't buy Joe's goodwill with *things*.
You could present him with bicycles, radios,
stereo units, footballs, anything you like. He'd
accept them and enjoy having them like any kid
of his age, but it wouldn't restore the relationship.
So that's no good.

Another thing that doesn't work is cheap, brief
expressions of affection or interest in the world
that he specially inhabits. Taking a few seconds
out of one's busy life to communicate a superficial
involvement in Joe's preoccupations cuts no ice at
all.

This presents particular problems to people
like me who, unfortunately, tend towards manip-
ulative control of others as opposed to whole-
hearted involvement. We learn our 'tricks' young,
and it can be quite a shock to discover that the
ones we usually find most useful, are no use at all
with folk like Joe.

Take sulking for instance.

Sulking doesn't work with Joe. He doesn't
notice it. This is a shame, because if there's one
thing I'm an expert in, it's making other people
feel guilty when I've done something wrong. If
ever sulking is included in the catalogue of Olympic sports I'm pretty well guaranteed a place on
the winners' podium. Gold or silver medal at the
very least.

I'm particularly proud of a rather fine shuddering sigh that's taken some years to perfect. When timed correctly it can actually confuse my wife into apologising to me for something that *I've* done! It hints at deep, incalculable hurt, or secret knowledge of impending tragedy, bravely borne for the sake of others. I have toyed with the idea of patenting this effect and instructing others in its use, possibly by correspondence course – it really is *so* effective, but it only works with selected people, and Joe is definitely not one of them.

Anger is a waste of time. It has the effect of reducing tension in me, but it makes no real impact on him, he simply retreats even further into himself and the situation is then worse than before.

There's only one way to repair a friendship with Joe. I know – I've done it a few times now. You have to go right into his world, committed to using plenty of what is nowadays called 'Prime Time' to be with him, genuinely involved with his interests, proving how much you value him by abandoning distractions for a significant period.

In practice this usually means a Saturday spent going into the local town – Eastbourne in our case – having lunch in some cafe, looking round the shops together, buying one or two quite small things, and talking *properly*; Joe chats like mad when you take him out on his own. What it really amounts to is just being together in a *real* way. One day like this is usually enough to get things back on a proper footing. After that it's a matter of ensuring that regular genuine contact is happening.

I realised some time ago that my relationship with God is very similar. It's no good me moaning about feeling separated from him if I'm not spending prime time with him; talking to him; listening to him; showing I love him enough to get involved. You can't buy God's friendship with good works. Superficiality, sulking and anger are no use. God is like Joe. He wants me to make real friends with him. It can be costly (it is with Joe), and I don't always manage it by any means, but I can tell you that it makes all the difference in the world.

The Inter-Denominational World Cup

With a house full of football fanatics like mine, 1990 was inevitably a very significant year. World Cup fever gripped most of us for the duration of the tournament in Italy.

To celebrate this major event, I include the following report on a rather less well-known tournament:

Commentator: Good evening and welcome to the inter-denominational football cup. We're halfway through the competition now; and we've already had some marvellous encounters in this exciting seven-a-side tournament.

Beginning with a sparkling

contest between the Strict and Particular Baptists – they're the ones who insist on showering before the match – and the lenient and not very fussy at all Baptists – they're the ones who would shower if they could remember what it was for in the first place.

Fascinating during that match to look around the arena and see other teams limbering up and waiting for their matches to begin. The Greenbelt team dribbling quietly in the corner, one of the Roman Catholic substitutes being given the reserve sacrament over at the rail, and John Wimber being offered a contract by one of the English teams; he doesn't quite know what's going on, he just signs and wonders. It's all happening here tonight.

The following match was a real humdinger between the Spring Harvest side – four centres but very little defence – and the anglo-catholic team, whose game is based largely on the use of high crosses and some very ornate setpieces. The Spring Harvest side took an early lead after Graham Kendrick took the ball the length of the pitch, shouting 'Make way!

Make way!', but the anglo-catholics fought back in the second half, assisted by the wind and the fact that they were now playing in the direction of Rome.

Other matches: The Church of England versus Methodist battle was postponed because, although the captains agreed on the rules, the other team members weren't so sure. Once they did get going it was dazzling stuff, except at the point when the Church of England captain stopped to read the notices just as a goal was about to be scored. Shortly after that one of the players was injured – Colin Urquhart ran on to the pitch with a wet sponge (unidentified as yet), only to be told by the injured Methodist that he wasn't sure he was ready yet for Revival.

The Pentecostal team, who reached the tournament finals by a process of Elim-ination, managed to overcome the House Church team, and were ecstatic. Experts agreed that the House Church side would have done a lot better if they hadn't all played with their arms in the air and their eyes closed. They were also penalised twice for moving the goalposts and marching around the edge of the pitch claiming victory for the Lord.

Impressive combination play by the U.R.C. team, although they were disqualified in the end for dangerous and illegal use of zimmers. A pity this, as they would have easily defeated the Bishop of Durham's private team, which, despite hard work and some very fancy footwork, scored a number of own goals, and insisted that the referee was only present in a symbolic sense.

The Famous Christian team, very popular here tonight, especially at the moment when their captain, Cliff Richard, after spending much of the evening shooting wide of the posts, sang frustratedly into his opponents' goal:

'But these miss-you nights are the longest . . .'

Terrific cheering now as the next match gets under way, and it could be a rather difficult one, two anglican synod sides, one in favour of allowing women to play, and the other not. The Archbishop of Canterbury, amazingly, attempting to captain both teams.

(LOUD CHEERS)

Great excitement here behind me! Let's find out what's going on from one of the supporters. (APPROACHES ONE) Why the big cheer?

Supporter: (WITH RABID EXCITEMENT) Yeah, one of the synod teams just passed a resolution agreeing in principle that a passing movement would be initiated, that might, in the context of

	sensitive awareness of popular response, eventually culminate in the scoring of a goal!
Commentator:	Electrifying! Well, that's where we have to leave it, I'm afraid. The final? Well, predictions suggest a clash between the fundamentalists and the liberals and that's one that's bound to be settled in the midfield. A final comment, endorsed by the managing director of our sponsor – Divine Products. Remember that denominations is an anagram of 'not made in Sion'. Goodnight.

A Professional Foul

There seems to be a fashion nowadays for exploding popular myths about famous events and people, past or present, living or dead. You know the sort of thing I mean, don't you?

The gunfight at the O.K. Corral was actually a game of tiddly-winks.

Genghis Khan was a home-loving, gentle type, with a talent for social work.

St Francis of Assisi regularly used his bird-charming skills to assemble the ingredients for pigeon pie.

No doubt scholarship will soon reveal that Winston Churchill was a German spy, Columbus was a chronic agoraphobic, Florence Nightingale was a poisoner, and Jack the Ripper's murders were definitely committed by Queen Victoria, sneaking around the East End on stilts with a bag full of knives.

Public figures are observed and examined by the Media of this age in a way that was impossible previously. Perhaps our discovery that nearly all idols have feet of clay has produced a sort of corporate resentment in us. If we can't have the kind of heroes that we want, then we're jolly well going to debunk all the ones that previous generations ignorantly elevated to super-star status!

Nevertheless, we still preserve a small stock of present-day heroes, and, presumably because they are few in number, we get very upset when our respect or admiration is shown to be misplaced.

Take the case of a certain professional footballer, famed as a Manchester United and England player, but also highly respected for an on-pitch behaviour record that was not blemished by a single instance of either being sent off or displaying rowdy behaviour – a real gentleman of the game.

Then, one morning, a daily newspaper devoted most of its back page to reporting a public statement by this same player, in which he stated quite openly that when a (euphemistically termed) 'professional foul' was the only way to stop an opposing player, he did not hesitate to use it. (A professional foul is one where a piece of deliberately illegal behaviour is disguised so as to appear blameless.)

This honest admission produced quite a reaction, not just from the footballing establishment, but from ordinary supporters as well. People like their heroes intact. This is, of course, very unfair on any ordinary human being – perfect people are rather few and far between.

I happened to be travelling on a train from London to Polegate when I read this 'shock-horror' revelation, and as I finished the article, I folded my newspaper, put it on the seat beside me, and gazed out of the window, lost in thought.

Leaving aside the ins and outs and rights and wrongs of the particular instance I had just read about, what, I wondered, were the kinds of 'professional foul' or its equivalent that I used in my own life? How might other people's perceptions of me change, if I opened up in the way that this footballer had done?

I don't think it would be appropriate to describe here some of the grimmer little ploys that I recognised as vices I had managed to disguise as virtues. Not that there weren't any. On the contrary, there were far too many. Even so, as I stepped off the train at Polegate Station, I felt that I had not quite identified any incident in my own life which paralleled the concept of the professional foul with *absolute* accuracy.

Still pondering this matter, I walked out into the station forecourt intending to engage one of the taxis that were usually queuing for customers when the London train came in. This time there was only one cab available, standing by the TAXI sign about fifty yards away. Between me and the sign there was just one person, an elderly lady moving very slowly with the aid of a stick in the same direction as me.

Somehow I *knew* that the elderly lady was heading for that solitary taxi, but I made an instant decision to pretend to myself and her and God and anyone else who might be interested, that I didn't really know that at all. After all, it was perfectly feasible that she was heading for the car park to pick up her own vehicle, wasn't it? How was I to know what she was doing? I wasn't a mind reader, was I?

Briskly overtaking my tottering competitor I reached the taxi and put my hand on the door handle. Suddenly I seemed to see an ethereal yellow card raised in the back of my mind.

A professional foul! Never mind how feasible anything was. My conscious intention was to do something selfish and deceptive. Remaining publicly intact was not the point at all. Removing my hand from the door I waited for the old lady to arrive, and helped her into the taxi. Just as I closed the door another cab drove into the forecourt and swept round the circular space to take up its position beside the TAXI sign. Gratefully, I settled into the passenger seat and was soon heading for home.

So, the business with the old lady and the first taxi hadn't really mattered after all, I mused, as we sped along the A22 towards Hailsham.

But of course it *had* mattered. The more I thought about that little incident, the more important it seemed. It had forced me to ask myself how many other times I had played this kind of game with my public and private morality. And, most significantly of all, perhaps, I realised that my sense of the reality of God's presence in my life was insufficient to prevent me from committing the kind of inward sins that are akin to the professional foul. Did I honestly think that God would be as easily taken in by my public posing as those people who were unable to see inside my head?

I am beginning to realise that openness with God and Man is not an optional extra. It's better to 'come clean' and admit that, whereas God is perfect, I'm not. I think I shall make a point of exploding my own myth before someone else blows the whistle on me.

Criticism

I have only ever once interrupted a sermon. It isn't an activity I would recommend or advocate, but perhaps it doesn't happen quite as often as it should. On this occasion, the speaker was talking about the Christian approach to personal finance, and the question of H.P. agreements in particular. This is, of course, very much in line with the current obsession with tidying up every aspect of something called 'The Christian Life'. I haven't yet seen any paperbacks entitled 'Loo-flushing the Christian way', or 'Pencil-sharpening in the Spirit', but I don't doubt they are being prepared at this very moment.

This time, though, it was the old 'never-never'

system for buying household and personal goods, that was under the microscope. In general, said the speaker, it was best for Christians to avoid transactions of this kind. Debt was debt, whether it was formally organised or not. Much better, he added, to buy what you can afford, using money you've actually got. I sensed a little shadow of guilt settling over my friend, Brenda, sitting next to me. I knew her very well. She lived on the nearby council estate, in a house that was almost exclusively furnished and equipped with goods bought on hire purchase. I knew for a fact that she was still paying for her washing machine and cooker. I could almost hear her brain clicking as she computed the sum of her debts. She laid a hand on my arm, and leaned towards my ear.

'Adrian,' she whispered, 'I owe close on three hundred quid for my stuff!'

Brenda only needs a little shove to make her leap into the black abyss of guilt. Years ago she lost all respect for herself, and the rehabilitation of her self-worth has been a long, slow process. God is doing it, but the job may not be completed this side of heaven. A thought struck me. I raised my arm quickly before I could lose my nerve.

'Excuse me, sorry to interrupt, but you didn't actually mention mortgages. I mean – you've got a mortgage, haven't you? So have I. We owe thousands and thousands of pounds between us, don't we? It's just a huge, glorified H.P. system really – don't you think?'

Mortgages, it appeared, were 'different'. Never mind. I could feel Brenda's shadow lifting. *She* had got the point.

But why didn't mortgages count? Why are people so easily able to see areas that need correction in other people's lives, and remain blind to similar problems in their own? In the case I've just mentioned, it's probably something to do with an illusion that frequently bedevils the Church; namely, that a very organised and materially successful life indicates spiritual solidity. It is interesting to note how those who are socially and financially 'Inferior', can become victims of an oddly predatory form of – so-called – ministry, from a certain type of 'successful' Christian.

Even more common, though, is that form of modern pharisaism where Christians home in on satisfactorily visible things, such as smoking and drinking, despite their inability to face invisible, non-public vices or sins in themselves. (I hasten to add, incidentally, that I don't consider smoking or drinking to be sins in themselves.) Occasionally, however, the fault-finder can come badly unstuck, as when, some years ago, a gentleman challenged a friend of mine about his pipe-smoking habit.

'I'm surprised at you,' he said, 'a Christian like you carrying on with a filthy habit like that!'

My friend has a *real* gift of knowledge; not the sort where you offer vague comfort in sixteenth-century English, but a specific, relevant, sometimes disturbingly accurate insight into unseen things. He looked keenly at the man who had spoken.

'Well,' he replied calmly, 'it's a lot better than *your* filthy habit.'

The erstwhile critic blushed to the roots of his hair, and departed hastily. My friend hadn't the faintest idea what the 'filthy habit' might be, but clearly the Holy Spirit had hit the nail right on the head.

I have been judgemental in just about every way that's possible at one time or another, but I specialise in something that I call 'The Spiritual Three-Step'. One of the steps is forward, and the other two are back. The 'dance' goes something like this.

For a long time, possibly days, or weeks, or months, or even years, I wrestle with, worry about, or live with, being spiritually low. It may be because of a particular issue, or it may be a whole set of problems. Then, one day, through prayer, or advice, or reading, or just growing up a little more, my chronic lowness is overcome, and I discover, to my intense relief, that I am experiencing a little of the joy and peace that Christians are 'supposed' to enjoy all the time. For a while, all I feel is a deep and honest gratitude to God for bringing me out of the pit. This is the one step forward.

What happens next, however, is that I feel a burning desire to advertise my 'rightness' with God. I start to tell people, patiently but firmly, that they need to 'get right with the Lord'. I avoid mention of the fact that I have only just found peace myself, but I do make it clear through my crinkly smile and other-worldly manner, that my own state is one of healthy spirituality. These are the two steps backwards. In my old gloomy state, I might have been a bit of a wet blanket, but at least I was recognisable as a human being. Now I am that most oppressive of beings, the Christian who is as incapable of normal communication when he is spiritually high, as he is incapable of normal participation when he is low. Pray for Christians like us who follow this kind of manic-depressive pattern. We need it! We are forever lecturing others about the sins and weaknesses that are all too familiar to us. The tendency is psychological and temperamental rather than spiritual, and it can be very destructive.

Why are we Christians so critical and condemnatory of each other at times? Often, it is the result of fear and insecurity. When children are left to organise themselves in situations where an adult would normally be in charge, they have a tendency to create rules and restrictions that are far harsher and less flexible than under the adult regime. Where there is fundamental lack of belief, this happens among Christian families and churches as well. Groups will develop a rigid structure of do's and don'ts, to protect themselves from the uncertainties and risks involved in grappling with the real world. Anyone who breaks one of the rules is threatening the security of the group, and must therefore be corrected or rejected.

This is understandable, but it has very little to do with the ideal outlook as Jesus taught it. He himself was a totally released and free person, one hundred per cent against sin, and one hundred per cent *for* the sinful individuals with whom he was so tender and forgiving. His most intense vituperation was reserved for the hypocrites – church leaders who burdened others with endless rules and regulations, and did nothing to relieve those burdens. The Christians I've met who walk closely with God don't make me feel bad. They make me feel as if I could be good. Their breadth and positivity have a creative, life-changing effect. They are like Jesus.

We are called to be '*doers*', not narrow-eyed guardians of a complex system of laws. Sin is more easily displaced than guarded against. Perhaps if our churches opened up to the world and the Spirit in a bolder way we would discover that there is an adventure with God waiting for us, that is far more exciting than sin, and a thousand times more useful than the detection of faults in our brothers and sisters. God will judge us all in time. Meanwhile, let's be positive. Let's look for the best in others, and let's not inhibit the spread of God's Kingdom by concentrating on the rulebook. We are only truly safe if we let go. The avoidance of sin on its own is safe but sterile. Where it is accompanied or made possible by *extravagant* goodness, it can change the world.

They don't smoke, but neither do they breathe fresh air very deeply
They don't drink wine, but neither do they enjoy lemonade; they don't swear, but neither do they glory in any magnificent words, neither poetry nor prayer;
They don't gamble, but neither do they take much chance on God;
They don't look at women and girls with lust in their hearts, but neither do they roll breathless with love and laughter, naked under the sun of high summer.
It's all rather pale and round-shouldered, the great Prince lying in prison.

George Target

Confession
Thou Shalt Not Eavesdrop

I suppose this book wouldn't be truly complete unless I included at least a couple of grovelling confessions. Well, here's one, and I hope you like it.

I am an inveterate eavesdropper. Not just because I happen to be a writer who is constantly scavenging for material (although I always think that sounds a wonderfully smooth excuse, don't you?) but because I really am fascinated by real conversation between real people in day-to-day situations.

I've been dropping eaves anywhere and everywhere for years and years. I'm the rather good-looking – all right, ordinary-looking, if you want to be boringly accurate – man with a beard, apparently deeply absorbed in his newspaper, sitting just in front of you on the bus.

Don't worry – you can carry on exchanging hissed imprecations with your spouse. I'm not listening. Well, you'd never guess that I was listening, anyway. Actually I can hear every exasperated word you and your beloved say. When you get off in a minute I might even make a few notes on the back of an envelope.

One good row could be a whole chapter in my next-but-one book – if I pad my jottings out to five thousand words, and set the whole thing in Russia, and make the fate of the Western world hang on its outcome.

Rather an honour for you, I should have thought; especially when you consider that the original argument was about whether the dog got fed or not before you came out.

Is eavesdropping a sin? I don't honestly know. 'Thou shalt not eavesdrop.'

It sounds a little odd, doesn't it? But until a blinding revelation convicts me unequivocally, I shall continue with my earwigging activities. After all, I can always repent later, can't I?

To be honest, most of the things you overhear are not very dramatic. Discussions, rows, jokes, gossipy chats – they're all interesting. But they don't have much 'shock value', if you know what I mean. That's why it was so exceptional one day when a mere snatch of dialogue overheard in a station buffet, chilled me to the narrow, and left me feeling deeply disturbed long after the initial impact had passed.

It doesn't matter when it was, except that it wasn't too long after the Press and TV news had been full of accounts of soccer violence at home and abroad.

The two people involved were very ordinary. One was the girl who worked behind the buffet counter, the other was a young British Rail employee, probably in his late teens or early twenties, quite unexceptional to look at, both of them.

They obviously knew each other. Being genuinely absorbed in my newspaper for once, I didn't register the first part of the conversation, but the bit I did hear went like this.

'Still livin' in the same place, Gary?'

'Yeah, but I'm movin' soon.'

'Oh, where you goin' then?'

'Movin' up to live with a mate at the other end of town.'

'Oh, why's that then, Gary?'

'It's better. There's more aggro up that way. . . .'

This last, stunning announcement was delivered in precisely the same tone that someone else might use to talk about superior housing or better recreational facilities.

In a modern, but not less grotesque version of the old werewolf legend, this young man called Gary was an inoffensive – probably very helpful – employee of British Rail by day, and a committed seeker after 'aggro' by night.

When evil is deep and uncompromising and consistent, it's somehow easier to face and combat. When, as in the case of Gary and his associates, something like violence has been elevated to the status of legitimate recreation – albeit within a limited social group – and can be mentioned casually as a desirable attribute of the area in which one plans to live, it's much harder to establish where the real spiritual battleground is.

This seems to me one of the most successful devil's ploys of this age. When the edges between black and white, evil and good, wrong and right, are blurred and confusing, we can end up spiritually paralysed, vaguely feeling that to do nothing is better than doing the wrong thing.

Now, more than ever, we need to make our priority a close walk with God, asking for *his* wisdom, and keeping our ears wide open. Sometimes our willingness to *listen* can make all the difference.

A friend of mine told the story recently of a girl who was counselling an older woman, when the words 'God hates mummies and daddies' came into her mind. Very wisely she refrained from immediately passing on this strange piece of information. 'Words from the Lord' can so easily turn out to be the product of wishful thinking or an over-active imagination. You know the sort of thing I mean:

'I saw, as it were, a frying pan, and within the pan did appear an egg, shaped like unto the land of Greenland, and behold the egg did speak . . . etc.'

You really do have to be very careful. The girl in this case talked and prayed about the words in question with a friend whom she respected and trusted. They decided that the message was from God, and with considerable trepidation the counsellor returned to the lady she had been trying to help and repeated the sentence that had come into her mind. To her consternation the woman collapsed in tears, explaining when she recovered that, as a young girl, she had been continually abused by her uncle who always prefaced his unwelcome advances with the words: 'Let's play mummies and daddies. . . .'

After many years the Holy Spirit had, at last, found someone whose ears were wide open enough to hear words that would bring the sympathy of God to a life that had been crippled by past hurts.

It's always worth trying to overhear what the Holy Spirit is saying. He doesn't mind us eavesdropping at all.

Political Repentance

Another confession.

I have not been political, and I repent.

My parents always voted Liberal if they voted at all, but I suspect that their understanding of politics was less than profound. I remember asking them to tell me the difference between the three major parties. As far as I can recall, they said that the Conservatives wanted to keep everything the same as it was now, the Labour Party wanted to abolish rich people, and the Liberals wanted to be fair to everybody.

This may of course be a more penetrating political analysis than appears at first sight, but at the time it failed to inspire me with any burning interest in the activities of politicians. As I grew older I learned how to conceal my ignorance beneath a thin veneer of sceptical derision.

'Naturally', my attitude seemed to imply, 'I'm pretty shrewd about the whole business, but if you understood it like I do, you'd know that it's really not worth bothering with.'

In fact, it was only fairly recently that I was jerked out of this absurd false complacency. It was during a period when my life had settled into a pattern of rather cosy little routines, one of which took me to London each week.

Every Wednesday morning during the early part of that year I caught a train at 6.30 from Polegate in East Sussex to Victoria Station, London. After a short but crowded journey by tube to Oxford Circus, I walked up Regent Street to a small sandwich cafe on the right, just before you come to the St George's Hotel and All Souls, Langham Place.

There, I ordered a black coffee and a bacon sandwich – made with brown bread and no butter because I was dieting – and read whichever magazine or newspaper I'd picked up at the station bookstall.

At about 8.50 I sighed heavily, folded my paper, paid the bill and walked round the corner to Broadcasting House. There I collected an admission sticker from reception and descended into the bowels of the building via two flights of steps.

Fifty yards or so along the corridor I pushed through two swing doors and found myself in the control room attached to Derek Jameson's 'bunker', the studio from which Radio Two's 7.30-9.30 programme is broadcast. A few minutes later I was sitting opposite Derek delivering my prepared script for the slot entitled 'Pause For Thought'.

What has all this got to do with not being political?

Well, typically, I was so absorbed in my own cosy little routine and the contribution I would be making, it never occurred to me that I might be challenged by something someone else was talking about.

Derek was conducting a series of phone-in voting opportunities on topical issues. The one that really penetrated my thick skull was concerned with the building of the Channel Tunnel between England and France – not where the rail link should run or anything like that, but whether it should be built at all.

The response was enormous, and the result unequivocal. The vast majority of people just didn't want it – as simple as that.

As I sat on the south-bound train later, I chewed this over in my mind and realised I didn't want the tunnel either. In fact I *hated* the idea of it. Not 'as a Christian' – I'm sure there isn't a correct Christian view of such an issue – but because on some very deep level I wanted Great Britain to keep its island status.

I didn't – and don't – want to be physically joined to the continent of Europe.

As my train flew past East Croydon and rattled through Gatwick I got angrier and angrier. By the time I got to my home station of Polegate I had a whole list of complaints going back several years, all concerned with valuable things sacrificed on the alter of efficiency.

'Just think,' I stormed at Bridget when I got home, 'all those things they've done without asking me!'

'Such as?' she asked dispassionately.

'Steam trains!' I replied. 'They got rid of them and brought in boring old diesels and non-corridor carriages and they never asked me!'

'But they were dirty and – '

'Currency!' I cried. 'While I wasn't looking they got rid of our lovely, curly, complicated pounds, shillings and pence and put nasty metallic, robotic, rotten old decimal currency in its place – scandalous!'

'But the children find it much – '

'I turn my back for a moment, and they abolish Rutland! And Huntingdonshire. Where's that gone? Who said they could go messing about with counties like that? I was never consulted, was I?'

'But – '

'And now this tunnel business! Everyone says they don't want a tunnel but we're having a tunnel anyway. I mean – you know!'

Sensing that like the railway system, I had run out of steam, Bridget spoke again.

'But you never did anything, Adrian. You've always gone on about politicians being silly and it being a waste of time thinking about that sort of thing. You knew all these things were happening really, you just couldn't be bothered to get involved!'

I get fed up with my wife being right, but she usually is. She was this time.

I suppose my life has tended to be like my weekly trips to the BBC, running along rather cosy ruts of non-involvement.

I think part of my Christian commitment should have been finding ways to express my discontent with loss of quality of life, even – or especially – over questions that have no obvious right answers.

I have not been political, and I repent.

Something Beautiful

I have already confessed that if eavesdropping was a capital offence I would have been hanged years ago. I don't know what the visual equivalent of eavesdropping is, but I'm afraid I have to plead guilty to that as well. I am continually entertained, distracted and absorbed by the things that people are doing in my immediate vicinity. Concentrated observation can function like a mental telescope sometimes, revealing large significance in small events – babies being born in stables, for instance.

Similarly, one of the most delicately beautiful things I ever witnessed was on the platform of Beckenham Junction railway station. An unlikely setting I agree, but that's where it was. Having just recorded a television sermon in a private house in Beckenham at a painfully early hour of the morning, I strolled down to the station to begin my journey home, contemplating as I went the very pleasant prospect of the rest of Saturday stretching ahead with nothing very arduous to be done in it.

It was a grey, overcast morning filled with the damp threat of rain, and I had nearly an hour to wait before my train was due to arrive. I didn't mind. Like Chesterton I have always (well, nearly always) enjoyed being stranded in railway stations. I bought a newspaper, sat on a bench near the ticket barrier, and was soon lost in the sports pages.

My attention was diverted after a few minutes by a clattering noise coming from the inside area where the tickets were sold. The noise stopped for a moment or two, presumably while tickets were being purchased, then it began again, becoming louder and louder, until a young couple appeared at the ticket barrier carrying a large wooden object between them. They lowered it to the ground while the man on the barrier inspected their tickets.

It was a table. I peered inquisitively at it round the side of my newspaper. It certainly wasn't a particularly distinctive piece of furniture – quite nice, but nothing special. One of those old-fashioned circular gate-leg tables, the kind that fold down on both sides, and are supported by carved spiral legs. It wasn't even in especially good condition. There must have been two or three generations' worth of stains and knocks on the bits that I could see. A good sanding and polishing prospect – if you had the time – but nothing special.

The two people were very ordinary looking as well. A young man and a girl, probably no more than twenty years old. I watched them carry their table on to the platform after the ticket inspector had agreed that it could travel on the train with them. He had seemed somewhat flummoxed at first by the fact that it was not a dog or a bicycle.

As the two young people came towards me I studied their faces. She was quite pretty, and they both had pleasant, open expressions. Their eyes declared that they were each enjoying exactly the same level of happiness, a quite reliable indicator that true love is present. They made me want to smile.

The table was lowered gently on to a spot roughly half-way between my bench and the edge of the platform. I folded my newspaper casually and pretended to stare vacantly at the opposite platform.

The girl took some coins out of her pocket, did what appeared to be a rapid calculation, then dashed out of the station again, presumably to buy sweets or a paper at the shop opposite the ticket office.

While she was gone, her friend embarked on a little, light-footed circular stroll around the table, clearly locked into orbit by the sheer pleasure of ownership. It was almost a restrained skip that he was doing. He did *try* to look casual and suitably bored, but he couldn't quite manage it. Every now and then he would stop, move a little closer, just touch the wood gently with the tips of his fingers, and smile a small, private, happy smile before going on to do another revolution.

When the girl returned the couple stood side by side, gazing fondly down at their piece of furniture like parents with a new baby. They stroked its top and pointed out bits of it to each other; they patted it and whispered about it and made arranging movements in the air with their hands, as though they were planning where to put it, all with a restrained delight that lit them both up like lightbulbs.

Unless I was very much mistaken that table was going to be the centrepiece of some newly ac-quired house or flat or perhaps even a bedsitter — they didn't look very well off. Something made me sigh a little as I imagined them arriving home and setting about the business of sanding and fixing and polishing their prize before finally putting it in different parts of the room to see how it looked.

There was such a glow in and around this little scene, that I stood up and moved a little closer, hoping (at least I'm honest) to overhear what they were actually saying. I think it was more than that, though. I wanted, silly as it sounds, to be nearer to the innocent joy of what was going on.

But, as it happened, their train came in at that moment, and seconds later, they carried their baby very carefully into one of the carriages and slammed the door behind them.

I felt all sorts of things at that moment: sadness, because I'd lost the kind of simplicity that produces the depth of pure appreciation I had just seen; pleasure, because it was just a lovely thing to watch; and a new understanding about what Paul the apostle meant when he encouraged us to look at whatever is beautiful. I could feel how good it was for me.

Perhaps, also, there was something about transfiguration, a word that, very broadly defined, means making things shine because of love.

I don't know if an old table could really shine, but I did have the absurd notion that the platform had become just a little darker as that train disappeared round a distant bend, on its way to the city.

Thou Shalt Not Kick the Cat

A final confession: I am emotionally handicapped in the area of 'conflict'. I don't know how to handle it.

A little while ago I was asked to speak on this subject. It wasn't an area I felt confident about, and I wasn't at all sure where to start. Eventually, after much moaning and growling and head scratching, I decided to go through Mark's gospel and list the occasions on which Jesus came into conflict with people or ideas or anything else. This catalogue of confrontation turned out to be much longer and more significant than I had anticipated. Jesus was in conflict with:

Demons: There was nothing polite about the master's way with these horrible in-dwellers.

Illness: Very early on in the gospel we read of Jesus healing Simon Peter's mother-in-law (much to the disgust of contemporary Jewish Les Dawsons, no doubt) and the leper, who so moved him to pity. Physical affliction was confronted and dismissed.

Weather: Jesus commanded a storm to 'be still'.

Nazarenes: The inhabitants of Jesus' home town were offended by the authority of his teaching and the claims he made. (How often do we fail to 'allow' people we know well to change, and thereby miss out on what God is offering us through them?)

The scribes and Pharisees: What a hard time he gave them! Not just through direct criticism, but also with witty, disconcerting replies to their trick questions. ('By whose authority do you do these things?' and 'Should we pay taxes to Caesar?')

His own disciples: He told them off on a number of occasions, usually when they had arrived at a committee-like decision about what ought to happen next, or what he really meant. At one point, after Jesus had talked of his imminent betrayal, death and resurrection, Mark tells us that the disciples 'didn't understand and were afraid to ask him'. Jesus was clearly determined that his followers were not going to turn his life into religion. (He's just as determined nowadays.)

Peter was admonished particularly strongly when he attempted to deflect Jesus from the dismally unattractive path of obedience. How many of us are doing the same thing in relation to people like Terry Waite? As well as praying for his safe return, should we not also be thanking God that this servant of his is in the right place at the right time, for reasons that we could not hope to understand at this stage?

His own father: At that terrible moment when our sin cut Jesus off from the roots of his own being, he was in sudden panic-stricken conflict with the person he had trusted most.

Because of those words – 'My God, my God, why have you forsaken me?', we can be sure that there is an experience of emptiness and rejection in the heart of God that compassionately echoes and empathises with similar darkness in the hearts of men.

That's only part of the list, and it doesn't include or mention the occasions when, much to his disciples' bewilderment, Jesus chose to avoid or withdraw from conflict when it seemed the most obvious option (the healing of the centurion's ear, for instance). Clearly, conflict is intended to be of positive use in our lives. So why do we see so little of it? What do we do with the legitimate confrontational impulses that spring up in us? I can only answer for myself.

(a) My family gets it in the neck instead of the person or people who should have been faced. This is the familiar 'kicking the cat' syndrome.

(b) I turn it inwards. I'm told that depression is unexpressed anger. Bottled up feelings can have a bad effect spiritually, mentally and physically.

(c) I release my aggression in the form of GOSSIP, one of the most destructive activities for a church community. Anger disguised as concern and passed on to others acts like poison.

'I like John – I really do. That's why it concerns me so much that he's beginning to. . . .'

'In confidence and just for prayer, but have you heard about Jill. . . .'

(d) I sulk. Instead of expressing displeasure or unhappiness openly, I play games, usually of the sort where the person I feel hurt by has to 'guess' that I'm feeling upset.

(e) I dilute the strength of my own convictions through fear of open conflict. This can happen when matters of faith are at issue, or when I ought to complain to the plumber yet again because the central heating *still* isn't working properly. I hear my own voice bleating out compromises when I should be sure and strong.

(f) I am very fortunate in that I am able to conflict with institutions and ideas through writing and speaking, but there are temptations here as well to be either too harsh or too soft.

So what can I do to change things?

First, I learn, through the way Jesus behaved, that there is a middle way of assertiveness between cowardice and outright aggression. Most of us find this approach quite difficult. It involves expressing the way we feel in a calm and clear fashion before we have let things continue for so long that we are only capable of exploding or gossiping or sulking. It will feel risky, because the person we address may not choose to meet us at the place where we wish to meet them. More often, though, I suspect that potentially explosive situations will be defused by such an approach and relationships actually improved. I wonder how many times I have impeded forward movement in my own Christian community by keeping quiet when I should have spoken, or speaking when I should have kept my mouth shut?

Secondly, and most important of all, I need to make sure that I am praying with concentration and urgency for real guidance about when to enter into conflict and when to withdraw. This is not an optional extra, but an essential.

Ultimately, I suppose, we are seeking to demonstrate the simplicity and straightforwardness of children, the sort of children who will not be afraid to say what they think, but will always be ready to receive guidance from wise parents.

Blushes and Bloomers

All right! One more little confession: I do have a certain tendency to get myself into embarrassing situations.

Years ago I was asked to read about the psychology of embarrassment as part of my teacher training course at Stockwell College in Bromley.

Most of the brain cells that collected this information seem to have dropped off since that time, but some of what I learned remains.

As far as I can remember, the theory presented to us was that embarrassment happens when people slip or are forced out of roles appropriate to the situation or environment they are in. This can produce 'role-conflict', which, said the books, is the real basis of the kind of uncomfortable confusion that we call embarrassment.

For example, if I am sitting in a theatre listening to a stand-up comic performing from the stage, role-conflict may easily occur. If the comedian's jokes are funny, and I laugh, then no embarrassment is caused. His role is to amuse, my role is to *be* amused. If, however, his act is so dire that I find myself unable to laugh at his jokes, then I may well squirm with embarrassment in my seat, all too aware that because he has failed in his role as an entertainer I am failing miserably in my role as an audience member. If the rest of the audience are as little amused as I am, then, of course, the performer himself will experience equal or perhaps even more profound embarrassment about the failures of his own role – poor chap.

One of my most memorably embarrassing real-life experiences happened on a single-decker bus travelling from Tunbridge Wells to Heathfield when I was quite a young man. The bus was crowded with shoppers, and I ended up sitting in a window seat, next to a young mother laden with various packages and carrier bags. She looked hot and tired, as young mothers so often do, and she had somehow become separated from her little girl who was sitting in the window seat directly behind me, completely blocked in by one of those enormously fat men who wear very short, tight pullovers.

As we approached a stop at around the half-way point in our journey, my neighbour gathered her assortment of belongings, stood up, and turned round rather worriedly, obviously about to ask the fat man to let her daughter out. Thinking that I could help, I also turned round and put my hands under the little girl's arms, intending to lift her over to her mother. Unfortunately, I misjudged the child's weight rather drastically. She was much lighter than I thought. The result was that I piledrove her into the roof of the bus, so hard that as she came down her eyes were crossed by the power of the impact. As the mother leaned across to rescue her daughter my cheeks burned. It must have looked so horribly deliberate.

Mother and child left the bus, and as we moved away again I glanced over my shoulder. The fat man was gazing reproachfully at me. 'Why', his expression seemed to ask, 'did you just commit that act of gratuitous violence against a poor defenceless little girl?'

Far from seeing me in the role of 'helper' he obviously saw me as a 'batterer'. I was embarrassed. I was *very* embarrassed.

Far more recently, during a family holiday in Europe, I was in trouble again. This time I made an idiot of myself in a cable-car on the way up to the top of Mont Blanc. The car was full of tourists, mainly French-speaking with a smattering of Japanese tourists who uttered very satisfactorily oriental gasps of awe and wonder as the panorama of snow-covered ranges came into view.

A benign, rather stout French lady of advanced years offered my two young sons a sweet each. They, of course, accepted, and it seemed to me an ideal opportunity to demonstrate my profound knowledge of the Gallic tongue.

My wife, sensing from my knitted brows and glazed eyes that I was composing a sentence in French, made frantic attempts to reach me in time to avert disaster, but she was on the other side of the car and didn't make it in time. Tapping the generous French lady on the shoulder I smiied warmly and said something that was supposed to mean 'You are obviously a grandmother yourself'.

The smile disappeared from the old lady's face as though I had slapped her. Grunts and clicks of disapproval emanated from the other French-speakers. I noticed that my wife gazed intently through the window at nothing at all.

'What did I say?' I hissed. 'Was the grammar wrong or something'

'Unfortunately,' said Bridget, from the side of her mouth, 'you sounded quite confident and fluent. That's what made it so awful!'

'Yes, but what did I say?'

It appeared that what I had said to the lady with the sweets was: 'Well, you *are* a large women, aren't you?'

More role confusion – more embarrassment!

The next step of our college education in this area concerned the nature and function of 'tact'. A tactful person, our lecturer told us, is one who restores or repairs roles that have become inappropriate, caused embarrassment or upset relationships.

'Perhaps he was only trying to help. . . . I'm sure he didn't mean it. . . . He might have been trying to help the little girl when he lifted her . . .' – that sort of thing.

The Christian faith is concerned with breakdown in the relationship between God and man. God created men and women to be in a loving relationship with him, and as long as individuals are not fulfilling this most appropriate of roles there will continue to be a sort of cosmic embarrassment.

I don't know if Jesus' death and resurrection can really be described as the ultimate exercise in tact, but it is the only way I know of repairing the damage that occurred somehow, way back in the past, when, as the Bible has it, Adam and Eve, having spoiled their friendship with God, suddenly recognised their own nakedness and were deeply embarrassed.

Performance
Fellowshipping in the Petrol

I used to be even more naïve than I am now. I honestly thought that the only thing a writer really needed was the ability to write. I now know that accountancy skills, legal expertise, a sponge-like readiness to read what my aunt's friend's second cousin has written with a blunt pencil on greaseproof paper, sufficient fortitude to provide the same answers to the same questions over and over again at local radio stations, and enough humble restraint to avoid hunting down adverse reviewers and mugging them in back alleys, are just a few of the extra talents that must be developed. They don't do evening classes in things like Forgiving Reviewers, so most of it has to be self-taught.

311

Take book-signing for instance. You-know-who's law operates here with a vengeance. If I undertake a speaking engagement and decide not to take any books to sell, invariably, as soon as I finish bleating, I'm descended upon by a howling mob, wolfishly intent on consuming every word I've ever written. Conversely, if, in a fever of confidence, I have large numbers of books delivered by my publishers to a venue, then I'm almost certain to end up staggering miserably on and off trains and buses with huge unwieldy parcels of books at the end of the day. When, by some miracle, supply and demand do happen to coincide, I find it essential to bear in mind one of the few lessons that has sunk in at last. You cannot sign books and take the money for them at the same time. Well – you might be able to, but I certainly can't.

I'm hopeless with money at the best of times. More than one taxi driver, after I've offered a note in payment and asked in magnanimous tones for a particular amount of change, has pointed out dispassionately that I've awarded myself a substantial tip. So, signing books with one hand and giving change with the other is completely beyond me. Not only does my left hand not know what my right hand is doing and vice versa, but my brain loses control over both. My consequent tendency to sign five pound notes and dump paperbacks in the cash tray is viewed with some alarm by the good Christian folk who approach with simple faith in my sanity. Nowadays I ask organisers kindly to provide someone to 'do the money'. This is an immense relief because I really enjoy meeting people and writing in their books – as long as that's all I have to do.

I read somewhere recently that the travelling Christian speaker is likely to face three main temptations. These are, in no particular order, sex, power and money. Well, all I can say is that I must be on the wrong circuit. I'm always on the look-out for opportunities to heroically resist the queue of seductive temptresses that should be waiting outside my hotel door, but so far not one has put in an appearance. I'm not complaining, Lord – honestly!

The desire to wield power over congregations,

313

readers and audiences is a temptation that is much more likely to come my way, but the fact that God has taken me by the scruff of the neck and said, 'Plass, your role in life is to be a sort of public idiot for me', has removed most of my chances for sinful indulgence in this area. I rather think that my family's jolly little satirical jibes might be a sufficient safeguard in any case, when it comes to taking myself too seriously as a writer or speaker.

As for money, I'd love to be in a position to turn down *most* of some unhealthily large sum, but no one's ever offered me one. On the contrary, a particular problem can arise in this connection, usually at the end of a speaking and signing session.

Many churches and organisations have a healthy and realistic attitude to expenses and fees for visiting speakers or entertainers. Their generosity touches and amazes me sometimes. But there are others, few but memorable, where gloomy treasurers enquire if they might 'have fellowship in the petrol', and it is in these situations that the afore-mentioned problem is likely to crop up. The scene is as follows.

The signing is finished, the people have gone, the evening is over. All that is left is me, my remaining books and the mournful distributor of precisely correct travelling expenses. Frowningly he filters out the appropriate sum from a small leather purse while I count the cash from the book sales. If a lot of books have gone there might be quite a pile of five and ten pound notes, as well as the usual collection of coins. Leaning over the table deep in calculation, I gradually become aware that the filterer is directing a sternly reproachful gaze at the wad of notes in my hand.

'What', his expression seems to ask 'is a Christian doing with all that money? Why?' it seems to enquire further 'are you taking expenses from our ill-provided coffers when you have already through your coarse marketing taken such huge sums from our ill-provided people?'

When I was a raw beginner, this would trigger me into defensive babbling about how much I had to pay for the books, how little profit I made on each one, how hard it was to support a wife and three children when you were freelance and how, as a Christian, money really meant nothing to me. There were times when I came very close to thrusting payment on the treasurer as a thank-offering for inviting me to speak.

I don't do that any more. I ignore gazes. It's another of those things I've had to learn about being a writer: Never answer questions you haven't actually been asked – especially about money.

So much to learn; but I'm getting there slowly. Perhaps if I really work at mastering all these extra skills, I shall be able to set aside a few hours each week to actually do a little writing.

Baptism of Fire

After speaking at the kind of event I've just described, I enjoy meeting people at the coffee and chat session before everyone goes home. During that buzzing half hour or so I've often been asked if I am a speaker who started to write, or a writer who started to speak.

The truth is that the writing came first. *Join the Company*, my initial faltering step into the world of books, was an almost instant worst-seller, but *The Sacred Diary of Adrian Plass*, which had already been appearing as a column in Family Magazine for a year or so, did very much better. As a result, I was invited to do some readings at the big Christian festival known as Spring Harvest. I thought I might be nervous when the time came, but I wasn't – I was terrified.

Shortly after returning from Minehead I recorded my nerve-wracking experience for posterity. I do hope it doesn't discourage potential speakers!

I am booked into Spring Harvest with my wife and three children. I am to read extracts from my *Sacred Diary* on the Fringe shows.

Only about three people have heard of my diary. I am very nervous.

We arrive very late at night. My seven-year-old son, Joseph, is sick just outside the main gate. This does not seem a good omen. Being a Christian, I ignore it. The weather is like that bit in *The Guns of Navarone*, just before they climb the cliff in the blinding rain.

We find the office and collect the key to our chalet. We find our chalet. There is a man n it. He is about as pleased to see us as we are to see him.

We say things like 'Praise the Lord!' and 'Where are you from, brother?' He is to share with us for one night. We are all hearty. Luckily, he is nice.

I am amazed by the chalet. It is new. It has a colour TV. It has a kitchen area. It has nice furniture. We settle in. Joseph is sick again. We go to bed. We sleep.

On Monday I go to a meeting of Spring Harvest staff. There are famous Christians there. We sing choruses. We get into small groups for prayer. There is a famous Christian leading mine. He suggests that we should thank God, one by one, for what he has done for us today.

I am the last to pray. Everyone else seems to have about fifteen things to say thank you for. I say to God in my mind, 'I can't think what to thank you for'. God sighs, and says, 'If only you knew, Plass. If only you knew!' I think of one or two things to say. I try to sound warm and devout. I actually feel rather sweaty and apprehensive.

Clive Calver, General Secretary of the Evangelical Alliance, speaks to us all. He exhorts us. He tells a joke. Everyone is very sympathetic. He tells us to divide into large, activity groups. We do. I am in the entertainment group. I turn to the person next to me and whisper, 'I don't go in for all this "famous Christian" rubbish, do you?' He looks a little disgruntled. I learn later that he is a famous Christian.

Later still, I tell my wife about the meeting. She suggests the reason I go on about famous Christians is that I'm annoyed because I'm not one. What nonsense!

The next evening I am due to do my first reading in the Multi Media Mega Show. I arrive early. I try to look cool. I am absolutely petrified. Soon, several hundred teenagers surge in through the doors with a mighty rushing sound. I gibber a silent prayer. God says, 'I am not a bottle of whisky, Plass'. I reply, 'I wish you were'. I repent hurriedly. God smiles. He can take a joke.

Steve Flashman, an old friend, has started the show. He is the host. He is very good. It is very good. Steve's wife, Sue, is very good. The teenagers enjoy it very much. Oh, heavens! Why should I spoil their pleasure?

Steve is very lively indeed. I consider the fact that he is the same age as I am. I decide that he must play squash or something.

There are videos and competitions and live performances and flashing lights. Suddenly it is my turn! Steve is introducing me. I yearn for sudden illness, natural disaster, the second coming, or anything to rescue me. Nothing does.

I climb up on the stage and look out towards the audience. There seem to be about a million teenagers jamming the auditorium. They are waiting in the dark to find out if I'm funny or not. The back of my throat sticks against the front. My stomach is full of cold, bubbling porridge. A muscle in the calf of my right leg starts to twitch uncontrollably.

I feel certain that I was only ever cut out to be a minor clerk in a huge firm, with no responsibility at all. If none of these two million horrible youngsters laugh, I will die. I ask myself what can have possessed me to believe I could ever stand up and read this appalling rubbish to three million killer-teenagers.

I have already paused for nearly four seconds since my quota of encouraging applause. If I do not start soon they will think I am a loony. I am a loony. Why else am I volunteering to destroy my self-image in front of four million people, all at a most unattractive age?

I begin. My voice clambers with an effort from between my tonsils. The first few words land like slabs of dough on the stage in front of me. Then, a wonderful, wonderful person near the back laughs loudly. Another person laughs. Several people laugh. Nearly everybody is laughing. Of course, I say to myself, I always knew I could trust teenagers. They are insightful people. A very attractive age group. As I complete the reading, I mentally resign from the minor clerkship and rehearse the expression of pleased but humble surprise that I shall adopt when confronted by the host of *This is Your Life* at some future date.

The applause is loud enough and prolonged enough to provoke me into performing a series of complicated spiritual gymnastics in order to remain humble. I fail. I climb down from the stage. My knees have turned to jelly. My stomach has turned to jelly. My brain has turned to jelly.

When the show is over, some of the teenagers come up to my wife and me. They say they thought my bit was good. I am pleased. One of the girls says to Bridget, 'It must be a real laugh living with him'. Bridget snorts. She says, 'Oh yes, it's a real laugh living with him, especially first thing in the morning.' I cough and suggest it's time we went. We go back to our chalet.

The week goes on.

Our children disappear every morning to their club. One is an 'ant', the other is an 'elephant'. Bridget and I miss them very much. That is not true.

We go to a talk by Winkie Pratney. He makes us laugh. We go to a talk by Lyndon Bowring. He makes us cry. We go to a talk by Eric Delve. He makes us laugh and cry, despite the fact that we have heard this one before in Luton. We go to a talk by Clive Calver. He makes us write a letter. We hear Chris Bowater sing. We are entranced.

We take an afternoon off and climb the hill behind Minehead to the place where Exmoor starts. We play a game among the trees with the children. It is as enchanted a place as any that A. A. Milne knew. Far below, the sea stretches away into the distance for ever. I ask God if this is a place where souls can be repaired. He says, 'Don't be sentimental, Plass. Just enjoy it.' I do.

I go to the New International Variety Show. It is hosted by Stuart Penny. I am to read a further extract from my diary later on. First, Stuart Penny holds a corny joke competition. The winner is the one who tells the corniest joke. A small girl enters. She comes up on the stage.

Everybody thinks she is sweet. They say, 'Aaah, isn't she sweet?' He holds the microphone close to the little girl's mouth.

She says, 'Why did the Romans build long straight roads?' Stuart Penny has not heard this joke before. If he had he would have pushed the sweet little girl off the stage at this point. Instead, he turns his head and smiles at the audience as if to say, 'Isn't she sweet?' He turns back to the little girl and says, 'Why did the Romans build long straight roads?' She replies, in a loud, clear voice, 'So the Pakis couldn't build corner shops'.

All the good Christians look concerned. All the others can't help laughing at the situation. I am one of the others. I laugh. Stuart Penny doesn't know whether to laugh or cry.

Somewhere in the audience the little girl's mummy and daddy are trying to cut their throats with the edge of their meter cards.

It is time to read my diary. I read some. I lose my place at a crucial point. The audience laughs far more at me losing my place than at anything I have actually read. I do not resent this. I forgive them. It is lucky there is not a machine gun handy.

I go into a Celebration one evening. I sit at the back. I look around. There are a lot of men with short, neat hair and hopeful expressions. There are quite a lot of beards. I have a beard. Most of the women look as if they have suffered more than the men.

I say to God, 'Is this your army, God?'

God says, 'I don't know if they're an army, but they're certainly mine. Why?'

I say, 'They're a bit odd aren't they?'

God says, 'You're a bit odd, Plass, but I put up with you, don't I? If *I* love them, then you'd better. All right?'

I say, 'All right, God, I'll try'.

Spring Harvest is going to sleep as I walk back through the darkness afterwards. I feel peaceful for once.

Heaven's Heroes

That first visit to Spring Harvest was very important to me. It was the beginning of a completely different way of life, and I shall never forget the pungent emotions of excitement and fear that accompanied my early experiences of entertaining and speaking. Over the year that followed I became quite insufferably fond of the sound of my own voice, until, having exhausted the novelty of 'being known', I settled down a little into the business of attempting to communicate for a living. In the process I began to learn (and am still learning) that unless my writing and speaking is rooted in real relationship with God and Man, there simply isn't anything to communicate. I have also begun to learn how passionately concerned God is with people, things and situations that may be small and insignificant in the eyes of the world, and even, at times, the Church.

Last year, for instance, four years on from my first encounter with 'killer teenagers', I was once more working for Spring Harvest at Minehead and Skegness (not simultaneously), and there were new lessons to learn in this respect.

Spring Harvest itself has not changed a great deal. It was the same big Christian knees-up, bringing together thousands from all denominations to enjoy teaching, worship and holiday-making. As usual, the thing I enjoyed most about this annual extravaganza was meeting old friends, making new ones and drinking free coffee in the team lounge. One of the friends I renewed acquaintanceship with was Andy Butcher, erstwhile editor of the monthly magazine *Christian Family*, now seeing his spirituality cubed daily as he worked for YOUTH WITH A MISSION in Holland. That was a pleasant re-union. It was Andy who suggested *The Sacred Diary of Adrian Plass*, a monthly column that later became a book which radically altered the direction of my life.

Spring Harvest, 1990, was even bigger and more dramatic than ever, especially during the Big Top worship, where huge numbers gathered each day.

For me, however, this particular year was marked by three rather undramatic events, the first of which happened before I even got there.

The evening before our departure I went to a meeting in my own church, St Mary's Hailsham, at about 7.30 p.m. By the time I came out at 9.45 the rain was bucketing down.

I had neither coat nor umbrella. Then Topsy offered me a lift in her taxi.

Topsy is an elderly and much loved member of our church who goes to just about every meeting throughout the week – despite the fact that she can only get around with some difficulty nowadays.

She took my arm and we moved very slowly along the church path and towards the taxi that was waiting a hundred yards away. My best suit was getting soaked – and so was I.

I could have done that distance in fifteen seconds flat. But then – I don't know what you think about God talking to people – I began to laugh because I could sense him saying to me, 'Hard luck, Plass, this is the pinnacle of your Christian achievement. You will probably never do anything much more important than this – including your bleating at Spring Harvest.'

The second thing happened the next day when I arrived at Butlin's, Minehead. I met a girl called Anita Hydes who was also working at the festival, but as a 'detached youth worker' – one of the most difficult and demanding tasks on site.

I'd met Anita very briefly before, and I knew she was the subject of a book called *Snatched From the Flames* but I'd never really had a chance to chat with her.

Anita is an attractive character, with a smile that lights up her face, but I have rarely met anyone in whom the marks of past grief and agonies are so evident.

Abused, beaten up and raped as a child, she went on to heroin at the age of fifteen and was an addict for seventeen years.

She was imprisoned for supplying drugs on more than one occasion, and was continually involved in acts of violence – often against the police.

At the end of the 70s she was admitted to hospital suffering from septicaemia and given three days to live.

Rescued and taken home by a friend who happened to be an ex-addict and a Christian, Anita spent the next three years recovering from the effects of drugs. During that time she made a Christian commitment herself.

Today Anita is a YMCA coffee-bar worker as well as being a regular prison visitor – especially concerned for those going through the same things as she did.

Much of her time is also spent replying to letters from people who've read about her and need help or advice themselves.

I spend quite a lot of time knocking the Church on a professional basis – but I don't knock God for what he's done with Anita. Hers is an amazing story.

The third event was so slight as to be hardly noticeable.

After two or three days at Minehead I met a teenage girl who described to me what happened after she read *The Lion, The Witch and The Wardrobe*, C. S. Lewis' book about a group of children who discover a different world through the back of an old wardrobe.

She was quite a little girl at the time, and very excited about the story.

Without telling anyone what she was doing, she climbed into the bottom of her parents' wardrobe, closed the door, and sat in the dark for an hour, waiting for the magic to start.

That simple little anecdote touched me very deeply. How many other people at that huge Christian get-together – children and adults – had been sitting in the bottom of their metaphorical wardrobes, waiting for the magic to start?

Topsy, Anita and the child at the bottom of the wardrobe – three people who reminded me that God's concern is for those individuals who may not be important in the world's eyes.

Not a bad thing to remember in a Christian world that still demands its heroes.

A Voice from the Past

You can never tell when or how God is going to teach you a lesson. It happened to me once when I was away speaking in Reading at the Greyfriars Centre in Friar Street. I was due to start my customary bleating at about eight-fifteen, but first I spent a very pleasant couple of hours at the home of John Brown, the centre manager.

John is a bluff, genial Northerner with a tough core, and a genuine determination to communicate Jesus in the real world. He also has a charming wife, Margaret, who I'm sure keeps him going with great love and expertise through the tough times; not to mention four very interesting children who are surprisingly clear about their projected careers. As far as I can remember, the

Brown household is scheduled to produce a Prime Minister, a chiropracter, a soldier and an American footballer.

It was the American Footballer's seventh birthday party on the day when I was there; great bumps and crashes from upstairs bore witness to the fact that Steve had 'a few friends round'. I met them a little later, when they war-whooped their way down to consume vast quantities of chocolate biscuits and sausage rolls and little sandwiches.

Later still, I ate an excellent supper with the political, medical and military elements of the family – known commonly as Rachel, Emma (she with designer holes in her jeans), and Tim, who had supervised most of the bumps and crashes.

Altogether it was an unusually relaxing prelude to the kind of evening event that had punctuated my life with increasing frequency over the preceding year. As we drove from John's house to the centre, I realised that I was getting a bit jaded generally. Trying to fit too many different things in, perhaps.

Like the Christian greengrocer or the Christian brain surgeon, however, I knew that the job had to be done, however I felt. It was nice to have started with the experience of being an honorary Brown, though.

I began my talk that evening as I often do, by speaking about how I was converted at the age of sixteen after hearing a sermon about the thief on the cross, preached by a man called Denis Shepherd who had served in the Merchant Navy before training for ordination into the Anglican Ministry.

I was a very awkward, unhappy teenager at the time, unsure about my own identity and generally mistrustful of others. Over the years I had cobbled together a personality of sorts, but it was a façade, and a thin one at that. Chaos reigned within, making me as vulnerable as many teenagers were in the sixties, to the wide variety of cut-price philosophies, religions and negative subcultures that abounded in towns like Tunbridge Wells, where I lived. Drugs, scientology, obscure eastern religions summarised in paperback, weekend violence and sexual experimentation were among the options open to young people like me.

I started going to an after-church youth meeting because there were girls there. I was interested in girls. Eventually the resident curate impressed me deeply with the sheer passion of his feelings about Jesus, and, in an attempt to track down the root or source of this passion, I began to attend the evening service at St John's church, always sitting at the back and always resisting the temptation to get too involved.

Then came Denis Shepherd's sermon. He talked about how one of the thieves who was crucified next to Jesus turned and saw in the face of this strange man a totally unexpected possibility of 'happy ever after'.

'Will you remember me when you come into your kingdom?' he asked.

The thing that impressed me was that Jesus didn't reply that it depended on his spirituality, or his theology, or his quiet-time, or his denomination, or his knowledge of the Bible, or how good he was able to be in the short time left to him; he simply said 'Yes', and promised that they would be together in heaven that very day.

After the service I prayed a very simple prayer with the preacher, and my relationship with Jesus began on that day. Much storm and calm was to follow over the years, but that was the beginning and it was very important to me.

I went on to tell the folk at Greyfriars about subsequent problems, and to attempt to identify the kind of 'rubbish' that had obscured the truth about Jesus for so many years of my life. It was three quarters of an hour later, when I was about to get going again after a short break, that something unexpected happened.

John Brown, no lightweight himself, ascended the platform and announced that he wanted to say a few words. He asked me if I'd ever seen *This Is Your Life* on television. My heart sank for a moment. Set up!

I imagined a succession of people from my past coming in through the side door and saying things like: 'Calls himself a Christian, eh? I can tell you a thing or two. . . .' I measured John Brown for a left-hook, followed by a flying drop kick, perhaps.

'Do you recognise this voice?' he asked. A tape-recording began to play through the loud-speakers. It was Denis Shepherd, the man who had preached that sermon nearly twenty-five years ago at St John's Church in Tunbridge Wells.

His message was one of greeting and encouragement. I was quite stunned! When the recording finished, John explained that Denis is a member of Greyfriars Church, working full-time as an evangelist for the Church Pastoral Aid Society. He was away for my visit, but had left a taped message to be played during the evening.

I felt quite shaken as I stood up to continue my talk. Later, as I sat in the passenger seat of a friend's car, speeding through the darkness towards Hailsham and home, it occurred to me that I'd been reminded of the two most important things in my life.

First, the Brown family brought my own houseful to mind. I knew that I would never be entrusted with a more important ministry than the one towards my wife and four children.

Secondly, the voice of Denis Shepherd had brought back that day, so long ago, when I met and loved Jesus for the first time.

Those were the really important things, and I would always be jaded if I was neglecting such essential priorities.

Failing Frankly

One of the questions that I faced when I began speaking publicly to Christian groups was the one about honesty. Just how truthful is it possible to be in a context where, traditionally, the chap up at the front is as near to a shining example as you are likely to get? Unrelenting frankness can have a curious effect on Christian groups, who expect their visiting speakers to fall into one of a limited number of familiar categories.

I spoke once in a jam-packed sitting-room to a band of local church members who were very mixed in terms of age and churchmanship. At the end of a lengthy session in which I described my own weaknesses quite graphically, I overheard a brief interchange between a mother and her ten-year-old son at the side of the room.

'Well,' said Mum, 'what did you think of him?'

After a short ponder, the boy replied.

'He was quite nice really – not like a Christian at all.'

I'm quite sure the lad was *not* saying that all the speakers he'd heard before were less than nice, rather that the way I spoke and the things I spoke about failed to match any model he had known previously.

Certainly, from the earliest days of my own Christian experience, I noticed – and still notice – that many preachers and 'professional Christians' appear to have only experienced problems in the past. By the time they stand up in the pulpit or behind the microphone everything is sorted out, tidied up and summarised in nineteen shiny points for the benefit of those who are still struggling. This can be quite intimidating for people like me, who are constantly grappling with an unruly queue of worries, bad habits, weaknesses and poultice-like responsibilities. Guidance and wisdom I certainly need from others to deal with these things, but it's much easier to accept help from one who travels with you, than from one who stands on a distant mountain-top offering detached advice from a great height.

Yes, platform immunity is a very wonderful thing. I know how it happens, though. There's something about standing up in front of a church full of Christians that seems to demand that your spirituality be cubed.

Present miseries and perplexities don't feel like a very good advert for God, whereas a comfortably retrospective look at difficulties overcome gives you, the speaker, a pleasant glow and persuades the listener – quite erroneously, really – that you are engagingly vulnerable and frank.

Often, as I sit down to write a magazine article, or prepare a talk, I feel shredded inwardly. Domestic conflicts over the previous twenty-four hours may have left me feeling wrung-out, inadequate and spiritually blob-like. Is it right on such occasions for me to share those negative experiences with the reader or listener? Some people think not.

A leading evangelical, writing in a magazine produced not a million miles away from the one that I contribute to, recently expressed the view that a current tendency to highlight the difficulties we all share in our Christian lives is not necessarily desirable or helpful. The Bible promises victory and that is what we should be preaching.

Well, I understand that point of view, and I'm all for preachers and writers who map out the route to victory in a practical, helpful and loving way, but – to change the metaphor with a screech of grammatical gears – I can also see the point of occasional dirty linen exhibitions.

Most of the Christians I know well – I would say all, but there may be some paragon I've forgotten – make mistakes, get things wrong, commit sins, get forgiven, get confused, read the Bible, stop reading the Bible, pray, don't pray, feel joyful, feel dismal, experience heaven and plunge into despair.

Being a Christian is a tough, gutsy business, shot through, for me anyway, by the radiance of truth. It seems sad to me that people often feel when they hit a low point that their testimony must be frozen until they have thawed out into a warmer moral or spiritual state.

The analogy of a hospital ward was once suggested to me.

As I enter this hypothetical ward I encounter, in the bed by the door, a patient who is completely encased in bandages from head to foot. Clearly he has suffered some appalling accident and has just been admitted.

He manages to convey to me through the slit left for his mouth that he knows next to nothing about the hospital or the doctor. He's just glad to be there.

A little further up the ward I meet another patient. This person is also very ill, but beginning to recover. He speaks warmly about the treatment he has received, and especially about the doctor who has tended him.

'The ones who've been here a long time tell me he's great,' he says, 'and I'm beginning to realise they're right.'

Towards the far end of the ward a bright-eyed, healthy-looking man is sitting up in bed. He smiles happily, and speaks rapturously about the doctor in charge.

'He's wonderful!' he enthuses. 'I'm completely well!'

In the last bed of all lies a bandage-covered figure just like the one in the first bed. I lean forward to hear what he has to say.

'It's my fifth time', he whispers. 'I keep having these blooming accidents! All my own fault really, but the doc's marvellous. Gets me back on my feet every time. Good job it ain't private!'

It would be very odd if the man in the first bed were to enthuse like the cured man in the third bed.

It would be equally odd if the man in the final bed were not to enthuse about the doctor who has brought him back to health so many times.

And perhaps that's the point really. We are not required to testify to us but to Jesus. If we are spiritually bright-eyed and bushy-tailed at the time, our words will ring with life and light. But if we feel as I sometimes feel, we shall simply say, in a small but hopeful voice, that he has pulled us out before and he'll pull us out again.

The truth is a powerful testimony.

Ministry and Mistaken Identity

A curious and almost undetectable process has occurred in certain sections of the Church, whereby words and expressions have become cloaks for human failure or self-delusion.

Take for example those occasions when church-based drama presentations or outreach evenings attract only a tiny fraction of the numbers hoped for.

'Well,' someone will say with a knowing smile, 'the Lord will have brought the ones he wanted to be here.'

Loosely translated this means either that the advertising was far from adequate, the whole concept was ill-judged, or that local folk are all too well acquainted with the usual standard of productions.

There's nothing deliberate or sinister about this kind of double-think. It's just that a sort of code has been developed to protect us from facing our own inadequacies.

Another, and perhaps even more common, example is the word 'ministry'. Some time ago a man phoned me to make certain money-making suggestions. He seemed to be some variety of Christian entrepreneur. His offers were wildly extravagant.

'After all,' he said, 'you can always use some extra money for your ministry, can't you?'

'My ministry?' I queried. 'What is my ministry?'

'Well – your ministry, you know.'

'But', I said, 'my main ministry is my family.'

'Yeah, quite!' he replied. 'Ministry – family, call it what you like. You can always use some extra cash, right?'

Personally, I think that selling cabbages can involve as valid a ministry as preaching to thousands, but the whole concept has become rather distorted.

The following verses are an attempt to sum up the problems in this area faced by those of us who habitually stand up in front of Christian audiences – I mean congregations.

I want to have a ministry.
I want to be profound,
I want to see the folks I touch
Go spinning to the ground.
I want to use a funny voice,
Mysterious and low,
I want to spot uneven legs,
I want to watch them grow.

I want to have a little team,
No more than two or three,
A totally devoted group
Whose ministry is – me!
They'd keep an eye upon my soul
And tell me how it looks,

And even more importantly
They'd sell my tapes and books.

I want to send my prayer list out,
The printed sort look flash,
The ones that say, 'I'm greatly blessed!
And could you send some cash?'
I'd send them out by first-class post,
And please the folk who got 'em,
By putting little written bits
In biro on the bottom.

I want to be a humble star
At national church events,
And lead obscure seminars
In great big leaky tents.
I want to say how I deplore
the famous Christian hunters,
I want to sign their Bibles
And refer to them as 'punters'.

I really want a ministry
I want to alter lives,
I want to pray for something dead
And see if it revives.
I do! I want a ministry,
I'm sure it's all been planned.
I'll make a start as soon as God,
Removes the job in hand.

The Christian world is still a very small pond in
which musicians, speakers and entertainers can
become very big fish, as long as they don't make

the mistake of swimming out into the huge secular ocean, where a whale can become a sprat in the twinkling of an eye. Very few people who begin as 'names' in the Christian arena make that transition successfully, and there are inbuilt dangers in the very concept of the 'famous Christian', both for the individuals concerned, and for those who provide an audience or congregation for them.

One of my most excruciating memories concerns an incident that occurred at a large Christian festival down towards the west of England. A worship meeting was about to begin, with a thousand or more people present. The leader of the meeting, a very enthusiastic gentleman, came to the microphone, made a couple of practical comments, then produced the following speech.

'I just want to point out to you, folks, that if you look over here' – he pointed – 'you'll see two people you all know well' – he named two famous Christians – 'and I just want to say how great I think it is that they're sitting down there among you all as if they were just ordinary people. Let's give them a round of applause . . .'!

I feel sure that those two people felt as bad as I would have done if I had been applauded for mixing with 'ordinary' people. We know there are *only* ordinary people in the Kingdom of God, but the idea still persists that some have made it farther than others, and are therefore significant in some way.

A couple of years ago I travelled many miles north on a train to speak at a large, modern anglican church. Several people were to be involved in the evening presentation, but it so happened that I reached the venue in the early afternoon, before anyone else arrived. There are few things more desolate than a deserted church complex on a grey afternoon. I trailed dismally around blank brick walls, hunting for an unlocked door.

At last, almost at the point where my circuit had begun, I located a door that squeaked open when I turned the handle and pushed, only to find myself in a small corridor with a door on each side. Putting down my trusty blue suitcase I considered for a moment. Which one should I try?

The clacking of a typewriter from my left decided me. Pushing open the swing door I peered into a room which looked as if it must be the church office. From behind a desk by the window a lady inspected me severely as she suspended her typing operations and removed her glasses. Behind her, on the wall, hung a poster advertising the event that was due to begin in a few hours' time. It featured a rather crude depiction of my face in cartoon form. I loathe pictures of me.

'Yes?' said the typist, her tone as sharp as a hatpin.

'Oh, well,' I foundered, 'I've come to – that is I'm part of the er . . . I'm involved in this evening's thing . . .'.'

'You're very early! We weren't expecting anyone until at least four o'clock.'

'Yes, I know', I writhed, 'I'm very sorry but my train just sort of got here, and er . . . here I am. I wonder if there's a room where I could just wait and . . . well wait?'

'Through the door on the other side of the corridor,' snapped the lady, gesturing dismissively with one hand and replacing her spectacles with the other. 'I believe that's the room they've allocated.'

The clacking began again. Clearly my audience was at an end. I withdrew, taking care not to let the door slam shut. After all, I didn't want my hand smacked.

At least she hadn't recognised me.

When I first began writing and speaking I experienced a pathetically intense thrill every time somebody approached me with the words, 'Aren't you . . .?'

As time has passed, however, the disadvantages of being recognised have become more and more apparent. When you are screaming irrationally at your child outside a tent or chalet at some Christian event, the last thing you want is someone coming up and saying 'Aren't you? . . .?' Besides which, my voice always goes into a sort of bleating neutral whenever I'm asked about my books or anything else connected with the work I do.

What happened half an hour after being sent to my 'allocated' room, though, was much harder to accept. I had just begun to doze happily on the teak edifice that supported me, when there was a gentle tap on the door and my secretarial friend entered with a quite different, coyly apologetic expression on her face. She must, I decided, have caught sight of that poster on the wall behind her desk.

'I'm awfully sorry', she said, continuing with the immortal words: 'I didn't realise who you were.'

Members of the small, loyal band who have grappled with my prose on a number of occasions will be aware that I suffer from the disease of politeness. On this occasion I overcame it.

'Actually,' I said, 'I'm exactly the same person that I was when we met the first time.'

Of course, I know what she meant, and I've done it myself, but what an easy trap it is to fall into. We pay lip-service continually to the principle that there are *no* unimportant people in the eyes of God, and that therefore we must consider all men and women equal; but how difficult it is in practice in the context of ordinary day-to-day interaction. Trained by our upbringing to make judgements according to the criteria of men, we are blinded to the starring role that every individual occupies in the family of God. There are no 'stage extras'.

Mother Teresa says that she sees Christ in every sick or starving beggar that she and her sisters try to help. I hope I can learn from her. I would hate it if, at the end of my life, I looked into the face of Jesus, recognised some humble soul whom I had dismissed as unimportant, and was forced to say, 'I'm awfully sorry, I didn't realise who you were . . .'.'

Television
Who Wrote the Script?

Some time ago I was watching one of our popular soaps. Which one? Well, here are two clues. First, the series is antipodean in origin. That hardly narrows it down at all.

Second, if you say it with an Australian accent it almost rhymes with 'rabies'. Got it? Good.

So, halfway through this particular programme, one of the characters – a girl with long blonde hair and rather simple eyes – gazed almost directly into the camera and said in a voice that throbbed with prefabricated passion. 'I don't understand what's happening to me. I'm not the same any more. Why have I changed?'

342

'Because, sweetheart', I replied, lounging back intelligently on the sofa with a diet-Pepsi in one hand and a fresh cream doughnut in the other, 'the scriptwriters have ordained that it should be so.

'You are trapped in a soap, and soap washes away all the grey areas. Trauma triumphs! Your destiny is not your own.'

My wife came in just then and asked me – in the sort of tone you use when you don't want to alarm someone who is on the edge of lunacy – why I was talking to the television.

My explanation, which grew quite complex as I warmed to my theme, went something like this:

Just imagine the strange and terrible world of the soap character. Grott and Scarlene, two of the main protagonists in this particular series, have been happily, faithfully married for a score of episodes.

Now, in the shadowy hinterland that such characters must inhabit between the sequences in which they are allowed actually to exist, they hold each other like frightened children, full of a nameless dread.

Scarlene grips a tear-stained script in one white-knuckled hand.

'They're making me fall in love with another man in the next episode!' she sobs. 'Oh Grott, I can't stand it. It turns out that I've been shallow and heartless all along!'

'What!' cries Grott, pulling her even more closely to him, 'despite that scene at Diphne's deathbed when the dialogue clearly established you as a person of deep integrity and warm compassionate maturity?'

'Yes, Grott, I'm nothing but a cheap little trollop!'

An alarming thought strikes Grott. 'What about me, Scarlene? How do I react?'

She clutches the crumpled script yet more firmly. 'Don't make me tell you, Grott!' she pleads.

'Tell me Scarlene! I'd rather you told me.'

She drops her head and speaks in a tense, barely contained whisper. 'You're depressed for three episodes, and then you face up to the fact that you're gay, and fall in love with my brother, Harry.'

'Gay!' screams Grott. 'What about all that suggestive winking and smiling they made us do every time we said goodnight? How can I be gay?'

'You've always been gay without realising it,' explains Scarlene, 'and my betrayal finally reveals what, deep down, you've always known. Oh, Grott, let's run away, somewhere where they can't make us do or be anything!'

'We can't Scarlene,' says Grott sadly, lifting her face to his for a final kiss, 'we're soap characters — we don't really exist. Oh Scarlene . . .'!'

'Oh Grott . . .'!'

'I can't stand here listening to your nonsense all day', interrupted my wife with her usual reverential regard for my ideas. 'I've got things to do.'

'Yes, but the point is . . .''

She'd gone.

The point I was going to make, if you don't mind me telling you instead of her, was that a sudden chill passed through me as I thought about the silly scene I'd just described.

It rang bells somewhere. The idea of living like a puppet, with some other powerful outsider pulling the strings, writing the script, making me do things that were foolish or wrong even when I didn't want to — pre-Jesus bells. And they still tinkle a little nowadays, but nowhere near as loud.

The alarming thing is that a lot of us, including me at times, would rather be in that helpless, driven situation, despite the subtle, underlying horror of it all. Is this because the fear of freedom and responsible choice is even greater? Perhaps more people would be attracted to a robotic Christianity that simply changed the programming, as it were, and marched us into heaven by remote control. Why should freedom be feared?

When I was working with children in care I encountered this problem fairly frequently. It caused great frustration among careworkers who were doing their utmost to help their charges. Many children who had endured appallingly traumatic early lives, followed by a long period of institutional residential placement, were passionately anxious to find foster parents who would offer the kind of loving, relaxed environment that they needed. Care-worker and child would take great trouble over preparation for such a move, including the compiling of a life-history, preparatory visits from and to prospective foster parents, and all the discussion and counselling that were so necessary to the process.

It was very difficult for care-workers (especially the inexperienced ones) to understand why so many children seemed to set out deliberately to sabotage the very thing they wanted so much, often at the point when they were just about to achieve it. One of the boys tried to explain it to me once.

'It's not that you don't want it to happen,' he said, 'and it's not that you don't feel excited and grateful and all that – it's just that you suddenly get frightened, and you think you're going to mess it up anyway, like everything else has always got messed up, so you just make it happen early.'

'But what is it that makes you so frightened?' I asked.

'Being in a family,' he said, 'not knowing what you do or say. Not knowing if they'll just pretend they like you or whether they really will. Besides,' he added, 'it's easier being in a home with all the other kids and staff and that. . . .'

Like many of those who yearn to be part of God's family, he was unable to take a gamble on the reality of love. Better the spiritual half-life of familiar day-to-day existence, than risky meetings with a God who might not turn out to be as loving or forgiving or understanding as his publicity suggests.

You only find out the truth by trying, and it's a terrible fate to be cast for ever in the devil's soap opera. I'm glad I got out when I did.

The Secret of the West Wing

I enjoy a lot of television programmes, but the news frightens me sometimes. The old cliché about good news being no news at all is almost one hundred per cent accurate. Occasionally a quaint or amusing anecdote will be tacked on at the end of a catalogue of woe (if a minute or so has to be filled in), but most of the information we are given is alarming or depressing. All the worst things happening in the world at any given time are condensed into periods of ten to thirty minutes on television. My children are growing up with a lopsided awareness of death and disaster. They move around a quiet Sussex market town with the threat of Middle East war rumbling through their heads. They walk to school with echoes of rape and murder reverberating through the space behind consciousness. The reality of mob violence trails them like a trouble-maker through crowded streets. They have heard of it all, but experienced none of it. I don't want them to be totally unaware of all these things, but I think their view of the world could be more balanced.

My own reaction to these real-life horror stories is more complex, and perhaps even more disturbing. Killing in Northern Ireland, brutal soccer violence, a woman murdered after breaking down on the motorway, someone thrown to his death in front of a moving lorry after a trivial argument; grotesque events of this kind provoke a response in me that contains, not only outrage, indignation and all the other common reactions, but also, and rather frighteningly, a sort of echo.

One evening, after a nauseatingly brutal and brutalised looking football hooligan had grunted something aggressively into the television camera, I turned to my wife and said, 'They should drop him down a manhole and weld the lid back on!'

Even as I spoke, I realised that this absurd Colonel Blimp-like response was just another part of my strategy for covering up a deep, cold fear that is permanently lodged in my innards. I don't think it's so much a fear of violence directed towards me (although I'm no keener on being bashed with lead piping than the next man), but rather, a dread of facing the violent impulses that exist *in* me and, I suspect, most other people as well. I am reluctant to face my own creeping awareness that something dark and dangerous is, increasingly, breaking through the shell of what we call civilised behaviour, particularly as my personal definition of civilisation is 'an agreement to pretend that we are not uncivilised'.

I feel sure I am not alone in believing that current types of legislation and policing can no longer contain these symptoms of wildness effectively enough to reassure me. The darkness is not in some conveniently distant sub-group. It exists potentially in all of us, and, in accordance with a cycle that human societies have never successfully broken, it is beginning to affect life in this country to a worrying extent.

Perhaps if we ignore it, it will simply disappear?

As a teenager I rather unwisely read several collections of what were described as 'horror stories'. I was almost addicted to them at one stage, especially the gothic Victorian tales, full of lamplit doom and despair. A theme that occurred more than once in these sombre narratives was that of the lunatic elder son, locked away in a secluded tower room at the far end of the West Wing by his embarrassed or protective family, fed and watered by some ancient family retainer, and much given to howling at midnight when some unsuspecting guest was attempting to sleep.

Those families would have faced terrible problems if a bored and, perhaps, unhappy member of the household had decided that a lunatic on the rampage was far more exciting than the monotony and restrictions imposed upon him by the rest of the family. If he knew where the key to the tower room was kept, and he used it, all hell might be let loose . . . .

The dark and dangerous secret will not just go away, and of course we have to deal with its manifestations on a practical level. I am the first to applaud genuine attempts to look for short-term solutions that will improve political and social structures, and thereby the moral health of our community.

There is no doubt in my mind that the police must continue to do what they do, as well as it can be done. Chaos is not an attractive prospect. Perhaps changes in the social and political climate *will* motivate more socially acceptable activities than soccer violence and other kinds of crude assault. Maybe vigorous efforts by public bodies will help. I hope so.

But I also remember G. K. Chesterton's comment that wife-beating is not 'the poker problem', just as soccer violence is not just a 'drink problem', and addiction is not just a 'drug problem'. They are all People Problems, and they are present, if only in embryonic form, in all of us.

Real individual change demands that we face the dark, secret place in our own personalities with courage and determination. It demands that we invite and experience personal revolution, death and resurrection on the deepest level. The shameful secret of the West Wing must be finally dealt with.

This kind of spiritual transformation is necessary for all of us, however virtuous we feel, or however mild our natures might seem, because the dark pool from which our sin is drawn finds the same level in the whole of mankind. Only the death and resurrection of Jesus happening daily and repeatedly in our lives can drain that pool and keep us clean.

We also need the kind of change that Jesus brings because it is the only type of transformation that has a real chance of surviving the decay of comfortable structures, and the frightening emergence of what we old-fashioned Christians might call 'Original Sin'.

Animals
A Single Sparrow

I've never been quite sure what to think about zoos. I have friends who put forward comprehensive and highly convincing arguments for the abolition of any kind of animal incarceration. Having listened to what they have to say I am amazed that anyone should even remotely consider it right to put wild creatures on display in this way.

'Yes!' I exclaim, 'Yes of course! You're absolutely right! How could I have ever thought otherwise?'

Unfortunately I have another friend, a zoologist, who speaks with equal passion and clarity about the *essential* role played by zoos in the protection and preservation of rare and endangered species. He also is totally convincing.

'How blind I have been!' I cry, when he explains his views to me. 'Thank you for opening my eyes to the truth – you are unquestionably correct in what you say. . . .'

Being in the rather curious position of believing that zoos should be both abolished *and* supported, and believing both things with passionate intensity, does not make it any easier to talk to my children on the subject. Consequently, when they wanted to see some 'wild animals' a couple of summers ago, we compromised and went to a safari park. In the end we got quite excited at the prospect.

We had to spend the equivalent of a month's mortgage repayment to get the six of us in, but we did it. Bridget and I were particularly keen on the big cats. Like thousands of others we wanted the thrills without the teeth.

Our monkeys, on the other hand, wanted to see their monkeys, and none of us were disappointed. Travelling through the animal enclosures in our antediluvian green box on wheels was an odd experience, rather like watching a wild-life programme from inside the television.

The lords of the jungle were impressive but not very lively slabs of lion, laid out in the sunshine, hardly twitching as the endless line of traffic wound slowly past them. Bored and superior, they completely ignored this ever-present phenomenon which experience had shown to be both harmless and invulnerable, unless someone was foolish enough to leave a car, or do something equally rash.

The monkeys were much more active. There was a sign at the entrance to the compound warning drivers that these nimble-fingered little creatures particularly enjoyed 'picking bits' off cars. We could proceed at our own risk.

The warnings were justified. Just in front of us a very smart nearly-new car was covered with the chattering vandals as they pulled out and removed the rubber strip running around the roof rim.

Billowing waves of seething monkey-hate emanated from the helpless car owner, who was prevented from accelerating by the vehicle in front of him. Our car, from which anything removable dropped off long ago, was clearly not an aristocrat amongst monkey targets.

One elderly, half-witted animal clambered laboriously up on to the back of our green box, and sat chewing dismally on little bits of rust before dropping off to confess to his equally ancient mate that he'd picked a duff one yet again.

We kept the windows carefully wound up. Those monkeys had no idea how dangerous Plass children could be.

Our car doesn't like travelling slowly. Mind you, it doesn't much like travelling fast either. In fact, given that its primary function is the provision of transport, it shows a marked reluctance to move at all. Most of all, though, it hates crawling along at a snail's pace. It gets very hot and smokes a great deal and the little temperature thing goes into the red bit and we all get rather jumpy. After we'd left the monkey enclosure we had to stop to let the engine cool down.

Just next to where we stopped, a sparrow was washing itself in a pool of water. The children craned out of the windows to watch and a little line of cars pulled up behind us to see what we were looking at.

The sparrow, sensing a rags-to-riches opportunity, put on the performance of its life; the most sensationally flamboyant piece of sparrow toiletry ever seen.

The other cars drifted slowly round and past us, their occupants looking slightly puzzled. At last we moved on, leaving the sparrow alone with his memories of greatness.

It might never happen again. But he would always know what it meant to be a star. From now on he would hob-nob with lions and swop show-biz anecdotes with warthogs.

Later, we abandoned our gasping vehicle, and set off across a large lake in a motor launch, together with twenty or thirty other people, to see the gorillas.

The two gorillas live on an island in the middle of the lake, and because they tend to become bored and fight they are furnished with their own television set, situated cosily in a little hut.

Their favourite programme, our guide informed us, was *East-Enders*. There was something vaguely hysterical about the idea of a boat load of *East-Enders* watchers peering inquisitively at two *East-Enders*-watching gorillas.

In fact, we could only just see bits of the creatures as they sat beneath a tree, presumably swopping ideas on what life will be like without Dirty Den . . . .

By the time we left the park, we were no clearer in our views on wild creatures in captivity than we had been before, but there was something about the scenes we had witnessed that reminded us irresistibly of something else.

The animals in the safari park get all the food they need, without trying. If they get bored there's always *East-Enders*. It's comfortable, but it's not natural. We saw them, but not at their untamed, resourceful best. The system looks after them and all they have to do is look as if they might do something dramatic.

Lions yawning, monkeys fiddling with cars, gorillas glued to the telly – they could have been Christians in the South-East of England.

I felt guilty. I'd rather be a sparrow . . .

Fear of Mint Sauce

I'm not very good at being tied down when it comes to the subject matter for speaking engagements, especially on those occasions when I am the 'visiting preacher' at a church. I can't preach to save my life – at least, not in any formal sense. I seem to be constitutionally incapable of assembling three points, all beginning with the same letter. You know the sort of thing I mean:

'My sermon this morning is divided into three sections under the headings – Peace, Power and Pork-scratchings. . . .'

You see? I can't even think of a sensible third one just to show you what I mean. I don't know how people do it.

That's why I panicked somewhat when, a year or so ago, I was asked to preach on the text: 'I am the good shepherd.'

As usual, when I've been given a specific title like this, my confidence nose-dived like some spluttering first world war bi-plane. I like big, broad headings that enable me to meander, and explore ideas and tell unrelated stories – those who have heard me speak will know, to their cost, exactly what I mean.

357

Just before my emotional Sopwith Camel hit the ground (have you ever regretted starting a metaphor?) I discovered a parachute in the form of a small zoo a few miles from our home, known as Drusillas. It isn't a Safari Park like the place I just mentioned, but it's very good. In the course of wandering around with my wife and our own small menagerie (no, I still hadn't worked out what to think about zoos), certain ideas occurred to me. Why, I wondered, did Jesus decide to portray us, his followers, as sheep? After all, the Bible is ankle-deep in all sorts of creatures. In Matthew's gospel Jesus says, 'Behold I send you out as sheep in the midst of wolves; so be wise as serpents and innocent as doves.' Quite a noisy little gathering if they all started bleating and howling and hissing and cooing at the same time.

So, why sheep? Obviously they were much in evidence in that part of the world. Was it just that they were the most available visual aid?

We lingered for a while at the tortoise pen. Twenty or more little armoured tanks were crawling under and over each other to get at the heap of food that had just been left for them. I pictured Jesus standing on a hillside and declaiming, 'I am the good tortoise keeper. My tortoises know my voice, and they come to me – very, very slowly . . . .'

Makes sense, doesn't it, especially when you think of the way Christians retreat into their shells when anything mildly threatening happens? Perhaps there weren't any tortoises in Judea.

The exotic birds who lived by a large, artificial lake suggested other possibilities.

'I am the good flamingo herder. My flamingoes know my voice, but every time anyone stares at them they stand on one leg and turn pink . . . .'

Or the monkey house.

'I am the monkey husbander. My monkeys hear my voice, but they chatter ceaselessly and perform unnecessarily complicated double somersaults whenever it becomes important to move higher or lower . . . .'

The porcupines.

'I am the good porcupine keeper. My porcupines may well know my voice, but they are almost exclusively concerned with defending themselves, and are very difficult to get close to . . . .'

Emus.

'I am the good emu-watcher. My emus know my voice, but they are so used to being grounded, that they've forgotten they were originally designed to fly . . . .'

I could go on for ever; there are lots of different animals and birds at Drusillas, but I'd better get on to the sheep. We came to a small enclosure, strewn with straw, and containing a ewe with her two recently born lambs. These knock-kneed little creatures, looking like something created out of pipe-cleaners, were clearly rather nervous of the spectators who ringed their small temporary home. One was simply standing and quivering beside his mother, while his brother or sister (well, can *you* sex lambs?) had hidden his face behind a small protruding piece of wood. He seemed to believe that if he couldn't see us then we probably couldn't see him. A tinge of ostrich in his ancestry, perhaps? Mother sheep was trembling constantly, her eyes flicking round fearfully from human face to human face. She looked as if she would have loved to find a herd to belong to, and a shepherd, perhaps. Maybe that's why Jesus described us as sheep; because we're nervous things who don't know where to go or who to follow. Milling around in crowds, separated into families, or isolated as individuals, the same shadowy problem has always existed in the hearts of men, women and sheep: 'I know that I belong to someone, but where shall I find that person, and will he greet me with love or mint sauce?'

I have to confess, as a relatively long-term bleater, that for many years I suffered from this mint-sauce view of God. Either he was fattening me for the kill, as it were, or else he was gritting his teeth and allowing me to hang around on the edge of his flock until such time as it became necessary to shoo me off into the wilderness. What a pathetically insecure little sheep I have been.

And now?

Well, I'm suffering a little thinning of the fleece, but the patient guidance of the good shepherd has warmed me into a reassuring confidence that I'm not going to end up on anyone's cosmic dinner table. Nowadays I find the rest of the flock

endearing, irritating, puzzling, lovable, confusing and infuriating. I'm sure they have an equally
diverse view of me, but the important thing is our
awareness that we belong to each other, and that
our mutual love and concern are top priorities.

We are a community of hope, not a perfect and
triumphant army: unsure about many things, but
united by our desires to be good, and a sheep-like
dependency upon the good shepherd.

Graffiti
The Devil's Aerosol

It's not easy to shake off the past. Wouldn't it be wonderful if conversion brought immediate, comprehensive repair and transfiguration? Instant perfection.

A bit of a shock for our nearest and dearest, though. Imagine waking up to find that 'Our Fred', whose every vice is as familiar as an old friend, has become a blazing torch of eternal light. Perhaps it wouldn't be so wonderful after all.

But why does the process of change take so long? Why are the labour pains of being born again so prolonged and acute for so many Christian people?

I have a friend whose ministry of healing and counselling has been stunningly effective. He is the smile on the face of God to a procession of needy people, but as his life goes on he is discovering layer upon layer of injury and pain related to the past, particularly in connection with his very early years when he suffered sexual abuse from his mother, and a very unhappy childhood generally.

Many of his buried memories have been uncovered and healed, but there are many more to come. How can we understand this process by which the past puts painful clamps on the present? Let me suggest just one way to look at it. It's summed up by a very modern word – graffiti.

The prophet Jeremiah announced God's intention to write his law on the hearts of his people, and the apostle Paul described the Corinthian Christians as a letter from Christ, written on the tablets of human hearts.

The problem though, assuming your heart is anything like mine, is that the negative graffiti accumulated over the years are so thick and indelible that there's not a great deal of space left for anything else.

The devil wields a pretty effective infernal aerosol can. Let me tell you about some of the scribbles I've discovered.

When I was a little boy of six I decided that I wanted to be an actor when I grew up. I announced this ambition to an aunt who happened to be staying at the time.

'Oh no,' she replied with sparkling aunty wit, 'you need to be good-looking to do that.'

Of course, Auntie Gertrude, or whatever her name was, had no intention of upsetting me – she was just being funny. But it's really and truly no exaggeration to say that the discovery that I was not good-looking wounded my self-image for years.

The next scribble – scraped out in capital letters, this one – happened when I was a teenager. I was in the middle of a combined Drama/GCE course at a college of further education in Tunbridge Wells.

One afternoon, as I sat talking to a couple of other students on the lawn at the back of the building, one of the lecturers strolled over and, quite gratuitously, told me that I was a 'waster'. Whatever chances and opportunities came my way, he said, I would misuse and simply waste. Then he strolled off.

I think he was trying to be helpful, but, as we all know, the road to Hell is paved with good intentions – or unposted letters in my wife's case – and those few words of his came very close to snuffing out the tiny spark of confidence that glowed faintly in my very insecure teenage heart.

Over the years that sentence has haunted me, and it has never had a constructive effect. It has often weakened my resolve, and still does very occasionally.

Sometimes the graffiti are in the form of conversational ruts, the same sort of verbal dialogue repeated again and again, eroding self-confidence and casting a shadow of defeat over the future.

Consider the following scene, for example, between a daughter and her father.

Daughter: Did you manage to get my bike done, Dad?

Father: I'm changing this plug for your mother, I've just mended the chair that your brother broke, and I've had your Auntie Phyllis on the phone for twenty minutes about next Wednesday. No, I have not got round to your bike yet and it's no use going on about it because I just haven't had time!

Daughter: I didn't mean you should have done it, Dad. I was just asking –

Father: Everyone's just asking. I've told you I'll do it, and I will do it just as soon as I can, so you'll just have to be patient.

Daughter: I don't mind being patient, Dad. I wasn't complaining about you not doing it, I was just wondering if you had got round to it. It was just . . . information I wanted.

Father: Okay! All right! I'll leave the plug. Let's not bother about what anybody else wants. Let's just get your bike fixed then you'll be all right and we can start seeing to other people's needs.

Daughter: But I don't want you to do my bike now. I told you, I was just . . .'.

Father: Well, if you don't want me to do your bike now, why have you been getting so het-up about it?

Daughter: I haven't been getting het-up about it! I wasn't anything when I first came in!

Father: *Well, what are you shouting at me for if you're not het-up?*

Daughter: I *wasn't* het-up!

Father: Well, you certainly are now, aren't you? Or is this what you call being calm and peaceful?

Daughter: Dad, when I came in I simply asked you quite quietly and nicely whether you'd done my bike or not. That's all I wanted to know – had you done my bike.

Father: Well, have you moved all your books off the landing yet?

Daughter: No, but that's not what we're talking about!

Father: Oh, I see! We're allowed to talk about me not having done what you wanted, but we're not allowed to talk about you letting me down. Don't you think that's a bit less than fair?
(PAUSE)

Daughter: That's stupid, Dad!

Father: Ah! Now we come it it, don't we? We usually end up with me being stupid don't we? Do you know what my father would have said to me if I'd ever *dared* to talk to him like that?

Daughter: I –

Father: Well, do you?

Daughter: (DEAD TONES) Yes, I do. You've told me about thirty-nine times. He'd have taken all your privileges away for the next two weeks, and you might have got the strap as well.

Father: There's no need to be sarcastic about your grandfather. At least he never set out to cause trouble in the family. He was a good man who never did less than his best. He loved you kids when you were little, and I'd be ashamed to have him standing here listening to the way you're going on! I don't know why you do it!

I don't know what's happened to you! We used to play games and have a laugh together. You used to look up to me and ask questions and I'd show you how to do things – we were best friends, dammit! What have I done to deserve you drifting off into being Miss Clever-clever?

Daughter: Dad – please! It's not fair. I didn't start any of this!

Father: Oh, you didn't start it. Who did then? The man in the moon? You come in here demanding that I do your blessed bike, you tell me I'm stupid when I talk about other people's needs, you mock your grandfather who's dead and can't defend himself, and then you tell me you didn't start

367

any of it! Well, I'm sorry but I think I'm too stupid to understand that, much too stupid!

Daughter: (ALMOST BREATHLESS WITH HURT) Look, Dad, I came in, right? And I said – exactly like this – I said, 'Have you managed to do my bike, Dad?' and you got all exasperated and went on about all the other things you had to do, but I – wasn't – complaining. I – was – just – asking . . . .

Father: Yes, like I've *just* been asking you for weeks and weeks to clear your books and stuff off the landing, and help your mother round the house and think about others a bit more than you do –

Daughter: (FURIOUS) That's not what we were talking about! That's not what we were talking about! You stupid, stupid man! You don't want to understand! You don't want to listen to what I'm saying! I didn't start it! I didn't start it! I didn't start it! (SHE CONTINUES TO SHOUT THOSE THREE WORDS OVER AND OVER AGAIN)

Father: (CALLS HIS WIFE) Sheila! Come and lend a hand. Dorothy's having one of her does again!

Mother:	Come on, Dotty, calm down, you'll only make your throat sore, calm down love, there's no point.
Father:	She's hysterical!
	(HE SMACKS HER ONCE ON THE FACE. SHE IMMEDIATELY STOPS SHOUTING).

I could make a long list of the graffiti that clutter my heart space. So could you. Things people have said, failures that have destroyed confidence, traumatic experiences, profound, unforgettable embarrassments – all sorts of things. Usually each one tells you a lie about yourself:

- You will never succeed.
- You are not lovable.
- God has cast you aside because of *that* sin.
- You're boring.
- People will only ever use you.
- Happiness is impossible.
- Your life has no purpose.

The almost invariable untruthfulness of these scrawlings should be sufficient indication of their ultimate authorship.

The father of lies is anxious that our souls should be covered by a confused mass of misinformation, some of it so deeply scored that it comes close to breaking our hearts.

Jesus promises that we shall be washed as white as snow. This may involve several years' work by the divine cleaning department in the case of you and me, but we have the promise and therefore we have the hope as well.

We may, like the friend I mentioned earlier, need specific healing of memories, we may just need to be loved for a good long time.

One of the things I like about God, and I've only discovered it relatively recently, is that he has relationships, not systems. When someone is converted he doesn't say, 'Right, Fred's come to faith, procedure number 39B, line 6, get on it, angels!'

He says, 'Fred's come home to me – wonderful! Now let's have a think about this. Old Fred's an awkward customer in some ways. Too much pressure and he just slips out sideways. What we need to do is . . . .'

And so a plan, specially, particularly designed for Fred, is set in motion. It will offer the best possible options, guidance and influence, and it will be alive with the love of God. Fred may mess it up at various points, but the plan is flexible and can be adjusted by Fred's new parent.

If God was a tailor there would be no off-the-peg suits in his shop, only bespoke ones, meticulously cut and designed to provide a perfect fit for each individual customer.

Our heavenly father knows everything there is to know about us, every worry, every hurt, every tiny scar, every line of graffiti that is trespassing in our lives. Let's try to relax a little, and ask him to show us his plan for clearing a space in our hearts.

The Worst Crime in the World

'What do you think is the worst crime in the world?'

One of my children asked me that question once, probably during Sunday lunch – they save up all their most difficult questions for Sunday lunchtime. I don't think I produced a very satisfactory answer at the time, but there probably is no final answer to a question like that, not one that everyone would agree with anyway. It made me think, though.

What is the worst crime in the world?

One of G. K. Chesterton's Father Brown stories is actually entitled *The Worst Crime in the World*. In this tale the ultimate sin was patricide, the murder of a father by his son, revealed as usual through the penetrating insights of the modest little Roman Catholic priest called Brown.

I imagine that many people would agree with this answer to my original question, the suggestion that illegal killing is the very worst thing that one could do, especially the kind of murder that Chesterton is describing.

The fact is, however, that a person's perception of what constitutes truly evil behaviour is very often conditioned by his or her particular circumstances and experiences.

I remember reading a book on the philosophy of education as part of my teacher-training course. I only understood one sentence in fifty, but it included a little anecdote that has stayed in my mind ever since. A class of junior children were given the task, by their teacher, of listing the ten worst things that anyone could do, in descending order of 'badness'.

Notable among the results of this exercise, was the list of a child who had written:

1. Murder.
2. Shouting in the corridor.

The latter sin never quite made it into the ten commandments, but for that child, it clearly ranked high above theft, adultery, and all the other trivial misdemeanours that our weak flesh is capable of. I'm rather glad I didn't go to that school.

Or, consider the case of a teenage boy whom we used to know. Alan was a frequent visitor to the little semi-detached house in Bromley that my wife and I shared with the curate of St Augustine's church, an old friend of mine called John Hall. None of us had any money, so the house was furnished, in the main, with items that had already been sold three or four times at the annual scout jumble sale. Indeed, local people who came to the house would often point out, with nostalgic pleasure, some item of furniture that had once been theirs.

Alan's house, by contrast, was like something out of a glossy magazine. His mother was not just house-proud, she was fanatically devoted to the brushing and dusting and scrubbing and hoovering of the brick-built god whom she served. Her family were annoying infidels who constantly undid all her good works.

Each evening, after the family meal, this sad woman insisted that her husband and son sat on camp chairs (fetched from an immaculate cupboard under the stairs) in order to avoid using the three-piece suite, her special pride and joy. Occasionally, she would arrive home to discover a tiny wrinkle in the fabric of the settee or armchair, and would then, in scandalised and accusatory tones, utter the immortal words: 'Someone's been sitting on the chairs!'

Unsurprisingly, Alan was a rather tense lad, though very pleasant company. He visited us a lot, perhaps because we were less than house-proud, to put it mildly, and not very bothered about 'things'. One day, however, he clearly thought that he had committed the worst crime in the world in the middle of our sitting-room.

Not long after our first meeting, he came in for coffee one morning, and, perfectly reasonably, sat down on an upright wooden chair beside the table. This chair was part of our latest jumble sale acquisition, a set of four heavily worn dining-room chairs which had cost the huge sum of five pence each. They had undoubtedly arrived at their final resting place.

As Alan relaxed his weight onto the chair he had selected, it collapsed completely, immediately and irreparably. It was no longer a chair and would never be a chair again.

Alan gazed up at us from the midst of the wreckage, physically unhurt as far as we could see, but white-faced with horror as he waited to see what our response would be to this abominable crime. After all, in his house, world war three broke out if you *sat* in the wrong chair. What kind of armageddon would erupt now that he had totally demolished one?

The expression on Alan's face as Bridget and I fell about laughing, moved from shock, through bewilderment to profound relief. We weren't about to beat him to death with a piece of ex-furniture. He really relaxed in our house after that.

I'm afraid that many Christians have a problem similar to that of Alan, and the child in the junior class. They have never committed the huge, cataclysmic sins or crimes such as murder, but they do have their own specific sin, vice or problem, which can easily seem like the worst crime in the world, depending on who supplied your moral yardstick in the first place. The junior child's was supplied by his teacher, Alan's by his mother, but it could be a denominational emphasis, or the influence of one Christian leader or parent or adviser.

It was a great relief to me, when I encountered one of these personal blocks, to go back to the gospels and remind myself of what I already knew in my heart.

Jesus condemned *all* sin. If the disciples were hoping for a bit of relaxation on some points then they must have been very disappointed indeed. You can't even lust after a woman in your heart, he told his followers. You are damned if you call your brother a fool, he went on to say. Far from easing up on the rules, he made Moses look like an anarchist. Not only did he not abolish the law, he made it absolutely clear that the standard demanded by God is *so* high that no one (except himself) had any chance of achieving that standard, let alone maintaining it.

Then, having made it clear that no human being would ever qualify for entry into the Kingdom of God, he voluntarily went to his death to save us from the consequences of breaking that law which he had insisted we must obey to the letter; very eccentric behaviour indeed for anyone but the Son of God.

As though it were a vast lake, we see only the surface of this mysterious act of atonement, but there is no doubt that if the sins of murder and messing up an armchair are thrown simultaneously into that serene expanse of water, they will sink at the same speed, and they will disappear with the same merciful certainty that they are gone for ever.

Failing to take advantage of that opportunity is probably the worst crime in the world – against ourselves.

Picking up the Pieces

Those who know Winchester Cathedral well, will be aware that it contains a quite extraordinary jigsaw puzzle.

Now, I'm something of an expert when it comes to jigsaws. I've got four children (which is about ten more than three, for those who don't know), and they range from cool sixteen to totally dominant three-and-a-half.

Sixteen years of assorted jigsaw puzzles have passed through the hands, toy-shelves and cracks in the floorboards of our offspring. Some are the very simple, thick kind that come in four pieces – those are the ones that little Katy or I do – and others are the huge two-thousand-piece sort where the sky drives you raving mad and the last three pieces look as if they couldn't *possibly* fit, but they do.

In a china pot upstairs I've got a sad little collection of orphaned jigsaw pieces. I can't help it! I can't bring myself to throw them away. I find them under stair-carpets, or blocking up the hoover, or even in the garden. They have a certain desolate, dog-eared charm, and, besides, any one of them might, one day, enable me to heal the anguish of some member of the family who has finished a long and difficult jigsaw only to find that ONE PIECE IS MISSING! Those lost pieces have a place somewhere and I just have this pathetic hope that they'll get back where they belong eventually, and mean something again.

Winchester Cathedral's spectacular jigsaw puzzle is, in fact, a huge window in the west wall, but it's unlike any other church window that I've ever seen. It appears to be made up of hundreds of pieces of glass, each of which is a different shape and size, but there is no overall picture or pattern. If you look very carefully you will see a foot, or part of a face, or some other small detail, but the sections of glass are arranged in such a random fashion that they seem to make no sense at all. Those who know the history of the cathedral will tell you that, once upon a time, they did make sense, and then something happened.

It was the seventeenth century and Cromwell's forces were in the process of securing the country for their leader. When the Puritan army came to Winchester many of the most beautiful works of art in the cathedral were brutally destroyed. The west window was completely smashed.

Aghast at this appalling act of vandalism, some of the local people collected the pieces of glass and hid them carefully, intending to put the window back when the soldiers had gone or the religious climate had relaxed a little.

When that time came, though, the task proved too difficult. Willing as the townsfolk were, they simply couldn't do it. That enormous jigsaw puzzle was too much for them. But that must have been a very stubborn group of people indeed. Their window was going back into the west wall of Winchester Cathedral whether it made sense or not! So, back it went, with the fragments of glass fastened together in crazy disarray, and there it still is, a monument to determination and community spirit.

Some people (Christian or otherwise) seem to float through life with few storms or disturbances to disrupt their progress. Whatever the reasons for this – temperament, background, personality or particular circumstances, I rejoice for these fortunate ones, but I also grieve for those who seem to encounter continual suffering.

For many people who read these words life may seem to have disintegrated, just as that vast window did more than three hundred years ago, into a jigsaw puzzle that doesn't seem to make any sense at all. I've been through that process of falling apart myself, and I know about the sobbing despair that can fill the nights and days with what feels like endless darkness. There are two things that might be worth considering.

First, like me at home, I feel quietly sure that God picks up and keeps the sad, lost parts of his suffering children's lives because he knows that they are pieces of the completed puzzle, however much of a mystery they may seem at the moment.

Secondly, it may be helpful to think about that cathedral window once again. Somewhere in that strange jumble of shattered images a potential picture still exists. We may not see it in its former state, not this side of heaven at any rate, but we know for sure that it is there. It is, I believe, not too optimistic to trust that the same God who says, 'Behold, I make all things new' will take every fragment – good and bad – of our disintegrated lives, and show us one day what an unexpectedly beautiful picture they were always intended to make.

Mary, the mother of Jesus, has always been a personal heroine of mine in this respect. Her personal collection of, apparently, unmatched jigsaw pieces was strange indeed.

First of all, as a young, unmarried girl, she is visited by an angel who announces that she is to become pregnant by the Holy Ghost. What an irregular shape to begin with! It was just as well that Joseph had it all authenticated by his own angelic visitor.

The next bit of the puzzle comes when Mary arrives in Bethlehem only to find that she is forced to bed down in a smelly old stable. She might easily have said, 'Look, God, this is a bit off! Are you losing your grip? You've blown the budget on the angels, there's nothing left for bed and breakfast.' But she didn't say that. Unlike many of us modern Christians she accepted everything that came alone – puzzled but willing.

After the birth of Jesus the other pieces of the puzzle came thick and fast; shepherds turning up to see the baby – very nice, but why? Wise men arriving with strange symbolic gifts; the meeting with Simeon in the temple; the flight into Egypt to escape Herod; the death of all those babies in Bethlehem.

Much later comes the business of the boy Jesus absenting himself from his parents' care for three days, to be discovered eventually discussing religious matters with doctors of the law.

'Didn't it occur to you', says Jesus to his distraught mother, 'that I would be in my father's house?'

The Bible says that Mary stored all these things in her heart, rather like the contents of that little pot of mine, lots of oddly shaped bits of jigsaw that seemed to mean very little at the time. Sometimes, when things are quiet, she must have taken those pieces out – as it were – and tried to fit them together. Some of them so starkly contrasted:

'Blessed art thou among women . . . .'

'A sword shall pierce thy heart also . . . .'

Then, when Jesus begins his ministry, there are the miracles and the conflicts, the teaching and the taking on of a very powerful establishment; the pain of hearing him say, 'Who is my mother?'; and that magical moment when, almost with his last breath, he looks at her from the cross with loving eyes and instructs one of his disciples to look after her when he is gone.

As she mourned at the foot of that cross, Mary must have wondered if the jigsaw would ever be completed now.

We seldom talk about it in the Church, but can you imagine Mary's feelings when she first saw her son alive and well three days after his dead body had been placed in the tomb? That moment, and the moment when the Holy Spirit came in tongues of flame and a mighty rushing wind, must have seemed like the last two pieces of the picture, a picture that showed Mary she had played a leading part in bringing God himself into the world, so that generation after generation would be able to go home to their heavenly father.

But, of course, the final piece of the jigsaw, for Mary and for each of us, must be our encounter with Jesus in the place where he sits at the right hand of his father. When that happens the picture will certainly be complete, but it may be very different from what we expected.

If you ever find yourself in Winchester, visit the cathedral for half an hour – take a look at that window . . .

Heaven
Far Pavilions?

For me, April shines like a jewel in the fascinating necklace of the year. It makes me think of two very important things. First, it's the time of year when God switches on the heavenly sprinkler system to prepare our cricket pitches for a new season.

I might possibly have let slip in previous writings a hint of the passion I feel for this superlative activity. If we were not Christians my three sons and I would undoubtedly worship the sport god, an energetic trinity composed of cricket, football and rugby.

For me, the greatest of these is cricket, so the alternative shine and shower of the fourth month fills me annually with exuberant expectancy and sends me burrowing through the junk in the cupboard under the stairs muttering things like, 'I know I put that bat in here! I just wish people wouldn't move things . . . .'

It's always where I left it, and I always find it, and I always stand for a moment caressing the wood with the tips of my fingers, making little half-witted cooing sounds as my mind is filled with anticipation of the red, white, green and blue of a perfect cricketing day.

'Earth hath not anything to show more fair . . . .' Oh, no, that's the view from Westminster Bridge isn't it? Sorry!

Now, in case you think this is all a bit over the top, I do realise that, for some people, cricket is the most excruciatingly effective cure for insomnia ever devised by man. But then, I might find your favourite activity completely incomprehensible.

Perhaps you are devoted to wrestling with aardvarks. I respect that. My ignorance of the finer points of aardvark wrestling may prohibit me from enjoying it as you do, but I understand enjoyment. Let us be tolerant of each other.

The second thing that April makes me think of is heaven.

I live almost at the base of the South Downs, which means that I'm constantly being drawn to the top of the South Downs. God goes up there a lot too, and I walk and talk with him if we meet.

We've also met in police cells and pubs and dark, dangerous places, but this is a different kind of encounter. Up on those swelling green hills in springtime I can taste the bubbling springs of heaven as I sense his yearning for the return of perfection to the world he made so long ago. I need those encounters because I've had trouble with the idea of heaven.

Perhaps I'm the only one who has experienced these fears about the after-life, but I doubt it.

Sometimes, on a Sunday morning, whatever the denominational setting, I have known a sudden surging panic as I imagine heaven being like an average morning service, but going on for ever. A small child inside me shouts, 'I don't want to go! I don't want to go!'

Then there are some of the rewards promised by scripture, many of them items in a sort of regulation Paradise kit, things like gold crowns and white robes. No doubt these were powerful incentives to Jesus' contemporaries, mainly poor folk enduring the humiliating fact of Roman occupation, but they don't attract me at all. I'd just as soon walk the golden streets of heaven in jeans, tee-shirt and no head covering at all if the divine quartermaster doesn't mind.

I find it interesting to conjecture how Jesus might have described heaven if he had entered the world as a man at the present stage in history. I feel sure that he would have selected symbols relevant to the age, but I wonder if he might have focused in on my particular preoccupation. Sometimes, in the course of those hill-top walks of mine, I have addressed God on the subject of life after death and the specific components of eternal bliss.

'God,' I've said, 'I don't really want a gold crown like it says in the Bible. I don't fancy sitting round for eternity singing choruses and – and all the other things.

'I like – love – so many things on this earth you made. When the new earth gets done, couldn't I have a little flat a bus-ride from The Oval? I love you, and I want to be with you, but . . . .'

Up on the hills I can hear God chuckling when I say that. 'The essence of everything you have loved will be yours', he says. 'Trust me. No eye has seen, no ear has heard, no mind has conceived what God has prepared for those who love him.'

And when I think about those words calmly and sensibly the truth is so obvious. Why should I expect God, who knows me and loves me like the best possible of fathers, to saddle me for ever with a burden of tedium and monotony? How intriguing to reflect that heaven is certain to contain the essence of all those things that I have loved and cared about most. What a joy it must be for our Heavenly Father to arrange individual mansions for each of his beloved children as they come to him, welcome visitors in his kingdom because the name of Jesus is always on their lips.

Suddenly it all begins to seem rather exciting.

Cricket and heaven – perhaps they're not mutually exclusive after all. We shall see . . .'.

I'm dying to live after living has ended,
I'm living for life after death,
Alive to the fact that I'm dead apprehensive,
I'll live to the end of my breath.
But what would life be were I no longer living,
And death were no longer alive,
How would I stick it without my cricket,
How would I ever survive?
Would I cross swords on some heavenly Lords,
With the angels of Holding and Hall,

Would I face up to Lillee without feeling silly,
And even catch sight of the ball?
Would a man with a beard who the bowlers all
  feared,
Redeem us from losing – a sin?
Yes, by Grace we'd be saved as his century
  paved
The way to a glorious win.
I promise you Lord, I'll never get bored,
I'll practise the harp, there, I've sworn,
If cricket's allowed, I'll be back on my cloud,
The moment that stumps have been drawn.

How easy it is for our image of heaven to be
distorted and darkened by the kinds of pictures
and stories that insist on hanging sterile religious
trappings over attractive Christian realities. Don't
get down about the after-life; it'll be heaven!

We'll Meet Again

Part of the joy of heaven will be reunion with
people we loved in this life.

My friend, Chris, loved his mother very much.
Widowed relatively early in life, she eventually
became unwell, and was diagnosed as having an
incurable disease. Chris and his wife Jean nursed
her through the final stages of what turned out to
be a rapidly spreading, wasting disease, until she
died in the spare bedroom of their little house in
Eastbourne.

It was a complex experience for Chris. The
pain of watching his mother's suffering was almost unbearable, especially as she grew thinner

and thinner, and more and more helpless. Increasingly, he felt as if he was parent in the relationship, and his mother a child, a child whose physical dependency became more pronounced with every week that passed. Occasionally his emotions would overwhelm him and he would sob uncontrollably at the side of the bed, forced into being a child again by the power of his grief. At such times, his mother was able to reach out an enfeebled hand and comfort him with her touch. Her mind and emotions were perfectly sound, and she knew exactly what her son was going through. Through this continual exchange of caring and receiving roles the relationship deepened and sweetened in a way that was quite new to both of them.

Death, when it came, did not seem harsh, and it certainly didn't feel like the end. United on one very important level by their Christian faith, Chris and his mother said their farewells in the sure and certain knowledge that they would meet again, not as parent and child perhaps, but in a new and more complete relationship. Some time after his mother's death, Chris asked me if I might write something about his feelings and experiences during those last few difficult weeks. The following poem is an inadequate attempt to do just that.

I mothered she who mothered me,
The body that I never knew,
(Though she knew mine so well when I was
small and she was all my need).

So plaintive now,
Her arms surrendered high to be undressed or
    dressed,
Like some poor sickly child,
Who sees no shame in helplessness,
Embarrassed once, but all too happy now,
To let me ease her weariness.
And yet, when I collapsed and cried beside her
    on the bed,
She was my mother once again,
She reached her hand out to the child in me,
She dried my tears,
And held me there till I was still.
So ill, so long
Until, at last, when endless days of hopefulness
    had faded finally
There came a night of harmony, a night of
    many psalms,
I mothered she who mothered me
And laid my sister gently
In our father's arms.

Love or Light-Sabres

I am told by some people that the anticipation of
union with Jesus will overcome fear of death. The
answers, they say, are in the scriptures. I don't
believe it is quite as simple as that.

When I was converted nearly twenty-five years
ago I began, with many others, a lifelong attempt
to understand what the Bible means, or should
mean, to Christians like myself.

Like many young Christians in the sixties I
began by swallowing whole lumps of information

without really chewing or digesting the things that I was told. Thus, at the tender age of sixteen, I was loudly and dogmatically arguing that the Bible was without question inerrant and infallible, and that anyone who disagreed with me was probably not saved and certainly in grave error.

As the years pass though, and I gradually learn how to relax into a genuine father-son relationship with God, I've come to realise that it can take decades for knowledge to become truly heartfelt. In my own journey towards understanding I have reached the point where I know in my heart that the Bible is a letter from God to me, and every word is meant to be there. It begins: 'Dear Adrian . . .', and it ends: 'Love, God'. I thank him for it.

Back in those early days also, I had what seems on reflection to have been a somewhat superstitious belief in the 'magical' power of scripture verses, again a distorted perception of a truth that was taught in an over-simplified manner. I developed, or inherited, or caught, the notion that in any problematic situation it was possible to wield portions of the Bible rather like the light sabres used in *Star Wars*.

On the many occasions when my holy incantations didn't work, I assumed that either I had backslidden in some way, or that I had picked the wrong scripture, or, after particularly dismal failures, that there was no God after all. I still understand virtually nothing, but my understanding in this area has at least matured a little.

It seems to me now that there are indeed times when scripture can be used like a sword to cut through worldly or satanic thickets, but it is not automatic and if we are, like Jesus, doing only what we see the father doing, it can never be a loose or random way of approaching problems. Sometimes we are given a specific scripture, not to thrust dramatically under someone's nose, but to show us what we must do. Let me give you an example of what I mean.

At the end of last year a man called Peter, whom I know a little, dropped round for coffee. Peter is a retired U.R.C. minister, a good man and a solid Christian. As we sipped our coffee he told me that his wife, Jean, had died two days previously. She had been ill for some time, finally discharging herself from hospital three years ago, a few months before Peter was due to retire. She had come home to die.

The illness was incurable and she was very frightened. As Peter lay beside his wife in the darkness, on the first night of her return, he asked himself and God what he could possibly do to ease the suffering of this woman who had given in to the prospect of imminent death, and whose body was rigid with the terror of its approach.

People talk very easily about receiving 'words from the Lord'. When little hangs on the outcome it can be a very inexpensive claim to make. That night, for one of the very few times in his life, Peter believed that God had placed a verse of scripture into his mind, and that it was connected somehow with his desperate prayer.

What was the verse? It was a very familiar one; one he had read and even spoken about many times in the course of his long preaching career. It occurs in the first epistle of John, and consists of just five words: 'Perfect love casts out fear.'

But what did it mean? Some people, well-meaning no doubt, would have switched the light on, and cheerily cried: 'Good news! The Lord's given me a word for you — "Perfect love casts out fear". Feeling better?'

But Peter didn't see it like that. The word had been for him, not Jean. He was supposed to do something. By the morning he knew what it was, and he knew how costly it would be; tremendous emotional expenditure on someone he was bound to lose eventually.

Peter cuddled Jean for breakfast and he cuddled her for lunch, he cuddled her for tea and he cuddled her for supper. For three months he was rarely more than three yards away from her. Maybe it wasn't perfect love, but it was the very best he'd got, and God was in it. At the end of that three months the fear had been loved out of Jean, and she was beginning to take an interest in where she and Peter might live after his retirement.

Peter held his wife's hand three years later as she died in late December, and knew as he did so that the fear was gone from her. He was able to say to God: 'I did do it, Lord. I did what you said. It might not have been perfect love, but I did my best and you topped it up. You were right in what you told me that night. Thank you. . . .'

Peter's experience highlights a truth that I have paid lip-service to for years without really absorbing its importance. Namely, that God will do what he will do, for his own good reasons, and that these 'doings' will frequently fail to fit with the personal theology I have cobbled together over the years. Peter and his wife needed that particular word, applied in that particular way, at that particular time, and God knew it.

Similarly, a friend of mine who is a pentecostal minister (his only fault!), was anxious that his father should become a Christian. With customary energy he set about expounding the scriptures to his ageing parent, threatening him with hell, promising him heaven, and generally giving him the 'works'. After a lengthy experience of this kind of approach the old man did his best to be out when he knew his son was likely to call. Conversion was definitely not on *his* agenda.

It was only when my friend stopped talking and started listening that God was able to whisper to him: 'When did you last tell your dad you loved him?'

'Never', thought my friend. 'I should have done, but I never have . . . '

The next day he went along to see his father, put his arm round his shoulders and, ignoring the flinch of resistance to what his dad obviously thought was going to be yet another evangelical blast, said those three words that are so difficult to use when they are not common conversational currency: 'I love you.'

My friend's father made a Christian commitment very shortly after that, and became a member of his own son's church.

God knows what will melt hearts much better than we do, and it may be different in every case. I hate the thought that my pet formulae might obscure or postpone the work that the Holy Spirit wants to do. Perhaps, rather, we should aim (as my friend Jo Marriott puts it) to find out what God is doing, and then join in.

He wants people in heaven much more than we do, and he knows how to achieve it.

Outsiders
What Oscar Did

'I never read anything but the Bible. That's the only book I need.'

I have heard that comment more than once whilst visiting churches or groups as a speaker. One shiny-eyed character informed me of this fact as I sat behind a table piled high with my own volumes, signing books for a steady stream of folk who had just endured more than an hour of my voice.

I tried to look abashed. At first this kind of restricted literary diet seemed as though it must be right. Then I was suddenly annoyed with myself. Of course it wasn't right! The depth and richness and beauty of good literature is a gift from God to be used and enjoyed. Obviously, some types of writing (the badly written as much as the obscene) are unhelpful, to say the least, but the secrets of the human heart are unveiled through the literary art in ways that are as diverse as they are enlightening.

By all means let us be selective, but let us not be narrow or prudish.

I wonder, for example, how my friend who only reads the Bible would view my choice of Richard Ellmann's biography of Oscar Wilde, as my favourite book of the last two or three years. It warmed my heart, and I would like to explain *why* it meant so much to me.

Some things never change.

As a small child I occasionally chanced upon a book so ravishingly, richly absorbing, that all I wanted was to inhabit that small universe within a universe, to the exclusion of all other activities and interests. My first choice reading spot was the foot of a pine tree at the top of a hill a mile from my home. That place is all houses now, but I still retreat a mile back from the front of my mind when the book is right and the phone is dead and the family are out and I haven't passed my latest deadline. I hardly left my pine tree from the moment I began to read Richard Ellmann's generous biography.

'What Oscar Wilde Did' was one in a long catalogue of pieces of information withheld by my parents and other adults until I was old

enough to understand. The politics of embarrassment, of course, but I didn't know that. I adored the beautiful fairy stores, the sparkling wit of the plays, and the shivering mystery of poems like *The Harlot's House*, which I loved for its sounds. My other heroes, Dylan Thomas and G.K. Chesterton, must have been equally problematic for my parents and early teachers. A homosexual, an alcoholic and a Jew-hater (what a load of rubbish by the way). They produced humour, beauty and excitement; all the things that proceed from and please the heart of God, and that was all I cared about really.

Crudely nudging my wife into buying Ellmann's book was the first step in my long-saved-up intention to find out about the man, as opposed to the works, which have been affirmed by time in a way that few other literary products of the period can equal. My fascination survived my ignorance (it is a very scholarly and erudite work) because the biographer is warm, witty and compassionate, not just about his subject, who turns out to be an unexpectedly kind and lovable personality in any case, but about the whole array of singular characters and events that gave flavour to the end of the Victorian age.

Oscar Wilde was made for television. There seems little doubt that his legendary skill as wit and raconteur is hardly exaggerated. At its best, there seems to have been an awesome power and fluency in his conversation, which left listeners breathless with excitement and admiration.

'An Audience with Oscar Wilde' would certainly have placed Dame Edna and even the excellent Peter Ustinov firmly in the shade. The 'box' would also have kept Oscar from penury. At most key points in his life he lacked funds and owed money. A generous man, he spent freely and saved nothing. His major talent was not so much in doing as in being. At the end of the last century there was no highly lucrative means of cashing in on verbal and stylistic pyrotechnics, even if you hadn't been exposed by that hypocritical nineties society as the only homosexual in the universe. Wilde would have endeared himself to modern mass audiences, not just because he was a brilliant mind, but because he was not harsh and he was always able and willing to attack his own arguments. Ellmann describes how, on an occasion when some fortune hunter launched a long and vicious verbal attack on the great man, Wilde sat 'like a lump', too kind to triumph in debate by using cruelty.

His downfall lay in his relationships, and a strange, tragic inability to withdraw from situations that were bound to hurt him. In particular, of course, it was his relationship with Lord Alfred Douglas that resulted in so much pain, of which the prison sentence was only a part. Wilde was unable to resist the greedy, beautiful, raging, cruel Douglas, who, in retrospect, seems such a slight object for such a self-damaging obsession. It is not a new story, and it is not about homosexuality. It is about being human and vulnerable.

Ellmann's detailed description of the last few exiled weeks in Paris made me weep. In particular I was moved by an account by Frédéric Boutet, a writer, of encountering Wilde seated at a café in torrential rain, soaked to the skin but unable to move because he had no money to pay for the three or four drinks that had postponed his return to squalid lodgings.

'Like dear St Francis of Assisi I am wedded to poverty,' said Oscar, 'but in my case the marriage is not a success . . . .'

Wilde died on 30th November 1900, his ever faithful friend Robert Ross at his side. He raised his hand shortly before his death when asked if he wished to be received into the Roman Catholic Church, and was baptised, annointed and absolved by the priest who had been called by a worried Robbie.

What does a Jesus-loving relativist like me make of such a life? Wilde told Percival Almy that Christ was not divine. 'It would', he said, 'place too broad a gulf between him and the human soul.' Most people's religion was too vulnerable to the quickness of his perception. Organised expressions of spiritual belief appealed to him as art and something more – he kneeled honestly to at least two priests and the pope – but as Ellmann points out, his views were scarcely orthodox.

The biographer in this case clearly loves his subject, and I believe that he succeeded in making me love him too. Love is *despite* as well as *because of*. Some aspects of Wilde's life repel me, but to understand all is to forgive all. God knows the details of Oscar Wilde's life better than I do, better even than Richard Ellmann. A hand raised just before death may be as efficacious as a few words from a thief dying on a cross. I hope so.

I would like to meet Oscar Wilde in heaven, and, as our God is gracious, I probably will.

Artistic Licence

Any attempt to form Christians into groups that have a secular focus is fraught with problems and dangers.

Not least among these is the tendency for such groups to become congregations after only a few meetings. Because there is no pressure to do specifically religious things, group members can sometimes feel an unexpected freedom to talk about the things that are puzzling or troubling them in their personal lives.

This is fine if the group is equipped and willing to deal with each other's 'entrail-displays', but it can be very frustrating to go along one evening, anxious to learn about the inner workings of the combustion engine, and to end up instead learning about the inner workings of Mabel Drummond.

Perhaps there is a lesson for the Church here. Church leaders who decide to re-title Evening Prayer 'Bee-keeping for Beginners' will probably find the church packed with people who want to talk and sing about God, and who couldn't care less about bees. People are confusing creatures.

A further danger is, or can be, the presence of a self-appointed spiritual chaperone, someone who feels 'burdened' to ensure that communal flirtations with, for instance, something as flighty as art, are not allowed to develop into vulgar and inappropriate relationships.

There is no defence for this kind of re-routing of other people's interests when they have met specifically to pursue those interests, even when the works of art in question are non-religious or, indeed, anti-religious. A communist may tour a stately home without being stripped of his red tie. In fact, he may emerge from his excursion into the world of the privileged classes even more determined than before to carry out his crusade for equality.

Apart from anything else, we need breadth of vision and involvement in the Church. Jesus himself was as fully integrated with the real world as he was untainted by it. There are few things less attractive than what Bernard Levin once called 'single-issue fanaticism', especially as practised by those Christians who tread the bleak, antiseptic passages of religiosity.

I belong to a Christian arts group myself, a regional branch of the Arts Centre Group, a London-based organisation that caters for Christians in the professional and semi-professional arts. Our local group has managed to survive and overcome most of the difficulties that such gatherings are prone to, including, from time to time, the ones that I've just mentioned. In the five years or so that we have been in existence, though, we have seen a bewildering variety of situations and personalities.

Any similarity between those personalities and the ones mentioned in the following verses is, naturally, entirely coincidental.

Our local Christian Arts Group
Meets at St Virginia's Hall,

The cost is not prohibitive,
You pay a pound, that's all.
It started last September
And it's been tremendous fun,
We meet alternate Fridays,
And we share what we have done.
Comments must be true or kind
For nobody is barred,
They range from 'Yes, that's really good!'
To 'Gosh, you have worked hard!'

There's Mrs Leith from Brassey Heath,
Divorced but never low,
Whose bosom mountainously shrouds
The fires down below.
Her many giant canvases
Are mostly purple sky,
She paints in tinted marmite,
No, we haven't asked her why.
At home her neon works of art
Are hanging high and low,
We've often wondered why her husband
Took so long to go.

Miss Duncalk from Cheyne Walk
Is very thin and tense,
She is a Carl André fan
She thinks his bricks make sense.
She educates our appetites
With extracts from Camus,
She says we get a lot from it –
We all pretend we do.
In matters of philosophy

She briskly puts us right,
We hope her inner comprehension
Keeps her warm at night.

Mr Grange is slightly strange
He's something small in eggs,
He always says 'The yolk's on me'
And looks at ladies' legs.
He brings along his only sketch
It's called *Reclining Nude*,
He says it is aesthetic,
But it's not, it's very rude.
Mrs Blair, our acting Chair,
Says, 'Yes, he's less than sound,
But unlike some more pure in heart,
He always pays his pound.'

Mr Smee is ninety-three
But vibrant and alive,
He's never late, unlike his mate
Who died in sixty-five.
He plays the bongos badly
At a quite frenetic rate,
It lasts for several minutes
We just have to sit and wait.
Mrs Leith says through her teeth
'I cannot take much more!
If left to me, then Mr Smee
Would not reach ninety-four.'

The sisters Verne are very stern
They always think the same,
They tell us Joyce is vulgar,

And Picasso is a shame.
Wordsworth was a pantheist
And Lawrence was depraved,
Muggeridge might be all right,
But was he really saved?
C.S. Lewis wasn't quite
A fundamentalist,
And Dylan Thomas? Hopeless,
He was permanently paralytic.

Last week the members all agreed
That we should make a start,
On planning some more public way
To share abroad our art.
And so the works of Leith and Blair
And Grange and Voke and me,
Will grace the public library
For all the world to see.
What greater satisfaction
Than to help the unsaved find,
A glimpse, through our creations,
Of the *great* creator's mind?

Who Am I?
The Sensitivity of Sid

Names are very important.

I know a man who refuses to be introduced to strangers by his Christian name. He believes that shallow intimacy is achieved far too easily and cheaply nowadays, and that the casual exchange of forenames is often the first step in this unwelcome process. Similarly, he insists that his nephews and nieces address him as 'Uncle', rather than following the modern fashion of using his first name only.

He sees his name as a personal possession, something he values and shares with those who are close to him.

I am certainly very aware of my name, but, far

from valuing it, I have always felt uncomfortable about it. I very nearly hated it while I was at school. 'Adrian Plass' – I thought it sounded like a mouthful of plumbing tools. Most of all, I hated it when other boys took the mickey out of my name. It seemed a very specific, personal attack, not only on me, but, in a vague sort of way, on my family. How silly that sounds, but it really did make me very unhappy and angry – I expect that's why they did it.

Several years later I inadvertently upset someone very much because of a mistake I made in connection with his name.

It was Christmas, and during my vacation from College I was, for the second year running, contracted to work for the Post Office in Bromley during their busy period. I was looking forward to it. The previous year had been very enjoyable. Contrary to my own expectations I found it quite exhilarating to get up in the early hours, and ride my rickety old bike down to the sorting office in the dark. There were quite a lot of other students milling around when I arrived each morning. It was a pleasant atmosphere.

This year, instead of being allocated a normal delivery round as I had been the previous Christmas, I was asked to join a full-time regular driver on one of the parcel rounds. After much delay and many cups of tea in the canteen I was collected by my new partner, and we set off in his van to begin work. He was a young man of few words and, unfortunately, neither he nor anyone else had told me what his name was. Being some-thing of a chinless wonder at the time I lacked the courage to ask for this information, so I was greatly relieved when we returned to the floor of the sorting office an hour or two later, to find that the problem was solved for me. My colleague seemed to be immensely popular.

'Hi, Sid! . . . wotcha, Sid, mate! . . . look, it's Sid! . . . Sid's 'ere! . . . had a good morning, Sid? . . .'

Cries of greeting went up from all sides. Every-one appeared to know and like my colleague. I couldn't quite see why. His response to all this warmth was ungracious, to say the least. He barely acknowledged the smiling welcome of his friends. Still, I reflected, at least I knew his name now. He was called Sid.

For the remainder of that working day I con-fidently addressed my workmate accordingly.

'Ill take this one, shall I, Sid? . . . cor, this is a heavy one, Sid! . . . Nearly time for tea, eh, Sid? . . .'

He was no more responsive to me than he had been to all those nice friends of his. In fact, if anything, he was getting grumpier and grumpier as the day wore on, until by the time we arrived back at the depot for the last time his expression was little short of thunderous. As he marched off towards the locker-room with a final grunt of farewell, I called out with unabated cheeriness:

'Cheers! See you tomorrow, Sid!'

The chorus of laughter from a nearby group of postmen that greeted this innocent cry was quite inexplicable to me. Sid stopped in his tracks, turned round and walked back towards me, his lips pressed angrily together, his cheeks flaming.

'My name's not Sid!' he hissed, his mouth about an inch from my ear.

'Not Sid?' I repeated, completely bewildered. 'But if you're not called Sid, why does everyone call you . . .?'

'Because,' he interrupted, 'I drove into one of the brick gateposts last week and knocked it down. . . .'

'But what's that got to do with . . .?'

'And there's a demolition firm in Bromley called Sid Bishop Limited. That's why they call me Sid. But my name's not SID!!'

'Oh.'

If I hadn't been quite so naïve I suppose I would have sensed what was going on much earlier. Poor Sid – I mean, poor . . . actually I never did find out what his real name was.

It was during that same holiday period that a grizzled old postman greeted me with the words: 'Hello, John!'

For some reason I had never encountered the name 'John' used as a generic term meaning 'mate' or 'friend'. My reply must have utterly confused the poor man.

'I think you've got it a bit wrong', I bleated, in my high-pitched, middle-class way. 'You must be thinking that I'm my brother John. I'm not John, I'm Adrian, but we are rather alike, so. . . .'

'Eh?' he said.

Nowadays, I don't really get very bothered about my own name but I am very conscious of the labels that people might attach to me. I seem to recall reading somewhere that Marx once said, 'I am not a Marxist'. I don't know if Jesus would say, 'I am not a Christian' if he returned in the flesh today, but one wonders. There are so many negative connotations attached to the 'religious' terms that we use all the time.

It intrigues me to think that there are many, many people outside organised religion, who would never come within the measuring scope of polls that set out to assess numbers of church-goers, but who would say they were Christians if the word had not become so devalued.

As for myself, I can't help being aware of the 'cringe factor' but I am very happy to be labelled as a follower of Jesus, albeit a stumbling one.

In fact, I'm more than happy, I'm genuinely proud to be associated with the name above all names.

If I belonged to a 'Believers Anonymous' group, I would stand up at the beginning of each meeting and say, 'My name is Adrian, and I'm a Christian'.

When Disaster Struck

But, what kind of Christian am I?

When things are easy, and the pressure of work has lifted temporarily, and I'm leaning back in my favourite armchair, and there are no emergencies, and the queue of worries has gone for lunch, and I *have* had a quiet time, and I've done the three vital things that I was supposed to do before my wife got back, and I haven't had a letter telling me that I write evil books, and I don't feel tired, and I've paid all the bills, and the dog has been walked, and it isn't what the British call a 'Glorious Day', and I haven't just realised that I've been booked to speak in Sunderland, Dudley and Tunbridge Wells on the same evening by three lots of people who've all been led by the Lord to ask me, and childhood spectres have taken a day off from haunting me, and I don't have indigestion, and every one of my four children is in a reasonably balanced state, and I'm not six months behind with unanswered post, and there isn't an

411

ominous little knocking sound in the engine of my – alleged – car, and I'm not covered in Tipp-Ex from a squeeze bottle that didn't work and then suddenly did, and I'm feeling reasonably confident that God likes me, and I'm pretty sure that I like him – then, when all these conditions are fulfilled, I call myself a 'Jesus-loving relativist'.

It sounds quite impressive, doesn't it? All it means is that I am unswerving and uncompromising in my attitude to Jesus, but that my expression of this personal association is related to the needs, personalities and circumstances of the individual people I encounter.

This may seem naïvely obvious, but, strictly applied, such a philosophy can take one along strange uncharted paths that do not appear on many of the rather small-scale theological or doctrinal maps. I'm not talking about heresies, but the infinitely varied ways in which God works with people on a day-to-day basis. The gospel accounts of Jesus' ministry are very large-scale maps, little unexpected paths and by-ways in addition to the broad main roads of orthodoxy.

That's the sort of Christian I am when life is rolling along smoothly. I can (and do) talk and write about it a lot. It's easy to do that when things are going well.

Most of the time, though, like nearly everybody else that I know, my Christian faith is a tangle of joys and despairs, faith and doubt, certainty and unsureness, and all the other pairs of opposites that writers use to fill up space. I

412

write and talk a lot about this muddled middle-path as well. It isn't quite so easy, but it is probably much more useful. Most of us know more about survival than victory.

What happens when disaster strikes? What sort of Christian am I when darkness and danger remove all my props and leave me helpless? What remains of the words and the ideas and the comfortable theorising when death stares me in the face?

In the summer of 1990 I had a chance to find out.

For our annual holiday that year we decided to take the car over to Denmark from Harwich on an extremely comfortable Scandinavian ferry. After a twenty-four hour journey we disembarked at the port of Esbjerg and drove north for a hundred miles or so to the little village of Stenvad in the Jurs peninsula, where our rented cottage awaited us.

Denmark was a land of rolling yellow corn-fields, green forest, enamel-blue skies and an unusually sparkling quality in the light. We were due to be there for a week before driving down through Germany to Holland, where I was to speak at the Flevo Festival for a day or two. On the third day of our Danish week we decided to visit a nearby theme park, known as Jurs Summerland.

We paid our entrance fees, parked the car, then explored the park, Bridget and I watching the children as they tried out the very large selection of rides and activities.

Halfway through the afternoon Bridget drifted off with Matthew, the eldest, while I queued with Joseph, David and Katy (eleven, ten and three at that time) to have a ride on the little circular boats that floated down an artificial river at quite considerable speed.

Hoping to balance our small craft, I sat the three children on one side and myself on the other. It still 'dipped' a little on my side, but it was reasonably trim. Away we went, our small craft spinning slowly round as it was swept along by the current.

Somehow, perhaps because safety regulations are quite rigidly enforced in most similar situations in this country, one expects that nothing much can go wrong. This time, everything went wrong.

As the boat reached a point where the river was straddled by a little brick bridge, the level of the water dropped abruptly and its speed increased slightly. Without warning the boat overturned completely, tipping all of us into the river and trapping me on my back under the water.

Lying there, my belt snagged by some projection on the riverbed, the weight of the upturned boat pressing like a coffin full of rocks on my chest, the following thoughts went through my mind.

First, quite incredibly, I said to myself: 'If I get out of this alive, it'll make a jolly good article or broadcast.' I suppose that just shows how pathetically desperate we writers are to find new material.

Secondly, eclipsing that ridiculous initial reaction, came blind panic. How was I, a non-swimmer, going to free myself to look for Katy? Where *was* Katy? Had she hit her head? Was she drowning? Was she already dead? What about the boys? Where were they? They were strong swimmers, but . . . .

Suddenly, the sheer horror of the situation screamed through my brain in the darkness. Like a small child I cried out in my mind to the only person who could help me.

'God, get me out of this . . . river!!'

With a final desperate heave I pushed the boat off my chest, thereby dislodging the other end of the craft, which was resting on the shelf in the riverbank that had caused the problem in the first place.

Standing up and gasping for breath, I pushed the wet hair away from my eyes and looked around. The two boys were swimming around unscathed, wild-eyed but safe. Katy had completely disappeared. Joe and David adore their little sister. The tearful panic in their voices as they called out to me was a perfect echo of the emotion that paralysed me for a moment as I tried to think what to do next. Where, oh where, was Katy?

I started to feel around under the water, hoping and dreading that I would find her there somewhere. In the space of a few seconds I saw the hypothetical events of the following few days as vividly as if they had already happened: the abrupt termination of our holiday: the miserable

return to England: telling everybody: the funeral
. . . .

'She's under the boat, Dad! She's under the boat!'

The boys had swum down to where the still upside-down boat was lodged against the bank. David could hear Katy calling me from inside the air-pocket between the surface of the water and the bottom of the inverted craft.

Frantically, I made my way down to where the boys were vainly battling to free their sister. Putting both hands under the rim of the boat I heaved with all my strength, but my efforts were useless. It wouldn't budge. Almost whimpering with frustration I threw out another silent prayer, gritted my teeth and heaved again. The boat lifted and turned in a cloud of spray as I fell back into the water again. Struggling back onto my feet, the first thing I saw was my daughter bobbing gently up and down in the water a few yards away. Her hair was hardly wet, and her expression was remarkably untroubled.

'Hello, Daddy,' she said, as Joe pushed and pulled her up on to the bank. 'I knew I'd be all right, 'cos you were here.'

When I finally held Katy I nearly squeezed her to death. It had, without any doubt, been the most alarming experience of my life.

On the positive side, though, it had answered my question about what kind of Christian I would be when disaster threatened, and ritual, churchmanship, theology and all the man-made paraphernalia of religion were irrelevant. The answer was that I became a frightened child who called out, with primitive trust, to the only person who could possibly help.

We cannot avoid physical danger, illness and other problems, Jesus made that quite clear. I thank God that Katy is still with us; other parents (Christians included) have not been so fortunate, and that is a dark mystery that I don't pretend to understand. But, whether or not disaster strikes in this world, I could ask for nothing more than to be the kind of Christian who says to God, rather as Katy optimistically said to me: 'I knew I'd be all right, because you were here.'

Falling Off

I fall off the bouncy castle from time to time – don't you? Also, like the pathetic prodigal son that I am, I take an occasional day excursion back to the 'pigs', drawn like an insect to the sticky-sweetness of sin. But when the feverish glow of self-indulgence has paled I feel dreadful. I used to feel frightened as well. Jesus' words about the unworthiness of people who put their hands to the plough and then turn back are rather alarming when you look around and see the haphazard and incomplete state of your own particular field.

But, returning from the world of pigs, insects and ploughs to our original bouncy castle image – why *would* I want to get off? Why exchange a clearer view of heaven for the stolid pseudo-realism of an earthly perspective? Am I mad?

No; I am unfit.

Why would I not last too long on a real bouncy castle? First, because I am overweight and unused to exercise. I would be puffing and blowing like a walrus after five minutes. The spiritual daily work-out requires a régime of regular prayer press-ups, and biblical bull-working, although the strictness of the discipline involved is really only intended as a framework within which I can be as daft as a brush with God – like a child on a bouncy castle in fact.

Secondly, my sense of balance is faulty. After bouncing around for a while I start to get dizzy and lose my footing. The rules for staying up-right in the Kingdom of Heaven are quite different from the ones we're used to. It can be quite a relief to plant your feet on familiar and apparently solid ground. It takes lots of practice, and not a little courage, to accept a completely different basis for being.

Thirdly, and this is one we don't hear very much about, I get bored after a while. Obsessional by nature, I am quite likely to do nothing but castle-bouncing once I'm fit enough, and I've learned to keep my footing. The analogy becomes a little er . . . deflated at this point, but it is undoubtedly a fact that many people fall away from faith after obsessionally enthusiastic involvement in one narrow aspect of church life or theology, usually because a particular need has not been met at a particular time. The fall can be tragically hard. In fact, of course, God is in all places and activities that can benefit from his presence; light and pleasant or dark and desperate. He is there, inviting us to give our hands for his use in an enormous variety of ways, some of which offer a chance of real adventure. It is the limits I draw around myself and God that can sometimes result in boredom.

Does God condemn us when we fail in these ways? If he does, then I was condemned a long time ago, and many times since (if that makes any sense).

No, I don't believe that God condemns his bouncy-castle children. I do believe he corrects, coaxes and disciplines us just as an earthly father would, and that his ultimate aim for each of us is total purity of motivation, behaviour and perspective. The chances of achieving such perfection on this side of heaven may be nil, but if things do go wrong we know that Jesus will plead for us more eloquently than we ever could. We need to go on believing that – like children.

So keep on bouncing!

See you on the bouncy castle.

CABBAGES FOR
THE KING

Contents

I Know What You're Going to Say

Redundant Rituals and Flimsy Fashions

TO THE READER

Why is this book called *Cabbages for the King*?

The simple answer is that, on one very important level, being a Christian who happens to speak and write about his faith is much the same as being a Christian who happens to run a greengrocer's shop.

The conscientious greengrocer buys and sells the best produce he can get, in as pleasant a manner as possible, at a price that is appropriate to the resources of his customers and the needs of his own family. He does not (unless he is a a greengrocer with private means) have the option of not coming in to work on those mornings when he feels spiritually barren. The public need their cabbages, and an unsanctified cabbage tastes much the same as a sanctified one. The believing greengrocer is an ordinary man trying to live up to his high calling. Day by day he does his best to provide people with what they need, and asks God to protect his customers and himself from his own shortcomings.

So do I.

When the greengrocer and I arrive in heaven together, we shall be equal in the eyes of God, except that I (hopefully) will be known by my fruit, whereas he will be known by his fruit *and* veg.

This book is a collection of the jokes, stories, sketches and verse that I, and more recently my wife and I, have flung at people from platforms all over the country. Most of them are humorous (or are supposed to be), a few are sad or serious, and the rest are beyond definition.

Such as they are, they are what I do for God – cabbages for the King. I hope you enjoy them.

TELLING THE TRUTH

Truth enters the mind so easily that when we hear it for the first time it seems as if we were simply recalling it to memory.

BERNARD DE FONTENELLE 1768

Truths and roses have thorns about them.

H. G. BOHN – Handbook of proverbs 1855

Truth stretches but does not break.

Spanish proverb

Telling the Truth

How do you start a book? I never know how to start anything. Quite often, when I stand up to speak in churches or halls or theatres, I haven't the faintest idea what I'm going to say. This doesn't matter so much nowadays because I don't get as frightened as I used to, but in the early days my nervous system took a terrible pounding every time.

Recently, after arriving at a venue by the skin of my teeth, I began with the following words:

"I just want to thank my lucky stars that . . ."

I stopped as I realized that among those present there would almost certainly be a number who were astrologically challenged. Most people laughed when I changed my remark to: "I just want to thank the Lord that . . .", but some did not.

Oh, dear!

Apart from the fact that I'm constitutionally incapable of putting together a logical sequence of ideas or points and then sticking to it (my tangential tendencies do occasionally cause a little conflict when my wife and I are working together), this inability to find a starting place is probably something to do with identity. I don't seem to fit into any of the traditional categories of Christian speaker. I'm not a preacher, I'm certainly not a Bible teacher and it's a long time since I've been allowed to just entertain. What I do have is a determination to live, privately and publicly, with the gap between what I am and what I think I ought to be. I don't mean that I won't change for the better – God is always making that possible in our lives – but I refuse to pretend that my virtue or spirituality is cubed just because I'm standing on a platform.

We shall never match our message, so I think it is probably more useful to tell the truth. Enthusiasm and optimism are no substitutes for reality.

I remember working with an evangelist in the Midlands once. It was an evening meeting and the large hall in which we were operating was about half full. I went on stage first and spoke for fifteen minutes or so, then he came on to do the main talk. Now, for those who don't know, evangelists are a fine body of men, but they find it very difficult to believe that anyone can absorb or understand any piece of information unless it has been repeated about thirty-nine times. This fellow was no exception. When, in retrospect, I add this tendency to the aforementioned inability to separate personal and divine truth, what followed was not really very surprising. I can't remember the exact wording of my colleague's address, but here is an approximation of one whole chunk of what he said.

"I don't worry, because I belong to God. I belong to God, so I don't have to worry. Why don't I worry? Well, it's because I belong to God. Who do I belong to? It's God, of course, and because of that I don't have to worry. Worry? Me? I don't! Why should I when I belong to God? You see, belonging to God means the end of worry, and that's something I don't do now that I belong to God . . ."

Several permutations later the evangelist concluded his talk, left the stage, and came into the wings where I was waiting. His whispered words took my breath away.

"I'm really worried," he said hoarsely, "I don't think I got through to them at all."

I was shocked. I hadn't been in the crinkly-eyed business for very long and I still believed that – by and large – Christian speakers were honest about themselves.

"Hold on a minute," I replied, "you just told all those

people out there that you don't worry because you belong
to God. What about that?"

"Ah, well," he said, "I was preaching then."

It's so easy to get carried away like that. I've done it
myself. But, balanced against experiences like the one I've
just mentioned, which might make one very cynical, are
some overwhelming truths.

First, nothing has changed. The message always was
going to be greater than we are. John the Baptist,
languishing in Herod's prison, wanted to know if Jesus
really was "the one". Only a short time ago, filled with the
Holy Spirit, he had confidently identified the Messiah in
front of crowds of people at the river bank. Now, crouched
in the confining darkness, faced with his own limitations,
he felt wretchedly uncertain.

God uses inadequate people. He has to. They're the only
sort available to choose from. He is committed to the risk
of entrusting his earthly image to idiots like you, me, and
my evangelist friend, people who will fail and make
mistakes from time to time.

Secondly, there are many wonderful and authentically
God-inspired events and miracles happening in the Church
nowadays. Sadly human nature is such that many people
notice absurdity, failure and vain empire-building much
more readily than the things of God. You, me and the
evangelist had better work even harder to keep silliness to a
minimum.

There's an illustration often used in philosophical
discussions on the subject of creativity. It concerns a cynic
who rips apart a beautiful picture.

"I told you so!" he exclaims triumphantly. "There is no
picture here. It's just a collection of wood, canvas, nails
and pigment. You're all deceiving yourselves!"

He's wrong, of course. There *is* a picture, and it's so
much more than the sum of its component parts.

The Church, the body of Christ, is exactly the same. Any

cynic could examine my life, or the strange antics of my Christian brothers and sisters, and say, "There's nothing here – there's just Adrian Plass and these other ridiculous bits and pieces. There *is* no Church. There is no body of Christ. There is no God!"

How sadly wrong he would be. The bride, the body, the face and hands of God on earth, quickened by the Holy Spirit, and led by the mind and will of Jesus himself must be a beautiful picture when it's viewed from Heaven. God loves to look at this work of art, and I'm so glad he's painted me into one small corner.

He has given me permission to be honest about him *and* myself, and that's what I shall go on doing.

It seems very fitting that this first selection of pieces should be concerned with Truth, because Truth is the wholesaler from whom most of my "cabbages" are obtained.

Am I the Only One?

One of my greatest fears as a young Christian was that, by some impossible means, the person I really was inside would be revealed to all the other people in my church. What would they say and think when they saw the swamp that my mind often became? How would they cope with the knowledge that I stopped believing in God altogether sometimes, or that my daily "quiet time" was not daily at all, but weekly, or fortnightly, or monthly, or even less frequent than that? Could they accommodate a mess?

Nowadays I'm much less bothered about people knowing what I'm really like, but I shall always experience a slight sense of loneliness about being the only person, in terms of personality and outlook, who is my unique shape. I will never find another me to compare notes with (what a blessed relief for the rest of the world!), but, unique as each of us is, we do all have an awful lot in common. In fact, it can be breathtakingly liberating to discover that you are *not* "the only one".

Am I the Only One?

Am I the only one
Who follows God,
Nottingham Forest,
Neighbours
And his own inclinations — usually in reverse order?
I do hope not.

Am I the only one
Who likes Norman Wisdom films,

Bat out of Hell,
Little House on the Prairie,
and *Silence of the Lambs?*
Probably.

Am I the only one
Who hasn't learned to drive,
Probably never will,
Doesn't want to,
And might well murder the next person who asks why not?
Maybe.

Am I the only one
Who checks his sitting-room carpet for big bits before
  hoovering it
Then afterwards finds the suction pipe blocked with dead
  dogs,
Half bricks, rolls of prairie wire, nests of tiddly winks,
Most of the *Sunday Times* and six pound fifty in small
  change?
I doubt it.

Am I the only one
Who talks to himself loudly when he's alone
Then suddenly realizes he isn't,
Feels like a loony,
And tries to make it sound like a song?
Surely not.

Am I the only one
Who hates all criticism,
Especially the constructive sort,
Because that usually means
I have to do something about it?
I don't think so.

Am I the only one
Who likes to have his cake,
Eat it,
Sick it up,
Then feel sorry for himself?
Possibly.

Am I the only one
Who loves and needs love,
And fails and falls and cries,
And takes the hand of anyone whose turn it is to be strong,
Whose turn it is to be Jesus for me?
Am I the only one?

Jenny

I wish that, as a Church, we were more willing to share our shadows as well as our shining. What a shadowy event the crucifixion must have been – and what a shining outcome.

People can accept the *whole* story, however grainy and granular it may seem, much more readily than a carefully edited one.

Not long after Jenny Larcombe was miraculously healed (only those who did not know her before and after her healing could doubt that) the sister of a very close friend of ours committed suicide after years of depressive illness. She happened to be called Jenny too. She was a follower of Jesus, struggling against all the odds to remain stable enough to lead a normal life. She tried very hard, but in the end she failed, just as those who are suffering from severe physical illnesses quite often fail to recover. I would like the Church to own *both* of these Jennys, because they both belong to Jesus, equal citizens in the Kingdom of God.

Of course the mystery remains, but it is a mystery with a heart.

Jenny

Our father who art in heaven,
Jenny walked in front of a train last night,
Hallowed be thy name, thy kingdom come,
She was only thirty-seven,
Thy will be done on earth, as it is in heaven,
You knew what she was going to do, didn't you, Lord?
Give us this day our daily bread,
She had no hope left,

And forgive us our trespasses as we forgive those who
    trespass against us.
Jenny is forgiven, isn't she?
Lead us not into temptation,
Lots of us are on the edge of darkness,
And deliver us from evil,
The only strength we have is yours,
For thine is the Kingdom,
And she's living there now,
The power and the glory,
She's yours, Lord,
For ever and ever,
Jenny,
Amen.

Diet

It is impossible to over-emphasize the connection between physical well-being and spiritual peace. I'm not, of course, suggesting that one depends upon the other, because many wonderful people have demonstrated great serenity of spirit in the midst of suffering. I'm simply pointing out that a number of people I know (including myself) have discovered that tiredness, too much alcohol, and over-eating, to name but three little items, have the effect of dulling one's awareness of spiritual things.

I know someone who felt far from God for years, and made no progress at all until she went on a strict diet and began to like herself again. This is not a moral statement that I'm making, although (forgive me) it becomes one as soon as we see the truth of it, but a matter of practical living.

I crouch miserably in my hovel of hypocrisy as I write these words. I get very tired. I do enjoy a drink. I expand and contract like a bull-frog's throat.

Read the words that follow, have mercy on me, and I'll have mercy on you.

Diet

expansion was not good business for my body
then I replaced the four sugars in my tea
with sweeteners no after taste eh funny
fat out fibre shovelled in or through
got a shade depressed a little blue
a friend told me alcohol inflates
gave up claret very nearly died
no more boozing nothing fried
full of tuna fish and dates
planned to cheat but then
a miracle I saw my feet
like other better men
fresh air was sweet
and nature smiled
I ran and leapt
soundly slept
happy child
so serene
so lean
a bit
fit
I
ate
a bit
a treat
or trophy
had a steak
a titchy cake
a glass of port
a prize I thought
for dieting so well
oh I smiled as I fell
suddenly I wanted chops
wild eyed I hit the shops
syrup jams and lemon cheese
spring into my trolley please
soggy doughnuts filled with jam
come and make me sticky here I am
chocolate fancy and chocolate plain
welcome to the orbit of my face again
crinkly crunkly crunchy fat fried chips
how I do desire to squelch you in my lips
expansion was not good business for my body

Christmas

Here's the scenario.

The angel Pongo appears in your sitting room at midnight on Christmas Eve, and makes the following speech,

"Greetings, highly favoured one. Behold, the Lord has appointed me to bring you news of great joy. Namely, that thou hast built up such a multitude of Brownie points with thy constant do-goodings and such, that he wisheth to offer thee anything that thy heart desireth, even unto a brand new motor or a holiday in the Algarve with bath and all facilities, or, if thou opteth for such, something more useful but less material, if thou getteth my drift."

"What, you mean like the knowledge that I am following faithfully in the steps of my beloved master?"

"Well, yes, that sort of thing. Most of them tendeth to go for a Porsche, actually, but what you said would go down like a dose of salts in terms of thy future standing with the boss, him being exceedingly big on humility and the like. Suit thyself, but bear in mind that the boss valueth the truth above silver and gold. If thou fancieth a Porsche but asketh for a cold bath and septic boils he will bloweth his stack — take mine word for it."

So, what would you choose if Pongo asked you?

What would *I* choose?

Whatever I wanted, eh?

Well, it wouldn't be a Porsche or anything like that. A Porsche would rust eventually, and then I would wish I'd asked for the thing I've always wanted — always.

You'll find out what it is at the end of this poem.

Christmas

Christmas happens anyway – it happened in our house
today,
It's good! And yet, I have to say, for me there's something
missing.
It's not that Santa didn't come; he floated past our worldly
locks,
He drank his sherry, ate his pie, left me a pair of purple
socks,
And lots of other things.
My daughter gave me half a beetle in a box, a touching
sacrifice.
There's no significance, I hope, in all the gifts of scent and
soap,
In mutant ninja turtle shapes!
And who sent exercising tapes?
That isn't very nice.
My son said, "Dad, I've spent a lot,
A portable word processor."
I really was excited till I got,
My pencil in a plastic pot.
But there were toys and Garfield mugs
And boxer-shorts and laughs and hugs,
And anyway, they always say, the thought's the thing that
really counts.
There's something missing, and it isn't here. I'm not sure
what it is.

The crib confuses me because – I see it as it surely was,
Divine confusion, shepherds visiting the new-born shepherd,
Mary proud but puzzled, Joseph close, concerned for her,
And what would tiny babies want with gold and
frankincense and myrrh?

Why did a million angels fill the sky, like snowflakes on a
   starry night?
I guess that no one quite knew what was going on,
Except that something *right* was happening,
And God was saying, and is saying still,
"Here is my son, do with him as you will.
Though you may kill him he will live for you forever now,
Not lost in rhymes or mimes or special times,
But in the human heart, where revolutions really start,
And struggles in the darkness never seem to cease.
He offered then, he offers now, the only gift you'll ever
   want or need,
The possibility of peace."

Jane Drain

This is the first of five short sketches involving a writer,
that you will find scattered through this book. The first one
highlights the difficulty of being truthful with a person who
appears to have the direct authority of God on her side.

What *do* you reply to someone who says "The Lord told
me . . ."?

Jane Drain

W: = WRITER
G: = GUEST

W: Now, Miss Drain –
G: Call me Jane
W: Jane Drain – right. Err . . . Jane, you wanted to see me
   to ask advice about writing. Yes?

G: Yes, well you're a writer aren't you?

W: (*Modestly*) Well . . . yes, I am.

G: The Lord has given me some poems (*She plonks a huge pile of papers on the table*) and in my quiet time last week he told me that *you* were going to help me get them published.

W: He, err, he's given you a lot, hasn't he?

G: Yes, and you're going to help me get them published.

W: Well, I'm not sure —

G: I get them all over the place.

W: What?

G: Poems. I never know when one's coming. I'll be lying in the bath —

W: (*Warily*) Mmm . . .?

G: And one just comes into my head and I have to jump out of the bath, all dripping and unexpected, and run round the house looking for a biro, and when I've found one I put it down quickly.

W: What?

G: The poem. I put it down as quick as I can.

W: When you say the Lord gives you these poems, Jane, do you mean —

G: Here's one I did this morning (*Takes sheet from pile*) It hit me in the shower when I wasn't expecting it. (*Reads*)

> When I into the Bible do look
> I think to myself what a jolly good book
> And there will be considerable joy
> For those who do it read, girl or boy
> In it we do learn that man a menace is
> Disobeying God since not far into Genesis
> Why do not we all ask God for his bounties
> Whether we hail from Scotland or the home
>   counties?
> Let us now to God show all due deference

In ways relating to our denominational preference
That way we might avoid a schism,
This was revealed to me in the shower which is a bit
    like baptism.

W: Well! That was . . . well!
G: What did you think?
W: Only *you* could have written that, Jane.
G: Which publisher shall we send my poems to, then?
W: Jane, the fact is that poetry, however, err . . . good, is
    just not a selling proposition.
G: Ah, yes, but these poems were given to me by the Lord,
    so they *will* sell, won't they?
W: Look, Jane –
G: I've written a little poem for you to read when you go
    out speaking and that (*Hands him a sheet of paper*).
W: (*Reads disbelievingly*)

That I do write books there is no doubt
Of thicknesses varied, some thin, some stout.
In them I hope that I do capture
The means by which we'll escape being left behind
    when it comes to the rapture.

That's – very moving, Jane. Certainly moves me. Tell
me, what exactly do you mean when you say that God
gives you a poem?
G: Well, I'll be lying in the bath, and –
W: No – no. I mean what happens in your head?
G: I dunno – the words just pop into my head and then
    pop out on to paper. Anyway, which publisher shall –
W: (*Claps hand to head*) Just a minute, Jane! I think it's
    happening to me. Yes, there's a poem coming through,
    and I think it's for you. Listen –

Thank you for writing your poems divine
They're part of you, so I guess they're mine.
But frankly, Jane, it would make more sense
To publish a few at your own expense.

END

Wooden Man

I had a very negative view of Christianity until I went through a stress illness a few years ago. Having been converted at a time when, generally speaking, one was taught that God more or less held his nose as he allowed filthy repentant scum to slip, lizard-like, into his presence, it never really occurred to me that the creator was bothered about anything but stopping his verminous followers from pursuing their foul, sinful activities. It wasn't until I heard a sermon by John Collins on the subject of Jesus' parable of the sheep and the goats in Matthew, chapter twenty-five, that it began to dawn on me that Jesus is far more interested in what we *do* than what we don't do.

That sermon was a very important step in my journey towards understanding that, actually, God is nice and he likes me.

What follows is an extract from a production called *Coming Home* that I wrote for our local inter-church group. It is about the *positive Gospel* of Jesus, and I make no apology for the fact that it ends rather inconclusively.

Wooden Man

A. All I can think about is how rotten I am inside. There seem to be so *many* sins. If you get rid of one, another one pops up to take its place. I don't think I'll ever be good enough to do anything really useful for God.

B. Nobody's perfect, y'know.

C. Well, nobody except my friend Donald. He's never committed a sin in his life.

A. There isn't anyone who hasn't done anything wrong – is there?

C. My friend Donald hasn't.
(*Pause*)

B. He's never done anything wrong? A perfect Christian?

C. My friend Donald – he'll be here in a minute so you can see for yourselves – he has never stolen, never murdered, never committed adultery, never envied, never lusted, never told a single lie, never been guilty of a cowardly act, never hurt anyone, never hit anyone, never hustled, harassed or hated anyone –

A. But surely –

C. Donald has never been greedy, slothful or avaricious, he's never dropped litter, disturbed the peace, driven with excess alcohol in his blood or destroyed other people's property. He's never had a single unkind thought, he holds no grudges, he never gossips, he's never late or lascivious or libellous. He has never caused, continued or condoned conflict of any kind. He never complains, he never blasphemes, he never gets drunk, he never overeats, he worships no false images, he's never mean or menacing or malicious –

B. But isn't that – ?

C. Donald never watches nasty videos, nor does he condemn people who do, he's never judgemental or over-sentimental, or harsh, or unforgiving. He's never sad, mad, bad or (*Hunts for words*) anti-oriental. He never smokes, he never swears, he's never rude, he never stares. Donald has never ever committed a single sin. Oh, and one other thing.

A. What's that?

C. He won't be going to heaven.
    (*Pause*)

A. Why not?

B. Because he's not very good company, I should think.

A. No, seriously – why not?
    (C. *Disappears and then reappears carrying Donald, a wooden figure*)

A. Because he's made of wood.

B. But you said –

A. You said he was the perfect Christian.

C. No I didn't – you said that. I just told you about all the things he's never done wrong. The trouble with old Donald here (*Pats him*) is that although he's never committed any of the sins I was talking about, he's never done anything else. He can't – he's made of wood. So – (*Looks at A.*)

A. So . . .?

C. So, it doesn't matter if you don't do anything wrong for the rest of your life. It won't make you a Christian and it won't get you into heaven.

A. What will then?

C. Now, that's a *very* interesting question . . .

Motivation

It's that writer again, only this time it's not Jane Drain he's having trouble with – it's himself. What really motivates him? Why does he do what he does? What a state he's in!

I remember asking a respected friend what he thought about motivation. He pointed out that when Jesus called Zacchaeus down from his tree he only wanted him to go and get the tea under way. He didn't demand an instant change of lifestyle; that came about as a natural progression from obedience. That seems to be the secret really. If you've been given a job to do, then get on and do it, and let God see to the fine-tuning.

Genuine obedience is just as much from the heart as more mushy things.

Motivation

W = WRITER
F = FRIEND

F: Hello, Rodney! You all right?

W: Hello, Viv – mmm, I've got a lot to be thankful for.

F: Oh, bad as that, eh? D'you want to stop rejoicing for a moment and tell me why you're looking so glum?

W: I dunno, Viv, I've been sitting here trying to write, and I suddenly thought – why am I doing this? (*Taps page*) Who actually wrote this stuff, me or God?

F: Let's have a look. (*Reads*) "Five pounds of potatoes, two and a half pounds of sprouts, six eggs and a packet of cornflakes." This is deep stuff, Rodney, I see your problem. Looks like your handwriting though.

W: Not my shopping list, you twit. I'm talking about my books –

F: Oh, sorry. Your books. Right.

W: I mean – *why* do I write books? I say it's for God, but is it? What's it for?

F: Money?

W: Oh come off it, Viv, you're not seriously suggesting

that I write about God for cash?

F: What do they pay you in, then – bananas?

W: No, but . . .

F: You told me the other evening – after your fourth glass of that wine you said was only slightly alcoholic – that you sift through the post every morning looking for cheques and you don't enjoy your breakfast much if there aren't any.

W: That was just the truth – I mean, that was just an exaggeration. You've got me confused now.

F: Maybe it's personal fame and glory, Rodney.

W: Maybe *what* is personal fame and glory, Vivienne?

F: Well, you know, the reason you write. Maybe you write so that people will think you're wonderful?

W: How long have you had this ministry of encouragement, Viv? Here, I didn't say anything about *this* after my fourth glass of wine, did I?

F: No.

W: Oh, good . . .

F: It was after your fifth –

W: Oh, blimey . . .

F: You said that, every now and then, you go down to the local Christian bookshop and look in the indexes of the new publications to see if you've been quoted.

W: (*Groans!*) Oh, I didn't say that, did I?

F: Was it true?

W: Well, it wasn't *un*true . . . (*She laughs*) So you don't think there's anything good and pure motivating me to write?

F: I didn't say that.

W: No, but you've taken an interesting, sophisticated problem and reduced it to sordid issues of money and vanity. Blow you, Viv. I was really enjoying my problem till you came along.

F: Look, answer me two questions, Rodney.

W: (*Sulkily*) I don't remember having a sixth glass . . .

F: No – no, listen! Do you believe God wants you to write books?

W: Well – yes, I do really. Yes, I do, definitely – I think. No, I do! I *do* think he wants me to write books. Why?

F: (*Holds up shopping list*) Who's going shopping for this lot?

W: What?

F: Who's doing the shopping?

W: (*Shrugs*) Probably send one of the girls down. Is there something wrong with that?

F: No, but hadn't you better check her motivation before she leaves? Have you ever tasted sprouts bought by someone whose motives are mixed? Yuck!
   (*Pause*)

W: Viv.

F: Yes?

W: Clear off – I've got some writing to do . . .

END

'Is this a motivationally deprived Sprout?'

Creed

Speaking at a local church a few years ago, I held up a jigsaw puzzle that had been specifically made for the occasion by a friend who is less ham-fisted than I am. It was the normal rectangular shape, but right in the centre of the puzzle was a large, tortuously shaped section that was nevertheless accommodated perfectly by the more orthodox pieces that surrounded it. Each of those surrounding pieces had needed to become a little bit irregular itself, but only on one side. I was making a plea for acceptance and tolerance of individual differences in members of the church community, and suggesting that the doctrinal frame of our faith is quite capable of holding and enclosing people as they are, and not as they should be.

Thank goodness God allows us to be what we are, and enables us to move towards becoming what we should be. We can be honest with him about the shape of our faith, even if it seems a bit irregular at the moment. One of my moments was shaped in the way that this poem describes.

Creed

I cannot say my creed in words.
How should I spell despair, excitement, joy and grief,
Amazement, anger, certainty and unbelief?
What was the grammar of those sleepless nights?
Who the subject, what the object
Of a friend who will not come, or does not come
And then creates his own eccentric, special dawn,
A blinding light that does not blind?
Why do I find you in the secret wordless places

Where I hide from your eternal voice?
I hate you, love you, miss you, need you, wish that you
　　would go.
And yet I know that long ago you made a fairy-tale for me
About the day when you would take your sword
And battle through the thicket of the things I have become.
You'll kiss to life a sleeping beauty waiting for the prince to
　　come.
Then I will wake and look into your eyes and understand
And for the first time I will not be dumb
And I shall say my creed in words.

STRENGTH AND
VULNERABILITY

The greatest weakness is the fear of being weak.

French proverb

Strength and Vulnerability

Quite early on in my writing career I was asked to work at an event called "Take Seven". (I think this referred to the number of spare tents each family needed to have because the weather was so appalling. Later, this kind of Christian festival became the basis for the section on "Let God Spring Into Royal Acts of Harvest Growth" in *The Sacred Diary of Adrian Plass*.) Originally I had been asked whether I would be interested in fronting the evening chat-show, but my ideas on how this might develop were not very well received. Unfortunately I was not told this at the time. Instead, it was suggested that I would be much *more* useful in the capacity of seminar speaker on the subject of "Parenting". As an inveterate coward of long standing I have every sympathy with the person who curved the truth in this way. He is a charming fellow and I forgive him from the heart of my bottom. Besides, I learned a very valuable lesson down there in Shepton Mallet, as you will see.

Flattered by this implicit trust in my parental expertise, I agreed to address a large group of Christian mums and dads on the subject of bringing up children. It seemed quite easy when I was sitting at home not doing it, but as the date of the festival came closer and closer I began to panic seriously. What could have possessed me to imagine that I had anything remotely useful to say about raising a family? I reviewed my qualifications:

● I had been a child myself; but then, so had everyone else.
● I had been raised by parents. Big deal!

• I had three children of my own, but although I loved and liked them very much the whole business of family had been a Columbus-like voyage of discovery for me. There was no method in my madness.

True, I had dealt with children in care for most of my working life, but such skills as I had acquired in that field seemed to be non-transferable when it came to my own little children's home.

Dismally, I came to the inescapable conclusion that I had nothing to say on a subject concerning which those trusting mothers and fathers would undoubtedly believe I was some kind of expert. How naive I was then! Later, of course, I realized that if a Christian becomes well-known as an expert on – let us say – gardening, he will almost automatically be asked to speak about the theology of fuel injection. You just buy a couple of books, get some notes together, make sure they're heavily laced with relevant verses and Bob's your auntie! Anyone can do it. A lot do. I didn't know that – being so very green.

Then a new and awful thought struck me. My children would be coming along, all three of them, solidly present and visible evidence of the efficacy (or otherwise) of my platform philosophy. A waking nightmare took possession of my mind. There I would be, standing up at the front in a great big leaky tent, lecturing others earnestly on various aspects of fatherhood, when, suddenly, I would become aware that my audience was no longer listening. Instead, their eyes and attention would be fixed on the open tent-flap behind me, through which my offspring would be clearly visible – trying to kill each other on the grass outside. Grim-faced, I dismissed the nightmare and gathered my little darlings together. They sat in a row of three as I addressed them thus:

"Listen! Daddy's doing seminars on Parenting, right? So I don't want any trouble. Gottit?"

"Yes, yes, yes!" they all said, "we'll be good, of course we will . . ."

The time came, and we set out in our big old green Peugeot tank. The car was stuffed tight with camping equipment, food in cardboard boxes, children, sundry sporting accessories and quite a bit of rubbish from our last major trip. I don't drive. My wife, Bridget, drives. I navigate. My oldest son says this is like asking Cyril Smith to break the world pole-vault record. He's a very silly person sometimes.

The fact that we ran out of petrol fifty yards from the house didn't trouble me too much. After all, Bridget was the captain of the ship, as it were, so we could blame her, and we did.

Some time later, however, things began to get a little more serious. Bridget stopped the car, turned to me as I sat with the map on my knees, and said, "Adrian, why is the road getting so small? Why are we in a village called Funtington?"

The children had been singing, "We're off to Shepton Mallet! – we're off to Shepton Mallet!" Now they started to sing, "We've ended up in Funtington! – we've ended up in Funtington!"

All parents know how angry it is possible to get with children in a car. The vehicle turns into a ghastly red-hot oven full of sub-human fiends whose only talent is torment. I got furious with the children because I felt guilty, Bridget got furious with me because she thought I should be getting furious with myself instead of getting furious with them, and finally I took refuge in a sulk, hoping that by the time I came out of it everyone would have forgotten that it was my fault in the first place.

Whatever the ins and outs of this charming little domestic scene, by the time we arrived in Shepton Mallet the Plass clan was in a BAD state. As we passed through the main gates of the festival showground the lad who was

checking tickets enquired in the mildest of tones, "Are you speaking on something?"

"Yes," I growled back venomously, "PARENTING!"

I decided that the best way to restore harmony was to get the tent up, a good communal effort. Yes, you're absolutely right – I know nothing about camping *or* communal efforts. The strange, recently bought, aggressively heavy slab of canvas that we dragged from the back of our exhausted car bore no resemblance to any tent that I had ever erected. It was like a dead thing that had gone to heaven and didn't want to be bothered with coming to life again. When we did, at last, work out what was meant to go where, it was discovered that Daddy (me) had forgotten to include an essential pole. My family stood round in a circle and stared at me in the same way that people stare at some electrical appliance that has finally gone beyond repair. My oldest son went off and somehow managed to scrounge a spare pole that supported our tent (and our marriage) for the rest of the week. Glumness reigned.

By the time the morning came I was ragged. The thought of standing up in front of all those Christian parents was just too awful to contemplate. If you have ever had to tell people about God immediately after being vile to some close member of your family you'll know exactly what I mean. You want to die, but you can't.

Up I got, clutching a piece of paper on which were listed nineteen wonderfully shiny points about being a good father. I glanced at it before beginning to speak, and silently said to myself, "Well, you don't do any of them".

It was then that a little voice seemed to say, "What about telling the truth?"

"No," I said to myself, "we've managed without the truth in the Church for years. Why should I go and spoil it all now?"

But I decided to give it a go. I described to those present the events of the last twenty-four hours. I talked about my bad temper and my sulks. I confessed that the last thing I felt qualified to do was to pontificate about parenting. I thought it might have depressed them, but it didn't. You should have seen their faces brighten! Obviously none of them were very keen on having their mistakes itemized in nineteen easy-to-understand sections! *I* wouldn't have fancied it either. What those people really needed was permission to be vulnerable, and my admission of failure had offered them exactly that. Being a parent can be so painful sometimes. The last thing most of us want or need is to be intimidated by the bright and flawless ones.

That experience at "Take Seven" was the beginning of an essential understanding that vulnerability is a strength rather than a weakness. That applies just as much to public ministry as it does to selling cabbages. Here comes the second batch.

Worry

Jesus was very hot on "not worrying", wasn't he? Storms, food, clothing, what to say when the time comes, nasty things that people say about us, death itself – these are just a few of the things we're not to get hot and bothered about. I suppose that if we had the same insight into things of the spirit that the master had, we would be all too keen to relegate this team of concerns to the foot of our table of priorities.

As it is, many of us are locked into constantly recurring patterns of worry, often about things that are almost certainly never going to happen. It's easy to say we shouldn't be troubled in this way, but how *do* we break these patterns and become free?

As usual (at least I'm consistent) I have no easy answers, only a couple of suggestions.

First, Jesus said that the truth (or "reality" as it can accurately be translated) will be the thing that sets us free. Perhaps a re-reading of the gospels, with some sleeve-pulling prayer, will give us new insight into what reality really means. Let's not be silly about this – nobody is going to abandon deeply ingrained habits of worry because someone says it's a bad idea. There has to be a genuine change of perspective and probably a touch of the spirit before anything radical happens.

Secondly, the "truth" demands that we look honestly at what our worries actually are. When we have faced them with (possibly) a little more courage than usual, we might talk to another person about them, and that might be the first step towards constructing a plan of escape.

Whole lives are wasted by worry – about the wrong things?

Worry

No burglars came again last night,
Just as they failed to come the night before
And for as many nights as I remember,
No burglars yet again
Although I listened, as I always do for them,
Once more they did not oil and ease the rusty bolt that
  holds the garden gate
Behind the shed beside the house,
Nor did I hear them moving in the yard at some heart-
  sobbing wretched hour.
It was the ticking of a clock upon my wall

That like the pad of evil steps a hundred feet
   away.
They did not creep inside,
Their blind-from-birth brutality reduced to stealth and
   whispers
Did not stand above me,
Were not there with threats and ugly promises,
Intoxicated by the scent of fear incontinent
Nor did they then, with weapons that I meekly placed into
   their hands,
Proceed to sever from my chilled insides
The screaming child who has evaded birth for so long now.
They did not come.
They were not here again last night
And what if they should never come?
A waste of nights – I might have slept
But if I had, I feel quite sure
They would have come, those burglars
Yes, they would have come.

Beams

I wish I didn't have such an appetite for gossip.

"Adrian, there's something I feel I have to say to you
about Mavis, but I'm very anxious that you don't feel I'm
just spreading stories around for the sake of it. We're both
fond of Mavis and I know your only concern will be for her
welfare. Are you with me?"

Oh, yes, yes, yes, yes, yes! A thousand times yes! Of
course I'm with you, whoever you are. Gimme the dirt on
Mavis and we can call it anything you like. I've put my
mature, non-judgemental, seriously-concerned expression
on, so let's get to it – what's she done, eh?

My wife, who is looking over my shoulder as I write this,

has just suggested that I'm being a little hard on myself.

"I agree with most of the negative things you write about yourself," she says (thank you very much, dear), "but you've worked hard on this gossip thing. I don't think you do it much any more."

"Unlike some people we could name, eh?" I reply.

She has left, slightly annoyed.

But Bridget is right, I think. Although the appetite remains, unabated, I have tried to make a habit of countering criticism with praise, and simply not co-operating with muck-spreading ploys. I still fall sometimes, but it hurts me so much when I hear about others doing it to me, that I don't want to do it to anyone else.

As far as the church is concerned gossip is a killer, one of those noxious dark fluids that ooze in to fill the vacuum created by absence of courage, security and reality. I read somewhere once that gossip is a psycho-social necessity. I'm not sure what that is — but I don't agree. It's a bad thing.

Beams

A: Just between the three of us
       There's something I should share
       It's in the strictest confidence
       And purely for prayer
       But I just saw young Martin Spence
       With Mrs Falloway
B: You mean they're having an affair?
C: You told us he was gay
A: I think he was until last week
       But now the healing touch
       Has reached him through our loving prayers
C: We must have prayed too much

B: I really like old Martin
A: I think he's great –
B: Me too
A: It's such a shame he's lost control
C: He sometimes has a few
B: But we don't condemn our brother
A: No! As one we sink or swim
            We've all been down that sinful road
C: But not as far as him . . .
            Hey, Martin, fancy seeing you!
B: Glad you made it, mate!
A: We've been unholding you in prayer
MARTIN: I'll tell you why I'm late.
            I've just been down the hospital
            With Mrs Falloway
A/B/C: Ah!
MARTIN: Her husband's in for treatment
            And she's visiting today
A/B/C/:   Oh!
MARTIN: But listen – just in confidence
            And purely for prayer
            You know the place where people wait
            Well, guess who I saw there.
A/B/C/:   Who?
MARTIN: Well, who believes that Christian folk
            Should not be sick or ill?
            Who would use a drop of oil
            Where others use a pill?
A: Mildred Smith!
B: A godly lass!
A: Her faith is sure and strong
B: She's full of hope and charity
A: She's good
B: She's kind
C/MARTIN: She's wrong.
A: Ah, Mildred, what a nice surprise!

	You're just in time for prayer
MILDRED:	I've just come from the hospital
MARTIN:	I know – I saw you there.
A:	Something wrong then, Mildred?
B:	We're concerned
C:	Allay our fears
MILDRED:	I visit there on Wednesdays
	I've been doing that for years.
MARTIN:	Oh!
MILDRED:	But if we're lining up for prayer
	Here's something for the queue . . .
A:	Is it something confidential?
B:	Is it just between us few?
MILDRED:	Yes, the vicar's looking desperate
	That man is never free!
	What with services and visiting . . .
C:	He never visits *me*.
MILDRED:	He told me he's exhausted
	But he doesn't want it known
A:	No!
B:	Of course not!
MARTIN:	We'll be very careful
C:	Where's the nearest phone?
A:	Let's pray!
B:	Oh, Lord, protect us!
C:	Don't put us to the test
MARTIN:	Forgive us all our trespasses
ALL:	As we forgive the rest.

Postmen

If we're going to be all metaphorical now, and it looks as if we are, then I have to say that my wife has been the most important "postman" in my life.

When Bridget and I did an evening together in the theatre tent at Greenbelt '91, the show was entitled "Mrs Plass and her husband".

Bridget came on first and recited the following lines:

Behind the greatest men, they say,
A woman humbly stands,
Her task to serve the genius she wed.
In all my girlish dreams,
I longed to be with such a man,
But then I married Adrian instead.
Perhaps I lack humility,
Perhaps I am too proud,
But if I were to stand behind him here,
The bountiful excess,
With which his stomach is endowed,
Would fill the stage and I would disappear.
The questions get me down,
How's Gerald? Are the Flushpools real?
I like that monk,
Is he a local man?
Exactly why was Leonard Whatsit borrowing the cat?
And how come you're called Bridget, and not Anne?
To those of you who feel
(And there are some of you who might),
That being Mrs Plass should thrill my heart,
He has a ghastly habit,
That would give you quite a fright,
It's –

At this point I made an appearance on stage just in time to cut short the awful revelation. But that bit of nonsense had some truth in it. Bridget has been an immeasurable source of support and strength as far as I'm concerned, and quite apart from putting up with those ghastly habits that she nearly mentioned, she has been the most reliable postman of all in my life, delivering common sense and the heart of God to me on so many occasions.

And now it's time for me to come out of the closet and confess to my post habit. Be strong – it's not a pretty story.

Postmen

I have become a post junkie. I can no longer live without my daily fix. Sundays are a nightmare. What will become of me?

It's not even as though I like much of my post when it does come. Bills are nasty, circulars are boring, letters asking why I haven't replied to the last two letters are guilt-inducing, and invitations to come and collect my prize at a local hotel from time-share salesmen drive me into a wild frenzy.

So why do I begin to salivate mentally at eight-thirty each morning? Why do I pace restlessly to and fro by the window of the upstairs sitting-room and gaze yearningly up the road in the direction from which the postman usually comes? Why, when the dog goes berserk and the letter-box clatters, and the mail lands with a muted thump on the front mat, does my heart leap up with joy and anticipation? I suspect that part of the answer lies in the random quality of post – anything could come from anywhere and anyone. It is a regular source of potential unexpectedness in a life which, with four children at school, is necessarily as ordered as people like us can manage.

It is also, as my oldest son would be quick to point out, because I am prone to developing loony obsessions. This same oldest son, knowing how I pant like a thirsty dog for my daily epistolatory dose, will sometimes sprint to the front door before I can get there, scoop up the mail in one

well-developed movement, and retreat to his bedroom.
There, behind hastily erected barricades, he can enjoy the
scratching, whining and bloodthirsty threat-making that
emanates from his sad, demented father as he laments for
that which he has not got. One day I shall push *him*
through the letter-box.

My mania reached new heights at a past address when it
began to seem to my feverish imagination that different
postmen were bringing different kinds of post. The same
part of me knew that this could not possibly be so, of
course, but sometimes the evidence appeared to be
overwhelming.

There were three postmen.

The first, and most regular one, was a grandfatherly
older man with kind eyes and a relaxed, benevolent aura.
He pushed a trolley around his "walk", as I believe it is
called, and he never seemed to be in a hurry. This excellent
postman could be relied upon to bring fat cheques, warm
letters from old, dearly loved friends, and invitations to
dinner parties with people we liked. A Father Christmas of
the postal world, he had nothing but goodies in his sack.

The man who regularly brought the second post was a
different type altogether. He was very much younger for a
start, no more than nineteen or twenty, and he conducted
himself with a carelessness that bordered on flippancy.
Often, from my post at the upstairs window, as the time
for second post approached, I would see this lightweight
young person swinging round the corner at the top of our
road on his bicycle, and watch as he then pedalled along
the straight stretch with his hands off the handlebars and a
dreamy smile on his face. I would have laid heavy odds on
his being involved with an unskilled but highly ambitious
rock band.

The post he brought was pathetic – predictably so. He
brought vouchers offering 10p off well-known makes of
washing powder; large, impressive-looking envelopes with

huge print screaming that you'd probably won £50,000, only you knew you hadn't; unsealed brown envelopes containing the quarterly bulletin of the Retired Gentlefolk's Association and addressed to the person before last who lived in your house. He just didn't try. He wasn't cut out to be a postman.

The third one was the worst of all! He filled in when the older man was ill or on holiday, and I dreaded his coming. Small, thin, horribly clean and unremittingly severe in his manner, he was, we happened to know, a member of the small but very stern religious group that met every Sunday in a little corrugated iron hut at the other end of the town.

During the weeks when he delivered to us the supply of fat cheques and warm letters simply dried up. I know why – they would have been bad for us. Instead, he brought knife-edged envelopes containing bills that were red with anger, postcards from the public library demanding the return of their books, letters from the bank charging fifteen pounds to point out that we hadn't any money, and ranting communications from members of obscure sects who, having read and disapproved of one of my books, wanted to point out that I would spend an eternity of misery with Satan unless I spent a lifetime of misery with them.

He was a terrible postman!

So what is the point of all this? Well, it's very simple really. I was wrong about the three postmen. It was just a fantasy. They all brought the same selection of post because they were all employed by the same firm. Howeer much I may have wished it otherwise, their character and temperament were irrelevant to the items that they actually delivered.

Sometimes I'm tempted to ignore or discount ministry that's offered to me through an individual or a church that isn't to my taste or liking, especially, in my case, if it's someone who is familiar and close to me.

Let us beware! God sends the messages *and* he runs the entire delivery service. The rest of us are just postmen.

Graces

I was rather pleased when a friend rang to ask if it would be possible for me to write a "grace" to be said before the meal at a local gathering of Licensed Victuallers. What a pleasure it was to produce something for a group of people who have probably never heard of Graham Kendrick – or Adrian Plass, for that matter.

What a lot of colour and life we miss by avoiding what we suspiciously refer to as "the world".

I was severely handicapped, of course, by my profound ignorance of alcoholic drinks, but after much anxious thought I suddenly remembered my friend, Eric Delve, mentioning that he had once had a small port in a Public House in Godalming. I hastened to ring him, and to my relief found that he recalled the incident quite clearly. What a memory he has! Even after such a great lapse of time Eric was able to recollect the names of several drinks that had been bought by other patrons of the bar.

Off I went, but after completing the Licensed Victuallers' Grace I got a bit carried away and did one for taxi drivers as well. The mania had me in its grip by the time that one was finished, and I steamed ahead with something suitable for British Rail employees. When my wife came in I looked at her with crazed eyes and held up a list of fifty or more different occupations.

"Look," I said, "I'm going to write a grace for every single one, even if it takes – "

"Three's enough, I would think", said my wife.

Here they are. I'm going to do some more when she's not looking.

Graces

1) FOR PUBLICANS:
   Lord, we meet together here,
   Mild and bitter, stout and pale.
   Grant, from now till final orders
   That our spirits never ail.
   With specific gravity
   We shall hock depravity,
   Please fill each hungry cavity
   Let gratitude prevail. Amen

2) FOR TAXI-DRIVERS:
   Simple thanks we offer now,
   No trace of ambiguity,
   For once we'll take this humble fare
   Expecting no gratuity. Amen

3) FOR BRITISH RAIL EMPLOYEES:
   Speed this food, Lord, as it comes
   On its journey to our tums.
   Let there be no long diversion
   Of this edible excursion,
   Unavoidably delayed
   Just behind the shoulder-blade,
   Or stranded in the lower back
   By lettuce leaves upon the track.
   May all traffic safely pass
   And our digestions be first-class. Amen

Lewis and I

You may have some difficulty in believing that the little story I'm about to tell you is true. I can understand that, but try to fight this lack of trust within yourself. Above all, please don't get the idea that I'm just cashing in on the Lewis industry as so many other people have done. We Christian writers are not afraid of our personal limitations, you know. Ha! The very thought.

After all, I *might* have met him.

Can you prove I *haven't* met him?

He was alive during my lifetime so I *could* have met him.

Were you there when I *didn't* meet him? (Not that I didn't – I did.)

Anyway, if that's the way you feel, nobody's *making* you read it.

Oh, go on – read it.

Lewis and I

I thank God that I am more restrained than other men.

Despite a flood of highly attractive offers from major international publishers I have, until now, refused to describe or discuss the intimate details of my encounter with C. S. Lewis. The memory is sacred to me, and were it not for the specific leading that I have recently felt, I would have quite happily taken my secrets to the grave.

It was, then, on a cold and blustery autumn afternoon in Oxford, as I was in the very act of purchasing a fresh cream doughnut in a small but interesting baker's shop near the centre of town, that I suddenly espied the great thinker and writer standing in the doorway of a shoe-shop on the opposite side of the road.

I was transfixed, as you may imagine, for the entire ninety seconds that elapsed before a car drew up and transported the creator of Narnia away to some other world. Hardly able to believe what had just happened, I took a pen from my pocket and begged a paper bag from the girl who had been serving me. Impressed perhaps by the luminous urgency of my expression, she pushed one into my hand and retreated into some back room or area of the shop.

That paper bag, covered in hastily scribbled notes, lies before me now, evoking memories as fresh as the cream in that distant doughnut, long ago consumed, but never to be forgotten.

Lewis was standing (my notes inform me) with his weight evenly balanced on both feet – and how fitting that was! One foot in fantasy and one foot planted, with exactly equal firmness, in the reality of what *is* and cannot be ignored or changed. It was the balance also between academia and that – oh, so profitable awareness that great truths must be taught with great simplicity by great minds. One would not wish to read over much significance into random events, but it seemed to me that there was what I can only describe as a sort of parabolic synchronicity in Lewis's decision to position himself in front of an establishment that sold footwear. For he himself was responsible through his writings for providing so many folk with the winged sandals, not of Hermes, but of free and unburdened access to the things of God. (It is interesting to note that immediately after Lewis's departure – the shop closed!)

Tears and jam blur a part of my next note, but the picture in my mind is too clear for recollection to fail. Lewis extended his right hand – palm upward – and gazed at the sky for a full five seconds or more.

Yes, the storm clouds were gathering, and yes, the

first fragmentary drops of October rain (God's "natural baptism" as G. K. Chesterton called it) were steadily beginning to fall on that hand whose sure grip had already penned so many and such varied works of literature.

In that moment I seemed to see both a resistance and a submission in Lewis's response to the wild weather of adversity, criticism and self-doubt. He did up one button of his jacket – but *only* one. He frowned slightly towards the clouds, but almost immediately withdrew even further into the shelter of the shop doorway, perhaps seeking in an instinctive way the surrounding comfort of those symbols of individual progress that thronged the windows on both sides of him. From, as it were, the casemented warmth of popular affirmation he would be able to emerge fearlessly (Lewis was *not* carrying an umbrella) into the inclemency of disapproval and difficulty.

Engorged with the richness of these unique insights, my doughnut still untouched, I hardly dared continue to watch as the final act of this fascinating drama began to unfold. Without any warning Lewis lifted his left wrist, cupped his right hand around his watch, and peered intently at it for a second or two before raising his head and nodding, as if to say: "Yes, it *is* time."

And, of course, it *was* time. It was Lewis's time. It was my time. It was and is and will be the time of those generations who have and shall and must benefit from the offerings of such a genius. It was with a smile of infinitely sweet sadness that Lewis greeted the arrival of the vehicle he was awaiting, a smile that bade farewell to the *then*, welcome to the *now* and patient resignation to the *not yet*.

It was a privilege to be there on that day, and it surprises me not one iota that responses to the leaking of this unique experience have been uniformly negative. Already an article has been published in America, claiming that Lewis was speaking to an audience of hundreds in a completely different country on the day in question, but that, I fear, is the voice of jealousy braying across the Atlantic.

Next year I plan to publish a paper examining the style and content of a note left by Lewis for his milkman in the late fifties. I believe in my heart that this recently discovered document will establish beyond all reasonably doubt that C. S. Lewis wrestled with an obsessional desire to control the working habits of others.

True scholars could not be other than appreciative.

Angels

I know very little about angels. I know that they are God's messengers – more than messengers. I know that they fight, and comfort, and protect, and that we might entertain them unawares.

I know also that they would like the opportunity to become sons and daughters of God – the opportunity that *we* have.

I wonder if it takes some of them a while to accept their limitations? Do you think God will forgive me if I undertake a brief, whimsical conjecture? I hope so, because here it comes.

Angels

Two angels were gossiping in the waiting-room of the buckshot clinic.

"I don't complain," said the larger one, "because I'm an angel, but if I wasn't I'd have something pretty sharp to say about the allocation of names to us heavenly beings. It's all right if you're called something like 'Gabriel' or 'Michael'. They've got a real ring to them."

"What are you called then?" asked the smaller angel.

"Pongo – that's my name. No wonder I didn't get any mention in the boss's book. 'The Angel Pongo appeared to Mary . . .' Doesn't quite have the same impact, does it? What's your name?"

"Biggles", replied his companion sadly. "My name is Biggles – forever."

Silence descended as the two angels contemplated an eternity of ignominious nomenclature.

"And another thing," said Pongo, after a minute had passed, "I was on that angelic sub-committee that was supposed to ratify the boss's plans for his son's visit to the third planet. They gave me that Prodigal Son story to comment on. But did they take any notice of what I said?"

"Well, did they?" enquired Biggles with real interest.

"Did they, heaven! You've seen the final draft. I would have been furious, if I was capable of negative responses. I put in a very full report. Look, I said, the whole thing needs tightening up and refocusing. First of all, there's the road that this prodigal's travelling on. It's so vague! Anyone would think that the boss is willing to travel down any old cart-track that these human wrecks come staggering up

once they've realized which side their bread's buttered on.
Narrow it down! That's what I recommended. Spell it out!
Create an orthodoxy! Pin 'em down!"

"They didn't listen?" Biggles shook his head sympathetically.

"If I was capable of criticism," said Pongo, "and the
boss was less than perfect, I'd say that this story embodies
the kind of flabby liberalism that makes life so difficult for
us angels. Why does the father come rushing down
towards this wretched son of his while he's still a long way
off? It gives the game away – that's what I said in my
report. Why not let the kid do the whole trip? Keep him
worried and guessing right up to the point where he

reaches home. Then leave him standing at the door for a few minutes. Let him stew. Send the least important serving girl to let him in, and when he does finally get to see his father, let the old man be distant – a little bit cool. The son has to earn his way back into his dad's good books. That's what I suggested."

"Instead of which . . .?" coaxed Biggles.

"Instead of which," continued the larger angel, "we have what is (let's be frank) this embarrassing portrayal of the boss going for Olympic gold as he sprints down the highway with a bag of presents, like Father Christmas on jet-propelled roller-skates. Too vulnerable!"

"Too obvious," nodded Biggles.

"Too easy," asserted Pongo.

"Too emotional," added Biggles, rather absently.

"Too generous," declared Pongo, really enjoying himself now.

"Too wonderful," said Biggles dreamily.

Pongo frowned and shifted in his seat. "I might as well have not bothered sending in a report at all," he muttered. "Why deliberately provoke those Jewish humans by having the prodigal end up working with the pigs? That's another of the points I made. Then there's the cultural context. What happens, I wanted to know, when we reach the twentieth century, and people start calling it The Parable of the Failed Father? To my mind the boss was laying himself wide open. Two failed kids. Poor parenting. See what I mean? And why so tough on the older brother anyway? Poor bloke, slogging away – doing his best without so much as a thank you. No wonder he wasn't very pleased when his dirty-stop-out brother got all that V.I.P. treatment. If I'd been him I'd have had something to say about – just a minute!"

He looked narrowly at his fellow angel.

"What?" said Biggles, innocently.

"You just said the idea of the boss running down the road was 'too wonderful'. That is what you said, isn't it?"

"Well," said Biggles, turning slightly pink, "I was just thinking that, *if* I was capable of feeling envious, I might have wished that I could walk up the road like the prodigal and see the boss rushing down towards me looking all excited and throwing his arms round me and giving me all those gifts and throwing a party for me and telling me he loved me and – and all that. He's crazy about those humans, isn't he?"

Pongo looked into his companion's shining eyes for a moment, then sighed and smiled a sad little smile.

"Yes," he said quietly, "I suppose that if I had been capable of feeling envious, I might have envied . . . all that."

Positive Graffiti

Once or twice people have suggested that I am too negative about life, the Church, and everything. It hurts me to say this, but they may be right. Some good things have happened in my life.

So here, to make the people who've suggested I'm too negative feel good, and to earn me an extra blessing for listening to criticism and acting on it, is – (*Roll of drums*) something positive!!!!

Positive Graffiti

I have discussed elsewhere they way in which Satan uses his infernal aerosol spray to cover our hearts with graffiti. Jeremiah said that God will write his law on our hearts, but where these devilish scrawlings are too deep and too numerous to be easily erased, it can be a very long time

before the Holy Spirit finally completes the cleaning job
and enables us to present a clean sheet to the divine scribe.

Abuse, harsh words, ridicule, failure, rejection – the
devil's negative graffiti come in many different forms.
Sometimes a few words, not intentionally harmful but
thoughtless and ill-chosen, can cause a wound that takes
years to heal, and leaves a scar that never quite fades. How
dangerous the tongue is!

It occurred to me recently, though, that, in my own life
at any rate, there have been correspondingly positive
experiences, events and influences that have counteracted
or even replaced some of the negative ones. These heavenly
graffiti come in many different forms, often through agents
who have no specifically Christian connection. They are
little gifts from God that may have a disproportionately
profound effect.

I can remember three without really trying.

The first happened when I was about five years old and
attending the little infants school in the village of Rusthall,
where I was brought up. I was a slightly worried child, not
particularly naughty, but given to occasional outbursts
when I felt driven into a corner. One day I did something
naughty in the playground, halfway through the dinner
hour. I can't remember exactly what it was that I did but I
do recall my awareness that it was "a fair cop". I was for
it! The lady who was on playground duty dragged me into
the top classroom and left me there while she reported my
crime to the headmistress. When she came back she told
me I was to wait on my own until the head sent for me.

I was terrified. My hair stood up and my blood drained
down. What tigers there were in this jungle of a world!

At last the headmistress appeared at the classroom door
and beckoned me to follow her through the corridor and
into her office. I stood facing her as she sat behind her desk.
I felt my bowels move ominously. What was going to
happen?

After a moment's silence the headmistress pointed to a bowl on her desk and said, "Come and sit down and have some ice-cream Adrian".

She picked up a second bowl, and we sat, side by side, eating ice-cream together. She never mentioned my dreadful misdemeanour, and I certainly wasn't going to bring it up. I didn't feel any satisfaction about "getting away with it". I was just puzzled and surprised and relieved to find that authority did not exclude mercy.

The second experience happened just outside Paddington Station in London. I was a raw, unsophisticated teenager, anxious to project a cool, confident image to the rest of the world. A porter carried my bags from the train on which I'd travelled, to the bus-stop just up the road from the station. As he bent down to put my luggage on to the pavement I felt in my pocket for some change. I knew what

to do now. When porters carried your bags you gave them a tip. How much? I didn't know – I'd never been in this position before.

Withdrawing my hand from my pocket I looked at the selection of coins. Airily I selected two florins (a florin was the same as a ten pence piece) and handed them to the porter, who was just straightening up. He stood quite still for a second or two, studying the two coins that lay in the palm of his hand, then, after a searching look into my face, he handed one of them back to me, and said, in a voice tinged with some mid-European accent, "Two shillings is quite enough".

Even I, naive as I was, knew how unusual it was for *anyone* to return any part of a tip. The porter had given me a little free lesson. It warmed my heart to know that his generosity extended to strangers. Perhaps he had a son of my age.

Thirdly, there was George.

George worked in a paint distribution warehouse near Bromley, a place where five or six employees plodded around behind metal trolleys, assembling orders to be delivered to retailers. It was a place of long alleys running between high shelving units, loaded with every conceivable variety of paint, a veritable maze.

George was not in love with his work; there was nothing very inspiring about piling tins on trolleys. In his mid-

forties and totally lacking in ambition, George was an expert in the art of disappearance. He knew the alleys like the back of his hand, and he spent the day playing hide and seek with the foreman, a little, frantic man with no top teeth who ran around the warehouse clutching a sheaf of overdue orders in his hand, and plaintively calling for one of the mole-like trolley-pushers to come and fill them. Occasionally George allowed himself to be spotted in the distance, passing across the far end of an alley, moving with considerable speed, and looking as if he had suddenly remembered where some obscure variety of paint was stored. George was a master of the art of doing nothing, and he did it all day.

I was working in the warehouse as a vacation job in between terms at the teacher-training college in Bromley. I was in my mid-twenties at the time. Unlike George, I worked very hard at assembling orders, mainly because it was so excruciatingly boring if I didn't. George and I got on very well, though, and one day he saved me from death by tedium.

At that time I was a fairly heavy smoker. It was one of the few things that made life in the warehouse bearable. One day I left my packet at home and was quite desolate. With no money to buy any more I steeled myself to an eternal, cigarettte-less day.

George, also a smoker, realized my predicament, and throughout that day, found me at regular intervals, handed me a cigarette without speaking, and returned to whichever bolt-hole he was occupying at the time.

Leaving aside the rights and wrongs of smoking, it struck me then, and it strikes me now, that George, with his redundant teddy-boy haircut, and his rather grey aimless view of life, did a very sweet thing for a fellow human being on that day.

My headmistress, the porter from Paddington Station and generous George, each offered me, in their own way, the cup of water that Jesus talked about his followers needing. And each will undoubtedly receive the reward that he also mentioned.

Thank God for positive graffiti, and those whom he uses to provide them.

YOU, ME AND US

There is little less trouble in governing a private family than a whole kingdom.

MICHAEL DE MONTAIGNE, *Essays* 1580

If you wish to study men you must not neglect to mix with the society of children.

Ibid.

You, Me and Us

A few years ago we enjoyed a family holiday in Denmark, and I can testify that there's a lot more to that ancient kingdom than bacon and Lego. The eastern peninsula that we explored was beautiful to look at and full of interest. More importantly from the point of view of our three boys, there was a football pitch and two practice goals just up the road from our holiday house in the village of Stenvad. It was a comfortable place to stay, with a "cricket-sized" garden at the back.

We had some very silly jokes from some members of the family. Worst of all was the suggestion that when we got home we should take our films into the chemist, then when we returned to collect them a few days later, we would say, "May we have Hamlet, please?"

"Hamlet?", the shop assistant would enquire.

"Yes," we would reply, "the prints of Denmark."

Gettit?

The best thing, as usual, was just being together as a family, arguing in peace for once.

Sometimes the holiday ethos allows quite subtle problems to rise to the surface.

One evening, after the younger members of the family had finally been coaxed, threatened and bribed to bed, my oldest son put into words an area of concern that had never occurred to me. He described how, as he listened to Bridget and me talking to the younger children, praising them for things they'd said or bought or done, he recognized in the words we used and the tone of our voices, the same kind of encouragement that had enabled him to feel valued and approved of as *he* grew up. Now, however, seeing how positive we were about quite small efforts and achievements on the part of the little ones, he started to feel a little insecure. Perhaps we had been less than sincere when we praised *him* in the past. What if his feelings of allrightness were based on a series of half-truths? Maybe we weren't really proud of him after all.

I didn't really know what to say in reply to this, but by the next morning the issue had resolved itself into a question in my mind: Which is more important in relationships – the love of truth, or the truth of love?

Should our response to the efforts of others be doggedly, uncompromisingly accurate, or should we let love mould and modify our reactions.

I tried to explain what I was thinking to my son, but it was only when I got down to concrete examples in his own life that he began to see what I meant.

"What about you with Katy?" I said (Katy was three and her biggest brother was potty about her). "What about when Katy brings you one of her drawings and asks what you think of it? Do you say, 'I'm sorry, Kate, but it's just a meaningless scribble'? Or do you say, 'Well done, Katy, that's really lovely!'? In fact," I went on, seeing his face soften, "would you be happy if you knew that the way I feel about you is the same as the way you feel about Katy?"

"Yes," he said "I would."

"That's good then," I said, "because it is."

The maintenance and repair of relationships with God, family, neighbours and fellow believers is an absolute priority in our lives, but what a tricky area this can be. I was about to say that this next cart-load of "cabbages" includes some ideas and issues that are rather personal to me, but I think I can safely say that most of us ratbags can easily identify with each other's problems.

So stay with me (unless your relationships are totally under control, of course).

Generations

G. K. Chesterton described atheism as a nightmare – a maze without an exit.

My own atheistic nightmare is concerned with the inexorable roll of the generations. So much birth and death and joy and grief, happening over and over and over like a constantly repeated film, in which only the faces change slightly each time. Grandparents who will probably never know their great-grand-children, and will certainly never know their great-great-grandchildren, and wouldn't be able to remember all their names anyway because there would be far too many of them.

"Oh, God, let it all mean something!" I have cried at those times when the darkness just won't go away. My heart would break if I ever seriously believed that all our relationships turn to dust. What would be the point of anything?

"Don't be afraid," said Jesus, "I have overcome death."

Generations

1) I took my daughter to the park last night
    She ran with a shout to the roundabout
    The roundabout went round and round
    But it never stopped anywhere very profound
    It just went round and round and round,
    It just went round and round.

2) I took my daughter to the park last night
    She bounced like a spring to the grown-up swing
    It swung quite high and it swung quite low
    But there wasn't any doubt where the swing would go
    It just swung high and it just swung low,
    It just swung high and low.

3) I took my daughter to the park last night
    Her eyes grew wide when she saw the slide
    She climbed up the steps and she slid back down
    But the same sun set on the same old town
    She just climbed up and she just slid down
    Just climbed and slid back down.

5) We're all going down to the park tonight
   Where the swings go high and the swings go low
   But there isn't any doubt where the swings will go
   And you climb the steps and you slide back down
   While the same sun sets on the same old town
   Where the roundabout just goes round and round.
   And never stops anywhere very profound
   It just goes round and round and round,
   It just goes round and round.

Waste of Days

Our writer is in an even trickier position now than he was before. Having sorted out the abominable Jane Drain, and worked out where he stands on motivation, he is now dead, and about to discover if the words he wrote so easily in life will do him any good at the gates of Paradise.

I suspect, although never having been dead I can't be sure, that God's idea of priorities may turn out to be very different from ours. Poor old Rodney Fuller finds that the books he's written are of far less importance than the way he has treated his family, especially in his use of time.

Recently I have become very conscious of the richness of days that most of us possess. So many mornings and afternoons and evenings to use as we wish. We can squander them or spend them wisely, and of course that will mean different things to different people. Walking on the Downs could be the best or the worst way to use a day; helping a neighbour can be selfish or unselfish; working without a break can be admirable or cruel. Our hearts tell us the truth if we want to listen.

Which reminds me – I said I'd go and play snooker with my son this evening.

Waste of Days

W = WRITER
A = ANGEL

W: (*Approaching desk*) Err . . . excuse me.
A: (*Brisk and pleasant*) Yes, sir?
W: Is this . . . heaven?

A: Front-desk, yes, sir. Did you want to come in?

W: Well, err, I'm a writer.

A: That doesn't automatically disqualify you, sir. We've admitted publishers before now. If I can just have your name.

W: My name's Rodney Fuller. (*No response*) I wrote Christian books. I've written lots of, err . . . Christian books. Are you an angel?

A: Yes, sir, I am an angel.

W: Well, I wrote a book about angels – a sort of novel – you know, about how things really are for angels.

A: (*Dryly staring*) Yes. I read it.

W: And I wrote another book called *Boldness before God: The Certainty of Salvation.* Err . . . do you think I *will* be allowed in?

A: I have your file here, Mister Fuller (*Studies it for a moment*) and all your books. (*Puts pile on desk*) These are all yours, are they not?

W: (*Encouraged*) Yes, yes they are. Writing was my ministry, you know.

A: Writing was your *obsession*, Mister Fuller. According to this file you robbed your family, your friends, your community and your church of a year and a half's worth of free time just so that *this* (*Holds up book*) could be written, for instance. (*Reads title*) *A Study of the Relationship between Hair-length and Heroism in the Pentateuch.*

W: That was described as "A very important book".

A: Yes. (*Consults file*) by the Latvian Christian Barbers In Exile Association's five-yearly news bulletin, which was only produced once because its seventeen subscribers had all died before the second edition was due.

W: Well, it was a bit of a minority –

A: And while you laboured away on behalf of seventeen octogenarian hairdressers your wife was putting the kids to bed, looking after visitors, cleaning the house, sorting out the bills, fending off door-to-door Spring Harvest salesmen, apologizing to needy people in the local community for your non-availability, writing an article about not having time to write a book, doing a part-time job, mowing the lawn, planting out vegetables, and putting up with your chronic bad temper – all because you had convinced her that you were engaged in the Lord's Work!

W: I was committed!

A: You were fanatical.

W: I was creatively absorbed!

A: You were self-indulgent.

W: I was spiritually driven!

A: You were an Anglican.

W: But I thought –

A: Mister Fuller, at birth your account was credited with sixty-nine years, three months and nine days. That is a very sizeable deposit. It has now been spent to the very last moment, and these records suggest that a large proportion of what you used to describe as your "writing career" involved the squandering of very valuable hours. Balance, Mister Fuller – that is what you failed to achieve – balance!

W: I'm not going to be saved by works, am I?

A: (*Pats books*) Well, not these, no. Up here, Mister Fuller, it's not what you've done or what you know, it's *who* you know.

W: (*Brightening*) I had tea with Eric Delve once.

A: I thought you *wanted* to come in.

W: I do, I was only joking. I – I know Jesus. I've written about him.

A: Oh! (*Examines file - pauses*) Well, let's hope he's written about you . . .

END

Today's News

I very rarely set out to be obscure in my writing. On the contrary, I can't understand why, in the vast majority of cases, writers would *not* want readers to know what they are getting at. I have to confess, however, that in the following lines, which are song lyrics, the images employed are quite deliberately selected with a view to offering the listener an impression of what I want to say, rather than a clear picture.

Why?

Good question. I suppose the answer is partly that I just enjoyed the freedom of communicating without accountability, and partly that fuzzy pictures can sometimes reveal more soul than photographs.

Having said that, some of the metaphors are quite obvious, and I promise that they all mean *something*. For instance:

> For her memory is blind
> To the one who touched her body
> In the middle of her mind.

This refers to child abuse, and the psychological mechanism that conceals painful memories from the conscious mind, but is unable to prevent the wounds caused by those forgotten events from festering, and poisoning the victim for years.

Can you work out what all the other images are about? Can you be bothered?

The general theme of the piece is that large-scale convictions, movements and principles, even if held and supported sincerely, are not much use if they never affect anything or anybody on a small scale. At least, I *think* that's what it was about . . .

Today's News

Today's news came on the wrong day
And the right day never comes
Though the man who is tied to the dragon
May smile as he does his sums
But he doesn't understand
That we just can't handle
The pain in the universe.
Someone'd better tell the man, he doesn't seem to care
If love's not down in the market square
It's not anywhere.
I'ts not anywhere.

The bear is called a pussycat
The cat's become a mouse
But it hasn't made a difference
To the feeling in our house
For mother's in the same old place
The baby's out the back
My brother hit the ceiling
Then he bounced into the crack
And the sun is getting hotter
And the sky is getting old
But the central heating's busted
So our feet are just as cold
It's not that we don't see the dead
A thousand years away
But there's someone in our upstairs room
Who might be dead today

    Today's news came . . . etc

Would-be-good, the watcher
Wanted poetry in stone
But the valley of the dwellers
Is already overgrown
By the pestilence upon her
For her memory is blind
To the one who touched her body
In the middle of her mind
The icemen love experiments
But this will never do
For the maze is getting difficult
The rats are coming through
And the voluntary patient
Hates the pattern that he's known
For the shape of it is uglier
Than anything in stone

    Today's news came . . . etc

Somewhere there's a city
Where the washing powder's been
All the citizens are sleepy
And defiantly unclean
But in the solid cells
Behind another city wall
There are people who are clean and grey
And never seen at all
Fifty million babies
Have been planted on the moon
And another stepping-stone
Will be a mausoleum soon
But here we step more warily
Across the wild park
For the city's getting dangerous
The city's getting dark

Today's news came on the wrong day
And the right day never comes
Though the man who is tied to the dragon
May smile as he does his sums
But he doesn't understand
That we just can't handle
The pain in the universe
Someone I'd better tell the man, he doesn't seem to care
If love's not down in the market square
It's not anywhere,
It's not anywhere

Clay

One of the wonderful things about Christian marriage is that you never have any rows or arguments, so when I wanted to write about conflict in relationships I had to go round all my friends asking them if they could tell me what it was like. At last I found some people who remembered having an argument some years ago, and they have kindly allowed me to record the details of that event in this book.

And if you believe all that, you'll believe anything!

Arguments in marriage are like pieces of music — harsh music perhaps, but with familiar and oft-repeated tunes. It seems to me a legitimate function of drama that it should face people with the truth of what they do to each other. Maybe it might even help them to change the music — something a little more harmonious, perhaps?

We must be careful with each other. We are only clay.

Clay

W: Well?

M: Well what?

W: Aren't you going to ask me how I got on?

M: How did you get on?

W: Well, don't sound too interested, will you? (*Pause*) What's the matter?

M: Nothing. Why?

W: I dunno, you just seem . . . funny.

M: How did you get on?

W: (*Excited*) I actually made a pot! I made one! It weighs about three and a half pounds, and it only holds about a thimbleful of water, but it's a pot! My pot!

M: (*Dully*) I thought you didn't go on the wheel for the first few lessons, or have I got it wrong?

W: No, we don't.

M: Oh, don't we?

W: I made this one with my hands, just, you know, squeezing and shaping. It was quite sensual!

M: It was what?

W: The feel of the clay – it's lovely stuff to handle – all squishy and thick and soft.

M: I thought the idea was to acquire a practical skill, not to have sensual experiences.

W: Oh, don't be so grumpy, darling. You're not jealous of a lump of clay, are you? (*Imitates him*). "I thought the idea was to acquire a practical skill, not to have a sensual experience . . ."

M: I don't think doing impressions of me is particularly helpful, do you?

W: What *is* the matter with you? (*Pause*) Have you not had a very good evening? (*Waits*) Michael?

M: I've just been here. Haven't really . . .

W: I thought you'd enjoy being on your own for a while. Was the dinner all right? (*Pause*) You have had your dinner, haven't you?

M: I couldn't work out the thingy . . . I dunno, I just couldn't be bothered in the end.

W: (*Genuinely distressed*) Michael, that was a lovely dinner! I spent ages getting it ready. All you had to do was turn it up for half an hour then take it out. What do you mean you don't know how to do it? – you've done it loads of times! Why didn't you –

M: Look, I didn't have my dinner, all right! It's hardly the crime of the century, is it?

W: No, but it's meant to punish the crime of the century, isn't it?

M: Don't be stupid! I –

W: The only thing is, we're not quite sure what the crime of the century is, are we? At least, I'm not! Is it my torrid affair with a piece of clay, or is it just that I left you alone to wrestle with the terrible complexity of an oven switch? Or is it something else?

M: (*Strategic sigh*) I'm beginning to wish I hadn't said anything at all.

W: I'm sure you are. Because you haven't actually got any real grievance at all, have you? I thought we left all this sort of stuff behind ten years ago. I just couldn't *stand* it if –

M: *Overwhelmed*) Look, can we just forget about it now please? I'm sorry! I wish I'd never – I mean – I'm sorry!

W: (*Pause*) Do you want to hear any more about my pot?

M: (*Back in the driving seat*) Yes, go on.

W: Well, it's brown.

M: Mmm . . . (*Nods*)

W: And ugly.

M: Mmm . . . (*Nods*)

W: Like you . . .

M: Humph!

W: (*Quietly*) Especially when you get like you got just now. What was going on? Please tell me.

M: There's no point in telling you.

W: Why not?

M: Because you don't really want to know. It's irrational, and you don't like that. If I tell you what I feel you'll just tell me how wrong I am to feel it.

W: No I won't.

M: Yes you will. You always do.

W: Well, I won't this time. (*Pause*) Try me.

M: (*Unconvinced!*) All right – I feel hurt and upset and threatened by you going out and doing something that doesn't involve me, and being all bright and happy about it and talking about – sensual clay, and . . . well, that's about it really.

W: (*Shaking head*) How can you *possibly* feel that?

M: See what I mean?

W: I mean – I just don't understand how you can say that. We *talked* about me doing an evening class. You said you thought it was a good idea. You were the one who persuaded me to get on and actually do it. Now you're spoiling it!

M: Look, you asked me what I was feeling so I told you. I said you wouldn't like it because it's irrational. It *is* irrational! I know it's irrational. But I'm stuck with being who I am and what I am because of all the – stuff in my past and all that. I didn't choose to feel what I felt this evening; it was just there. If you hadn't asked me what was the matter, I wouldn't have told you, then we wouldn't have had a problem would we?

W: (*Temporarily conned*) I'm sorry, Michael. I didn't mean to stir things up. I was just upset that you felt – (*Pause*) Wait a minute! What am I talking about? It's just like the old days. I've ended up apologizing for what you've done to *me*!

M: What?

W: Well, you say we wouldn't have had a problem if I hadn't asked you what was wrong, but that's not true, is it? You were in your "Guess what's the matter with me" mode from the moment I walked through the door. All morose and moody and (*Whines*) "couldn't work the thingy on the oven so I didn't have any dinner". Poor little boy!

It's true, isn't it? You were determined to show me how miserable you were. Tell me the truth for once!

M: (*Apparently deeply hurt and offended*) Are you saying that I usually tell lies?

W: Oh, dear! Have I exaggerated? I do apologize. What a convenient thing to latch on to. We're not *talking* about *my* exaggeration. We're talking about you! When I first met you, you'd just emerged into the adult world with "A" Levels in sulking, self-pity and – (*Searches for a word*)

M: You can't think of a third word beginning with the same letter, can you?

W: I warn you, Michael! I'm not going back to all that. If I can't do things on my own without you trying to punish me every time . . .

M: Yes?

W: (*Quietly*) I don't know. (*Pause*) I'm going out. I can't stay here at the moment.

M: Where are you –

W: I don't know where I'm going. I've got my pot in the boot. I might go down to Brighton for a dirty weekend.

M: Don't be silly . . .

W: What, irrational, you mean? Well, I'm sorry, Michael, but it's all because of my dreadful past. I'm stuck with being who I am, you see, and you don't have to make any effort to control yourself. I thought you knew that. It's just unfortunate if it affects anyone else. Ring round the hotels if you want to find me. Just ask for Mrs Clay (*Pause*) Oh!! I'll see you later! (*Exits*)

M: Hmm (*Longish pause for thought*) I think I'll have some dinner . . .

(*Blackout*)

I KNOW WHAT
YOU'RE GOING TO SAY

I Know What You're Going to Say

It's dangerous to assume that we know all there is to know about a close friend or marriage partner. I once acted in a play featuring a married couple who disagreed about the type of house they occupied. She was convinced that they lived in a two-storey house, while he was adamant that it was a bungalow. He had refused to go upstairs for years, because it would prove her point.

This deliberately absurd situation amusingly highlighted the stagnation that can occur when long-term relationships are reduced to a set of predictable, constantly repeated verbal and behavioural shapes. Whole chunks of personality are put into cold-storage because they never became part of the relationship pattern at an early stage.

I always find it so sad to see a couple sitting in a cafe or restaurant, especially on holiday, gazing blankly into the distance because there's no point in trying to communicate when you know exactly how your partner is going to respond. Yes, I know it's a good thing to be able to sit in companionable silence, and no, Bridget and I *don't* always talk animatedly in cafes and hold Wildean conversations in restaurants, but you know what I mean. So sad.

One of the ways in which I annoy Bridget is by suddenly saying, apropos of nothing: "Who are you?"

I do put it on a bit, but that occasional question is born out of the sudden, genuine realization that this person who is so close to me that I can hardly see her, is actually a quite separate, complex, total human being who I don't know half as well as I think I do. I find those moments rather exciting in a number of ways.

Heaven preserve my relationship with my wife, and with God, from the illusion that I can be totally sure what either of them is going to say.

I Know What You're Going to Say

WOMAN: John, I've been thinking.

MAN: Mmm?

WOMAN: I've made a decision.

MAN: Uh-huh?

WOMAN: I'm going to stop work in September.

MAN: Well –

WOMAN: I know what you're going to say. How are we going to manage on one salary? Well we did it before and we'll do it again. We're far too extravagant anyway. It'll do us good.

MAN: I –

WOMAN: It's no good coming out with that old line about "How are you going to manage without your holidays and little treats?" It really infuriates me when you say that. You're virtually accusing me of being a simple-minded bimbo, which, for your information, I certainly am not!

MAN: You –

WOMAN: Don't bother telling me I've got some secret reason for stopping work, either. I haven't, and, quite frankly, I take exception to your view of me as a devious, self-seeking female.

MAN: Could we –

WOMAN: No, don't try to smooth me over. You can't call someone a neurotic simpleton and then make it all right with a few glib phrases. No doubt you'll claim you "didn't mean it". Well, if you didn't mean it you shouldn't have said it! How would you feel if you'd come to me with a carefully thought through plan and just had it steamrollered? Because that's what you've done.

MAN: I –

WOMAN: No, please don't insult my intelligence by denying it, because I simply won't listen. You've had your say and now it's my turn! Or perhaps I don't get a turn. Well, I'm going to take it anyway. I've told you I want to stop work, but you didn't seem to hear me. Or rather, you did hear me, but all you could do was go on in your usual style about holidays and treats and not being able to manage. So negative as usual! You don't agree with me, so that's the end of that.

MAN: It's –

WOMAN: You don't have to say any more. I get the message. Well, all right – I *won't* stop work! But just you bear in mind that it was you who bullied me into carrying on.

MAN: When –

WOMAN: It's useless trying to back-track now. It's too late! You've got your own way, now you can live with it. Keep on slaving away! Those are your orders to the resident servant. Well, okay, I will. But I loathe you sometimes, and one day I'll find the words to tell you how much – if I ever get a word in edgeways, which is unlikely.

MAN: But –

WOMAN: I'm sorry, I don't want to hear any more. You may not have finished, but I have! I'm going out. Goodnight! (*Exit*)

MAN: If only I'd kept my mouth shut . . .

Navigation

Having undertaken to do a seminar on "Sex" at Greenbelt
'91, I began to lose my nerve. What on earth was I going to
say on this thorny subject? Parenting had been bad enough
at Take Seven a few years previously, but Sex?

"I'll have to call in sick," I said to my wife, "I don't
know what to say. I can't come out with all that old 'God
created sex – it's a beautiful thing – but only within the
context of marriage' stuff. It may be true but it's hardly
original, is it? What am I going to do?"

"Calm down," said Bridget, "I'll think of something."

And she did.

"What is it", she asked a little later, "that we've had
more rows about than anything else while we've been
married?"

I went through a list of five or six things that it might
have been, but they were all wrong.

"Come on!" said Bridget, "think hard. What is it that's
brought us nearer to physical conflict than anything else?"

And then it clicked. Of course! How could I have been so
slow? There was absolutely no doubt about the cause of
our most virulent arguments.

MAP READING.

And not just us. I have got into a car before now with the
most saintly couple you could hope to meet. Never heard
so much as a raised voice from either of them. Then it
begins.

"*Why* didn't you tell me there was a turning coming
up?"

"Well, last time I told you there was a turning you got
cross with me and said you didn't need to hear about every
little wrinkle on the map!"

"For your information, that 'little wrinkle' we just

missed was our last opportunity to leave this road for the next thirty miles. Thank you very much, I *don't* think!"

"How you can be so unreasonable, I just don't know!" (SHE CRIES)

And so on, and so on . . .

"The thing is," said Bridget, "that vicars and curates and elders and ministers and people like that ought to counsel engaged couples on map reading. The sex would follow on naturally from that."

"Err . . . the seminar, Bridget?"

"Yes, well what you need to do is write a sketch that combines sex and map reading. We'll start the seminar with that."

So I did – and here it is.

Navigation

VICAR: Well, now, Sally and Slim, this is the last of our marriage preparation sessions. We've already covered an awful lot of ground –

SALLY: Metaphorically.

VICAR: Yes, metaphorically, we've already covered an awful lot of ground. Last week Slim shared with us that he couldn't actually recall asking you to marry him, Sally, and that he was profoundly horrified by the prospect of spending the rest of his life with you, to the extent that (and I think he put it rather picturesquely) he would rather be stung slowly to death by killer bees than face you over the breakfast table every morning for the next fifty years. And I think we sorted that one out okay last Thursday. One of those little worries that needs to be aired, and err . . . well done, you, for airing it.

Now, your turn this week, Sally, to throw up –

SALLY: Not literally?

VICAR: Not literally, no . . . err, your turn to throw up any little last-minute worries or problems. (*Pause*)

SALLY: Well, there was one thing, and – well it ruined my parents' marriage, so I wondered if we could talk about it.

VICAR: Of course we can, Sally. What is it? (*Pause*) Is it err . . . alcoholism?

SALLY: No.

VICAR: Err . . . finance?

SALLY: No.

VICAR: Exegetical incongruity?

SALLY: No, we sorted that out with a pair of curling tongs.

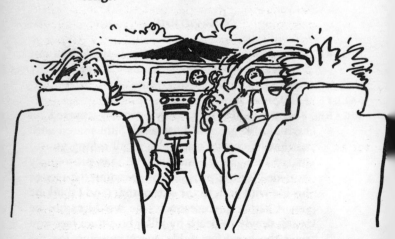

'If you took it more slowly Stim, the trip would be more enjoyable for both of us'

VICAR: Ah! So you're talking about —

SALLY: Yes, navigation.

VICAR: Yes, indeed, and I can tell you, Sally and Slim, that many marriages founder on the rock of navigational ignorance and conflict. Something that should be a natural and joyful experience can so easily end in trouble and tears.

SALLY: (*Tentatively*) We were wondering about (*Pause*) positions . . .

VICAR: Yes, well, traditionally the man — that would be you in this case, Slim —

SALLY: (*Taking out pencil and notebook*) Can I just make a note of that . . .?

VICAR: Traditionally, the man would sit in the driving seat, while the woman would sit in the passenger seat with the . . . map . . . on her knees. Nowadays, many couples prefer to do it the other way round, and there's absolutely nothing wrong with that. As long as both partners are comfortable and happy with what's happening, that's all that really matters.

SALLY: We're going to Leeds for our honeymoon in the car. Do you think we ought to navigate our way up there beforehand, just to see if we can manage it all right?

VICAR: I'm going to say the same thing to you as I say to all young engaged couples. It's perfectly proper to make short trips and excursions in the general direction of Leeds, but I must counsel you against going all the way at this stage. I think Milton Keynes is quite far enough. And once you get as far as Nottingham it's very hard to stop.

Times have changed, of course, since I was a young man. When I was driving out with a young lady it would never have occurred to me to leave Littlehampton, let alone attempt to navigate all

the way to Leeds. Not that I wasn't interested, I hasten to add. I well remember getting a terrible roasting from my father when he found a street map of Huddersfield hidden under my mattress.

Now, any other little questions or problems? Once you're married you'll gradually get to know each other's needs and it won't be long before you're reaching your mutual destination very harmoniously on every single occasion.

SALLY: We wanted to ask if it's possible when we actually start navigating to Leeds – I mean – if we get stuck at a junction, and Slim says it's my fault for reading the map wrong, and I say it's Slim's fault because he wasn't sensitive to the road signs, and Slim says he wishes he'd never married me in the first place, and I hit Slim with the emergency flashlamp that we've asked Uncle Vernon and Auntie Grace to buy us for a wedding present, and we crash because Slim temporarily loses consciousness, and we're on the verge of giving up navigation altogether . . .

VICAR: Yes?

SALLY: Well, can you help us then?

VICAR: No, but I know a man who can, and he drives a patrol car in the sky.

SALLY: Literally?

VICAR: Err . . . no, metaphorically.

SALLY: Thank you, Vicar. You're a very nice man. You're a very, *very* nice man . . .

Dear Family

One of the pointless questions I ask myself from time to time is whether I would opt for mental or physical pain if I had to choose. It's difficult, isn't it – until you start to live through one or the other, that is. Then you know for sure that you would choose the kind of suffering that you are not being afflicted with.

My own experience has been that, for years, I was quite sure nothing could be worse than extreme physical pain. After all, you can always find a way to distract yourself from mental anguish. That's what I believed, and for most of my early life it was true.

Then I had a family. They have brought me much joy, but also the discovery of a new kind of pain; something to do with observing the gradual death of innocence; even

more, I think, to do with my own shortcomings as a father
and a husband. Being a morbid beggar by nature I've
always made a bit of a meal of these things, but I have
known excruciating pain at times, and I've lost the knack
of distracting myself.

I'm sure that if I suddenly developed a chronically
painful illness, I would long for those good old days of
mental torment, but I still can't quite answer that original
silly question of mind.

I do feel sorry for Jesus at Gethsemane.

Family

Dear family, I write to you in this campfire place
Where temporary flames repel the savage things
Whose glowing, hungry eyes appear from time to time.
They know, as I do, that a campfire only burns as long as
    fuel lasts.
My stocks are low as ever, and these devils never rest.
But I have light and time enough to write to you
Dear family, asleep, for once, beside me here in peace,
To say how I regret the need to share such fearful travelling
    with you.
I know that monster-ridden darkness is my own affair
I have no right to take you there.
The battle I shall face tonight will threaten you
But certainly it never was your fight.
God knows I wish that it was otherwise
That we could strike our camp and head for home.
I have some choice
But when those creatures leap I find I am clean out of
    choice
And they draw blood so easily.
Dear family, as you awake,

And eye my campfire ashes nervously
I want to say how I am wretchedly aware
That others would protect and lead you properly.
They would be strong and confident and sure
They would be many things that I will never be
I only know they could not love you more.

REDUNDANT RITUALS AND FLIMSY FASHIONS

Fools may invent fashions that wise men will wear.

THOMAS FULLER, *Gnomologia* 1732

Rituals, liturgies, credos, Sinai thunder: I know more
or less the history of these; the rise, progress, decline
and fall of these. Can thunder from all the thirty-two
azimuths, repeated daily for centuries of years, make
God's laws more godlike to me? Brother, no.

THOMAS CARLYLE, *Past and Present*, III 1843

Redundant Rituals and Flimsy Fashions

Some months ago I spent a morning at a small independent evangelical church in Kent. I was speaking about the need for each individual to experience the kind of explosively joyful encounter that we read about in the parable of the prodigal son; that moment when the father throws his arms round his returning offspring and showers him with love, forgiveness and a host of practical gifts. Trying to follow Jesus without that experience, I was trying to say, is difficult, if not impossible, because love is the greatest motivator of all.

After I had finished, everyone broke off into small groups (where would the Church be without small groups?), to discuss three or four questions relating to the talk. As they "discussed" I ambled around nervously, hoping that people were suitably stimulated and not sneaking covert glances at their watches every five minutes. Fortunately, all the groups seemed quite animated and had to be metaphorically prised apart so that we could enjoy our picnic lunch at one o'clock.

After lunch there was a brief feedback session (where would the Church be without brief feedback sessions?), and a short period of worship and prayer to round off the day.

"Good," I said to myself, as the last "amen" sounded, "I can relax now. The talk went all right, the discussions went well, the people were nice – time to go home."

It was as I lingered in conversation with a small group of elderly people at the back that I realized how miserably I had failed to convey my main point, at least as far as one person was concerned.

Her name was Beth, and she was one of those white-haired, attractive eighty-year-olds whose eyes are deeply crinkled from years of smiling. As I sat with Beth and two of her contemporaries someone mentioned outreach.

"I've always admired the old Sally Army," said the venerable gentleman on Beth's right, "the way they go into pubs and that with their papers. Maybe we should get to know people in the locals – then we could talk to 'em, couldn't we?"

"Not me," said Beth, the crinkles disappearing as she sat up a little straighter in her chair, "I would *never* do that!"

I looked at her for a moment.

"Suppose", I said, "that Jesus were to come through that back door now – today – and say 'Beth, I want you to come down to the King's Head with me.' Would you go?"

"I would not", replied Beth, compressing her lips and folding her hands together decisively in her lap.

"But, Beth," I persisted, "we're talking about Jesus, the son of God, asking you personally if you would go with him. Would you not go?"

"I have never set foot in a public house in my life," said the old lady adamantly, "and I'm not about to start now."

"But if Jesus himself asked – "

"It's a good witness," interrupted Beth, "alcohol has never passed my lips and it never will."

"Okay," I said, warming to my theme, "he doesn't want you to actually drink anything intoxicating, he just wants you with him in the King's Head, and – "

Beth shook her head firmly: "No!"

"Jesus, God himself, the creator of everything, the reason why we're all here today – he comes in and he says, 'Beth, I really need you to come to the pub with me today, so *please*, please make an exception, just for me.' Would you go with him?"

A tiny crack of uncertainty was undermining Beth's wall of principle. Her brows creased and her fingers twisted together as she mentally surveyed this rather unlikely scenario.

"I suppose", she said at last, "if he *really* did have a *really, really* good reason for asking, I *might* go."

Afterwards, as I travelled home, I thought about Beth and the way in which her principles seemed to be a more powerful motivating force than the relationship she had with Jesus. I realized that my own sticking points were often more personal than spiritual. Was I so aware of the love of God that I would follow him wherever he went? Or would I, like the rich young man in the Bible, go away sorrowing because there was some principle or issue or sin or religious habit concerning which I simply would not budge?

The alarming truth is that these "blocks" may well turn out to be respectable, laudable, even spiritual convictions or practices that have been elevated to the position of false gods.

Man-made fashions, fads and patterns can cause a lot of trouble as they work their way through the life of the Church. Here are quite a few examples in this last consignment of "cabbages".

Cabbages

I don't suppose God really minds what kind of spiritual activity we indulge in as long as we are expressing ourselves from the heart. The problem is that even the most impressively devout-sounding prayer, praise or worship might easily be nothing much more than a religious pattern.

Take prayer, for instance.

Two or three times a year I speak at dinners organized by a very energetic and effective body whose members are committed to outreach all over the world. I always enjoy these occasions, but I have noticed that a certain style of prayer seems to be mandatory for organizers and speaker before the evening gets going.

We stand in a tight circle with our arms round each other, like a small, introspective rugby scrum, bouncing on our heels (why?), shouting aggressive prayers towards the bottom of the well that is formed by our bodies. Eventually, someone will say something that sounds very much like: "One hundred and eighty!!"

Then we get on with the meal.

There's nothing wrong with this kind of prayer — who am I to criticize, anyway? It's just that habit can breed hollowness.

I couldn't help wondering what would happen if one of these violent-prayer merchants took over a greengrocer's shop, and, at the same time, happened to have no outlet for his religious fervour.

It might be a bit like this.

Cabbages

Scene: A Greengrocer's, Shopkeeper, Customer and a pile of cabbages.

SHOPKEEPER: Good morning, madam. How may I help you?

CUSTOMER: I'd like a nice cabbage, please.

SHOPKEEPER: A nice cabbage?

CUSTOMER: Yes, please (*indicating*). That one will do nicely, thank you.

SHOPKEEPER: Just one moment, sister. That one will *not* do nicely.

CUSTOMER: It won't? Well, how about — ?

SHOPKEEPER: I think we should seek the will of God here. Do you witness to that, sister?

CUSTOMER: Well, I just want a cabbage really. I'm not sure —

SHOPKEEPER: Let's take it to the Lord. Let's just take it to him. (*Starts to pray*). Lord, we know that you chose a cabbage for our sister here before the world began, and we pray for your guidance now. We know that the world sees the outside of these cabbages, but, Lord, you see the inside. You see the heart. We pray that our sister's cabbage will have a heart for you, Lord.

We *claim* this cabbage! We *seal* this cabbage! Take dominion over your greens, Lord!

Lord, we ask that, like these fruits of thy bounty, we shall happily be sliced, boiled, drained and consumed for you, Lord. Bless your chosen cabbage to our sister, Lord, and our Sister to her rightful cabbage. Whether it be a companion to the sausage, Lord. Or, Lord, a neighbour to the fish-finger. Or peradventure Lord, an accessory to the veal cutlet: they and we are but cole-slaw in your hands, and we just ask now that we shall make a decision according to your will.

Lord, we know that in your eyes there is no such thing as a Methodist cabbage, or a Pentecostal sprout, or a Strict and Particular turnip, or a Quaker carrot, or a United Reformed aubergine, or a Salvation Army swede, or a Baptist leek; or a Anglican potato. Lord, we're all just vegetables in your sight. And now we pray for your guidance on our sister's behalf.

And we say to the caterpillars of doubt and the slugs of uncertainty – we say "Go! Right now! We rebuke you and we dismiss you and we cast you out from among these cabbages – right now!"

And now, Lord, we ask that your servant's appointed cabbage will just *rise up*! (*One cabbage springs into the air and is caught by the shopkeeper who drops it*

casually into a bag and hands it to the customer) That'll be seventy-five pence, please.

CUSTOMER: Thank you! 'Morning! (*Exit*)

END

Doors

The language of the Bible and the Church (and the world, for that matter) is full of richness. Why, then, do so many choose to live in poverty? Are we frightened of language? Do we fear a serious distribution problem when, after taking all we need, we are left with twelve gloriously, extravagantly superfluous baskets of delicious, assorted words?

Take metaphor, for instance. We've only got about two. Here's one of them that may well have passed its sell-by date.

Doors

INTERVIEWER: Now, Mr Williams, you and your wife have a recent experience of seeking guidance. Tell us about it, will you?

WILLIAMS: Well, what happened was – we tried one door that we thought the Lord was opening for us, but when, as it were, we pushed it, we found that it was shut. So we tried another door and this time it did open, so we passed through, and on the other side there was another door, but this one was shut like the first door. And when we turned round and tried to go back through the previous door – that is, the second door – we discovered that it had shut behind us, so we were in fact trapped between the two doors, so we had to climb out, as it were, through the

skylight, and we came down through another skylight and found ourselves in front of, err . . . a fourth door. This door was slightly ajar so I pushed it, but it was on a very strong spring, and it swung back and hit me quite hard on the face. So I did rebuke the door – and all the other doors, actually – at that stage, and we did wonder whether doorways might create openings through which something demonic can come. So we decided

                              then to seek the Lord's will by laying a
                              fleece, but . . . well, the Lord shut that
                              door.
INTERVIEWER: Mr Williams, what exactly were you and
                              your wife seeking guidance over?
WILLIAMS: Whether to have an open-plan house or
                              not . . .

Allegory

I am a great admirer of C. S. Lewis's Narnia books. Quite
apart from pure entertainment value, they open up all sorts
of ideas and perspectives that are interesting to juggle with.
Most children love them, whatever some sniffy people
may say, and you don't need to know anything about
Christianity to enjoy them.

What about modern so-called "Christian Books" for
children? There are some good ones, of course, but I find
the punch-in-the-mouth metaphors employed in some
publications quite repellent, and I don't know what the
point of such shallow writing could possibly be.

I could ramble on in this vein for page after page, but
I've already written on the subject in one or two other
books, and you're probably asking yourself how I can
criticize other people for being shallow when I don't mind
being boring.

All right! I give in – here is my own "Allegory".

Allegory

"Where on earth is Flossy-Anne?"

Pimply's voice floated into the drawing-room from the patio outside the open French windows. Sticky and Fangio looked up from the sea of home-made bread, fresh eggs, boiled ham, farmhouse butter, thick strawberry jam, rich plum cake and creamy cow's milk that Auntie Enid made them plough through every time they came home for the hols.

Sticky was a sturdy twelve-year-old with an open, frank expression under fair sticking-up hair. Auntie Enid had called him Sticky since he was a little boy, not just because of his hair, but also because of a certain moistness in his handshake.

"I haven't seen Flossy-Anne for ages", muttered Fangio. "Sisters are nothing but a nuisance, aren't they, Sticky?"

The two friends grinned at each other. Sticky loathed eleven-year-old Pimply just as much as Fangio detested ten-year-old Flossy-Anne. Fangio was a dark, moody boy capable of manly impulses, but only very infrequently.

"I think she's still up in Auntie Enid's wardrobe", called Sticky through a mouthful of half-masticated farmhouse butter.

"Oh, no, she's not looking for secret worlds again, is she?" Pimply's voice conveyed a mixture of exasperation and fondness as she ducked into the room. Well over six feet tall, Pimply had been given her nickname by Auntie Enid to take attention away from her height, but as her complexion deteriorated so she had seemed to "grow into her name", as Auntie Enid put it.

"Well, what if I was? We haven't had a decent allegory for ages."

The high, lisping voice coming from the doorway that

led into the hall announced that the fourth member of the party was present. Fangio's younger sister, Flossy-Anne, was a fluffy-haired little girl with bulging eyes and a permanent expression of surprise on her face. One of her arms was slightly longer than the other.

"So there you all are!" The voice was muffled.

All eyes swivelled upwards towards the skylight, as Auntie Enid's face appeared behind the glass. Swinging the window open she dropped a rope-end into the room and was soon lowering her bikini-clad figure to the floor.

"I want a word with you lot!" she said. "I've been trying to relax on the roof, and all I can hear is crashing noises. What's going on?"

Flossy-Anne turned bright purple and tried unsuccessfully to hide a small axe behind her back. The other children grinned at each other. Flossy-Anne always seemed to select the wrong arm!

"I'm afraid that was me," she said. "I was knocking out the back of your wardrobe, looking for Narnia. It wasn't there", she added, looking so half-witted that even Auntie Enid had to laugh.

"You children and your allegories", she smiled. "Can't we have just one school holiday when you do something a bit less symbolic?"

Auntie Enid looked at her four charges with a mixture of fondness and exasperation. They all grinned at each other. Sticky, Pimply, Fangio and Flossy-Anne had been spending their school hols with Auntie Enid for the last twenty-four years. None of them ever grew any older, and they had never yet been known to use a lavatory.

"Look at what happened yesterday," said Auntie Enid, "Sticky tried to get into the picture on his bedroom wall, didn't you, Sticky?"

Sticky grinned.

"And the day before that I had to call the fire brigade to rescue Fangio from the bottom of that old hollow oak tree at the bottom of the garden."

Fangio looked at her with a mixture of fondness and exasperation.

"It's all very well for you, Auntie Enid," he said, "you're an adult Christian. Life is one long spiritual adventure for you. We kids have difficulty understanding that. We need to experience reality through synchronistic fantasy. Besides, after twenty-four years we're allegory junkies. We need our fix, and that's why we're all hunting for this summer's secret entrance. I'm going to have a look down the lavatory bowl tomorrow – after all, it's quite hygenic because we never use it."

Auntie Enid sighed. "Well, I don't know what to say. I've grinned, and I've looked at you with a mixture of fondness and exasperation. What more can I do?"

"Well, I think Auntie Enid's right", said Pimply earnestly. "Why can't we stay here and go to church and have real adventures with God like the grown-ups do?"

Although Fangio detested his sister he was very fond of her as well. He hated to see her make a fool of herself.

"Pimply", he said kindly, "it's got to be allegory because allegory sells where spiritual adventure won't. Think secular, think W. H. Smith, think Waterstone's, think Dillons. If nobody reads us we don't exist, right?"

"I'll check the cellar for secret doors tomorrow", said Pimply.

They all grinned at each other.

Playing Games

Our writer now seems to have been resurrected. He's back on earth and getting a bit worried about his royalties – if there are any.

In every area of specifically Christian work the tension

between commercial and spiritual considerations can produce all sorts of games that have to be played out appropriately before a resolution can be reached.

I do hope old Rodney gets what he really needs.

Playing Games

W = WRITER
P = PUBLISHER

W: Hello, Crystal, it's Rodney here – Rodney Fuller.

P: Rodney! Great! How *are* you? Great to hear your voice!

W: I'm fine, Crystal. I was just ringing to ask how the book's going.

P: The book! Well –

W: Yes, my children's allegory – *Slubglab's Splod*.

P: Ah, right! Well, Rodney, we feel tremendously encouraged!

W: You do? By the sales, you mean?

P: We regard your book as a very significant addition to our back-list.

W: Oh! But in terms of sales – I wondered – I mean – things are a bit tight. I wondered if there are going to be royalties coming up when –

P: Rodney, we're all of us – publishers and writers – part of the Lord's team in this, aren't we? That's my priority, anyway.

W: Mmm . . . it's just that you don't seem to have put much into publicity, really.

P: You have to bear in mind that publishing is a commercial operation, Rodney. We can't afford to be airy-fairy, can we? Publicity is expensive.

W: Well, how many copies have actually been sold?

P: We're tremendously encouraged!

W: Yes, you said that before, but you still haven't told me the actual figures.

P: Okay, let me put it like this – the moment we hit the five thousand mark we'll be reprinting immediately – or sooner!

W: I've sold nearly five thousand then?

P: Well, no, but if we ever did hit the five thousand mark we'd –

W: Crystal, how many books have I sold?

P: What do we get from tiny acorns, Rodney?

W: Mighty oaks! How many books have I sold?

P: How many people did Our Lord use as a basis for the world-wide Church?

W: Twelve! How many books – wait a minute! Are you saying that I've sold *twelve* copies! Twelve! You told me that this book was going to change the face of children's literature in the twentieth century! How's it going to do that if only twelve people have bought it?

P: Of course I didn't mean that, Rodney. We have had a little problem – err . . . just after your book came out we found there was already a children's book on the market called *Slodglub's Slab*, which is not unlike *Slubglab's Splod*, so that did create a titchy-witchy problem. But, no, your sales are well up in the high, err . . . well, err . . . well, well, we're tremendously encouraged.

W: I'm fed up with this, Crystal! I might as well tell you – I've got myself an agent.

P: You've what? An agent? Rodney, this is terrible! This is – wait a minute. Is he a Christian?

W: Yes, he is.

P: Ah, that's all right then . . .

END

Trapeze

When I first started writing I was advised to "study the market". This is very good advice, especially for anyone who wants to write for a particular type of magazine or journal. I bought all the Christian magazines and newspapers and looked through them to see what sort of thing I should be producing.

As far as I could see, the most popular type of article was one in which someone who had just written a book lectured his or her readers, gently but firmly, on the subject of their failure to perform satisfactorily in some crucial area of their lives. The article would be accompanied by a box containing five, eight or even ten handy points to remind readers how it should be done. I tried to write such an article myself, but I didn't feel very comfortable about it.

It was only Andy Butcher's inventiveness and Mary Reid's courage that enabled something as unusual as the *Sacred Diary!* to appear, as it originally did, in column form in *Family Magazine*.

My advice to a new writer nowadays would be very similar to that which I received, except that I would add something. Once you have studied the market and thoroughly understood it – do something different. Do something that reflects what, where and who you are. Find out who created whatever boundaries you come across and, if it wasn't God, look at them very carefully indeed.

I very much enjoyed writing the piece that follows, but I do hope the style and content that I am caricaturing will go the way of the dinosaurs before too long. If you want an example of Chrisitan literature with a real edge – try the Bible.

Trapeze

Trembling with fear, the elderly lady gripped the trapeze bar so tightly that her knuckles whitened under the pressure. Glancing down at the sawdust floor a hundred feet below the tiny platform on which she balanced, she silently asked herself yet again, why, at the age of eighty-three, she was about to leap into space, supported only by the slender length of wood that her arthritic hands were clutching with such nervous intensity. Moistening dry lips with the tip of her tongue she tried hard to remember the advice that Dave and Sheena had given her.

"Don't look down – concentrate on what's happening up here. Remember that God created gravity as well as everything else . . ."

Suddenly it was time to go. Gently but firmly, Dave's hands pressed into the small of her back until she toppled over the edge of the platform and found herself swinging out and across the open space beneath the canvas ceiling of the huge tent. There was a moment's exhilaration followed by a stab of fear as she felt the bar sliding slowly but inexorably from her grasp. Dimly she was aware of Sheena's encouraging smile as the opposite trapeze swung past, and then she was falling down and down until, with a bone-shuddering jar her body hit the safety-net, bounced two or three times, then came to rest like a pound of sausages in a string-bag. A few bruises, a minor fracture here and there perhaps, but, as the octogenarian acrobat was lifted carefully from the net, there was a smile on her face. A faint cry of "Hallelujah!" from the platform high above indicated Dave's awareness that he and Sheena had yet another satisfied "customer"!

It is ten years since Dave Bolden, now a slim and well-preserved man in his early forties, first realized that God was telling him, in no uncertain terms, that acrobatics on the high trapeze are for the whole Church, not just for a specially selected few.

"I fought against it for a while," says Dave, his handsome face breaking into a grin as he remembers, "but after a couple of falls from a hundred feet without a safety net I began to think very seriously about the direction I was going in. The Lord has such a sense of humour!" he chuckles.

What about scriptural support for these revelations?

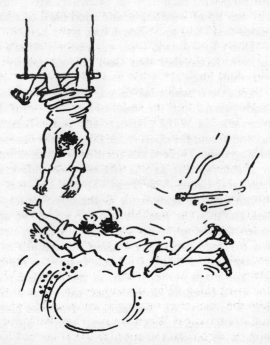

WHAT WAS THAT ABOUT GENTILES, PETE?

"Let's face it," avers Dave wryly, "you can prove or disprove just about anything you like if you don't mind twisting Bible verses to make them fit the truth as you want to see it. I have to say, though, that my own reading of Acts in particular suggests that, possibly Peter, and certainly Paul the apostle, were very fine performers on the flying trapeze in their own right. In fact, it seems clear to me that aerial acrobatics was a normal and acceptable part of day-to-day life in the early Church. It's fallen into disuse in this age and we just want to do something about it."

Did Dave encounter any special problems in setting up his ministry?

An awe-struck expression appears on Dave's well-chiselled features. "It was a real miracle, especially when it came to getting a big-top." He shakes his head in disbelief. "I was literally led step by step. I bought a magazine called *Big Tops for Sale* – quite by chance, you understand – and I was flicking idly through it one day, when an advert seemed to leap off the page, and hit me between the eyes. It said 'Big Top for sale' and there was a telephone number."

Dave's attractive and expertly made-up wife, Sheena, takes up the story, her green eyes shining with excitement.

"I dialled the number and when I spoke to the man at the other end I could hardly believe my ears. He had a big top for sale! The amount of money he wanted was almost exactly the amount of money that we had to spend."

Dave picks up the thread.

"We weren't quite sure what to do then, so we rang around our Christian friends for advice." Tears well up in Dave's eyes as he continues. "It was amazing! They *all* said the same thing. Why not suggest to the man that we give him the amount of money he wants and he gives us his big top in exchange? When we rang him back and put this to him he agreed on the spot, and that seemed like a sort of final confirmation. We were so excited that Sheena leaped up on to my shoulders and did a double backward somersault with pike and triple twist into my paternal grandfather who was staying at the time."

Sheena giggles, showing two rows of perfectly formed teeth.

"I did get a little excited," she confesses with a mischievous twinkle, "but grandpops understood – once he regained consciousness."

They laugh and look into each other's eyes. This couple are still very much in love.

Over the course of the last decade many folk have "swung for God" as Dave pursues his deeply held conviction that the Lord would have all his people involved in high trapeze work. Have some sections of the Church been less ready to respond than others?

Dave nods seriously. "The elderly infirm have been very sluggish in their response, so too have partially-sighted and blind folk. They are particularly reluctant to step off the platform once we get them up there." His normally cheerful face clouds over suddenly. "I guess it's a matter of trust. The world says it makes no sense to step into space a hundred feet above the ground when you're blind and have no experience of trapeze work, but we are not of the world and ought to be different really."

Are there dangers?

The old smile returns to Dave's face. He catches Sheena's eye and they both laugh. They've been asked this question many times in the past.

"Let me put it like this", he explains, "it's far less dangerous than strolling across the M25 with a blindfold on when the traffic is moving at maximum speed. Why do anything as risky as that when you could be here doing something really worthwhile?"

The question seems unanswerable and, in any case, there is no time for a reply. In the distance two men can be seen stretchering in the next candidate for high-flying obedience. With a flashing smile from Sheena, and a friendly wave from Dave, the trim couple are gone. Christians are often told that it's a good thing to keep their "feet on the ground". People who know Dave and Sheena Bolden are not quite so sure!

Dave Bolden's Five Helpful Hints

1) **DO** contact your nearest circus and ask how accessible they are prepared to be to church members. Christians have a God-given right to the use of trapeze equipment.

2) **DON'T** be afraid to insure your life before "taking the plunge". Christians are not called upon to abandon commonsense just because they're doing what God has told them to do!

3) **DO** speak to your vicar, elder, or church leader about wanting to perform acrobatics a hundred feet above the ground. He will certainly have some helpful things to say.

4) **DON'T** be put off by "horror stories" spread by others. People who talk about death and serious injury are very rarely the ones who have actually suffered such things.

5) **DO** remember that non-believing circus employees will be watching as you ascend to that little platform. If you're up there with a long face, and "I FEEL TENSE" written all over you, what are they going to make of the Christian faith? Enjoy yourself – and let it show!

Starting a Meeting

I have included the following piece at the last moment because it was inspired by a sermon that I heard just the other day. If you can imagine Basil Fawlty, converted but not changed, making his convoluted way through the business of starting a meeting in a very "unadorned" church, then you will easily picture the chap who is delivering this "message".

I would have included the rest of his talk, but a book can only be so long, and I fear your head would spin off and go into orbit. It might anyway.

Starting a Meeting

Can I start by suggesting that if I come back *now* to something I shall have said earlier, it will save a great deal of time in a minute? Is that clear?

I'm going to begin by telling a humorous story. The purpose of this is to relax you, the congregation, so that you will be more receptive to the serious points that I shall subsequently make. So, if you are taking notes I would suggest that you refrain from recording any of the first section because it will *be* the humorous story. Do, however, feel free to record the humorous story if you would like to pass it on to somebody else after the service, though naturally there will be no point in passing on the humorous story to anyone who is present now because, of course, they will have already heard it, unless, that is, they have to leave in the middle of the humorous story, before its climactic peak has been reached.

After the humorous story is concluded, and the laughter

thus engendered has died away, I shall speak under three headings, each beginning with a "P". Plague, Punishment and Pestilence – three areas which, I believe, beautifully illustrate the love of God.

But first, as promised, the relaxing humorous story. Those of you who are feeling tense this morning will, in a minute or so, be relaxed enough to hear scriptural judgement pronounced upon those of us for whom it is intended.

This humorous story is one which, in its original form, is quite unsuitable for the elect. I have therefore adapted the content so that it is no less humorous, but considerably more edifying.

It concerns a male person who questions another male person in the following fashion.

"Who was that lady I saw you with last night?"

The other male person replies in tones of righteous, but quite justifiable, indignation, with these words.

"The lady in question happens to be my marital partner, and has been so for some three decades."

I shall wait a few moments now while the laughter provoked by the humorous story runs its course. Settle down please.

Well, that is the end of the fun section and now I feel sure that most of us are more than ready for our first "P" of the morning.

Plague! And how we do need it in the Church today . . .

Images of God

The worship of false images is not a sin that tends to be discussed very much in the twentieth-century Church. When it *is* mentioned it's usually equated with excessive attachment to possessions, such as cars or houses. After all, you don't see too many golden calves or images of Baal in your average British sitting-room.

There is, however, another, and more subtly destructive way in which this commandment continues to be disobeyed – by Christians.

We all do it to a lesser or greater extent. Because of individual upbringing, life experiences and inherited patterns of response, we tend to invest our personal images of God with attributes that have more to do with us than with God as he actually is.

Often, and perhaps more commonly, people have difficulty in separating the concept of God as father, from memories of their own unsatisfactory parent. Earthly fathers can be cruel or over-indulgent or emotionally chaotic. The child in us clings unconsciously to these negative recollections, unable to allow the idea of God as a perfect father to sink successfully from head to heart.

Within any one congregation a strange and varied selection of God-images will be prayed to and worshipped each Sunday.

I have recorded elsewhere how a friend of mine on hearing Bishop Peter Ball talk about his faith, said, "He knows a different God to the one I do – his God's nice!"

There are many distorted views of the divine personality. Here are three of the most common ones.

Images of God

1) God as bank manager.

> Ah, Mr Brown, do please sit down,
> Now what are we to do?
> For, once, you banked with us, but now,
> We seem to bank with you.

Your sin account is overdrawn,
With lust and sloth and pride,
And, dear, dear, dear, there's little here,
Upon the credit side.
Against the veritable sea,
Of evil you have done,
There's one small act of kindness,
Back in nineteen-sixty-one.
In fact your banking record,
From the moment you were born,
Is such that we may well decide,
Your Access is withdrawn.

2) God as a senile old man

Hello! Yes, this is God – speak up!
Hello! What's that you say?
Well, if you say you did, you did,
I didn't hear you pray.
You say you asked me several times?
Well, nowadays I find,
That even quite important things
Just seem to slip my mind.
Oh, yes, that is a problem,
But there's little I can do,
My angels are quite elderly,
They've all got fowlpest too.
I wouldn't bother being good,
You'll only end up bored,
It's not exactly heaven,
In a geriatric ward.

3) God as a hippy

Nothing's wrong and nothing's right,
And nothing's in between,

All this "Heh, you broke the rules",
Has never been my scene.
People go for different things.
Like Mecca and Nirvana,
Some find me in worry beads,
Or hash, or a banana.
Don't let people steer you wrong,
It's cool to sin and doubt,
Whatever gives you groovy vibes,
Just let it all hang out.
Heaven's what you make it, man,
Freedom gives you power,
Love and peace and jelly-beans,
No hassle – have a flower.

Connections to Paradise

People often ask me where writers get their ideas from. The answer, of course, is – British Rail. No, I'm only joking, although, when you travel by train as much as I do, you do hear some wonderful things. Take the other day, for instance. I was sitting on a train, in a fairly crowded compartment, when the guard's voice came over the loudspeaker system. It began in that flatly repetitive tone beloved of guards everywhere, but it quite quickly turned into a strangled bleat.

"Like to advise customers that the next station stop will be Darnley Halt. (*Pause*) Darnley Halt has a very short platform. (*Longer pause*) Customers wishing to alight at Darnley Halt should move to the front of the train. The front of the train (*Worried pause*) is situated (*Very worried pause*) at the end (*Pause indicative of realization that there is no way out of sentence with honour*) farthest (*Pause of utter panic*) from (*Pause as guard plays wildly with alternative endings to his sentence, such as: " . . . The Platonic Ideal", or "Patagonia") the back . . ." (Miserable silence as guard covers head with arms and vows to stay locked in little guard compartment for rest of journey)*

No, it isn't always British Rail, but it's certainly true that most of my ideas spring from relatively ordinary day-to-day incidents.

"Yes," says the questioner when I explain this, "but nothing ever happens to me – nothing worth recording in detail, anyway."

I don't think this is true. Lots of different things happen to all of us; the difference, perhaps, is that the writer makes a conscious mental (or written) note of his or her experiences and, even more importantly, goes on to forge or discover the kind of connections that add depth and significance to quite ordinary observations.

Let me give you an example.

Connections to Paradise

One morning I was travelling by train from Polegate, in Sussex, down to Southampton for a day of promotion in connection with my latest book. I knew I had to change at Brighton, but I wasn't quite sure whether the journey was straight through after that. I went into the travel-centre on Brighton station to check.

Travel-centres are strange places. They seem to be staffed by people who go off sick in packs of four. They always leave behind a nice but nervy person who will burst into tears if too much pressure is put on them. In addition, the queue in front of you invariably consists of a ninety-year-old Ukranian who speaks no English, weeps passionately but inexplicably at regular intervals, and needs to get to Clitheroe via Taunton on a sleeper in six weeks' time, and a very, very lonely person who always comes down there on that day, at that time, to while away an hour or so with the nice, nervy person who doesn't mind because it never involves any nasty, awkward questions about train times.

Thank goodness Brighton travel-centre is nothing like that. I had no trouble at all.

"Change at Hove, sir," trilled the young girl behind the counter, "you'll pick up a Southampton train there."

"Thank you!" I called over my shoulder as I went back out to the station concourse.

On my way to the appropriate platform I glanced up at the electronic information board, just hoping for a little comfortable confirmation. No such luck!

"*Passengers for Southampton should change at Worthing*", announced the board in large white letters.

Somewhat dismayed, I stopped at the ticket barrier and spoke to the bored young man who was slumped on a stool inside his little shelter.

"Tell me," I said, "if you were me, where would you change for Southampton on this train?"

"Portsmouth", he replied with gloomy certainty.

"Portsmouth?" I repeated. "Are you sure?"

"Change at Portsmouth for Southampton", he said, in that wearily sarcastic manner that people reserve for those who haven't understood the first time.

Muttering thanks I hurried along the platform to board my train, and was just about to get on when I surrendered to a wild impulse to ask just once more for this surprisingly elusive piece of information. An elderly, white-haired, rather avuncular looking British Rail employee was pushing a trolley past me. This was a man to be trusted – a man who would know!

"Excuse me", I called.

The man stopped his trolley and beamed at me with fatherly kindness. "'Ow can I 'elp you, sir?" he said.

I explained that I had been offered three quite different pieces of advice and wasn't sure which one to follow. He chuckled tolerantly.

"Bless 'em, sir, they don't know nothin', these young things. If you take this train you wanna change at Havant for Southampton, sir. You'll pick one up there all right."

"Oh well," I said to myself as I settled down in the corner of a carriage at last, "at least I know now – change at Havant . . ."

A few minutes later the ticket inspector arrived. He was a youngish man with a heavy Indian accent.

"Change at Havant for Southampton, don't I?" I enquired lightly, certain that he would agree.

"You need to go upstairs, sir," he replied, "upstairs for Southampton."

I stared at him for a moment, my senses reeling. Upstairs? Upstairs for Southampton? Had I, without realizing it, boarded some kind of new double-decker train, the top half of which went to Southampton, while the bottom half didn't? How could that be . . .?

"Upstairs? " I repeated faintly, "I don't . . ."

"Upstairs at Portsmouth station," continued my informant, "upstairs to the upper platform for the train to Southampton, sir. That is what you must do."

And that piece of advice was, I'm pleased to say, absolutely correct.

That is what happened, and it is completely true.

Connections? Well, it occurred to me afterwards that my succession of advisers, all employed by the same company, and all offering diverse views on the same subject, were rather like the Christian denominations, each with its own clear idea about how people should get to the place where they are going, and each adamant that their way is the only one worth considering.

Where *do* we change for Paradise?

Precious

For years I tried to exercise ministries that I had not got. It didn't work.

I did *not* have a ministry of reconciliation. I had a ministry of making things worse, and ending up with everyone disliking me as well as each other.

I did *not* have a ministry of wisdom and special insight. I had a ministry of getting things wrong and upsetting people.

I did *not* have a ministry of prayer. I had a ministry of promising people I would pray for them, and then forgetting to do it, and getting very embarrassed when they thanked me and said that they knew my prayers had helped, and feeling guilty because I couldn't quite bring myself to tell them the truth.

I did *not* have a ministry of evangelism. I had a ministry of putting forward arguments so hopelessly ill-prepared and half-baked that I became progressively less convinced myself as I went on speaking, and ended up in a state of miserable agnosticism.

I did *not* have a ministry of prophetic absailing, although it broke my heart to have finally to face that realization.

Perhaps there are signs of a genuine ministry developing nowadays, but I'm certainly not going to put a name to what I think it might be.

Here's a ludicrously exaggerated version of what goes wrong when a "ministry of encouragement" is exercised so liberally that the encouragement becomes devalued to the point of being rather meaningless.

Precious

Leader, Stanley, George (a newcomer), Veronica and Penelope are sitting in a semi-circle. They all have open Bibles on their laps.

LEADER: Right, now, we've read the passage of scripture that tells us the story of Zacchaeus, and I'm going to ask that we might share our insights as we feel led so to do.
(*Pause*)

STANLEY: Well, I was thinking . . .

LEADER: Yes, Stanley, go ahead.

GEORGE: Yeah, go fer it, Stan!

STANLEY: Well, I was thinking that Zacchaeus was up a tree, and a tree's got leaves, right?

LEADER: Yes?

STANLEY: Yes, and God *leaves* us to deal with certain things on our own. He *leaves* us, doesn't he?

LEADER: Well, isn't that interesting? *Isn't* that interesting? Do you know – I never made that connection before. Leaves on the tree, and he

leaves us. *Isn't* that interesting? (*Pause*) Any
other insights to share?

VERONICA: I noticed that Zacchaeus begins with the last
letter of the alphabet, and, when you think of
it, the last thing God wants us to do is
disobey him. It's the *last* thing he wants us to
do, and Zacchaeus begins with the *last* letter
of the alphabet.

LEADER: Isn't that special? That's *very* special. The
last thing God wants is disobedience, and
Zacchaeus begins with . . . that's very special
– *very* special. Veronica has given us something very special, hasn't she, everybody?
(*All nod except George, who shakes his head
in puzzlement*)

PENELOPE: May I share?

LEADER: Please do, Penelope. Mmmm!

PENELOPE: I feel that this passage is really about serving.
Zacchaeus was asked to serve – not just serve
the food, but to serve the Lord. We should all
serve. He's called us to serve, and when we
do serve we in our turn will be served. Not
just serving because we're told to serve, but
serving with joy because we want to serve the
one who served us.

LEADER: Isn't that precious? What a precious thing to
share. We're called to serve – we're all called
to serve each other. What a new and precious
thought. Bless you, Penelope, for that very
precious gift to us. (*Pause*) George, you're
new here, but have you any err . . .

GEORGE: Well, I'm not sure I've got the 'ang of this,
but I was thinkin' that once old Zack was –

LEADER: Zacchaeus.

GEORGE: Once old Zacchaeus was – like – back on the
ground . . .

LEADER: Yes?

GEORGE: Well, everyone must've realized 'e was a scone short of a cream tea, mustn't they?

LEADER: A scone short of . . .? Do you mean that he was mentally deranged?

GEORGE: Yeah, that's right, yeah.

LEADER: And why must everyone have realized that?

GEORGE: Well, s'obvious, innit? Because . . . (*Pause*) 'e was out of 'is tree! Out of 'is tree – gettit? 'E was out of 'is tree!
(*Laughs raucously*)

LEADER: (*When George has finished laughing*) Well, isn't that silly. That's *very* silly. That was a silly thing to share, wasn't it, everybody?

GEORGE: Why? 'Ow come 'is was interestin', an' 'ers was special, an 'ers was precious, but mine's silly? Anyway, Precious laughed, didn't you Precious? Old Special looked a bit upset, but Precious was well away, weren't you, Precious? Couldn't 'elp it, could yer?

PENELOPE: (*No longer laughing*) If you call me Precious one more time I shall break my chair over your head!

GEORGE: Well, that's special, innit? That's interestin'. That's a very precious gift to me, innit? Breakin' a chair over me 'ead! (*To Penelope*) Thank you for offering to share your chair with me. What d'yer make of that, chief? I bet old Zacchaeus wouldn't 'ave done that once 'e got Jesus 'ome an' sat down at the table – crept up behind 'im an' broken a chair over 'is 'ead. I bet –

STANLEY: May I share an urge?
(*Pause*)

GEORGE: (*Warily*) That's interestin', innit?

STANLEY: I'd like to suggest that we forgive our brother

	George fully and freely, just as Zacchaeus was forgiven for all his past offences.
LEADER:	Well, isn't that lovely. *Isn't* that lovely! Isn't that a lovely unselfish thought, everybody?
GEORGE:	Yeah, that's lovely all right. Only reason I'm 'ere is 'cos old Stan 'adn't got a lift tonight, an' 'e knows 'e won't get 'ome unless 'e does a grease-job on yours truly. That's a lovely unselfish thought, Stan, old mate. That's —
LEADER:	Just a minute. Did you really give Stanley a lift here tonight, George? Did you do that for him?
GEORGE:	Well . . . yeah, I did.
LEADER:	Well, isn't that . . . That's really . . . (*Searches for appropriate word*)
PENELOPE:	Surprising?
LEADER:	Now, now, Precious — I mean — Penelope, there is something very beautiful about George bringing Stanley here in his car without any thought of personal cost. Isn't that beautiful, everybody?
STANLEY:	He charged me the same as a taxi would have done — Sunday rate. That's double.
LEADER:	Oh! Well, that's not quite so beautiful, is it?
GEORGE:	Ah, well I *'ad* to charge 'im, see?
LEADER:	You had to?
GEORGE:	Yeah! I needed the money for the same reason that old Zacchaeus 'ad to climb the tree.
LEADER:	And that reason was . . .?
GEORGE:	Well, like old Zacchaeus . . .
LEADER:	Yes?
GEORGE:	I was a bit short. Gettit? A bit short! (*Laughs*)
LEADER:	Let's close by joining together in a physical attack on George. Won't that be lovely?
STANLEY:	That's a very interesting prospect.

VERONICA: Very special.
PENELOPE: Precious!
          (*They cònverge on him*)

END

Gig-Along-A-God

Our writer has now had a stroke of really bad luck. The poor fellow has been renamed Cedric Spamrumbler (as if he hadn't got enough problems already). He is about to come face to face with the "famous Christian" machine, that strange mechanism that takes very ordinary people and turns them into *well-known* very ordinary people.

The significant point, of course, is that dear old Cedric is very anxious to meet his hypothetical public halfway. Once he's established he'll be free to say that fame and popularity were never motivating forces in his "ministry".

Oh, Cedric!

Gig-Along-A-God

W = WRITER
A = AGENT

W: Good morning – err . . . is this the agency?
A: Yes, indeed, sir, we are the "Gig-along-a-God Christian Performance Agency: Charismatics for Conferences, Prophets for Parties, Evangelicals for Events, Bible-scholars for Beanos, Mystics for Mainstage, Marquees and Marriages, Healers for Hoe-downs, Parsons for Picnics and Theologians for Theatricals: Bless-O-

Grams a speciality: all prices include VAT and will be tithed at source." Is your social engagement heading for disaster? My name is Grace. How may I serve you?

W: Well, err . . . I want to be a cult.

A: You want to be . . . ?

W: I want to be on the fringe at Green Harvest and Springbelt. I want to be famous! I want to be recognized! I want some respect! I want to be a star!! (*Pause*) for the Lord . . .

A: Our brochure does guarantee humility in *all* performers, Mister err . . .

W: Spamrumbler – Cedric Spamrumbler

A: Well, that would certainly keep *me* humble. So, Mister Spamrumbler – what is your normal occupation?

W: Well, I'm a Christian writer – it's a very lonely job y'know. I thought maybe a bit of public exposure might make life a bit brighter and push the sales a bit and – (*Suddenly crazed*) I wanna sign autograph books! I want to be endearingly self-effacing when I'm interviewed in front of hundreds of people! I want –

A: Mister Spamrumbler, what was the title of your last book?

W: It was called *An exegetical analysis of philosophical infrastructures in post-alluvial didacticism – Volume nine.*

A: Hmmm . . . not the sort of thing you can turn into a musical, is it? Are there any funny bits in it?

W: There are some references to mythical incongruity in the context of evolutionary antitheses that certainly make me chuckle.

A: Mmm, yes, what a hoot . . . I'm not sure we're quite getting there yet, Mister Spamrumbler. What about something juicy in the past that you've had a wonderful deliverance from? That always goes down very well. Ever been on drugs? Drink? Contact with the occult? Been in prison? Ever been involved with some big scandal in the papers – "Playboy Peer Slams Neo-nazi Darby and Joan Club" — that sort of thing?

W: The only thing I can remember (*Glances guiltily round*) well — last year I slightly over-filled my salad bowl during a visit to my local Pizza Land restaurant. I don't know why I did it. I — I just lost my head!

A: Mmm, yes, I think we can do something with that. "Greed Leads Top Christian Academic to Defraud Huge Food Chain". I'll get that in the Christian press for the month after next. Tomorrow morning I'll get on to a contact at the publisher's and have a contract drawn up for — let's say — a 40,000 word paperback, thousand pound advance. Title — let's see; something like: "From Gluttony to God — one man's journey from the gutter of slavering, greed and lust to the peace of personal renewal". Be out by next spring — and we should have you doing seminars on Dieting, Gluttony, Anorexia, Cookery, Significance of bread in the New Testament, and Occult influence on the pizza — by, well, by autumn at the earliest. How does that sound, Mister Spamrumbler?

W: Well, it sounds fine! What about money? How much will I have to pay you?

A: It's customary to pay a percentage to the agent, Mister Spamrumbler.

W: I see. Well, do you think we ought to pray about what the percentage should be?

A: Err . . . yes, all right. Let's err . . . pray that we will be told the appropriate figure.
   (*They both pray*)

W: Ten per cent!

A: (*Almost simultaneously*) Fifteen per cent! Mmm, let's give it a few more seconds . . .
   (*They pray*)

W & A: (*Simultaneously*) Twelve and a half per cent!
   (*They stand and shake hands*)

END

Anglican Rap

When I told my children I was contemplating the writing of a "Rap" they were far from impressed. I think they had visions of me performing some sonorous piece of badly scanning verse whose aim was to show the youth of today that the Church is relevant to their culture. They needn't have worried. I have a deep and abiding dislike of arranged marriages between two concepts that repel each other on sight.

We have enough things in the Christian faith that are authentically and uniquely ours, without having to caper foolishly to the world's tune. Don't misunderstand me – I'm all for minimum silliness and proper cultural integration. It's the Saatchi and Saatchi approach that puts me off. Why construct a false presentation of something that's true anyway? Much better, surely, to strip away the man-made nonsense that has obscured the truth, a truth that always *was* relevant. I would rather go to a properly conducted bar, selling all the normal alcoholic drinks, and run by Christians, than crouch over my vimto in a so-called "Christian bar". But, of course, I may be quite wrong in taking that view, and how fortunate I am that those of you who *do* disagree with me will freely forgive me for my error.

The Anglican Rap is a light-hearted look at what might result from my own church's attempt to preserve itself in its most turgid form by using a "modern" device.

Anglican Rap

Let's kneel, let's stand,
Let's be terribly bland,
Let's sing quite loud with a dignified clap,
Let's process around the church in a victory lap.
Check us on the old denominational map,
From the Isle of Wight to the Watford Gap,
Everybody's doing it – the Anglican rap.
Come along and boogie to the Anglican beat,
Just grab your hermeneutics and exegete!

Take a cruise to the pews, have a snooze, read the news,
Don't go looking for disaster with a pentecostal pastor,
There'll be tongues and revelations with bizarre
   interpretations.
Don't smile when life's vile in the house-church style,
Or linger with the lost under old Rob Frost.
Do you fancy looking barmy with the silly Sally Army?
Don't meet above the baker's with the Shakers and the
   Quakers,
Or shiver in the water like the Baptists say you oughter,
We don't baptize in the bottom of a tank,
Our font is Norman, and our vicar is Frank.
We're well aware of modern theological trends,
But Frank and Norman are still good friends.
We're modern and we're modish, have you seen our
   groovy cassocks?
And we're open to the option of inflated rubber hassocks.
Be a real cool cat, be an Anglican dude,
Every now and then we're *almost* rude.

Let's kneel, let's stand,
Let's be terribly bland.

Let's sing quite loud with a dignified clap,
Let's process around the church in a victory lap.
Check us on the old denominational map,
From the Isle of Wight to the Watford Gap,
Everybody's doing it – the Anglican Rap.
Come along and boogie to the Anglican beat,
Just grab your hermeneutics and exegete.

Don't falter at the altar, have a rave in the nave,
Have a smile in the aisle, have a lapse in the apse,

Have a thriller by the pillar, eat an apple in the chapel,
Have some oysters in the cloisters, read some Auden to the
    warden,
Climb the font if you want, feel the power up the tower,
Light a torch in the porch, start a fire in the choir,
Raise your arms in the psalms, mind the gorgon at the
    organ,
Swap your knickers for the vicar's, check you're zipped in
    the crypt.
Some of us speak through tightly clenched teeth,
And lots of us look like Edward Heath. (And that's just the
    ladies)
Anglicans hurry to the old God-shack,
To be first in the queue for the seats at the back,
We're a very broad church, we're home from home,
You can chat up the vicar, or flirt with Rome.
The leader of our gang is big and scary,
He's no spring-chicken, but his name is Carey.

Let's kneel, let's stand,
Let's be terribly bland,
Let's sing quite loud with a dignified clap,
Let's process around the church in a victory lap.
Check us on the old denominational map,
From the Isle of Wight to the Watford Gap,
Everybody's doing it – the Anglican rap.
Come along and boogie to the Anglican beat,
Just grab your hermeneutics and exegete!

Dear Craig

A friend of mine who happens to be gay and a Christian
went through hell in his early attempts to find counselling
and constructive assistance from various sections of the

Church. Elementary formulae and simplistic ideas were not just unhelpful — they were sometimes terrifying. Now, thank God, he has found people and places that offer hope, because they are dealing with *him*, rather than one aspect of what he is.

That is the Jesus way.

Perhaps we should think before we produce clichéd responses to very deep problems. The following letter is extremely silly but . . .

Dear Craig

Dear Craig,

First of all, let me say how much I appreciate the fact that you have trusted me with such a delicate and personal problem. I only hope I can help a little!

Craig, I'm going to say something to you now that may surprise you. I very much doubt that you really are the only person in your church who owns a trombone. Recent and quite reliable research shows that at least one in twenty-five of all British males is in possession of a brass instrument of some kind, and yours is a large congregation. I am quite sure you are not alone.

And now for a little personal testimony. This is a private letter, so you will understand that what follows is not for sharing. A few years ago, Craig, I inherited the possessions of an elderly uncle whom I had known only slightly. When I arrived at Uncle Brendon's house to look through the items that were now mine, I discovered that my uncle had himself been the covert owner of a brass instrument. For some reasons that I do not understand I was both repulsed and fascinated by the object. Throwing all moral considerations to the wind I raised the instrument to my lips (I will not mince words with you, Craig) and blew one

indulgent blast that shattered the silence of my deceased uncle's bedroom.

Guilt encased me like a diving-suit, Craig.

Later that day I arrived home, sat my wife quietly down in the kitchen, and, taking both her hands in mine, told her as gently as I could that I now had a malignant tuba.

Clarissa and I have worked through that problem as man and wife, and I think I can honestly say that it *is* under control. I shall always have my tuba, but it has not left the closet since that day.

I inherited my wind instrument, Craig, and some people claim that they cannot be acquired in any other way. You do not say in your letter anything about the origin of your brass instrument, but I am convinced in my own mind that inheritance is not the only means by which younger *and* older folk become involved in such pursuits. (I once counselled a tone-deaf pensioner who had embezzled a tenor saxophone).

Craig, let me make the most important point of all. No one can condemn you or anyone else for owning a trombone and desiring to play it, but performance would be a sin. We love the sinner, but we hate his trombone, don't we? Let's not be misled by those who have openly formed brass-bands for performance in the church. You and I will be strong, Craig, and one day the rest of the church will know just what a debt of gratitude they owe us.

Yours in mutual restraint,

Babies and Bathwater

The Protestant Church has thrown out far too many healthy babies in its panic-stricken fear of being polluted by dirty bath water. We have suffered loss and deprivation as a result.

Negative, knee-jerk responses to Mary, the mother of Jesus, have left us with an impoverished appreciation of the female elements of divinity, and an unattractively disrespectful attitude to a very special and heroic lady.

A couple of years ago I took a midnight walk over the Downs with two friends, both from a very low-church background. As we climbed those softly-curving, motherly hills beneath the moon, I expressed my view that Mary was regarded slightly neurotically by many evangelical Christians.

People will say things on the Downs at midnight that they might not say anywhere else.

"It's funny you should say that", said one of my companions, a self-employed builder. "I was working up on a roof this week with some other blokes, and they were telling jokes and saying things that I just didn't want to hear. And then, suddenly, I felt as if a woman's hands had been placed over my ears."

We walked on in silence for a moment, then my other friend spoke.

"It *is* funny you should say that. The other day, when I was leading our church meeting, I said something or other about Mary, something sarcastic, I mean, and – I don't know how to describe it – it was as if God slapped me on the wrist. That's how it felt."

We didn't discuss those experiences any further. There was no point. None of us were about to embrace Rome. We were just opening one or two doors marked "private".

Confession is another example. Terrified of being trapped in a box with a man who is trying to do God's job for him, we heedlessly sweep away the entirely scriptural business of confessing our sins to one another. Spiritual and psychological health can sometimes depend on this process.

Often, the baby that we discard grows up elsewhere in a distorted form. Healing goes and Christian Science grows. Spiritual gifts are neglected and a doctrine of "no salvation without tongues" appears.

Death, and the whole question of communication between heaven and earth, went down the theological waste-pipe a long time ago. These issues are determinedly and consistently prevented from gurgling back to the surface by those sections of the Church whose members have managed to perfect the corporate magic act of concealing fear beneath aggressive or frenetic "now-ness". Everyone does it. Last year one of the breakfast programmes spent a week discussing the problem of road accidents involving children. A huge number of kids are killed and injured every year on our roads. Everything was discussed during that week – road safety, careless driving, the evils of drink, proper car maintenance, everything you can think of, except death. Where are all those children who have died? Does it matter? How do we educate our children in an understanding of death? No one seemed to think these questions worth asking.

Spiritualism and absorption in the occult are the mutant and very unwelcome growths that tend to fill the vacuum that is created by this kind of denial in the world and the Church.

Let's hope that we can rescue some of these "babies", wash the dirty water away and examine them carefully and calmly. Perhaps, then, people like myself, who peep fearfully out from behind the blinds of fear and prejudice, will allow Jesus to shine light into dark corners and amaze us with new and deeper discoveries.

Back to the Future

A couple of years ago we took our bicycles down to Newhaven, crossed by ferry to Northern France, and spent a few enjoyable days pedalling from town to town along the river valleys. Our last day was set aside to explore the port of Dieppe before recrossing the channel that evening.

Just after lunch we entered the cool interior of a big church near the centre of the town. I lost touch with the others for a while, but after a few minutes I discovered Katy aged four staring at a life-size sculpture of Mary, the mother of Jesus, holding her son's dead body in her arms and looking into his face with an expression of real pain and loss. Katy turned and saw me.

"Daddy, why has Jesus got a hole in his side?"

Stumblingly, I explained that a Roman spear had been responsible. Katy was horrified. She studied the sculpture again.

"Daddy he's got holes in his feet. Why has he got holes in his feet?"

"Look", I pointed to a small crucifix on the wall above us. "They nailed his feet to that piece of wood called 'a cross, and those are the holes where the nails were."

"Nailed his feet?!"

She turned to look at the stone figures again. Her voice broke a little as she spoke.

"Daddy, he's got holes in his hands as well. They didn't nail his hands as well did they?"

Sadly, I explained. Katy moved closer to the sculpture, put her arm around Jesus, and rested her face down on his knee.

Suddenly I longed to go back to the time when I first understood that Jesus died for me and it really hurt, before I covered my faith in words and worries. I wanted to be like a child again.

But I felt like a cabbage.

> New to me
> But old in years
> When he came
> Examined tears.
> Antique love
> Regard me now
> Love so good
> Kiss my brow.
> Complete release
> Chance to start
> Eventually
> Forgive my heart.
> Now the peace
> Waits for me
> Rest in hope
> Maybe free.